VIBRANT PUBLISHERS

GRE®

VERBAL REASONING SUPREME:

STUDY GUIDE WITH PRACTICE QUESTIONS

First Edition

- ◆ **695** practice questions to prepare for every possibility in the GRE Verbal section

- ◆ **3** full-length practice Verbal tests

- ◆ Detailed overview of GRE Verbal Reasoning section

- ◆ Indispensable guidelines and advice

- ◆ Dozens of handy tips and tricks

GRE® Verbal Reasoning Supreme:
Study Guide with Practice Questions

Paperback ISBN 10 : 1-946383-45-7
Paperback ISBN 13 : 978-1-946383-45-7

Ebook ISBN 10:   1-946383-95-3
Ebook ISBN 13 :   978-1-946383-95-2

Library of Congress Control Number: 2020939594

Vibrant Publishers books are available at special quantity discount for sales promotions, or for use in corporate training programs. For more information please write to bulkorders@vibrantpublishers.com

Please email feedback/corrections (technical, grammatical or spelling) to spellerrors@vibrantpublishers.com

To access the complete catalogue of Vibrant Publishers, visit www.vibrantpublishers.com

Dear Student,

Thank you for purchasing **GRE® Verbal Reasoning Supreme: Study Guide with Practice Questions**. We are committed to publishing books that are content-rich, concise and approachable enabling more students to read and make the fullest use of them. We hope this book provides the most enriching learning experience as you prepare for your GRE exam.

Should you have any questions or suggestions, feel free to email us at reachus@vibrantpublishers.com

Thanks again for your purchase. Good luck for your GRE!

– Vibrant Publishers Team

GRE Books in Test Prep Series

Verbal Insights on the GRE General Test
(ISBN: 978-1-946383-36-5)

GRE Analytical Writing: Solutions to the Real Essay Topics - Book 1
(ISBN: 978-1-946383-26-6)

GRE Analytical Writing: Solutions to the Real Essay Topics - Book 2
(ISBN: 978-1-946383-29-7)

Analytical Writing Insights on the GRE General Test
(ISBN: 978-1-946383-39-6)

Math Insights on the GRE General Test
(ISBN: 978-1-946383-38-9)

GRE Reading Comprehension: Detailed Solutions to 325 Questions
(ISBN: 978-1-946383-30-3)

GRE Text Completion and Sentence Equivalence Practice Questions
(ISBN: 978-1-946383-32-7)

6 Practice Tests for the GRE
(ISBN: 978-1-946383-34-1)

GRE Word List: 491 Essential Words
(ISBN: 978-1-946383-40-2)

GRE Master Word List: 1535 Words for Verbal Mastery
(ISBN: 978-1-946383-41-9)

GRE Words in Context: List 1
(ISBN: 978-1-946383-42-6)

GRE Words in Context: List 2
(ISBN: 978-1-946383-43-3)

GRE Words in Context: Challenging List
(ISBN: 978-1-946383-44-0)

Conquer the GRE: Stress Management & A Perfect Study Plan
(ISBN: 978-1-946383-45-7)

GRE Words In Context: The Complete List
(ISBN: 978-1-949395-18-1)

GRE Analytical Writing Bible: Solutions to 134 Real Essay Topics
(ISBN: 978-1-949395-16-7)

GRE Verbal Reasoning Bible: Study Guide with Practice Questions
(ISBN: 978-1-949395-14-3)

For the most updated list of books visit
www.vibrantpublishers.com

Chapter **1**

Overview of the GRE General Test

The Graduate Record Examinations (GRE) General Test is required for admission to most graduate programs. The most competitive programs tend to require comparatively higher scores. This book is designed to prepare students for the GRE General Test. The GRE revised General Test was renamed in 2016 and is now known as the GRE General Test, but content and scoring of the test remain the same. Note that some graduate programs require applicants to take specialized GRE Subject Tests which will not be covered in this book. Before preparing to take the GRE, please review the admissions criteria for the programs that you are interested in applying to so that you know whether you need to take subject tests in addition to the GRE General Test. To learn more about subject tests, visit the Subject Tests section at ets.org.

The GRE General Test is not designed to measure your knowledge of specific fields. It does not measure your ability to be successful in your career or even in school. It does, however, give a reasonably accurate indication of your capabilities in certain key areas for graduate level work, such as your ability to understand complex written material, your understanding of basic mathematics, your ability to interpret data, and your capacity for reasoning and critical thinking. By using this book to prepare for the GRE General Test, you will not only improve your chances of scoring well on the test, you will also help to prepare yourself for graduate level study.

Format of the GRE General Test

Whether you are taking the paper or computer version of the GRE General Test, the format of the test will be essentially the same. The test consists of three main components: Analytical Writing, Verbal Reasoning and Quantitative Reasoning. The total time for the test will be between 3 hours 30 minutes and 3 hours 45 minutes, depending on the version you are taking.

The first section of the test is always the Analytical Writing component which is broken into two sections. In the first, you will be asked to write an argumentative essay that takes a position on an issue of general interest. In the second, you will be asked to analyze an argument for logical validity and soundness. You will be given 30 minutes for each section.

The remainder of the test will be split between sections devoted to Verbal Reasoning and sections devoted to Quantitative Reasoning. There will be two sections devoted to Verbal Reasoning, and another two devoted to Quantitative Reasoning. You will be given between 30-40 minutes to complete each section, and each section will contain approximately 20 questions. At any point during the test, you may be given an unscored section on either Verbal or Quantitative Reasoning; since this section will not be identified, it is important that you try your best at all times. Also, it is possible that you will be asked to complete a research section that will allow ETS to test the efficacy of new questions. If you are given a research section, it will appear at the end of your General Test. Unscored and research sections may vary in number of questions and time allotted.

Outline of the GRE General Test

The following will briefly introduce the three main components of the GRE General Test.

Analytical Writing Assessment

The first section of the GRE General Test is the Analytical Writing assessment. This component of the GRE is designed to test your ability to use basic logic and critical reasoning to make and assess arguments. The Analytical Writing assessment is broken into two assignments, each of which must be completed within 30 minutes. In the first assignment, you will be asked to develop a position on an issue of general interest. You will be given an issue and a prompt with some specific instructions on how to approach the assigned issue. You will be expected to take a position on the issue and then write a clear, persuasive and logically sound essay defending your position in correct English. You will be assessed based on your ability to effectively defend your positions with supporting evidence and valid reasoning, your skill in organizing your thoughts, and your command of English. In the second assignment, you will be presented with a passage in which the author sketches an argument for their position on an issue. Here, you will be expected to write an essay that critically evaluates their argument in terms of the evidence they use and the logical validity of their reasoning. You will be assessed based on your ability to parse the author's argument and effectively point out the strengths and weaknesses of their reasoning using good organization and correct English.

Task	Time Allowed	Answer Format
Analyze an Issue	30 minutes	Short essay on an issue of general interest that clearly and carefully addresses the prompt
Analyze an Argument	30 minutes	Short essay that analyzes another person's argument for validity, soundness and supporting evidence

The Analytical Writing assessment tests your ability to:

- coherently develop complex ideas

- write in a focused, organized manner

- identify relevant evidence and use it to support your claims

- critically evaluate another person's argument for clarity and effectiveness

- command the elements of standard written English

Verbal Reasoning

The Verbal Reasoning portion of the GRE assesses your reading comprehension, your ability to draw inferences to fill in missing information, and your vocabulary. You will be given two sections on Verbal Reasoning, each consisting of approximately 20-25 questions and lasting 30-35 minutes. Verbal Reasoning questions on the GRE General Test are mostly multiple-choice and will be drawn from the following three types: Reading Comprehension, Text Completion, and Sentence Equivalence. Reading Comprehension questions will ask you to read a short passage several paragraphs long, and then answer questions about the passage. Text Completion questions will have a short passage with 1-3 blanks which you will need to fill in by choosing the best of several multiple-choice options. The Sentence Equivalence section will ask you to fill in the blank in a passage using the two words that will complete the sentence in such a way that the meaning will be as similar as possible.

Task	Question Type	Answer Format
You will have 30-35 minutes to complete the entire section, which will include a mixture of different question types	Reading Comprehension	Multiple-choice: select one answer choice Multiple-choice: select one or more answer choices Highlight a section of text
	Text Completion	Multiple-choice: fill in one or more blanks to complete the text
	Sentence Equivalence	Multiple-choice: select the two options that produce two sentences with the most similar meanings

The Verbal Reasoning section tests your ability to:

- comprehend, interpret and analyze complex passages in standard written English

- apply sophisticated vocabulary in context

- draw inferences about meaning and authorial intent based on written material

Quantitative Reasoning

The Quantitative Reasoning section of the GRE evaluates your ability to use basic mathematics, read and interpret graphs and figures and engage in basic reasoning involving math and numbers. You will be given two sections on Quantitative Reasoning, each with about 20-25 questions. You will have 35-40 minutes to complete each section. There are two basic question types, multiple-choice and numerical entry. For multiple-choice questions, you will be asked to choose the best answer or answers from several possibilities; for numerical entry questions, you will be asked to enter a numerical answer from your own calculations. Some questions will be designed to test your knowledge of basic algebra and geometry; others will be designed to test your ability to read and interpret different presentations of data.

Task	Question Type	Answer Format
You will have 35-40 minutes to complete the entire section, which will include a mixture of different question types	Multiple-choice	Select one answer choice Select one or more answer choices
	Numeric Entry	Solve the problem through calculation and enter a numeric value
	Quantitative Comparison	Evaluate two quantities to decide whether one is greater than the other, whether they are equal, or whether a relationship cannot be determined
	Data Interpretation	Multiple-choice: choose the best answer or answers Numeric entry: enter a value

The Quantitative Reasoning section tests your ability to:

- use mathematical tools such as basic arithmetic, geometry, algebra and statistics

- understand, interpret and analyze quantitative information

- apply basic mathematical and data interpretation skills to real-world information and problems

Paper Based and Computer Based GRE General Test

Paper Based GRE General Test

If you are taking the paper-based version of the test, the format will be slightly different than the computer-based version. The typical format for the paper version of the test will be as follows:

Component	Number of Questions	Time Allowed
Analytical Writing	1 Analyze an Issue 1 Analyze an Argument	30 minutes 30 minutes
Verbal Reasoning (2 sections)	25 questions per section	35 minutes per section
Quantitative Reasoning (2 sections)	25 questions per section	40 minutes per section

Note that if you are taking the paper-based test, you will not be given an unscored section or a research section. You will enter all answers in your test booklet, and you will be provided with an ETS calculator for doing computations. You will not be allowed to use your own calculator.

Computer Based GRE General Test

If you are taking the computer-based version of the test, the format will be slightly different than the paper-based version. Also, unlike the paper-based test, the Verbal Reasoning and Quantitative Reasoning sections of the computer-based version is partially adaptive. This means that the computer will adapt the test to your performance. Since there are two sections each of Verbal Reasoning and Quantitative Reasoning, the difficulty of the second section will depend on how well you did on the first section. The format for the computer-based version of the test will be as follows:

Component	Number of Questions	Time Allowed
Analytical Writing	1 Analyze an Issue 1 Analyze an Argument	30 minutes 30 minutes
Verbal Reasoning (2 sections)	Approximately 20 questions per section	30 minutes per section
Quantitative Reasoning (2 sections)	Approximately 20 questions per section	35 minutes per section
Unscored	Variable	Variable
Research	Variable	Variable

While taking the computer-based GRE General Test:

- You can review and preview questions within a section, allowing you to budget your time to deal with the questions that you find most difficult.

- You will be able to mark questions within a section and return to them later. This means that if you find a question especially difficult, you will be able to move on to other questions and return to the one that you had trouble with, provided that you stay within the time limit for the section.

- You will be able to change or edit your answers within a section. This means that if you realize that you made a mistake, you can go back and correct yourself provided you stay within the time limit for the section.

- You will have an onscreen calculator during the Quantitative Reasoning portions of the test, allowing you to quickly complete any necessary computations.

Registering for the GRE

Before you register to take the GRE, be sure to consider your schedule and any special accommodations that you may need. Be aware that the availability of testing dates may vary according to your location, and that paper-based testing only takes place on certain set dates. Be sure to give yourself plenty of time to prepare for the GRE and be sure that you know the deadlines for score reporting and application deadlines for all the schools you are applying to. For general information about deadlines and the GRE, visit GRE section at ets.org. For more information on how to register for the GRE, visit the Register for GRE section at ets.org. For information on special accommodations for disabled students, visit Disabilities section at ets.org.

How the GRE General Test is Scored

Scoring for the Analytical Writing Section

In the Analytical Writing section, you will be scored on a scale of 0-6 in increments of .5. The Analytical Writing measure emphasizes your ability to engage in reasoning and critical thinking over your facility with the finer points of grammar. The highest scores of 5.5-6.0 are given to work that is generally superior in every respect - sustained analysis of complex issues, coherent argumentation and excellent command of English language. The lowest scores of 0.0-0.5 are given to work that is completely off topic or so poorly composed as to be incoherent.

Scoring for the Verbal and Quantitative Reasoning Sections

The Verbal and Quantitative Reasoning sections are now scored on a scale of 130-170 in 1-point increments.

General Strategies for Taking the GRE

There are strategies you can apply that will greatly increase your odds of performing well on the GRE. The following is a list of strategies that will help to improve your chances of performing well on the GRE:

- Review basic concepts in math, logic and writing.

- Work through the test-taking strategies offered in this book.

- Work through mock GRE tests until you feel thoroughly comfortable with the types of questions you will see.

- As you are studying for the GRE, focus your energy on the types of questions that give you the most difficulty.

- Learn to guess wisely. For many of the questions on the Verbal and Quantitative Reasoning Sections, the correct answer is in front of you - you only need to correctly identify it. Especially for questions that you find difficult, you should hone your ability to dismiss the options that are clearly wrong and make an educated guess about which one is right.

- Answer every question. You won't lose any points for choosing the wrong answer, so even a wild guess that might or might not be right is better than no answer at all.

Preparing for Test Day and Taking the GRE

How you prepare for the test is completely up to you and will depend on your own test-taking preferences and the amount of time you can devote to studying for the test. At the very least, before you take the test, you should know the basics of what is covered on the test along with the general guidelines for taking the GRE. This book is designed to provide you with the basic information you need, and give you the opportunity to prepare thoroughly for the GRE General Test.

Although there is no set way to prepare for the GRE, as a general rule you will want to

- Learn the basics about the test - what is being tested, the format, and how the test is administered.

- Familiarize yourself with the specific types of questions that you will see on the GRE General Test.

- Review skills such as basic math, reading comprehension, and writing.

- Learn about test-taking strategies.

- Take a mock GRE test to practice applying your test-taking skills to an actual test.

Remember, you don't need to spend an equal amount of time on each of these areas to do well on the GRE - allot your study time to your own needs and preferences. Following are some suggestions to help you make the final preparations for your test, and help you through the test itself.

Preparing for Test Day

- In the time leading up to your test, practice, then practice some more. Practice until you are confident with the material.

- Know when your test is, and when you need to be at the testing center.

- Make a "practice run" to your testing center, so that you can anticipate how much time you will need to allow to get there.

- Understand the timing and guidelines for the test and plan accordingly. Remember that you are not allowed to eat or drink while taking the GRE, although you will be allowed to snack or drink during some of the short breaks during testing. Plan accordingly.

- Know exactly what documentation you will need to bring with you to the testing center.

- Relax, especially in the day or night before your test. If you have studied and practiced wisely, you will be well prepared for the test. You may want to briefly glance over some test preparation materials but cramming the night before will not be productive.

- Eat well and get a good night's sleep. You will want to be well rested for the test.

The Test Day

- Wake up early to give yourself plenty of time to eat a healthy breakfast, gather the necessary documentation, pack a snack and a water bottle, and make it to the testing center well before your test is scheduled to start.

- Have confidence: You've prepared well for the test, and there won't be any big surprises. You may not know the answers to some questions, but the format will be exactly like what you've been practicing.

- While you are taking the test, don't panic. The test is timed, and students often worry that they will run out of time and miss too many questions. The sections of the test are designed so that many students will not finish them, so don't worry if you don't think you can finish a section on time. Just try to answer as many questions as you can, as accurately as possible.

- Remember the strategies and techniques that you learn from this book and apply them wherever possible.

Frequently Asked Questions

General Questions

What changes have been made to the GRE revised General Test?

The GRE revised General Test (introduced on August 1, 2011) is now known as the GRE General Test. Only the name of the test has changed. Content and scoring have remained the same. Study materials that reference the GRE revised General Test are still valid and may be used for test preparation.

Why did the name of the test change from GRE revised General Test to GRE General Test?

The name of the test was changed from GRE revised General Test to GRE General Test in 2016 because the word "revised" was no longer needed to distinguish the version of the GRE prior to August 1, 2011. The scores from that version of the test are no longer reported.

How do I get ready to take GRE General Test?

To take the GRE General Test, there are several steps you'll need to take:

- Find out what prospective graduate/professional programs require: Does the program you're interested in requiring additional testing beyond the GRE General Test? What is the deadline for receipt of scores?

- Sign up for a test date. You need to sign up for any GRE testing. For computer-based testing, there will generally be numerous dates to choose from, although acting in a timely manner is essential so that you have plenty of time to prepare and are guaranteed that your scores will be sent and received on time. For paper-based testing, testing dates are much more restricted, so if you know that you will need to take the paper-based GRE General Test, make arrangements well in advance of the application deadline for your program.

- Use this book and the resources provided by ETS to familiarize yourself with both the format of the GRE and the types of questions you will face. Even if you are confident about taking the test, it is essential to prepare for the test.

Does the GRE General Test measure my proficiency in specific subject areas?

No. The GRE General Test is designed to measure general proficiency in reading, critical reasoning, and working with data, all abilities that are critical to graduate work. However, you won't be tested on your knowledge of any specific field.

Where can I get additional information on the GRE General Test?

Educational Testing Service (ETS), the organization that administers the GRE, has an informative website entirely devoted to information about the test at the GRE section at ets.org. There, you can find links that further explain how to sign up for testing, fees, score reporting and much more.

Preparing for the Test

How should I start to prepare for the test?

The first thing you should do is thoroughly familiarize yourself with the format of the GRE General Test. Once you've decided whether you're taking the paper-based test, or the computerized version, learn exactly what you can expect from the version of the test you're taking - how many sections there are, how many questions per section, etc. You can find general information about the structure of the test earlier in this chapter.

How do I prepare for the questions I will be asked on the GRE General Test?

There are plenty of resources by Vibrant Publishers, including this book to help you prepare for the questions you will face on the GRE General Test. A list of books is provided at the beginning of this book. For the most updated list, you may visit www.vibrantpublishers.com.

How much should I study/practice for the GRE?

Study and practice until you feel comfortable with the test. Practice, practice and practice some more until you feel confident about test day!

Are there additional materials I can use to get even more practice?

Yes. ETS offers a free full-length practice test that can be downloaded from the GRE section at ets.org. Also, after you have signed up for testing through ETS, you are eligible for some further test preparation materials free of additional charge.

Test Content

How long the GRE General Test is?

- The computer-based version of the test is around 3 hours and 45 minutes including short breaks.

- The paper-based version of the test will take around 3 hours and 30 minutes.

What skills does the GRE test?

In general, the GRE is designed to test your proficiency in certain key skills that you will need for graduate level study. More specifically:

- **The Analytical Writing section** tests your ability to write about complex ideas in a coherent, focused fashion as well as your ability to command the conventions of standard written English, provide and evaluate relevant evidence, and critique other points of view.

- **The Verbal Reasoning section** tests your ability to understand, interpret and analyze complex passages, use reasoning to draw inferences about written material, and use sophisticated vocabulary in context.

- **The Quantitative Reasoning section** tests your knowledge of basic, high school-level mathematics, as well as your ability to analyze and interpret data.

What level of math is required for the Quantitative Reasoning section?

You will be expected to know high school level math - arithmetic, and basic concepts in algebra and geometry. You will also be expected to be able to analyze and interpret data presented in tables and graphs.

Scoring and Score Reporting

How are the sections of the GRE General Test scored?

The GRE General Test is scored as follows:

- **The Verbal Reasoning section** is scored in 1-point increments on a scale of 130-170.

- **The Quantitative Reasoning section** is scored in 1-point increments on a scale of 130-170.

- **The Analytical Writing section** is scored on a scale of 0-6 in increments of .5.

When will my score be reported?

It depends on which version of the test you are taking, and also when you decide to take the GRE General Test. In general, scores for the computer-based version of the test are reported within two weeks; for the paper-based test, they are reported within six weeks. Check the GRE section at ets.org for updates on score reporting and deadlines.

How long will my scores be valid?

In general, your score for the GRE General Test will remain valid for five years. The following are some specifications about score validity:

- For those who have yet to take the test, or have taken it on or after July 1, 2016, scores are valid for five years after the test administration date.

- For those who have taken the test between August 1, 2011 and June 30, 2016, scores are valid for five years after the testing year. For example, scores from a test taken in April 2015 would be valid until June 2020.

- Scores from August 2011 are valid until June 30, 2017.

Other Questions

Do business schools accept the GRE instead of the GMAT?

An increasing number of business schools accept the GRE as a substitute for the more standard test for admission to an MBA program, the GMAT. Before you decide to take the GRE instead of the GMAT, make sure that the programs you are interested in applying to will accept the GRE. You can find a list of business schools that currently accept the GRE in the GRE section at ets.org.

How is the GRE administered?

The GRE is administered at designated testing centers, where you can take the test free from distraction in a secure environment that discourages cheating. The computer-based version of the test is administered continuously year-round at designated testing centers. In areas where computer-based testing is unavailable, the paper-based version of the test is administered at most three times a year on designated dates. For information on testing centers in your area and important dates, visit the GRE section at ets.org.

I have a disability that requires me to ask for special accommodation while taking the test - what sort of accommodation is offered?

ETS does accommodate test-takers with disabilities. For information on procedures, visit the GRE section at ets.org.

Will there be breaks during testing?

Yes. You will have a 10-minute break during the test. On the computer-based version of the test, the 10-minute break will fall after you have completed the first three sections of the test. On the paper-based version, you will be given a 10-minute break following the Analytical Writing sections.

Will I be given scratch paper?

If you are taking the computer-based version of the test, you will be given as much scratch paper as you need. If you are taking the paper-based version of the test, you won't be allowed to use scratch paper, however, you will be allowed to write in your test booklet.

Should I bring a calculator to the test?

No. If you are taking the computer-based version of the test, there will be an onscreen calculator for you to use. If you are taking the paper-based version of the test, an ETS-approved calculator will be issued to you at the testing center.

This page is intentionally left blank

Chapter **2**

Introduction to Verbal Reasoning

The Verbal Reasoning component of the GRE is designed to evaluate your skill at reading, interpreting and analyzing sentences and passages written in standard English. The GRE General Test will have two Verbal Reasoning sections of about 20 questions each. You will have 30-35 minutes to complete each section. Each section will consist of three distinct types of question: Reading Comprehension, Text Completion, and Sentence Equivalence. This chapter will provide an overview of the types of questions you will face on the Verbal Reasoning portion of the GRE and list some general techniques and strategies for approaching Verbal Reasoning questions. In addition, it gives a more detailed look at each type of question, providing worked examples with in-depth explanations and strategies.

- The Verbal Reasoning portion of the GRE features three distinct question types: Reading Comprehension, Text Completion, and Sentence Equivalence

- Text Completion and Sentence Equivalence will be in multiple-choice format; Reading Comprehension will consist of some multiple-choice and some questions where you will be asked to highlight a section of text

- There will be two Verbal Reasoning sections, and you will be given 30-35 minutes for each (depending on which version of the test you are taking)

Reading Comprehension Questions

For Reading Comprehension questions, you will be asked to read a passage and answer several questions on the passage. Passages may cover topics from the physical, biological or social sciences, the arts, the humanities, business or everyday life. Passages will be between one to five paragraphs in length. After reading the passage, you will be asked to answer several questions on the passage. In some cases, the questions will require you to identify key aspects of the passage or draw inferences about meaning or the author's intent. In others, you will be asked to highlight the section of the passage that addresses a particular consideration or identify components of the passage that point to a given conclusion.

Reading Comprehension Questions will have three formats: multiple-choice in which you choose the single solution that best answers the question, multiple-choice in which you choose one or more solutions that best answer the question, and passage highlighting, in which you highlight the portion of the passage that best addresses a given question. To do well on the Reading Comprehension questions in the Verbal Reasoning component, you will need to be able to quickly read a passage and identify key points and the central themes of the passage.

- Reading Comprehension questions will be based off a short passage, one to five paragraphs long

- Some questions will be multiple-choice, others will ask you to highlight an appropriate section of the passage. Multiple-choice questions will either ask you to select a single option, or one or more options

- Reading Comprehension questions test your ability to understand and interpret complex passages and quickly determine key points and details

Text Completion Questions

Text Completion questions consist of a short passage one to five sentences long with one or more blanks. The passages will cover topics from the physical, biological, or social sciences, the arts, the humanities, business or everyday life. You will be asked to choose the best option from several to fill in the blank or blanks to complete the passage. Text Completion questions are designed to test your vocabulary and your ability to draw plausible inferences about the intended meaning of passages written in standard English.

All Text Completion questions are multiple-choice: the number of options you are given will vary from five (usually for passages with a single blank) to three (usually for passages with two or more blanks). To do well on Text Completion questions, you will need to review vocabulary, be able to draw quick inferences about the intent of a passage and be able to choose the word that completes the passage best given the context.

- Text Completion questions will ask you to fill in one or more blanks in a short passage, usually one to five sentences long

- All questions will be multiple-choice

- Text Completion questions test your ability to apply sophisticated vocabulary in context and to draw inferences about the meaning of passages based on incomplete information

Sentence Equivalence Questions

Sentence Equivalence questions consist of short sentences with a single blank. The sentence will be on a topic from the physical, biological, or social sciences, the arts, the humanities, business or everyday life. You will be given six possible answer options to fill in the blank. You must choose the two options that (a) complete the sentence grammatically and (b) produce two completed sentences with the most similar meanings. Sentence Equivalence questions test your understanding of correct English grammar and your vocabulary.

All Sentence Equivalence questions are multiple-choice and will ask you to choose the best two options from a total of six. To do well on Sentence Equivalence questions, you will need to review vocabulary and be able to identify words with similar meanings, and you will also need to review basic rules of English grammar.

- Sentence Equivalence questions will ask you to fill in a single blank in a short passage

- All questions will be multiple-choice; you will be asked to choose the two options out of six that complete the sentence and produce two sentences having the most similar meanings

- Sentence Equivalence questions test your knowledge of basic rules of grammar, draw correct inferences about the meaning of a passage based on incomplete information, and identify words with similar meanings

Tips for Verbal Reasoning Component

The Verbal Reasoning portion of the GRE tests your command of certain key areas of written English. Doing everything you can to solidify your vocabulary, your grammar and your ability to understand complex passages will help you prepare for the Verbal Reasoning Section of the GRE. Below is a list of general strategies that will help you with the verbal portion of the test:

- Familiarize yourself with the types of questions that will be asked. There are a limited number of possible types of question; once you know the format, you won't be faced with anything unfamiliar

- Read any instructions on the test carefully - always be sure that you are answering the question that you've been asked

- Brush up on your vocabulary. You can find a list of common GRE words in this book - carefully review that list. Also, using the examples provided in this book, you can get a good sense of the kinds of words you will encounter on the GRE. Be sure that you know what they mean

- Work on your critical reading skills. For anything you read while preparing for the GRE, try to ask yourself: what are the key points? What is the author trying to say? What information supports the author's claims?

- Work on identifying key words - words like "although", "moreover", "therefore" - that signal important information or shifts in perspective. Doing this will help you quickly grasp the sense of a passage even if some information is missing

- Use basic logic and common sense to draw inferences about the passage you are working with

- If you are unsure of how to answer a multiple-choice question, you can often use process of elimination. Often by getting rid of answers that are obviously wrong, you can get the right answer, even if you're not sure about some of the options

Chapter 3

Introduction to Reading Comprehension

Reading Comprehension questions are designed to test your ability to understand, interpret and analyze what you read. You will be asked to read a short passage between one or more paragraphs long and then answer several questions about the passage. To answer them you will need to recognize what the passage explicitly states and be able to draw inferences about the implications of the passage.

The passages used for Reading Comprehension questions will be drawn from a variety of topics, including the physical, biological and social sciences, the arts and the humanities, business and everyday life. To answer the questions on these passages, you do not need to be an expert on the topic covered; you need only read the passage attentively enough to answer basic questions about it. You will not be asked to evaluate the passage for truth or falsity; you will only need to understand what the author said, and what implications can be drawn from what the author said.

The Verbal Reasoning portion of the GRE will generally have about 10 passages that you will need to read. Some will be several paragraphs in length, others just one paragraph. You will be asked to answer 1-6 questions per passage, with longer passages generally corresponding to more questions. The questions -will appear in three formats: two types of multiple-choice and highlighting a section of the passage. The first type of multiple-choice will ask you to choose the single best answer from several options. The second type of multiple-choice will ask you to choose one or more answers from several options. For select-in passage, you will be asked to highlight the section of text that best addresses the question.

What does a Reading Comprehension question look like?

Reading Comprehension questions will always be based off a short passage of one or more paragraphs. You will be asked to read the passage and then answer 1-6 questions about it. Below is an example of what a Reading Comprehension question will look like on the GRE General Test:

Questions 1 to 3 are based on the following reading passage.

Sometimes hype can create impossible expectations. Nowhere is this phenomenon more pronounced than in the world of popular music. Two bands that came to prominence in the first years of the 2000s exemplify this. New York's The Strokes and England's Arctic Monkeys were both hailed by critics as the leaders of a garage rock revival, and more grandiosely, as saviors of rock music. Despite successes and considerable popularity, neither band has entirely lived up to these overblown expectations. Although both bands helped to bring greater awareness to the burgeoning indie music scene, rock music still struggles to compete with other genres of popular music. And although both bands have gained considerable popularity, they still don't have the ability to fill stadiums and arenas the way that some of their older and less heralded peers do.

Select only one answer choice.

1. Which of the following statements best characterizes the main idea of the passage?

    Ⓐ Popular music is more diverse than many people realize

    Ⓑ The Strokes and Arctic Monkeys are both highly successful bands

    Ⓒ A single band can revolutionize popular music

    Ⓓ Critics of popular music sometimes create exaggerated expectations for bands

    Ⓔ Older bands draw bigger crowds than newer bands

Consider each of the three choices separately and select all that apply.

2. The author most likely uses the phrase "saviors of rock music" to:

    [A] characterize the strokes

    [B] make a plea for the future of the genre

    [C] indicate the hyperbolic expectations created by music critics

3. Select the sentence that suggests rock music's struggles competing with other types of popular music.

Answer Key

The correct answers to the questions are:

1. D. Critics of popular music sometimes create exaggerated expectations for bands

2. C. indicate the hyperbolic expectations created by music critics

3. Although both bands helped to bring greater awareness to the burgeoning indie music scene, rock music still struggles to compete with other genres of popular music.

What skills do Reading Comprehension questions test?

Reading Comprehension questions test your ability to understand, interpret and analyze complex passages of the kind you will encounter in graduate school. Some key skills that are tested include your ability to:

- understand a text holistically and be able to determine the meaning of individual components

- distinguish major and minor points

- succinctly summarize the meaning of an entire passage

- use inference to draw conclusions about implied meaning and intent

- understand how individual parts of a text support the key points

- identify an author's assumptions, biases and perspective

- determine the potential strengths and weaknesses of the author's position

Key Facts about Reading Comprehension questions

- Questions will be based on short passages of one or more paragraphs

- There will be approximately 10 passages on the Verbal Reasoning portion of the test; you will be required to answer 1-6 questions per passage

- Passages will be on a variety of topics including the physical, biological and social sciences, the arts and the humanities, business and everyday life

- Questions will be answerable based on the passage alone - you will not need any prior knowledge of the subject matter being discussed

- Questions will ask you to select one or more correct answers from several, or highlight a relevant portion of the passage

Strategies for Reading Comprehension questions

Depending on what version of the GRE you are taking, you will have 30 or 35 minutes to complete each Verbal Reasoning section. To complete a section successfully, you will need to budget your time well, and this is especially important with Reading Comprehension questions. It is essential that you not lose too much time reading passages too carefully. Remember, to do well on Reading Comprehension questions you do not need to have a mastery of the material covered in a given passage - you just need to be able to answer a few highly directed questions about the passage. If you are able to read the passage both thoroughly and quickly, so much the better; however, if you find yourself taking too much time over a passage, it is better to gather key information quickly than to grasp absolutely everything and lose too much time. As you read passages for Reading Comprehension questions, your reading should be goal-oriented: read quickly and "loosely" and focus only on information that is important. Remember, you won't need to remember anything about the passage after the test, and you only need to grasp key points while taking the test.

Another key consideration is how to approach passages that cover unfamiliar material. Remember, passages can be drawn from many different fields, and chances are you will come across a passage that deals with something you are unfamiliar with. However, the questions about the passage will not demand any prior knowledge of the subject matter. Don't panic if you are asked to read about something that you know nothing about, since the questions will not ask you to evaluate the truth of the claims made in the passage. By the same token, don't let any expertise that you may possess lead you to make unnecessary judgments about the passage. Focus your attention on answering the questions and always keep in mind that your knowledge or lack of knowledge about the subject matter will have no bearing on how well you are able to answer those questions.

Finally, keep in mind that the key skills for Reading Comprehension are skimming and paraphrasing. To skim effectively, you will need to read quickly and gather key information. To paraphrase, you will need to be able to summarily restate the key points of the passage in other words. Skimming will help you quickly understand what the passage is about while paraphrasing will allow you to recognize which possible answers are the best.

- Don't lose too much time reading a passage carefully; read quickly, and read with the goal of answering the questions

- Don't worry too much about understanding everything - remember, you don't need to learn the material covered in the passage thoroughly, you simply need to answer a few highly directed questions

- Don't let your knowledge, or lack of knowledge, of the subject matter distract you - every question you are asked will be answerable solely on the basis of the information in the passage

- Use your abilities to skim and paraphrase to your advantage; gather relevant information rapidly, and be able to reformulate it to determine what answer choice best answers the question

What follows are some more specific strategies for answering Reading Comprehension questions. Later in this book, you'll have a chance to put your skills to the test and learn how to hone them in several in-depth practice questions.

Determine What the Passage is About

Your first task as you read a passage should be to find out what is being discussed. You should immediately look for clues as to what the main idea of the passage is - doing so will help you address any broad questions about the big picture that the passage is trying to convey. The following three questions will help you find the main idea of the passage:

- What is the passage about? This question should be the easiest of the three to answer, and could be fairly broad (e.g. "European history")

- What is the scope of the passage? This question asks how narrowly/broadly the passage addresses its subject matter

- What is the purpose of the passage? Here you are asking why the author wrote the passage to begin with - is it to educate? To persuade? Who is the intended audience, and what reaction is the author trying to get?

- Some of the questions you will be asked will be directly answered by answering one or more of the above questions.

Skim the Passage

You need to gather key information quickly to do well, and one of the best ways to do that is to skim. As you skim the passage, keep several key points in mind. First of all, skim to determine what the passage is about. You shouldn't need to read every word carefully to be able to address the questions listed in the section above. Also, as you skim the passage, try to keep in mind how the passage is organized - try to have a general idea of what information can be found where. Some questions will ask you to refer to very specific sections of the text - by skimming effectively, you can form an idea of where you'll need to look to address specific questions. Finally, don't be afraid to skip over sentences or phrases that you don't understand. In many cases, you will be able to learn all you need to from a passage without understanding every word. In those rare cases when a question directly addresses something that you didn't understand on the first read-through, you can always read the section again more carefully when you are trying to answer the question.

As you are reading the passage, try to get a quick feel for the structure of the text. If there is more than one paragraph, how are the paragraphs organized? What is the topic and purpose of each paragraph? How is evidence and supporting material presented?

Understanding the Questions

After skimming the passage as described above, you will need to be prepared to answer questions about it. You can use the following strategies to help you answer the questions well:

- Read the question carefully. While you usually don't need to read more than a small part of the passage carefully, it's important that you read the question and the possible solutions with care - you need to have a clear sense of what you are being asked in order to find the right answer

- If the question is in multiple-choice format, read every possible answer choice. Even if you think you can identify the right answer immediately, make sure you read all of the options

- If the question is general and asks you to describe what the passage is about, or what the purpose is, you should already have a pretty good idea of what the answer is from skimming and determining what the main idea of the passage is

- If the question is specific, you may need to find a particular section of the passage and read over it more carefully. Make "mental bookmarks" as you skim the passage to give you some idea of where to find which idea, so that when you're asked to answer a question on something very specific, you'll know where to find it

- Be prepared to use the information in the passage to draw an inference to a conclusion that was not explicitly stated. Sometimes you'll be asked to determine the next step in a passage - given what's said in the passage, what sort of conclusions can be drawn?

- Paraphrase. Sometimes you will find that you just can't understand the way that a particular question applies to the passage. By trying to reformulate the question, or the relevant section of the passage, or both, in your own words, you can often grasp the key idea that you need to address

Answering the Questions

Once you have read and understood the questions, you'll need to select the best answer (or in some cases, answers).

- Be sure you know what kind of answer you need to find. Some questions will be straight multiple-choice, where you pick only one answer; others will allow you to choose more than one answer, and still others will ask you to highlight a portion of the text. Be aware of what you're expected to provide in your answer

- Be sure you are answering the question that was asked. Just because an answer choice is true, doesn't necessarily mean that it is right. Sometimes you will have more than one option that correctly addresses a point made by the passage - be sure that you choose the option that answers the question asked

- Don't allow any personal opinion or prior knowledge of a topic to distract you - again, you should only answer the question as it bears on the passage. You are not being asked to express your opinions about a passage, or critique the content

- Use logic. To correctly answer some questions, you will need to use basic logic. Learn to recognize implicit assumptions made by the author, and draw inferences to see what unstated conclusions might follow from a passage

- Apply the process of elimination. For multiple-choice questions, you will often be given several potential answers that are more obviously wrong than others. Be sure to dismiss these answers first of all, since even if you don't know which of the remaining options the right answer is, you'll increase your odds of choosing it by dismissing those that are clearly wrong

Types of Questions

There are several types of Reading Comprehension questions that you can expect to find. Reviewing the kinds of questions, you can expect to be asked, and looking at strategies for answering them, will help you prepare for the test. The following is a list of typical questions:

- What is the main idea?

- What is the purpose?

- Identify specific details

- Identify the purpose of specific details

- Infer a conclusion based on evidence presented in the passage

- Identify assumptions made by the author

- Identify additional evidence that might undermine/bolster the author's argument

- Highlight a specific section of text that addresses a question

- Other

Main Idea

Some questions will be quite straightforward - you will be asked to answer a "big picture" question about the passage, such as questions about the main topic, intended audience, and scope.

Assuming that you have skimmed the passage well and answered the questions listed above in the section on determining what the passage is about, answering this type of question should be quite easy. Practice reading passages to quickly grasp the key points, and then have confidence in your ability to apply this skill on test day.

Purpose

Some questions will ask you to say something about the purpose of the passage. Here you are being asked to make an educated guess as to why the author bothered to write the passage - did they intend to educate? To entertain? To undermine a commonly held belief? To develop an argument as to why their perspective is better than another?

When answering questions about the purpose of a passage, look for clues in structure and wording. Does the author develop and then dismiss a certain view? What is the tone - is it adversarial or merely stating facts? Does the passage present a course of action, or does it simply present information? Answering questions such as these will help you determine some basic points about the passage, such as whether the author is advocating something or just trying to educate. You can then look of over some of the details of the passage to gain a sense of exactly what position the author is advocating, or who the intended audience might be for the information given.

Details

Some questions will ask you to identify specific points within the passage. Here you are being asked to find the place in the passage where the author discusses some particular aspect of the main topic or a detail that supports something that they have said.

To answer these questions, you will need to have developed good skimming skills. As you skim, learn to mentally bookmark the passage so that you know where to find certain information whether or not you have read it carefully or understood it perfectly. Doing this will allow you to quickly refer back to the right section of the passage to find the specific point you are being asked.

Purpose of Detail

Some questions will ask you to identify why the author chose to use certain details in their discussion. If the author is making an argument, you will need to think why they chose to include a certain point to support it; if they are attempting to educate, you will need to decide why they thought a given detail would help make the discussion more informative.

To do well with these types of questions, you will need to have a good grasp on the topic and purpose of the passage, and you will need to know where to find the relevant detail to see where and how it fits into the whole discussion. As you read through the passage, try to read actively rather than passively - ask yourself why the author has chosen to include particular information, and how it fits into the piece as a whole. If you can get a good sense of how and why things hang together in the passage as you skim through it, you will be able to answer this type of question much more rapidly.

Additional Conclusions

Sometimes you will be asked to put together the evidence provided in a passage to draw a conclusion. In some cases, the author will have stated a clear conclusion and you will be asked to use the evidence presented to find other implied conclusions. In others, the author will have left their conclusions implied, and you will be asked to say something about them given the evidence.

To answer questions about implied conclusions, you need to have grasped the main idea of the passage. There is no way to answer questions about what conclusion you might draw from the passage without knowing the basic big picture information about the passage. Once you have that, you can use clues from the author's tone and the details they provide to determine what conclusions can be inferred.

Assumptions

Some questions may ask you what assumptions are implied in the passage. Here, you will need to consider what the author is assuming to develop their position - what do they consider so completely uncontroversial that they rely on it without even mentioning it?

To answer questions about assumptions, you will need to have a solid grasp of what the author is trying to say and why, and how they have structured the passage. You need to focus on ideas or points that are essential to what the author is trying to say but have been left unstated.

Bolster/Undermine

Sometimes you will be asked to identify another point that would either strengthen or weaken the author's case in the passage. Here you are looking for any additional evidence that can be brought to bear on the passage.

To answer this type of question, you need to have a clear grasp of the main idea, purpose and structure of the passage. Focus on only those potential answers that have a direct bearing on the topic and weigh how the additional information would affect the development of the passage.

Highlight

Sometimes you will be asked to find a specific point in the passage and highlight it. For these questions, rather than being given possible answers, you will need to find the answer in the text and highlight it.

If you have skimmed the passage well and know where to find different points, these questions will be quite similar to multiple-choice questions that ask for specific details. Focus your attention only on those parts of the passage that deal specifically with the question asked, and answer the question based on that.

Other

You may be asked other types of question about passages, although any additional type of question will test the same skills that the types listed test. To answer other question types, apply the techniques discussed above in the appropriate combination.

Test Taking Strategies

- Be sure that you read the instructions for the question carefully. Remember that Reading Comprehension questions can appear in three distinct formats, and to correctly answer a given question, you'll need to understand the format first of all

- For all types of multiple-choice questions, always review every potential answer before you choose the correct answer or answers

- For multiple-choice questions that ask for the single best answer select only the option that best addresses the question

- For multiple-choice questions that ask you to select one or more answers don't be alarmed if more than one of the options looks correct. For this type of question, you can select all of the options that accurately answer the question

- Don't be deceived by answers that are only partially true, or do not completely address the question - make sure that you select only those answers that fully and appropriately answer the question you were asked, especially for those questions that ask you to select a single option out of several or a passage

KEY STRATEGY # 1

Always use process of elimination. Many multiple-choice questions of any type will have some options that are more obviously wrong than some others - perhaps they fall beyond the scope of the question, perhaps they produce an absurd result. If you are not immediately certain of the correct answer, dismiss those answers that are obviously wrong first of all and work with what remains. Even if you end up having to guess the right answer, you'll increase your odds of guessing right by eliminating answers that are obviously incorrect.

KEY STRATEGY # 2

Some questions on the test are designed to make you waste time if you haven't read effectively. If you did not do a good job of skimming the passage, you could easily waste minutes searching through the passage trying to determine which answers are right and which aren't. Don't let this happen. Hone your skimming skills so that you already have an idea of which information is right and which isn't before you look back over the passage for any final confirmation.

KEY STRATEGY # 3

You should be careful not to let "fancy" options that sound like they relate to the passage fool you. Some answer choices will be designed to take advantage of the way your mind tends to associate information with the topic. Be wary of this and be sure to ask yourself whether you actually saw anything in the passage that substantiates a possible answer.

KEY STRATEGY # 4

As you work on Reading Comprehension questions, remember to use elementary logic to your advantage. One very basic rule of logic is the following: for two propositions p and q, if p then q and not q entails not p. In other words, if you know that it is true that proposition p implies proposition q, and you know that proposition q is not true, then you know that proposition p is also not true. Use this and other strategies from basic logic to answer Reading Comprehension questions that require reasoning.

This page is intentionally left blank

Chapter **4**

Practice Questions for Reading Comprehension

This chapter is devoted to helping you develop your skill with Reading Comprehension questions using practice questions. You will find sets of passages related to subjects namely *Arts and Humanities, Biological Sciences, Business, Everyday Topics, Physical Sciences and Social Sciences,* that are similar to the sorts of passages you will encounter on an actual GRE test. Each passage has a set of questions and a detailed explanation of the solution to each question. The questions and their solutions will be presented as follows:

In each set:

- A passage related to a particular subject similar to what you can expect on an actual GRE test

- Several questions about the passage similar to those you will encounter on an actual GRE test

In Explanatory Answers for each set:

- In most sets, a quick summary that paraphrases the main issues of the passage and points out important words or phrases that indicate the meaning or intent of the passage. Being able to answer a few basic questions about Reading Comprehension passages before you even see any of the questions is a key skill that will help you answer questions more quickly and more accurately. The summaries provided here will give you some sense of how to approach summarizing when looking at actual questions.

- Detailed solutions that explain what the correct answer is, and what strategy or strategies you could use to determine the correct answer. Explanatory answers will usually refer back to the summary.

Practice Set 1: Arts and Humanities

Passage 1

Questions 1 to 4 are based on the following passage.

Dmitry Shostakovich's first visit to the United States was an appearance at the Cultural and Scientific Conference for World Peace in New York City in March 1949. He was serving as one of five delegates from the Soviet Union, and as a delegate he listened as his translators read a prepared speech, mumbled brief answers to a few awkward questions, played on the piano once, attended a few concerts, and then left with cartons of cigarettes under his arm. The conference was described in the popular press as pro-Communist propaganda, and protestors picketed the streets outside the Waldorf. Many Americans, however, were familiar with Shostakovich's music, and many knew about the recent banning of his works in the Soviet Union.

For Questions 1 and 2, select only one answer choice.

1.   Which of the following best describes the author's assessment of Shostakovich's first trip to the United States?

    Ⓐ   The Cultural and Scientific Conference for World Peace was essentially pro-Communist propaganda and Shostakovich viewed it as such.

    Ⓑ   The Cultural and Scientific Conference for World Peace was designed to present Shostakovich's works to the world for the first time, but his debut was overshadowed by the controversy surrounding the event.

    Ⓒ   The Cultural and Scientific Conference for World Peace proved to be an inauspicious U.S debut for Shostakovich.

    Ⓓ   Shostakovich's visit focused public attention on his music and the recent banning of his works in the Soviet Union.

    Ⓔ   Despite several problems, Shostakovich's visit boosted his popularity in the United State

2.   What is the author's purpose in closing this passage with the sentence, "Many Americans, however, were familiar with Shostakovich's music, and many knew about the recent banning of his works in the Soviet Union?"

    Ⓐ   To note that despite the lack of attention and exposure given to Shostakovich at the Conference and despite the perception of the Conference as propaganda, the composer's work and political plight were already known in the United States.

    Ⓑ   To note that the presence of Shostakovich, whose work and political plight were known in the U.S., lent credence to the popular perception of the Conference as propaganda.

    Ⓒ   To suggest that those Americans familiar with Shostakovich's work and political plight did not share the view that the Conference was pro-Communist propaganda

    Ⓓ   To suggest that the knowledge of Shostakovich and his political plight led to the protests against the Conference

    Ⓔ   To suggest that Shostakovich's political troubles were the primary reason for his fame in the United States

Consider each of the three choices separately and select all that apply.

3.   Which of the following statements about Shostakovich's first visit to the U.S. are implied by the passage?

      [A]   The performance of Shostakovich's music was not given priority at the Conference.

      [B]   Shostakovich participated in the conference reluctantly.

      [C]   Shostakovich was a smoker.

4.   Select the sentence which provides the most information about Shostakovich's musical compositions.

Passage 2

Questions 5 to 8 are based on the following passage.

In the Americas, paganism provided a convenient initial excuse for conquest and enslavement of indigenous people. However, as Indians were gradually Christianized, race replaced paganism as a justification for Spanish domination. Furthermore, gender functioned as a facilitator of political negotiation and inter-ethnic relations in the New World. Because more than 80 percent of Spanish immigrants to the Indies between 1492 and 1580 were male, race and gender ideologies interacted to reinforce the political and cultural hegemony of the Spanish in the New World.

For Questions 5 to 7, select only one answer choice.

5.   The passage addresses which of the following issues related to the large percentage of male Spanish immigrants during the 16th Century?

      (A)   The question of whether gender issues were more influential than racial ideologies upon the relationship between Spanish immigrants and indigenous peoples

      (B)   The contention that the Spanish immigrants' efforts at converting natives to Christianity were inspired largely by gender ideology

      (C)   The implication that racial attitudes toward the native population might have been different had there been a higher percentage of female Spanish immigrants

      (D)   The contention that gender ideology, in combination with the Spaniards' attitude toward race, was a significant facilitator of the Spanish domination of the indigenous population

      (E)   The suggestion that the Spaniard's attitudes towards gender, as well as race, evolved from the largely successful effort to convert the natives to Christianity

6.   The passage makes which of the following assertions with regard to racial issues?

   Ⓐ   Racial attitudes tend to shape gender ideology when two cultures meet for the first time

   Ⓑ   While the Spaniards originally felt superior to the natives because the natives were not Christian, a belief in racial superiority eventually became a long-term influence upon their policies

   Ⓒ   Racial attitudes tended to support the political dominance of the Spanish, while gender issues tended to support cultural hegemony

   Ⓓ   The racial attitudes of the natives toward the Spanish interacted with the Spaniards' belief in their own racial superiority to reinforce the cultural hegemony of the period

   Ⓔ   The pagan beliefs of the native peoples served as a justification for the Spaniards' racial attitudes toward them

7.   In the final sentence, the word "hegemony" most nearly means in the context of the passage:

   Ⓐ   The distinctive characteristics of one ethnic group

   Ⓑ   The predominant influence of one group or ideology over another

   Ⓒ   The decline of a civilization

   Ⓓ   The tradition of white, male dominance in Western culture

   Ⓔ   Policy based upon religious precepts

Consider each of the three choices separately and select all that apply.

8.   Which of the following does the passage suggest was a primary influence upon the Spanish domination of the Indians?

   Ⓐ   Political hegemony

   Ⓑ   Racial ideology

   Ⓒ   Gender demographics

Passage 3

Question 9 is based on the following passage.

   It is little realized how slowly, how painfully, we approach the expression of truth. We are so variable, so anxious to be polite, and alternately swayed by caution or anger. Our mind oscillates like a pendulum: it takes some time for it to come to rest. And then, the proper allowance and correction has to be made for our individual vibrations that prevent accuracy. Even the compass needle doesn't point the true north, but only the magnetic north. Similarly, our minds at best can but indicate magnetic truth, and are distorted by many things that act as iron filings do on the compass. The necessity of holding one's job: what an iron filing that is on the compass card of a man's brain!

Select only one answer choice.

9.   One of the following sentences provides support for the conclusion about "truth". Which one?

Ⓐ Desperation causes people to do things they wouldn't normally do.

Ⓑ Compasses sometimes lack accuracy, just like people.

Ⓒ Truth is not "black or white", it only exists in shades of grey.

Ⓓ Past experiences have a significant effect on a person's behavior.

Ⓔ People are often very dishonest, and seldom can be trusted 100%.

Passage 4

Questions 10 to 13 are based on the following passage.

"GOOD!" cried the Idiot, from behind the voluminous folds of the magazine section of his Sunday newspaper. "Here's a man after my own heart. **Professor Duff, of Glasgow University, has come out with a public statement that the maxims and proverbs of our forefathers are largely hocus–pocus and buncombe**. I've always maintained that myself from the moment I had my first copy–book lesson in which I had to scrawl the line, 'It's a long lane that has no turning,' twenty–four times. And then that other absurd statement, 'A stitch in the side is worth two in the hand'—or something like it—I forget just how it goes—what Tommy–rot that is."

"Well, I don't know about that, Mr. Idiot," said Mr. Whitechoker, tapping his fingers together reflectively.

"Certain great moral principles are instilled into the minds of the young by the old proverbs and maxims that remain with them forever and become a potent influence in the formation of character."
"I should like to agree with you, but I can't," said the Idiot. "I don't believe anything that is noble in the way of character was ever fostered by such a statement as that it's a long lane that has no turning. In the first place, it isn't necessarily true. I know a lane on my grandfather's farm that led from the hen–coop to the barn. There wasn't a turn nor a twist in it, and I know by actual measurement that it wasn't sixty feet long.

For Questions 10 and 11, select only one answer choice.

10. Which of the following statements best reflects the author's main point in this passage regarding the validity of maxims and proverbs?

    (A) These popular phrases are antiquated and useless.

    (B) Common phrases such as the ones mentioned in the passage are confusing and vague.

    (C) Phrases that are passed down through generations in still important messages in society through repetition.

    (D) People who misunderstand the significance of proverbs simply do not understand them.

    (E) Proverbs and maxims present literal messages for social improvement.

11. The bold–faced sentence contributes to the Idiot's main argument regarding the insignificance of popular sayings in all of the following ways EXCEPT:

    (A) It provides evidence to support his opinion.

    (B) It summarizes his main point.

    (C) It introduces his opinion.

    (D) It offers an alternate explanation to support his opinion.

    (E) It presents an argument.

12. Select the sentence in the passage that best depicts the author's view of the Idiot's lack of intelligence regarding the meaning of proverbs.

Consider each of the three choices separately and select all that apply.

13. Which of the following words could be used to indicate the author's attitude towards people who misuse and misunderstand proverbs and maxims?

    [A] Derisive

    [B] Satirical

    [C] Light-hearted

Passage 5

Question 14 is based on the following passage.

Together with the Mayans, the Andean peoples weave their stories and myths into their clothing. They attire themselves in their myths, legends, and folk stories which, at times, are displayed in their clothing. Histories merge with these tales, augmenting a powerful tradition. The visual metaphors that evolve link these indigenous peoples through their ancestors and varied cultures to the beginnings of time forging an identity and creating a sense of security and order. The daily dress cultivates this harmony. Thus, it can be said that weavers are bearers of tradition and are representatives of the Archetypal Feminine.

14.   Select the sentence that suggests the ways in which the traditional attire promotes a sense of emotional well-being.

Passage 6

Question 15 is based on the following passage.

For Africans, movement is a great way of communicating with others. Because of this, the dances often utilize symbolic mime, gestures, masks, props, visual devices, and body painting. Most of the basic movements of African dances emphasize the use of torso, upper body, and feet. There are also complex dances that use intricate action and various body parts. Team dances are common but there are also times when the dance involves 2-4 individuals taking turns on the dancing ring. There are also different formations used by the dancers like columns, serpentine, circular, and linear

15.   Select the sentence that suggests that some dancing exhibitions may be competitive in nature.

Passage 7

Questions 16 to 19 are based on the following passage.

After the splendid outburst of painting in the first half of the fourteenth century, there came a lull. The thoughts and sentiments of medieval Italy had been now set forth in art. The sincere and simple style of Giotto was worked out. But the new culture of the Revival had not as yet sufficiently penetrated the Italians for the painters to express it; nor had they mastered the technicalities of their craft in such a manner as to render the delineation of more complex forms of beauty possible. The years between 1400 and 1470 may be roughly marked out as the second period of great, activity in painting.

For Questions 16 to 18, select only one answer choice.

16. Which of the following best describes the author's primary purpose in this passage?

    Ⓐ To describe and explain the progress of Italian painting from the 13th to the 14th centuries.

    Ⓑ To describe the influence of Giotto upon painters of the 14th century.

    Ⓒ To describe the technical superiority of 14th century paintings to their 13th century predecessors.

    Ⓓ To describe the end of the Revival around the middle of the 13th century and the beginning of a new era of art in the 14th century.

    Ⓔ To compare and contrast two important eras of Italian painting.

17. The author implies that a second great period of Italian painting began around 1400 for which of the following reasons?

    Ⓐ The influential painter Giotto finally established a simple and sincere style for others to emulate.

    Ⓑ Medieval Italian culture could not be effectively expressed artistically before this time because artistic expression had been limited by the influence of Giotto.

    Ⓒ Revival Italian culture had had time to ferment and artistic technique had had time to develop.

    Ⓓ Once Medieval Italian culture had been thoroughly explored in art, painters were able to progress into a new era.

    Ⓔ New painting techniques were developed around this time, enabling artists to create more complex works.

18. Which of the following is clearly implied by the author?

    Ⓐ Italian painters of the Revival period expressed Italian culture as effectively as painters of the Medieval period.

    Ⓑ Italian paintings of the Revival period were aesthetically superior to those of the medieval period.

    Ⓒ There were very few Italian paintings produced during the second half of the 14th century.

    Ⓓ Italian paintings of the Revival period tended to be more complex than those of the medieval period.

    Ⓔ Italian painters of the medieval period were satisfied with a simpler style and not interested in more complex techniques.

Consider each of the three choices separately and select all that apply.

19.   The author gives which of the following as a reason for the artistic "lull" described in the passage?

        ☐A   Revival culture was too new and unfamiliar for artists to incorporate effectively into their work.

        ☐B   Medieval culture had been thoroughly explored artistically.

        ☐C   New artistic techniques take time to develop.

Passage 8

Question 20 is based on the following passage.

A pleasant and elevated spot being fixed upon, Sheddad dispatched a hundred chiefs to collect skilled artists and workmen from all countries. He also commanded the monarchs of Syria and Ormus to send him all their jewels and precious stones. Forty camel-loads of gold, silver, and jewels were daily used in the building, which contained a thousand spacious quadrangles of many thousand rooms. When finished, Sheddad marched to view it. Suddenly was heard in the air a voice like thunder, and Sheddad, looking up, beheld a personage of majestic figure and stern aspect, who said, "I am the angel of death, commissioned to seize thy impure soul." Sheddad exclaimed, "Give me leisure to enter the garden," and was descending from his horse, when the seizer of life snatched away his impure spirit, and he fell dead upon the ground. At the same time, lightning flashed and destroyed the whole army of the infidel, and the rose garden of Irim became concealed from the sight of man.

Select only one answer choice.

20.   Which of the following is an explanation for concealing the rose garden of Irim from the sight of man?

        Ⓐ   To prevent theft of the precious metals and gems used in its construction

        Ⓑ   To reserve its spectacular beauty for God and His angels

        Ⓒ   To prevent Sheddad's heirs from claiming it as their own

        Ⓓ   As a preventive against using the riches of other countries to promote oneself

        Ⓔ   As a moral lesson about the sin of excessive pride

Passage 9

Questions 21 to 24 are based on the following passage.

I was satisfied with San Francisco, with my interest in the lumber yards, and with my partnership with Colonel Stevenson on the North Beach. My interest in my brig, when it came down, and my prospective interest in what was to be the city of Toulom, and my associations with Mr. R., who was building the first brewery on the Pacific, which I was backing up with my endorsement, and I was to have one–third interest when it was completed, if I wanted it, at first cost, looked like a very favorable investment for me at that time. I was living an active and enterprising life, with bright hopes of future fortune. One morning when I went down to the North Beach, I found there had been a house erected on our land in the night. I, of course, informed the colonel at once. He informed me it was a man by the name of Colton, who pretended to have a title under what he called the "Colton Grant," and that it was bogus, and that he had the building erected to try and force his title. The colonel said he would see the judge of the court in the city and get an order for its removal. In about two hours he sent a messenger with an order from the judge authorizing us to remove it. He instructed me to employ all the men that were necessary, and have the material removed from the premises and he would pay the bill, which I did, and our title was not disputed after that.

21.   Select the sentence in the passage that implies that the Colonel Stevenson enjoys a significant level of respect in San Francisco.

For Questions 22 and 23, select only one answer choice.

22.   Which of the following is the best description of the author's attitude concerning his experiences in the San Francisco area?

Ⓐ choleric

Ⓑ earnest

Ⓒ objective

Ⓓ sanguine

Ⓔ sincere

23.   Which of the following is likely to be a topic in the text that immediately follows the passage presented here?

Ⓐ Steps taken by the government in San Francisco to prevent further bogus land claims.

Ⓑ The process by which the author built a house on his land in the North Beach.

Ⓒ The outcome of the author's enterprises in California.

Ⓓ The arrival of the author's brig.

Ⓔ The completion of the brewery.

Consider each of the three choices separately and select all that apply.

24.   Which of the following statements is a reasonable explanation for Colton's attempt to poach the
       author's claim to the land?

       [A]   The rapid growth of San Francisco and the towns surrounding it created an urgency to obtain
              plots of land suitable for building homes.

       [A]   The rights of squatters were seriously considered when encouraging settlement in the early days
              of San Francisco.

       [A]   An unscrupulous speculator sold the land to Colton under false pretenses.

Passage 10

Question 25 is based on the following passage.

   The aim of this little work is, therefore, limited to the gathering of such facts and phenomena as may serve
to throw light upon the nature of the magic powers with which man is undoubtedly endowed. Its end will be
attained if it succeeds in showing that he actually does possess powers which are not subject to the general
laws of nature, but more or less independent of space and time, and which yet make themselves known
partly by appeals to the ordinary senses and partly by peculiar phenomena, the result of their activity. These
higher powers, operating exclusively through the spirit of man, are part of his nature, which has much in
common with that of the Deity, since he was created by God "in His own image," and the Lord "breathed
into his nostrils the breath of life and man became a living soul.

Select only one answer choice.

25.   Based on the information in this passage, what makes it likely that the author will find it difficult to
       conduct an objective investigation?

       Ⓐ His belief in God

       Ⓑ His preconceived idea that man has magical powers

       Ⓒ The lack of previous research on the subject

       Ⓓ The refusal of the church to cooperate in his endeavor

       Ⓔ The likelihood that the public will scoff at his ideas

Passage 11

Question 26 is based on the following passage.

   I must confess, though, that I am a bibliophile with War books. Any book about the Great War is good
enough for me. I am to that class of literature what little boys are to stamps. Yes; I know well the dread

implication. I am aware of the worm in the mind; that I probe a wound; that I surrender to an impulse to peer into the darkness of the pit; that I encourage a thought which steals in with the quiet of midnight, and that it keeps me awake while the household sleeps. I know I consort with ghosts in a region of evil. I get the horrors, and I do not repel them. For some reason I like those ghosts. Most of them have no names for me, but I count them as old friends of mine; and where should I meet them again, at night, but amid the scenes we knew.

26. Select the sentence that suggests that the writer may be performing a cathartic act in this passage.

Passage 12

Questions 27 and 28 are based on the following passage.

Out we drove at last. It was December, but by luck we found a halcyon morning which had got lost in the year's procession. It was a Sunday morning, and it had not been ashore. It was still virgin, bearing a vestal light. It had not been soiled yet by any suspicion of this trampled planet, this muddy star, which its innocent and tenuous rays had discovered in the region of night. I thought it still was regarding us as a lucky find there. Its light was tremulous, as if with joy and eagerness. I met this discovering morning as your ambassador while you still slept, and betrayed not, I hope, any greyness and bleared satiety of ours to its pure, frail, and lucid regard. That was the last good service I did before leaving you quiet. I was glad to see how well our old earth did meet such a light, as though it had no difficulty in looking day in the face. The world was miraculously renewed.

Select only one answer choice.

27. In the context of this passage, which of the following is the best definition for "lucid"?

   Ⓐ Easily understood

   Ⓑ Shining or bright

   Ⓒ Rational or sane

   Ⓓ Clear, transparent

   Ⓔ Evident

Consider each of the three choices separately and select all that apply.

28.   Select the statement that can replace the second sentence of the passage without altering the overall meaning of the author's words.

A   Although it was December, we were fortunate to discover tranquil weather that seemed a better fit for a warmer month

B   It was December, and we discovered a holiday celebration that we had neglected to observe earlier in the year

C   Because it was December, we felt as carefree on that morning as we had in the summer month

Passage 13

Questions 29 and 30 are based on the following passage.

Friends - This lecture has been delivered under these circumstances: I visit a town or city, and try to arrive there early enough to see the postmaster, the barber, the keeper of the hotel, the principal of the schools, and the ministers of some of the churches, and then go into some of the factories and stores, and talk with the people, and get into sympathy with the local conditions of that town or city and see what has been their history, what opportunities they had, and what they had failed to do - and every town fails to do something - and then go to the lecture and talk to those people about the subjects which applied to their locality. "Acres of Diamonds" - the idea - has continuously been precisely the same. The idea is that in this country of ours every man has the opportunity to make more of himself than he does in his own environment, with his own skill, with his own energy, and with his own friends.

For Questions 29 and 30, select only one answer choice.

29.   Based on the information in this passage, select the word that best describes his purpose in delivering his presentation, "Acres of Diamonds".

(A) Information

(B) Confirmation

(C) Innovation

(D) Motivation

(E) Intimidation

30. What is the relationship of the last two sentences to the preceding portion of the passage?

    Ⓐ They invalidate the process of the writer's visiting local officials and work places.

    Ⓑ They contrast the universality of the idea with the specificity of the points for each town or city.

    Ⓒ They cast aspersions on the officials and townsfolk that he has visited.

    Ⓓ They summarize the information that he has discovered from his visits to officials and work places.

    Ⓔ They support the assumption of failure on the parts of the town's inhabitants.

Passage 14

Questions 31 and 32 are based on the following passage.

Nowhere is there anything just like them. In his best work - and his tales of the great metropolis are his best - he is unique. The soul of his art is unexpectedness. Humor at every turn there is, and sentiment and philosophy and surprise. One never may be sure of himself. The end is always a sensation. No foresight may predict it, and the sensation always is genuine. Whatever else O. Henry was, he was an artist, a master of plot and diction, a genuine humorist, and a philosopher. His weakness lay in the very nature of his art. He was an entertainer bent only on amusing and surprising his reader. Everywhere brilliancy, but too often it is joined to cheapness; art, yet art merging swiftly into caricature. Like Harte, he cannot be trusted. Both writers on the whole may be said to have lowered the standards of American literature, since both worked in the surface of life with theatric intent and always without moral background, O. Henry moves, but he never lifts.

Select only one answer choice.

31. Consider the words of this critic and select word or phrase that best identifies what is missing from O. Henry's writing.

    Ⓐ Tension

    Ⓑ Style

    Ⓒ Subtlety

    Ⓓ Plot

    Ⓔ Conflict resolution

Consider each of the three choices separately and select all that apply.

32.   Which of the following statements, if true, would have altered this critic's opinion of both O. Henry's and Harte's literary endeavors?

[A]   The readers of the stories crafted by Harte and O. Henry are left with a sense of satisfaction

[B]   Harte's and O. Henry's stories continue to appear in secondary school anthologies

[C]   The themes in the works of both writers provide significant insight into the motivations of human behavior

Passage 15

Questions 33 to 38 are based on the following passage.

Men's ideas root pretty far back. Their religious creeds are very old. By means of interest and hope and largely fear, they manage to hang on to the old, even when they know it is not true. The idea of man's importance came in the early history of the human race. He looked out on the earth, and of course he thought it was flat! It looks flat, and he thought it was. He saw the sun, and he formed the conception that somebody moved it out every morning and pulled it back in at night. He saw the moon, and he had the opinion that somebody pulled that out at sundown and took it in the morning. He saw the stars, and all there was about the stars was, "He made the stars also." They were just "also." They were close by, and they were purely for man to look at, about like diamonds in the shirt bosoms of people who like them.

This was not an unreasonable idea, considering what they had to go on. The people who still believe it have no more to go on. Blind men can't be taught to see or deaf people to hear. The primitive people thought that the stars were right nearby and just the size they seemed to be. Of course, now we know that some of them are so far away that light traveling at nearly 286,000 miles a second is several million light years getting to the earth, and some of them are so large that our sun, even, would be a fly-speck to them. The larger the telescopes the more of them we see, and the imagination can't compass the end of them. It is just humanly possible that somewhere amongst the infinite number of infinitely larger and more important specks of mud in the universe there might be some organisms of matter that are just as intelligent as our people on the earth. So, to have the idea that all of this was made for man gives man a great deal of what Weber and Field used to call "Proud flesh."

Man can't get conceited from what he knows today, and he can't get it from what intellectual people ever knew. You remember, in those days the firmament was put in to divide the water below from the water above. They didn't know exactly what it was made of, but they knew what it was. Heaven was up above the firmament. They knew what it was, because Jacob had seen the angels going up and down on a ladder. Of course, a ladder was the only transportation for such purposes known to Jacob. If he had been dreaming now, they would have been going up in a flying machine and coming down in the same way.

Our conceptions of things root back; and that, of course, is the reason for our crude religions, our crude laws, our crude ideas, and our exalted opinion of the human race.

For Questions 33 to 35, select only one answer choice.

33. In the context of this passage, which of the following definitions most closely fits the use of the word "crude" in the last sentence of the passage?

    Ⓐ Lacking in intellectual subtlety, perceptivity

    Ⓑ Unrefined or natural

    Ⓒ Lacking finish, polish, or completeness

    Ⓓ Lacking culture, refinement, tact

    Ⓔ Undisguised; blunt

34. What purpose is served by the author's using the speed of light in the second paragraph?

    Ⓐ To reveal the author's level of education

    Ⓑ To demonstrate how man's understanding of the universe has increased

    Ⓒ To help the reader understand the context of the passage

    Ⓓ To explain how distant the stars actually are

    Ⓔ To show the value of telescopes

35. What does the author's use of the words "blind" and "deaf" in the second paragraph reveal about his attitude toward his topic?

    Ⓐ They make evident his optimism for the human race

    Ⓑ They demonstrate his fear for the human race

    Ⓒ They show his scorn for members of the human race

    Ⓓ They reveal his feelings of superiority over other men

    Ⓔ They reinforce his sense of hopelessness about science in general

For Questions 36 and 37 consider each of the three choices separately and select all that apply.

36.   Which of the following is akin to the story of Jacob's ladder?

   [A]   President Kennedy's declaration that the United States would send a man to the moon by the end of the 1960's

   [B]   The belief that the Earth is the center of the universe

   [C]   Columbus' calling the natives of the New World Indians

37.   What does the author imply when he says at the beginning of the third paragraph that man can't get conceited from what he knows today?

   [A]   Man has failed to make significant progress in knowledge

   [B]   Man's current knowledge will be made insignificant by the knowledge of future generations

   [C]   The knowledge that man possesses is not used for the advancement of the human race

38.   Select the sentence that supports the author's opinion that man is conceited.

Passage 16

Question 39 is based on the following passage.

Is human nature intrinsically good or inherently evil? One of the most prominent and influential arguments for the latter was put forward by the British political philosopher Thomas Hobbes. In his seminal work, Leviathan, Hobbes established his theory of the social contract, in which he claimed that humans without government exist in a state of nature where each individual has a right to everything, engendering a "war against all". This environment creates a constant fear of death and prevents humans from both obtaining and hoping for the necessities needed to survive. It is only through the establishment of a civil society by way of a social contract that individuals are able to unite and thrive collectively. For Hobbes, society is what tames and controls the ultimately selfish and corrupt natural state of the human being.

39.   Select the sentence that best illustrates Hobbes' view on human nature.

Passage 17

Questions 40 and 41 are based on the following passage.

The Pop Art movement is generally seen as the aesthetic expression of capitalism, its motifs and imagery centering on mass production and consumer culture. The hallmark of Pop Art is its ability to make the viewer feel that it is pretend and not worthy of serious critique. A good example of such a work is pop artist Andy Warhol's images of Campbell's Soup cans. While Pop Art seems superfluous at the surface level, it is actually produced with marked intentionality and has a message that splinters in two directions. In Britain,

Pop Artists use the capitalist aesthetic to mock and critique the vapidity of American consumer society while American Pop Artists tend to use their work as a celebration of reality and a slight re-imagining of familiar surroundings.

Select only one answer choice.

40.   How does British Pop Art differ from American Pop Art?

Ⓐ   There is no difference

Ⓑ   British Pop Art lampoons American consumer culture while American Pop Art focuses on re-creating reality

Ⓒ   British Pop Art is not worthy of serious critique while American Pop Art is highly valued as a legitimate form of aesthetic expression

Ⓓ   British Pop artists are more famous than American Pop artists

Ⓔ   British Pop artists avoid exploring capitalism in their work while American Pop artists use their work to address issues related to capitalism

Consider each of the three choices separately and select all that apply.

41.   What traits of capitalistic culture does Pop Art seek to explore?

[A]   Consumerism

[B]   Mass production

[C]   Free markets

Passage 18

Question 42 is based on the following passage.

One of the defining features of the Art Nouveau movement was its desire to distance itself aesthetically from previous methods of artistic expression. Art Nouveau arose at the turn of the 20th century as a reaction to the Neoclassicist movement's propensity to simply mimic the style of the Greeks and Romans. Art Nouveau artists sought to create a truly new and distinct way of representing the world and this is best exemplified in their architectural approach. They used asymmetry and curvy lines and forms in conjunction with leafs, vines, and other unusual patterns to construct and decorate their buildings in a way that had never before been seen.

42.   Select the sentence that best describes why Art Nouveau artists were looking to radically alter artistic expression.

Passage 19

Questions 43 and 44 are based on the following passage.

Jacques Derrida famously proclaimed, "There is nothing outside the text." By this he meant that analyzing a work of literature could only be done by way of investigating its labyrinthine relationships to other contexts. As a literary critic and founder of deconstructionist theory, Derrida advocated the position that there is no true or objective reference that can serve as a hermeneutical springboard; narratives can only be understood by deconstructing the various frameworks that inform the interpretive process.

Select only one answer choice.

43.   It can be inferred that Derrida prefers a subjective approach to literary analysis because

      Ⓐ   textual analysis is dependent on deconstructing complex narratives

      Ⓑ   all texts are context sensitive and thus subjectivity is a more illuminating approach to finding meaning than objectivity

      Ⓒ   subjectivity accounts for the different ways readers experience and interpret a text

      Ⓓ   deconstructionist theory is predicated on the inner experience of each reader

      Ⓔ   subjectivity allows for a wider array of interesting interpretations of a given text

Consider each of the three choices separately and select all that apply.

44.   Derrida's claim "There is nothing outside the text" can be taken to mean that

      ☐A   texts are connected to the myriad of contexts that contribute to their overall meaning

      ☐B   texts cannot be studied as independent entities

      ☐C   there is no reality outside of the text

Passage 20

Question 45 is based on the following passage.

Modernist literature bloomed at the beginning of the 20th century and was characterized by concise language and precise imagery. Modernist writers such as Ezra Pound and T.S. Eliot used their poetry and prose to express sentiments of radical individualism and methodical order. However, this conviction quickly deteriorated from praise of autonomy to a more introspective, darker look at humanity and the role of the individual as the exactitude of form that modernists so cherished in their writing came to represent the meticulousness with which the industrialized world could extinguish human life during World War I and World War II.

Select only one answer choice.

45. Given the information in the passage, all of the following are true relative to modernist writing except

    Ⓐ Modernist writing evolved to mirror cultural changes

    Ⓑ Modernist writing lauds the primacy of coherent form

    Ⓒ Modernist writing is at its crux deeply reflective.

    Ⓓ Modernist writing eschews florid prose

    Ⓔ Modernist writing is mechanical in nature

Passage 21

Questions 46 and 47 are based on the following passage.

Sun Tzu's The Art of War is one of the earliest and most celebrated books on military strategy in the world. The Art of War covers a variety of topics related to success on the battlefield and, astoundingly, people at nearly all levels of Chinese society in both the past and present are familiar with the text. One of the most influential themes in the book is its emphasis on the ability to evolve and change plans in the present moment instead of focusing solely on developing rigidly thought-out, long-term strategies. This efficacious strategy defined success as the ability to evolve and utilize a quick wit when the situation calls for such action.

For Questions 46 and 47, select only one answer choice.

46. The author's personal opinion on The Art of War can be best described as

    Ⓐ light-hearted

    Ⓑ aloof

    Ⓒ unaligned

    Ⓓ inert

    Ⓔ phlegmatic

47.   The author intends the term "efficacious" in the passage to be analogous to

    Ⓐ ambitious

    Ⓑ useful

    Ⓒ potent

    Ⓓ adequate

    Ⓔ unorganized

Passage 22

Question 48 is based on the following passage.

The latter half of the 20th century witnessed the rise of a new epistemological approach in the humanities: postcolonial theory. Postcolonial theory was a reaction to the Western meta-narratives of European Imperialism that had been deeply entrenched in global society. It sought to give the colonized and their experience a voice in literature, cultural studies, politics, and philosophy in order to illuminate the fact that global reality had been constructed by European cultural power and that cultural space is really a fluid interaction of a "multiplicity of positionalities."

Select only one answer choice.

48.   According to the passage, what was the primary consequence of European Imperialism?

    Ⓐ European imperialism created norms that dictated the structure of global society

    Ⓑ European Imperialism made it difficult for diversity to thrive

    Ⓒ The colonized were unable to participate in the political systems erected by colonial societies

    Ⓓ European Imperialism had little effect on global society

    Ⓔ European Imperialism promoted a cultural space comprised by a variety of cultural perspectives

Passage 23

Questions 49 to 54 are based on the following passage.

Authorial intent is a vehemently debated topic within the realm of literary criticism. Some critics, such as the Marxists, believe that the author's intentions and ideological leanings shape the content of his or her work while others insist that the text is a completely independent artistic entity, impervious to external influences. Many scholars engaged with the New Criticism school of thought are proponents of the latter approach to textual analysis.

Narrowing the scope of the authorial intent debate, Franz Kafka is a writer whose narratives lend themselves well to this literary tiff. Kafka is widely regarded as one of the most prolific and inventive writers of the 20th century and is credited with changing the way many readers and writers viewed the form, content, and limits of fiction. His works are penetrated by alienation, persecution, and a metaphysical sense of magical realism that leave the doors wide open to the debate on whether or not Kafka's prose was an ideological tool or autonomous artistic expression. However, the consensus among scholars tends to hover around the conclusion that Kafka's texts were intentional metaphors for his ideological beliefs and experiences. Kafka's use of the law in his stories provides a compelling example of why this might be the case.

As a trained lawyer, Kafka was well aware of the ins and outs of the legal system in his native Prague - at that time a part of the Austro-Hungarian Empire. In his fiction, particularly in the aptly named The Trial or The Penal Colony, Kafka often portrayed the legal system as rigid, absurd, and tyrannical, as evidenced by arrests for unspecified crimes or the construction of elaborate tools for punishment. The images and metaphors that Kafka infuses his prose with regarding the law and the legal process are what constitute not only the meaning of his fiction but also his personal view on the law. His fiction is written with intention - the intention to show that the legal system is comprised of arbitrary signs and symbols that neither the lawmen nor laymen seem to understand. Thus, the images and themes in Kafka's works are intentionally placed to promote a deliberate message to the readership.

Kafka's use of the law is just one example of why many literary critics hold fast to the idea that every author produces a narrative that has intentional meaning - it is difficult to imagine that a writer can produce a text without having some kind of interpretive goal or objective in mind. However, since no hermeneutical approach to a fictional work's meaning is ever set in stone, the authorial intent debate, like all points of contention in literary criticism, is now and always will be open to a multiplicity of interpretations

For Questions 49 to 51, select only one answer choice.

49.   Which of the following can most reasonably be inferred from the passage?

    Ⓐ Kafka was anti-authoritarian

    Ⓑ The Marxist's have the best method of textual inquiry

    Ⓒ Kafka's fiction impacted the practice and implementation of law in the West

    Ⓓ Authorial intent can always be determined by properly analyzing the form and content of a piece of narrative fiction

    Ⓔ Literary criticism concerns itself primarily with the search for objective truth

50.   Given the information in the passage, how would the author define the concept of authorial intent?

      (A)   Authorial intent is the aggregate of the author's personal opinions and experiences that can influence the meaning of a given text

      (B)   Authorial intent is best defined as the author's main impetus for writing a text

      (C)   Authorial intent is the sum of an author's subjective thoughts that always create the meaning of a given text

      (D)   Authorial intent is the term coined by the New Critics for a specific kind of writing style

      (E)   The passage does not give enough information to define authorial intent

51.   The author intends the term "hermeneutical" in the last sentence to be analogous to

      (A)   Methodological

      (B)   Intentional

      (C)   Epistemological

      (D)   Explicative

      (E)   Remedial

For Questions 52 and 53, consider each of the three choices separately and select all that apply.

52.   What postulation does the passage put forth to argue that Kafka's works convey his personal opinions on law and legality?

      [A]   Kafka used metaphor to describe how difficult it was for laymen to understand the law and legal process

      [B]   Kafka used images and themes of absurdity and tyranny in his fiction to reinforce his belief that the legal process was based on arbitrary authoritarian signs and symbols

      [C]   Kafka used his prose to show that he did not like the legal system because he was a reluctant lawyer

53.   According to the information given in the passage, Kafka believed the legal system to be

      [A]   Intransigent

      [B]   Incongruous

      [C]   Inane

54.   Select the sentence that delineates Kafka's tropes.

Practice Set 2: Biological Sciences

Passage 24

Questions 55 to 58 are based on the following passage.

Just how much muscle a boy should have will depend upon his physical make-up. The gymnasium director in one of our largest colleges, who has spent his whole life in exercise, is a small, slender man whose muscles are not at all prominent and yet they are like steel wires. He has made a life-long study of himself and has developed every muscle in his body. From his appearance he would not be considered a strong man and yet some of the younger athletes weighing fifty pounds more than he, have, in wrestling and feats of strength, found that the man with the largest muscles is not always the best man.

For Questions 55 to 57, select only one answer choice.

55.   Which of the following is an assumption upon which the author's claim rests?

Ⓐ   While some bodybuilders have impressive muscle structures, they may be resorting to illicit methods to reach these goals

Ⓑ   The college gymnasium director is a typical case

Ⓒ   The college gymnasium director stands out as an unusual case

Ⓓ   Eating right is the key to strong muscles and good health

Ⓔ   Exercising consistently has proven results

56.   The lesson to be taken from the passage is most nearly:

Ⓐ   Long-term longevity is correlated to health and fitness

Ⓑ   Appearance does not prescribe one's level of physical activity

Ⓒ   Developing exercise habits will manifest itself in lifelong health

Ⓓ   Physical activity does not prescribe one's appearance

Ⓔ   Reliable gauges of health may include physical appearance

57. The logic in the passage is best shown by which of the following situations?

    Ⓐ An expensive motor performs with lower output than expected

    Ⓑ A small car's engine performs at high horsepower

    Ⓒ A large tractor has a surprisingly inefficient motor

    Ⓓ A small car has enough room for its passengers

    Ⓔ A cheap car has a limited warranty on its motor

Consider each of the three choices separately and select all that apply.

58. The passage suggests which of the following qualities as essential to building strength?

    ☐A Capability for introspection

    ☐B Dedication to weight training over aerobic activity

    ☐C Forgetting about traditional training methods

Passage 25

Questions 59 to 62 are based on the following passage.

The Danger theory of immunity holds that the immune system does not recognize between self and non-self but discriminates between dangerous and safe by recognition of pathogens or alarm signals from injured or stressed cells and tissues. It contradicts the conventional models which state that the immune system distinguishes between self, which is tolerated, and non-self, which is attacked and destroyed. Danger theory states that when tissue cells are distressed because of injury, infection, oncogenic transformation and so on, they start to secrete the so-called danger associated molecular patterns (DAMPs).The Danger model has brought new insights on adaptive and innate immunity. In the past the innate immunity was suggested as a minor part of immune system and the adaptive part was thought to be the most important and effective arm. According to danger theory there is no adaptive immunity without the innate part. This is because DAMPs lead to activation of antigen presenting cells (APC) to process antigens, induce expression of other required molecules and present antigen to T helper cells which are major effectors of adaptive immunity.

For Questions 59 to 61, select only one answer choice.

59.   Which fact, if true, would undermine the argument in this passage?

(A) Scientists discover that DAMPs double the activation of antigen presenting cells

(B) Scientists discover that tissues do not secrete danger associated molecular patterns

(C) Scientists discover that innate immunity is essential for adaptive immunity

(D) Scientists discover that T cells are helpful for destroying non-self-tissue cells

(E) Scientists discover that there is a new antigen that boosts T cell production

60.   The bolded and underlined word "expression" most nearly means in the context of the passage:

(A) depiction of emotions

(B) formation

(C) compression

(D) evidence

(E) feeling

61.   Which statement best summarizes how the Danger theory contradicts conventional views of immunity?

(A) The Danger theory states that the self and non-self are identical, while conventional views state that the immune system only tolerates the self

(B) The Danger theory states that the self and non-self are indistinguishable, while conventional views state that cells only recognize the non-self

(C) The Danger theory states that cells only recognize the self, while conventional views state that the self and non-self are identical

(D) The Danger theory states that the self and non-self are indistinguishable, while conventional views state that cells recognize the self and non-self

(E) The Danger theory states that cells only recognize the self, while conventional views state that cells recognize neither self nor non-self

Consider all three answer choices separately and select all that apply.

62.   Which of the following must be true in order for the Danger theory of immunity to be correct?

        [A]   Cells must go through a specific process that leads to new molecular patterns

        [B]   There must be successful human experiments showing cell tissue change

        [C]   Cells with adaptive immunity must have innate immunity

Passage 26

Questions 63 to 66 are based on the following passage.

In evolutionary biology, mimicry is the similarity of one species to another in characters like appearance, behavior, sound and scent which protects one or both the species involved. Mimicry occurs when a group of organisms, the mimics, evolve to share common perceived characteristics with another group, the models. The evolution is driven by the selective action of a signal-receiver, such as birds that use sight to identify palatable insects. As an interaction, mimicry is in most cases advantageous to the mimic and harmful to the receiver and may or may not have any effect on the model depending on the situation. An example is the moth ash borer (podosesia syringae), which is a mimic of the common wasp in appearance but is not capable of stinging. A predator that has learned to avoid the wasp would similarly avoid the Ash Borer. The most widely accepted model for evolution of mimicry in butterflies is the two-step hypothesis. The first step involves mutation in modifier genes that regulate a complex cluster of linked genes associated with large changes in morphology while the second step consists of selections on genes with smaller phenotypic effects, leading to increasing closeness of resemblance. The observation that only a few single point mutations cause large phenotypic effects while there are numerous others that produce smaller effects supports this hypothesis.

For Questions 63 and 64, select only one answer choice.

63.   The author's primary purpose in the passage is:

        (A)   to give the reader basic information about mimicry

        (B)   to persuade the reader that mimicry contributes to organisms' evolutionary pathways

        (C)   to provide a case study of the moth ash borer

        (D)   to introduce the importance of evolutionary biology

        (E)   to highlight the genetic mutations that help butterflies adapt

64. All of the following would be helpful information to help show how mimicry is beneficial EXCEPT

    (A) a table showing the different organisms that have evolved to mimic other groups

    (B) a chart showing a decreasing population after organisms increase closeness of resemblance

    (C) a case study of stick insects and how mimicry helps them avoid predators

    (D) a chart showing decreasing numbers of moth ash borers caught by predators

    (E) a graph showing increasing populations of stick insects after adapting a gene increasing closeness of resemblance

Consider each of the three choices separately and select all that apply.

65. The passage suggests that mimicry provides which of the following benefits

    [A] Increases reproductive rates of organisms that adapt using mimicry

    [B] Reduces the numbers of organisms captured by predators if the organisms use mimicry

    [C] Allows organisms to develop faster in order to escape predators

66. Select the sentence that best explains the different ways in which an organism can express mimicry.

Passage 27

Question 67 is based on the following passage.

When we examine a simple cell, we find we can distinguish morphological parts. In the first place, we find in the cell a round or oval body known as the nucleus. Occasionally the nucleus is stallate or angular; but as a rule, so long as cells have vital power, the nucleus maintains a nearly constant round or oval shape. The nucleus in its turn, in completely developed cells, very constantly encloses another structure within itself—the so-called nucleolus. With regard to the question of vital form, it cannot be said of the nucleolus that it appears to be an absolute essential, and in a considerable number of young cells it has as yet escaped detection. On the other hand, we regularly meet with it in fully-developed, older forms, and it therefore seems to mark a higher degree of development in the cell.

Select only one answer choice.

67.   All of the following would help to clarify the author's point and to improve the passage EXCEPT:

         (A) A diagram specifying cell parts and their locations

         (B) A brief glossary of infrequently used phrases that the reader is unfamiliar with

         (C) Further explanation of or informed speculation about the function of the nucleolus

         (D) Differences between old and young cells in an organism

         (E) Scaling back the explanation of the nucleus and its functions

Passage 28

Questions 68 to 71 are based on the following passage.

In biology, phylogenetics is the study of evolutionary relationships among groups of organisms discovered through molecular sequencing data and morphological data matrices. Evolution is regarded as a branching process, whereby populations are altered over time and may split into separate branches, hybridize together, or terminate by extinction. This may be visualized in a phylogenetic tree, a hypothesis of the order in which evolutionary events are assumed to have occurred. National Science Foundation funds the Assembling the Tree of Life activity (A To L) project to resolve evolutionary relationships for large groups of organisms. Phylogenetic methods depend upon an implicit or explicit mathematical model describing the evolution of characters observed in the species included. In general, the more data that are available when constructing a tree, the more accurate and reliable the resulting tree will be. Missing data are no more detrimental than simply having fewer data, although the impact is greatest when most of the missing data are in a small number of taxa. Concentrating the missing data across a small number of characters produces a more robust tree. However, there is no way to measure whether a particular phylogenetic hypothesis is accurate or not unless the true relationships among the taxa being examined are already known.

For Questions 68 and 69, select only one answer choice.

68.   The passage provides information on all of the following EXCEPT

         (A) the concept of a phylogenetic tree

         (B) effects of missing data on phylogenetics

         (C) significant drawbacks to phylogenetic methods

         (D) the role of modeling in phylogenetics

         (E) different outcomes of evolution for a population

69. The bolded and underlined word "robust" most nearly means in the context of the passage:

   (A) vibrant

   (B) extensive

   (C) thriving

   (D) detailed

   (E) blossoming

Consider each of the three choices separately and select all that apply.

70. Which of the following conclusions can be drawn from this passage?

   [A] Phylogenetics is a mathematical approach to studying evolution in organisms

   [B] Phylogenetic hypotheses always show the correct order of evolutionary events

   [C] Scientists need complete data sets before using phylogenetic methods

71. Select the sentence that best explains the specific tool or tools used in phylogenetics to describe the evolution of organisms.

Passage 29

Questions 72 to 75 are based on the following passage.

Systems biology is a biology-based inter-disciplinary field of study that focuses on complex interactions within biological systems, using a holistic perspective than traditional reductionism. One of the outreaching aims of systems biology is to model and discover emergent properties of cells, tissues and organisms, typically involving metabolic, transcriptional or cell signaling networks. The formal study of systems biology, as a distinct discipline, was launched by systems theorist Mihajlo Mesarovic in 1966 with an international symposium at the Case Institute of Technology in Cleveland, Ohio entitled "Systems Theory and Biology". With the birth of functional genomics and proteomics in the 1990s large quantities of high-quality data became available and the computing power exploded, making more realistic modeling possible. These investigations are frequently combined with large-scale perturbation methods, including gene-based and chemical approaches using small molecule libraries, and robots or automated sensors are used for data acquisition. These technologies are still emerging and many face problems in the quality of large-scale of data produced. A wide variety of quantitative scientists are working to improve the quality of these approaches and to create, refine, and retest the models to accurately reflect observations.

For Questions 72 to 74, select only one answer choice.

72.   The passage could be improved by the addition of what information?

    Ⓐ A glossary explaining the scientific words mentioned

    Ⓑ Images of the robots and automated sensors used to collect data

    Ⓒ A brief history of computers, leading up to their use in systems biology

    Ⓓ More information on Mesarovic's discoveries in 1966

    Ⓔ Studies currently being undertaken by systems biologists

73.   The author's primary purpose in this passage is:

    Ⓐ to inform the reader of systems biology and its history

    Ⓑ to highlight important discoveries in the field of systems biology

    Ⓒ to question recent scientific advances in biology

    Ⓓ to praise the role of technology in scientific discovery

    Ⓔ to summarize recent data obtained about genes and molecules

74.   The bolded and underlined word "perturbation" most nearly means in the context of the passage:

    Ⓐ confusing and complicated

    Ⓑ lacking an exact numerical answer

    Ⓒ unclear or unfinished

    Ⓓ purposely difficult

    Ⓔ lacking sense, direction, or reason

Consider each of the three choices separately and select all that apply.

75.   The passage could be described as which of the following?

    🄰 An overview of the birth of the systems biology field

    🄱 An explanation of recent advances in systems biology

    🄲 A treatise on the usefulness of systems biology

Passage 30

Question 76 is based on the following passage.

We may note here the meaning of certain terms we shall be constantly employing. The head end of the rabbit is anterior, the tail end posterior, the backbone side of the body-- the upper side in life-- is dorsal, the breast and belly side, the lower side of the animal, is ventral. If we imagine the rabbit sawn asunder, as it were, by a plane passing through the head and tail, that would be the median plane, and parts on either side of it are lateral, and left or right according as they lie to the animal's left or right. In a limb, or in the internal organs, the part nearest the central organ, or axis, is proximal, the more remote or terminal parts are distal. For instance, the mouth is anteriorly placed, the tongue on its ventral wall; the tongue is median, the eyes are lateral, and the fingers are distal to the elbow. The student must accustom himself to these words, and avoid, in his descriptions, the use of such terms as "above," "below," "outside," which vary with the position in which we conceive the animal placed.

Consider the answer choices separately and select all that apply.

76.   Select the scenario below that best reflects the writer's purpose in this passage.

   A   Sailing a yacht in the America's Cup race

   B   Performing brain surgery

   C   Repairing a truck engine

Passage 31

Question 77 is based on the following passage.

From this you can see that it is especially important to know all you can about the life of injurious insects, since it is often easier to kill these pests at one stage of their life than at another. Often it is better to aim at destroying the seemingly harmless beetle or butterfly than to try to destroy the larvae that hatch from its eggs, although, as you must remember, it is generally the larvae that do the most harm. Larvae grow very rapidly; therefore, the food supply must be great to meet the needs of the insect.

Select only one answer choice.

77.   Consider the information in this passage and select what relationship it likely has to the text that
       precedes it.

       Ⓐ It functions as the conclusion

       Ⓑ It functions as an explanation of an idea from the preceding paragraph

       Ⓒ It functions as a warning about a situation mentioned in the previous paragraph

       Ⓓ It serves as a transition between the previous paragraph and the conclusion

       Ⓔ It reinforces the idea presented in the previous portion of the text

Passage 32

Questions 78 to 80 are based on the following passage.

We have already given a description of the mammalian skull, and we have stated where the origin of
the several bones was in membrane, and where in cartilage; but a more complete comprehension of the
mammalian skull becomes possible with the handling of a lower type. We propose now, first to give some
short account of the development and structure of the skull of the frog, and then to show briefly how its
development and adult arrangement demonstrate the mammalian skull to be a fundamentally similar
structure, complicated and disguised by further development and re-adjustment.

For Questions 78 and 79, select only one answer choice.

78.   Which of the following is the most appropriate audience for the information in this passage?

       Ⓐ Herpetologists

       Ⓑ Zoologists

       Ⓒ Endocrinologists

       Ⓓ Thoracic surgeons

       Ⓔ Craniologists

79. Select from the following list the definition of "fundamentally" that most closely matches the use of the word in this context.

   (A) Primarily

   (B) Basically; underlying

   (C) Of or affecting the foundation or basis

   (D) Originally

   (E) Indispensably

Consider each answer choice separately and select all that apply.

80. Based on the information in this passage, which of the following is likely to be true about the study of human anatomy.

   [A] Every aspect of human anatomy has a corresponding structure in a lower life form

   [B] Examining amphibian anatomy leads to a better understanding of human anatomy

   [C] Examining anatomical structures of other life forms may lead to a better understanding of human anatomy

Passage 33

Questions 81 to 83 are based on the following passage.

Many attempts have been made and are still being made to increase the length of the staple of the upland types. The methods used are as follows: selection of seed having a long fiber; special cultivation and fertilization; crossing the short-stapled cotton on the long-stapled cotton. This last process, as already explained, is called hybridizing. Many of these attempts have succeeded, and there are now a large number of varieties which excel the older varieties in profitable yield. The new varieties are each year being more widely grown. Every farmer should study the new types and select the one that will best suit his land. The new types have been developed under the best tillage. Therefore, if a farmer would keep the new type as good as it was when he began to grow it, he must give it the same good tillage, and practice seed-selection.

81. Select the sentence in the passage that justifies the writer's purpose in this piece.

For Questions 82 and 83, select only one answer choice.

82.   Which of the following is a reasonable conclusion based on the content of the passage?

Ⓐ Hybridization is a long and costly endeavor

Ⓑ The benefit or a hybrid is that it can adapt to any conditions

Ⓒ Fertilization produces the best results with hybrid plants

Ⓓ Overlooking one of the cultivation criteria will reduce the success of a hybrid seed

Ⓔ Farmers should select the hybrid that demands the highest price after harvesting

83.   The use of the word "tillage" in this context implies that which of the following is most important to insure crop success?

Ⓐ Good soil preparation

Ⓑ Correct nutrient application

Ⓒ Sufficient use of pesticides

Ⓓ Adequate irrigation

Ⓔ Widespread application of mulch

Passage 34

Question 84 is based on the following passage.

The reason for mixing clover and grass is at once seen. The true grasses, so far as science now shows, get all their nitrogen from the soil; hence they more or less exhaust the soil. But, as several times explained in this book, the clovers are legumes, and all legumes are able by means of the bacteria that live on their roots to use the free nitrogen of the air. Hence without cost to the farmer these clovers help the soil to feed their neighbors, the true grasses. For this reason, some light perennial legume should always be added to grass seed.

84.   Select the sentence in this passage that demonstrates that growing clover is preferable to adding nitrogen-rich fertilizer to the soil.

Passage 35

Questions 85 to 87 are based on the following passage.

It may seem somewhat superfluous to say that fish cannot live in any water unless that water contains the food supply necessary for them to thrive upon, and yet this is the point most often overlooked in stocking waters with fish. Small attempts at stocking with creatures suitable for food, particularly after the fish have been already introduced, are not at all likely to succeed. Such an important matter when treated as a small afterthought is almost sure to end in failure of the whole business of stocking.

85. Select the sentence that most closely exemplifies the adage, "An ounce of prevention is worth a pound of cure".

For Questions 86 and 87, select only one answer choice.

86. What assumption about fish is the reader apt to make after reading this passage?

(A) Fish have specific diets

(B) Fish in a pond with no food source will be easier to catch

(C) Fish are slow to adapt to a new food source

(D) Fish become cannibalistic when deprived of a natural food source

(E) Fish will migrate to a source of food

87. In a presentation on stocking a pond with fish, where, in the sequence, is the best place for the information in this passage?

(A) The introduction

(B) The conclusion

(C) Immediately following a discussion of the types of food necessary for fish to thrive in a pond

(D) Immediately prior to a discussion of the types of food necessary for fish to thrive in a pond

(E) Immediately prior to a discussion of the vegetation needed in the pond

Passage 36

Questions 88 to 90 are based on the following passage.

Whether, therefore, a tree might possibly continue living and growing forever is a question of less entertainment than the question of its possible duration in the common state of nature and under the irreversible conditions of climate, soil, and the elements. What age may we ascribe to some of our largest specimens, either still existing or recorded in trustworthy history? Is the period of one thousand years, the favorite figure of tradition, a common or probable period of arboreal longevity, or have our proudest forest giants attained their present size in half the time that is commonly claimed for them?

In the discussion of this question we have but few known data to guide us, since statistics of the rate of growth, as afforded by careful measurement, date only from about the beginning of the eighteenth century. Of such statistics we may dismiss at once measurement of height or of the spread of a tree's boughs, the measurement of girth being far easier and more conclusive.

88.   Select the sentence that implies that the ages of apparently old trees were arbitrarily determined.

For Questions 89 and 90, select only one answer choice.

89.   Select the most accurate definition of entertainment as it appears in the first sentence of this passage.

   (A) Amusement

   (B) Something affording pleasure

   (C) A performance

   (D) An agreeable occupation of the mind

   (E) Consideration

90.   Use the progression of ideas in this passage to select which of the following is the most probable topic of the writer's next paragraph.

   (A) Other means of determining the age of trees

   (B) How soil and climate conditions contribute to arboreal longevity

   (C) The progress made in aging trees between the end of the eighteenth century and the end of the nineteenth century

   (D) An argument for replacing the one-thousand-year measurement for very old trees with a more moderate five-hundred-year measurement

   (E) The part of the world that is home to the oldest trees

Passage 37

Question 91 is based on the following passage.

   Research on barn swallows gives us insight into the ways in which hormones affect the behavior of various species, including our own. Male barn swallows with the most vibrantly colored feathers are most attractive to females and thus mate much more frequently than their dull-feathered male counterparts. Scientists, however, have discovered that simply darkening the feathers of the lusterless males with a marker can change their hormone levels, turning beta males into alpha males since their mating rates increase dramatically. This is due not only to an increase in attractiveness to females but also an increase in the confidence of the males, consequently engendering higher levels of testosterone.

Select only one answer choice.

91.   Given the information in the passage, what is the relationship between confidence and hormones in male barn swallows?

    Ⓐ Confidence plays a minor role in the increase of certain hormones in male barn swallows

    Ⓑ Physically attractive male barn swallows are more confident and thus experience higher levels of testosterone

    Ⓒ Only inherently attractive alpha male barn swallows have confidence due to high testosterone levels

    Ⓓ Confidence is the sole factor in raising the testosterone levels of male barn swallows

    Ⓔ Confidence plays no role in the hormonal patterns of male barn swallows; mating is the key factor in fluctuating hormone levels

Passage 38

Questions 92 to 94 are based on the following passage.

According to anthropologists, observing primates in Senegal is like opening a window to the world of understanding the behavior of early humans, particularly related to sharing. They have found that the chimpanzees display an intentional willingness to share food and rudimentary hunting tools with each other, an important detection since it was previously thought that chimpanzees usually only shared meat. However, this sharing is not altruistically motivated. Since it is an exchange that primarily takes place from males to females, anthropologists have postulated a "food for sex" theory. This claim is further backed up by the fact that sexually receptive females in their reproductive years were most likely to receive food and supplies from males.

For Questions 92 and 93, select only one answer choice.

92.   What is inferred by the "food for sex" theory in primates?

    Ⓐ Attractive females have the best chances for survival

    Ⓑ Sexual gratification is the primary motivation of male primates

    Ⓒ Male primates are ultimately exploitative

    Ⓓ Primates display a high level of magnanimity

    Ⓔ Male primates are lazy

93. According to the passage, understanding group behavior in primates is important because

   Ⓐ Primates are closely related to humans and thus can help us better understand our own species

   Ⓑ Group behavior in primates can help us understand specifically the way males and females share

   Ⓒ Primates can help humans see why it is important to learn to be altruistic

   Ⓓ Group behavior in primates is the key to understanding behavior patterns in all species

   Ⓔ The sexual habits of primates can enlighten humans as to their own motivations for sex

94. Select the sentence that makes use of the rhetorical device of the trope.

Passage 39

Question 95 is based on the following passage.

Starvation-induced antibiotic resistance is one of the primary reasons many bacteria are elusive when it comes to treatment and as a result some infections are actually impossible to cure. This situation proves paradoxical to scientists, as many of the bacteria that are antibiotic-sensitive still exhibit remarkable survival skills. As soon as bacteria, which typically gather in clusters, sense that their supply of nutrients is waning, they issue a chemical warning that causes them to modify their metabolic rates as a means of defending against starvation, which in turn halts their growth. Many forms of antibiotic treatment, which target active bacteria, are then rendered ineffective since starving bacteria stall cellular growth and lie dormant.

Consider each of the three choices separately and select all that apply.

95. According to the passage, starvation protects bacteria from medications by

   Ａ Modifying its growth patterns

   Ｂ Making it impervious to antibiotic attack

   Ｃ Changing its chemical composition

Passage 40

Questions 96 to 98 are based on the following passage.

Ocean acidification due to the absorption of atmospheric carbon dioxide is a major threat to coral reef ecosystems worldwide and scientists are looking for ways to both understand and combat this phenomenon. This is an especially vital area of exploration since coral reefs are home to 25% of all marine species. Studies pertaining to ocean acidity and the coral reef have been conducted at the submarine springs near the Yucatan Peninsula in Mexico, a perfect environment due to the naturally occurring high acidity (low pH). They have found that the type of coral that serves as the foundation of the reef is unable to calcify and grow in high acidity, which means that the continued absorption of carbon from the atmosphere could halt or dramatically change the growth of the ocean's coral reefs - a terrible catastrophe for the delicate balance of life undersea.

For Questions 96 and 97, select only one answer choice.

96.   From the information given in the passage, what are the implications of the continued occurrence of low pH levels in the world's oceans?

   Ⓐ   The atmosphere will continue to absorb carbon from the high acidity ocean

   Ⓑ   At least 25% of all marine species will die

   Ⓒ   The low acidity will negatively impact the growth of the foundation of the coral reefs

   Ⓓ   Since many types of coral can grow in high acidity, coral reefs are not in any dramatic danger

   Ⓔ   Continued acidification will make it difficult for coral reefs to grow and support marine life

97.   The rhetorical goal of this passage is

   Ⓐ   To delineate the danger atmospheric carbon dioxide poses to the world's oceans

   Ⓑ   To invoke an emotional response in the reader relative to ocean acidification

   Ⓒ   To persuade the reader that ocean acidification is harmful

   Ⓓ   To delve deeper into the specifics of how pH levels affect coral reefs

   Ⓔ   To persuade the reader that the coral reefs are in grave danger

98.   Select the sentence that best describes the importance of coral reefs in the ocean ecosystem.

Passage 41

Question 99 is based on the following passage.

Malaria is a mosquito-borne disease that attacks its victims by way of parasites within the red blood cells that cause serious illness that can result in coma and death. Researchers have recently gained a crucial understanding of the disease after discovering why people who have sickle-cell anemia, a prominent hereditary mutation of the red blood pigment hemoglobin, are immune to malaria. The successful transmission of malaria requires that the red blood cells infected by the parasite establish a trafficking system that allows the parasite to access the exterior of the blood cells via its adhesive proteins known as adhesins. However, the mutated hemoglobin present in sickle cell anemics causes these adhesions to occur rarely and often not at all. Thus, mutated hemoglobin (which does not only occur in sickle cell anemia) protects the human body from the malaria parasite.

Consider each of the three choices separately and select all that apply.

99.   Which of the following, if true, would weaken the author's contention?

> [A]   Hemoglobin mutations facilitate the bonding of adhesins

> [B]   Adhesins have the ability to attach to blood cells

> [C]   Malaria is able to infect the blood cells of sickle cell anemics

Passage 42

Questions 100 to 102 are based on the following passage.

Oxytocin, also known as the love hormone, bonds mothers to their children and promotes intimacy and relationships in various species including humans. Researchers have recently discovered that administering oxytocin nasally enhances prosocial choices among macaque monkeys. Exposure to the oxytocin caused the monkeys to more frequently share their juice without the expectation of receiving something in return. Scientists believe that it is important to understand how the hormone can impact the behavior in a positive way and monkeys provide valuable information in this regard since they are so closely related to humans.

For Questions 100 and 101, select only one answer choice.

100.   Based on the information given in the passage, what can be inferred about the scientific motivation to study oxytocin relative to humans?

> (A)   Humans are closely related to macaques and thus will behave in the same way as them under the influence of oxytocin

> (B)   Understanding the behavior of macaque monkeys under the influence of oxytocin can help scientists discern how oxytocin can potentially affect behavior in humans

> (C)   Scientists can find ways of treating antisocial behavior in humans with oxytocin

> (D)   Scientists can learn how to reproduce oxytocin synthetically as a treatment for depression

> (E)   Humans are not the focal point of scientific motivation for studying oxytocin

101. What is meant by "prosocial choices" in the second sentence?

   (A) Choices that promote the well-being of others

   (B) Choices that are made as a result of higher levels of altruism

   (C) Choices that create a hierarchy in the community

   (D) Choices that influence hormonal patterns

   (E) Choices that cannot be made without the influence of oxytocin

102. Select the sentence that best describes why oxytocin is a crucial component of social attachment.

Passage 43

Question 103 is based on the following passage.

Scientists have taken another step in the direction of better understanding the biological underpinnings of various psychiatric disorders. They have homed in on the gene named RNF123 because of effect on the hippocampus, the area of the brain that is altered in people with major depression. They hope to be able to then ascertain more information about the relationship between the gene, the hippocampus, and the subjective experiences of the patient in order to establish a more holistic approach to understanding the delicate amalgamation of nature vs. nurture in psychiatry and mental health treatment.

103. Select the sentence that best indicates scientists' initial interest in the role of genetics in depression.

Passage 44

Questions 104 to 106 are based on the following passage.

Stem cells are found in all multicellular organisms and their value in research is their ability to differentiate into specialized types of diverse cells as a result of mitosis (cell division). Medical researchers are convinced that human embryonic stem cell therapy has the potential to treat or cure various diseases and physical ailments from cancer to muscle damage; many even go as far as to claim it is a miracle treatment. However, many people stand in opposition to embryonic stem cell therapy, as they believe it is interfering with and exploiting natural life. Furthermore, some scientists believe that stem cell therapy could potentially aggrandize medical conditions rather than cure them. Thus, human embryonic stem cell research remains a highly controversial method of medical treatment.

For Questions 104 and 105, select only one answer choice.

104.   Mitosis is a specifically important factor in stem cell research because

(A) Mitosis allows scientists to use large quantities of stem cells since they reproduce so quickly

(B) Stem cells after mitosis are stronger and easier for scientists to study

(C) Mitosis generates cells that can be manipulated for a variety of medical purposes

(D) Mitosis is not really an important factor in stem cell research

(E) Stem cells undergo mitosis and become diversified as a result

105.   The author would agree with all of the following except

(A) Stem cell therapy is a sensitive issue

(B) Medical benefits sometimes come at a cost

(C) The outcomes of scientific research do not always align themselves with social mores

(D) The exploitation of natural life is the white elephant in the room of stem cell therapy debate

(E) Stem cells are a testament to the regenerative nature of the human body

Consider each of the three choices separately and select all that apply.

106.   According to the passage, stem cell therapy is an ethical conundrum because

[A]   Some believe that, despite its efficacy, it is the immoral treatment of natural life

[B]   Many maintain that it promotes a culture of death, despite the fact that it is an extremely useful form of medical treatment

[C]   Despite its flexibility as a treatment, stem cell therapy can also have adverse effects

Passage 45

Questions 107 to 110 are based on the following passage.

It has been a long-held belief within the field of biology that our DNA is fixed and unchangeable. While environmental factors may cause us to gain weight, lose a limb, or contract a virus, our underlying genetic sequence will remain constant. However, this popular view among scientists is beginning to shift towards a more fluid definition of the human genome; a new subfield within genetics, epigenetics, is exploring how environmental factors can actually change the expression of our genetic code throughout the course of our lives.

Epigenetics is the study of heritable changes to the cellular phenotypes of the DNA sequence, changes that have occurred as a result of external environmental factors after conception. Environmental factors are able to stimulate a particular gene, switching it on or off or altering it in some way. Through cellular division, the changes to the gene then have the potential to be passed on as heritable traits in subsequent generations. One way that scientists are delving into epigenetic inquiry is by studying heritability in animals. Scientists have been able to show that when a rat is subjected to a stressful environment during pregnancy, epigenetic changes to the fetus can engender behavioral problems in the rat's progeny as they mature and reach adulthood.

Scientists are also using human twins to better understand epigenetics and a related process called DNA methylation. DNA methylation causes genes to be expressed either stronger or weaker. By testing DNA samples taken from identical twins, scientists are able to identify areas where DNA methylation has impacted the expression of a particular gene in the sequence. Since identical twins have identical DNA, creating a methylation profile for each twin allows scientists to account for any subtle to extreme differences in behavior, opening the window to understanding how epigenetic processes affect both our personalities and our genetic code.

Epigenetics is still in the nascent stages of its development as a field of biological study, but it is nonetheless an incredibly exciting and groundbreaking area. It throws a wrench into Darwin's theory of evolution since it demonstrates how evolutionary changes can occur within one generation instead of spanning thousands of years. The possibility of such rapid evolutionary changes has major implications for how we think of not only life on earth but also the power we have to impact it, for better or worse.

For Questions 107 and 108, select only one answer choice.

107.   What is meant by "nascent" in the last paragraph of the passage?

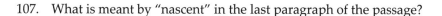

    Ⓐ   Nascent means that epigenetics is an old and established field of study within the biological community

    Ⓑ   Nascent means that epigenetics should not be seen as a valid method of biological inquiry

    Ⓒ   Nascent means that epigenetics should be seen as a valid method of biological inquiry

    Ⓓ   Nascent means that epigenetics is in the early stages of its development as a biological field of study

    Ⓔ   Nascent means that epigenetics is at a confusing stage in its development as a method of biological inquiry

108. According to the passage, why are DNA methylation profiles of identical twins important to epigenetics?

> Ⓐ The DNA methylation profiles of identical twins are not important to epigenetics

> Ⓑ The DNA methylation profiles of identical twins can be compared to see how epigenetic changes affect the genetic code of identical DNA

> Ⓒ Investigating the DNA methylation profiles helps scientists better understand the process of cell division and how it affects the genetic code

> Ⓓ The DNA methylation profiles of identical twins help scientists understand how twins inherit their genetic code

> Ⓔ DNA methylation profiles show where DNA methylation has affected the gene sequence

Consider each of the three choices separately and select all that apply.

109. According to the information given by the author, why do scientists use twins in epigenetic studies?

> Ⓐ Twins have identical DNA

> Ⓑ Twins are ideal for testing the DNA methylation process and its effects on the genome

> Ⓒ Twins look alike and thus it is easier for scientists to identify the expression of a particular phenotype

110. The claims of epigenetics have major implications for the future of the field of biology. Select the sentence form the passage that best describes why.

Practice Set 3: Business

Passage 46

Questions 111 to 114 are based on the following passage.

He says: "If under changed conditions of life, a structure, before useful, becomes less useful, its diminution will be favoured, for it will profit the individual not to have its nutriment wasted in building up an useless structure... Thus, as I believe, natural selection will tend in the long run to reduce any part of the organization, as soon as it becomes, through changed habits, superfluous." **If, as Darwin powerfully urges (and he here ignores his usual explanation), ostriches wings are insufficient for flight in consequence of the economy enforced by natural selection, why may not the reduced wings of the dodo, or the penguin, or the apteryx, or of the Cursores generally, be wholly attributed to natural selection in favor of economy of material and adaptation of parts to changed conditions?** The great principle of economy is continually at work shaping organisms, as sculptors shape statues, by removing the superfluous parts; and a mere glance at the forms of animals in general will show that it is well-nigh as dominant and universal a principle as is that of the positive development of useful parts. Other causes, moreover, besides actual economy, would favor shorter and more convenient wings on oceanic islands. In the first place, birds that were somewhat weak on "the wing would be most likely to settle on an island and stay there. Shortened wings would then become advantageous because they would restrain fatal migratory tendencies or useless and perilous flights in which the birds that flew furthest would be most often carried away by storms and adverse winds. Reduced wings would keep the birds near the shelter and the food afforded by the island and its neighborhood, and in some cases would become adapted to act as fins or flappers for swimming under water in pursuit of fish."

111. Select the sentence in the passage that states the thesis whose exclusivity as an explanation for changes in an individual the author amends here.

Consider each of the three choices separately and select all that apply.

112. Which of the following statements is a main idea expressed by the author of this passage?

   [A] Rather than adapting, some organisms seek a habitat that is favorable to traits they already possess.

   [B] Despite their habitats, some organisms discover a means to make all of their features or characteristics useful.

   [C] As characteristics become superfluous, organisms stop using them.

For Questions 113 and 114, select only one answer choice.

113. The theory of economy as expressed in this passage includes which of the following pair of concepts?

   (A) Adaptation and extinction of organizations.

   (B) Evolution and mutation of organizations.

   (C) Environmental effects and genetic influences.

   (D) Reduction and development of features based on usefulness.

   (E) Reduction and removal of features based on the environment.

114. Which of the following describes the author's tone in the sentence bolded in the passage?

   (A) Critical

   (B) Provocative

   (C) Disdainful

   (D) Reverent

   (E) Cynical

Passage 47

Questions 115 and 116 are based on the following passage.

Time is an asset that is critically important to the health of a business, particularly in the upper management domain; wasted time can be especially noxious to an organization's overall success. Despite the prevalence of the platitudes "time is money" and "time is of the essence", many people working in the higher echelons of a company are unaware of how they distribute their time relative to the tasks that they need to accomplish. Such oversight of fundamental management principles can cause a business to stagnate because it shows a lack of self-reflexivity that leads to disorganization, wasted resources, and a lack of solid leadership.

Select only one answer choice.

115. Based on the information in the passage, the reader can infer all of the following except

   (A) Upper management in an organization is often characterized by disorganization

   (B) The principles of business theory are not often practiced

   (C) Time management skills correspond to money management skills

   (D) A lack of organizational leadership is a harbinger of poor time management

   (E) Successful organizations have the ability to critically evaluate themselves

Consider each of the three choices separately and select all that apply.

116. Poor time management is paradoxical in businesses because

   [A] Upper management is the guilty party

   [B] Businesses know that time is a valuable asset

   [C] It leads to poor business decisions

Passage 48

Questions 117 and 118 are based on the following passage.

Industry is becoming more information-intensive and less labor and capital-intensive. This trend has important implications for the workforce; workers are becoming increasingly productive as the value of their labor decreases. However, there are also important implications for capitalism itself; not only is the value of labor decreased, the value of capital is also diminished. In the classical model, investments in human capital and financial capital are important predictors of the performance of a new venture. However, as demonstrated by Mark Zuckerberg and Facebook, it now seems possible for a group of relatively inexperienced people with limited capital to succeed on a large scale

For Questions 117 and 118, select only one answer choice.

117. Based on the information in the passage, which of the following statements best defines the word "capital" in this context?

Ⓐ material wealth owned by an individual or business enterprise and wealth available for or capable of use in the production of further wealth

Ⓑ any assets or resources, especially when used to gain profit or advantage and the nominal value of the authorized or issued shares

Ⓒ the ownership interests of a business as represented by the excess of assets over liabilities and material wealth owned by an individual or business enterprise

Ⓓ the nominal value of the authorized or issued shares and the abilities and skills of any individual

Ⓔ wealth available for or capable of use in the production of further wealth and the abilities and skills of any individual

118. Including the example of Mark Zuckerberg and Facebook at the end of the passage achieves which of the following purposes?

Ⓐ It supports the claim that industry is becoming more information – intensive.

Ⓑ It illustrates the rapid growth of social media as an important component of modern industry.

Ⓒ It contrasts with the idea that the amount of human and capital investment in a company is proportional to the success of the company.

Ⓓ It suggests that a company doesn't have to be especially productive to be successful.

Ⓔ It supports the idea of getting more work from employees while providing lower salaries

Passage 49

Questions 119 to 122 are based on the following passage.

Politeness and civility are the best capital ever invested in business. Large stores, gilt signs, flaming advertisements, will all prove unavailing if you or your employees treat your patrons abruptly. The truth is, the more kind and <u>liberal</u> a man is, the more generous will be the patronage bestowed upon him. **The man who gives the greatest amount of goods of a corresponding quality for the least sum will generally succeed best in the long run**. This brings us to the golden rule, "Whatever you want men to do to you, do also to them" and they will do better by you than if you always treated them as if you wanted to get the most you could out of them for the least return. Men who drive sharp bargains with their customers, acting as if they never expected to see them again, will not be mistaken.

For Questions 119 and 120, select only one answer choice.

119. The bolded sentence performs which of the following roles in the passage?

    (A) It provides an insight and a result

    (B) It shows a trait and a reward

    (C) It suggests a strategy and an outcome

    (D) It shows a tip for longevity and the financial benefits

    (E) It suggests an equation and its negation

120. The underlined and bolded word "liberal" means most nearly in the context of the passage:

    (A) Open-minded

    (B) Larger than life

    (C) Considerate

    (D) Generous

    (E) Thoughtful

Consider each of the three choices separately and select all that apply.

121. The passage implies that which of the following strategies would be effective in creating a successful business?

    A Dedicating resources to an employee mediation department for the company

    A Performing in-person follow-ups with employees

    A Providing refunds to unsatisfied customers

122. Select the sentence that gives the most specific and concrete instructions for ensuring the success of one's business.

Passage 50

Questions 123 to 126 are based on the following passage.

The transfer of land in England requires an uncertain time and cost - usually some weeks or months, and 5 to 25 percent on the purchase money. The common idea is that this peculiar difficulty, delay, and cost in the transfer of land arise from the law of inheritance and the legal machinery of entail; but stock in the funds can be virtually entailed and made to "follow the estate," and yet this stock can be transferred just as readily as any other stock.

The point is that, under English law, the trusts in the case of stock attach to the trustees, not to the stock; in the case of land, the trusts attach to the land itself as well as to the trustees. Hence, when I purchase stock of trustees, I need not trouble about how they apply the purchase money; in the case of land I have to go into the whole title.

It follows, therefore, that if, with a Government Land Registry Office, you required the purchaser only to get in the legal estate, i.e. holding him not responsible for the trusts or the application of the purchase money, then land could be transferred exactly as money in the funds is now, in spite of all the complications of our law (or rather custom) of entail.

For Questions 123 to 125, select only one answer choice.

123. This passage would most likely be found in:

    (A) A newspaper article

    (B) A textbook on foreign laws

    (C) A land title for a farm

    (D) The back of a legal document

    (E) A guide for new English citizens

124.   The author presumes that the reader is familiar with all of the following EXCEPT:

Ⓐ Land titles

Ⓑ The Law of Inheritance

Ⓒ Selling commercial shares

Ⓓ Trusts and trustees

Ⓔ Basic land rights

125.   The author's primary purpose in the passage is to show:

Ⓐ How lengthy the land transfer process is in England

Ⓑ An overview of the process of transferring land rights

Ⓒ A summary of important English law

Ⓓ Requirements of the purchaser in land transfer

Ⓔ Downsides to acting as trustee in land rights cases

Consider each of the three choices separately and select all that apply.

126.   The passage allows the reader to draw which of the following conclusions?

A Land rights vary globally, especially in Europe

B English land rights should be simplified

C Owning land is occasionally risky

Passage 51

Questions 127 to 130 are based on the following passage.

The history of money-getting, which is commerce, is a history of civilization, and wherever trade has flourished most, there, too, have art and science produced the noblest fruits. In fact, as a general thing, money-getters are the benefactors of our race. To them, in a great measure, are we indebted for our institutions of learning and of art, our academies, colleges and churches. It is no argument against the desire for, or the possession of wealth, to say that there are sometimes misers who hoard money only for the sake of hoarding and who have no higher aspiration than to grasp everything which comes within their reach. As we have sometimes hypocrites in religion, and demagogues in politics, so there are occasionally misers among money-getters.

For Questions 127 and 128, select only one answer choice.

127.   Which of the following social hierarchies does the author suggest?

   Ⓐ Laypeople > money-getters > priests

   Ⓑ Money-getters > laypeople > misers

   Ⓒ Misers > money-getters > laypeople

   Ⓓ Money-getters > scientists > laypeople

   Ⓔ Politicians > laypeople > money-getters

128.   The passage uses all of the following to make its point EXCEPT:

   Ⓐ Social standings

   Ⓑ Moral stance

   Ⓒ Figurative language

   Ⓓ Formal tone

   Ⓔ Analogy

Consider each of the three choices separately and select all that apply.

129.   The passage suggests which of the following conclusions?

   [A]   Money-getters benefit society, but the arts and sciences have longer-lasting impacts.

   [B]   Society should thank money-getters but should frown upon misers for failing to acquire money.

   [C]   An excellent money-getter should be immune to greed and selfish interests, as those could lead to being a miser.

130.   Select the sentence that best states the legacy of money-getters.

Passage 52

Questions 131 to 135 are based on the following passage.

Economists tend to assume that liberalizing markets is almost always a good thing. However, evidence suggests that deregulation is more of a mixed bag than orthodox economic theory would admit-sometimes it works well, and other times it doesn't. A case in point is capital market liberalization in developing economies. In nations moving toward more open markets in the late 1990s, capital market liberalization—the process of making the cross-border exchange of financial instruments more open-was a mixed blessing.

Capital market liberalization can have tremendous benefits for a developing economy. By allowing foreign capital to flow into developing nations, capital market liberalization can help to finance foreign trade and domestic investment opportunities that would likely be impossible otherwise. However, liberalization can also pose significant risks. Foreign capital can easily flow out of a country as fast as it flows in, putting the nation's financial sector under strain and adversely affecting foreign exchange rates.

Because of the unique combinations of benefits and risks posed by capital market liberalization, developing nations are often faced with difficult policy-making decisions. For instance, during the 1990s, Chile restricted borrowing from abroad in an attempt to prevent capital from flowing in and out of its economy too rapidly. However, by the beginning of the 21st century, stiffer competition for foreign investment from other Latin American nations forced Chile to reconsider its policy and deregulate its capital markets.

By over-regulating, developing economies make themselves less attractive to potential investors and thus effectively get left behind in economic development. On the other hand, too much deregulation can put economies at risk for abuses and capital flight. Because of the highly delicate balance between under and over-regulation, economists have tended to suggest that developing economies focus on effective regulation of their domestic financial sector while allowing gradual capital market liberalization.

Select only one answer choice.

131.   Which of the following best describes the scope of the passage?

    (A)   explanation of the macroeconomic situation in developing countries

    (B)   a discussion of the history of development economics

    (C)   a discussion of the impact of capital flows on the Chilean economy in the 1990s

    (D)   a discussion of the benefits and risks of a particular kind of market liberalization

    (E)   all of the above

Consider each of the three choices separately and select all that apply.

132.   Based on the passage, which of the following is likely true?

    [A]   Free market capitalism is the only economic system that efficiently distributes goods and services

    [B]   Economies that liberalize their capital markets face a risk of capital flight

    [C]   Capital market liberalization can help to finance foreign trade and stimulate investment

Select only one answer choice.

133. Which of the following best characterizes the author's reason for mentioning Chile?

   Ⓐ The passage is mainly about Chile

   Ⓑ Chile has recently been a dictatorship, and the passage is about the economic conditions in countries emerging from dictatorships

   Ⓒ Chile is an example of a country that has experienced negative consequences from capital market deregulation

   Ⓓ Chile has a more developed economy than other Latin American countries

   Ⓔ Chile exemplifies the dilemma that developing countries face when trying to decide whether to liberalize their capital markets

134. Select the two sentences that best explain the potential benefits and risks of capital market liberalization.

Consider each of the three choices separately and select all that apply.

135. Based on the passage, all of the following are likely true EXCEPT

   Ⓐ developing nations should open their capital markets to foreign investors

   Ⓑ developing nations should not regulate their capital markets at all

   Ⓒ foreign capital always has a positive effect on a nation's economy

Passage 53

Questions 136 and 137 are based on the following passage.

The normal situation is that the business enterprise is aiming at net profits, having an interest in large sales, heavy transactions and gross profits only so far as these are expected to lead finally to net profits, the real goal. Now these net profits are, of course, the remainder of earnings left on hand after providing for all costs and expenses, for depreciation and every other factor causing loss, destruction, and deterioration during the business period under consideration. In short, the business capital as it was at the beginning of the period is first fully restored and made intact at the end of the period before a net profit emerges. This net profit therefore becomes in a true sense a creation of new capital and may indeed be retained in the business as an addition to capital funds. Even when it is paid out in dividends, partly or wholly, it becomes new capital in the hands of the individual stockholders who then in their private capacity may of course spend it, but by proper investment may keep it permanently stored as capital. It is the creation of capital then that is in reality the ultimate money-making making aim of the business enterprise.

Consider each of the three answer choices separately and select all that apply.

136. Which of the following statements is true based on the information in this passage?

    [A] Large sales, heavy transactions and gross profits lead inevitably to net profits

    [B] Gross profits must be greater than the initial capital in any fiscal period in order to create net profits

    [C] Investors benefit most by spending their dividends from a company

Select only one answer choice.

137. Which of the following actions has the potential to increase net profits even though gross profits remain the same?

    (A) Freezing wages and salaries

    (B) Concealing losses

    (C) Reducing inventory

    (D) Installing energy efficient lights

    (E) Staying open more hours

Passage 54

Questions 138 to 141 are based on the following passage.

Men should be systematic in their business. A person who does business by rule, having a time and place for everything, doing his work promptly, will accomplish twice as much and with half the trouble of him who does it carelessly and **slipshod**. By introducing system into all your transactions, doing one thing at a time, always meeting appointments with punctuality, you find leisure for pastime and recreation; whereas the man who only half does one thing, and then turns to something else, and half does that, will have his business at loose ends, and will never know when his day's work is done, for it never will be done. Of course, there is a limit to all these rules. We must try to preserve the happy medium, for there is such a thing as being too systematic.

For Questions 138 to 140, select only one answer choice.

138. Which of the following best summarizes the passage?

⒜ One must be systematic, as this ensures that one will have excellent management strategies.

Ⓑ To be an excellent businessman, one should be rigidly systematic in one's work.

Ⓒ A man should be systematic but maintain temperance.

Ⓓ The benefits of organization can be felt in varied areas of life.

Ⓔ Systematic men will be respected in business for their organization.

139. The underlined and bolded word "slipshod" means more nearly in the context of the passage:

⒜ Bedraggled

Ⓑ Slovenly

Ⓒ ncorrectly shod

Ⓓ Absentmindedly

Ⓔ Painstakingly

140. Which of the following must be true in order for the author's claim to be valid?

⒜ Systematic methods always improve one's working ability

Ⓑ One can excel by performing one task at a time, or by taking short breaks between tasks

Ⓒ The most successful businessmen developed organizational strategies early in life

Ⓓ It is more important to follow a routine than an organization strategy

Ⓔ To be systematic, businessmen should utilize employees beneath them

Consider each of the three choices separately and select all that apply.

141. The author would probably support which of the following statements?

Ⓐ Systematic business practices will lower one's overall stress levels.

Ⓑ One must carefully budget time between projects instead of spending hours at a time on one.

Ⓒ Successful men will not change their organizational methods.

Passage 55

Question 142 is based on the following passage.

Older workers have prospered in the recent economic downturn. Currently, workers aged 55-64 account for 12% of the nation's workers, an increase of nearly 2% since 2000, and by 2010, nearly one in three workers will be at least age 55. A number of factors and trends are contributing to the increase in older adults in the work force including demographics, financial concerns, changing concepts of retirement, longer and healthier life spans, and demand for the knowledge and skills possessed by the current generation of older workers. Older adults in the work force are not the only ones who remain engaged in productive activities. Many adults who have retired look for expanded opportunities and options - either paid or unpaid - that may represent "a new chapter in life embodying a new definition of success". For these older adults, retirement represents another stage of life - which may extend for as much as 25 years - in which to accomplish many things. Because they have differing abilities, desires, and needs in terms of both paid and unpaid work, adults in late midlife are not homogeneous. As a group, however, they typify some of the changing conceptions of career.

Select only one answer choice.

142.   What additional information does the reader need to calculate the impact of older citizens' remaining in the workforce on younger people's ability to obtain employment?

   (A) The number of people in each demographic group that is currently in college

   (B) The average annual salary of workers aged 55-64

   (C) The average amount of debt carried by workers aged 55-64

   (D) The percentage of the total population represented by workers aged 55-64

   (E) The geographic areas in which most of the workers aged 55-64 live

Passage 56

Questions 143 to 148 are based on the following passage.

By the early 20th century, paper currency was in widespread use all over the world. The failures in paper currency were not really due to the fact that the paper money wasn't adequately backed by gold or silver. Although many nations clung to the gold standard well into the 20th century, all money amounts to is a medium of exchange, allowing the citizens of a country to engage in transactions. The US finally completely abandoned the gold standard in 1971. All nations now use "fiat currencies", money which has no intrinsic value and is not backed by precious metals.

The problem with paper currencies was not that they were often inadequately backed by precious metals. The money circulating in a society, in a sense, mirrors the material wealth of a country. It is relatively easy to print more banknotes, but not so easy to increase the overall material wealth of a nation, and so if twice the number of banknotes is printed given the same amount of wealth, the value of each banknote is more or less cut in half. This happened automatically, as if by magic, every time a government cheated on the system. The most famous example was the Wiemar Republic that ran post-World War I Germany, where inflation took place by a factor of trillions. It was actually done more or less deliberately, to reduce the burden of foreign war reparations payments, at the expense of wiping out the savings of the citizens. More recently, the African nation of Zimbabwe printed their currency into worthlessness, to finally establish the US dollar as the national currency.

The idea that there is an "inherent" value even to gold and silver is something of an illusion. A money supply based on precious metals is not absolutely more stable than one based on paper. When the Spaniards and Portuguese conquered much of what would become Latin America in the 16th century, they seized large quantities of gold and also obtained rich gold and silver mines, with the result that the value of their gold and silver currencies plunged to about a third of their original value.

Some astrogeologists have calculated the value of the metals in a single typical metallic asteroid; if some future generation were able to nudge one into orbit around the Earth and then render it down, the haul would be so huge that it would dramatically devalue every precious metal in circulation. Even without such a monstrous kick in the teeth, the price of gold tends to fluctuate drastically, dropping or rising relative to relatively stable fiat currencies. Money, as the saying goes, "is worth what everyone thinks it's worth", and that rule applies just as much to gold as to paper bills. The real concern is discipline in the printing of money. If too much money is printed, it becomes devaluated. If too little is printed, it stifles commerce.

Mainstream economists will admit that it may be harder to cheat with a gold standard but point to its restrictiveness as a crippling flaw; some accuse those who push the gold standard of simply trying to restore a system that would give them personal control over the money supply by hoarding gold. There is still a school of thought that believes money should at least have some hard currency backing, but it's well off the mainstream. In 1998, the highly respected US Federal Reserve chairman Alan Greenspan commented: "I am one of the rare people who still has some nostalgic view about the old gold standard, but I must tell you I am in a very small minority among my colleagues on that issue." As for advocates of a strict gold standard, mainstream economists regarded them as pushing "the economic equivalent of leeching.

For Questions 143 to 145, select only one answer choice.

143. In this context, the word "fiat" most closely matches which of the following definitions?

   (A) Decreed

   (B) Sanctioned

   (C) Acceptable

   (D) Solvent

   (E) National

144. What is implied by the information in the first sentence of the third paragraph?

    (A) Gold is the most appropriate foundation for a monetary system

    (B) Gold is an arbitrary choice of foundation for a monetary system

    (C) Latin America has greater quantities of gold than other areas of the world

    (D) Gold is an unreliable foundation for a monetary system

    (E) Spanish and Portuguese conquerors are responsible for gold's acceptance as the foundation of modern monetary systems

145. Based on your understanding of the information in the passage, what would be the likely result of the discovery of twenty previously unknown paintings by the nineteenth-century artist, Van Gogh?

    (A) They would be found to be counterfeit

    (B) They would be appraised based on the completeness, originality, and the quality of the work

    (C) The value of already known works of Van Gogh would be reduced

    (D) The value of already known work of Van Gogh would be inflated

    (E) They would be donated to a museum for tax purposes

For Questions 146 and 147, consider each of the three answer choices separately and select all that apply.

146. Which of the following scenarios has an effect similar to that of the Weimar Republic's devaluing its currency after World War I?

    [A] A clothing store putting its seasonal merchandise on sale at the end of the season

    [B] High-school students taking Advanced Placement courses to raise their GPAs

    [C] A college admissions' policy that adds 100 points to the SAT scores of applicants from culturally deprived areas

147. Use the information in this passage to determine which of the following is an example of a medium of exchange.

    [A] Replacing a traditional baby-shower gift with a coupon for 5 hours of free babysitting

    [B] Revising a writing assignment for a higher grade

    [C] A mechanic providing a free oil change for the electrician who did not charge him for replacing a faulty switch in his office

148. Select the sentence that explains the weakness inherent in the use of the gold standard.

Passage 57

Question 149 is based on the following passage.

In 1980, the federal government began encouraging academic-industry relationships by creating a uniform federal patent policy, allowing federal grantees to collaborate with commercial interests to promote inventions, and permitting universities to retain the title on inventions developed through government funding.

As a result, as many as 90 percent of life-science companies now have a financial relationship with academia. Corporate licensing of academic inventions account for more than $20 billion of the universities' annual revenue. In most cases, the researchers making the discoveries get some portion of the money. Another recent byproduct of the increased privatization of research has been the right of companies under patent law to refuse to allow foreign competitors to create generic -- and often significantly cheaper - treatments for life-threatening diseases. Poorer countries in Africa, particularly, say they need the less-expensive generic drugs to fight AIDS, leaving the federal government in the awkward position of equivocating between protection of U.S. corporate interests and global humanitarian interests.

Select only one answer choice.

149. Select a word from the following list that would be a better choice than "equivocate" in the final sentence of the passage.

(A) Hesitate

(B) Prevaricate

(C) Pontificate

(D) Vacillate

(E) Abrogate

Passage 58

Question 150 is based on the following passage.

The United States has been the largest producer of greenhouse gases, so what we do makes a big difference. And the U.S. has been reluctant to act aggressively on curbing emissions, worried about the economic consequences. But this is generally agreed to be a global problem requiring worldwide action. Many European nations like Britain and France, and Japan as well, have acted much more aggressively on cutting emissions. They rely more on nuclear power and relatively clean natural gas than we do. They have also mandated significantly higher fuel efficiency standards for cars and invested more in mass transit and rail. The story is mixed in developing countries, especially the economic powerhouses like China and India.

Because their economies are growing so rapidly, they are using much more energy and producing more greenhouse gases than they have in the past. At the same time, they have the chance to start fresh with cleaner and more efficient technologies if they can be persuaded to do so.

Select only one answer choice.

150.   Use your understanding of this passage to determine which of the following can be inferred about the challenges faced by rapidly growing economies.

   (A) They cannot train enough workers to meet the demands of industry

   (B) They are reluctant to use examples set by other nations

   (C) Their isolation makes them unaware of more efficient technologies

   (D) They cannot institute more efficient technologies fast enough to keep pace with their growth

   (E) They do not recognize their impact on global warming

Passage 59

Question 151 is based on the following passage.

A nation's GDP (Gross Domestic Product) at purchasing power parity (PPP) exchange rates is the sum value of all goods and services produced in the country valued at prices prevailing in the United States. This is the measure most economists prefer when looking at per- capita welfare and when comparing living conditions or use of resources across countries. The measure is difficult to compute, as a US dollar value has to be assigned to all goods and services in the country regardless of whether these goods and services have a direct equivalent in the United States (for example, the value of an ox-cart or non-US military equipment); as a result, PPP estimates for some countries are based on a small and sometimes different set of goods and services. In addition, many countries do not formally participate in the World Bank's PPP project that calculates these measures, so the resulting GDP estimates for these countries may lack precision. For many developing countries, PPP-based GDP measures are multiples of the official exchange rate (OER) measure.

Select only one answer choice.

151.   Based on your understanding of the information in this passage, which of the following statements is likely to be true?

(A)   The difference between the OER- and PPP- denominated GDP values for developing countries is generally much smaller

(B)   The difference between the OER- and PPP- denominated GDP values for most of the wealthy industrialized countries in generally much greater

(C)   The difference between the OER- and PPP-denominated GDP values for countries who do not participate in the World Bank's PPP project is generally much greater

(D)   The difference between the OER- and PPP-denominated GDP values for countries who do not participate in the World Bank's PPP project is generally much smaller

(E)   The difference between the OER- and PPP- denominated GDP values for most of the wealthy industrialized countries is generally much smaller.

Passage 60

Question 152 is based on the following passage.

In recent years, the business world has placed increasing emphasis on the inner-work lives of their employees. A recent study published in McKinsey Quarterly has shown that productivity, commitment, and creativity increase in the work place when employees' experience in the office includes a positive flow of emotions, motivations, and perceptions. This environment can best be fostered by leadership that promotes the connection between meaning and work tasks through active engagement and positive, consistent feedback.

Select only one answer choice.

152.   Which of the following rhetorical strategies is employed by the author to discuss the work environment and the inner work life of employees?

(A)   Logos rhetoric

(B)   Pathos rhetoric

(C)   Ethos rhetoric

(D)   Comparative rhetoric

(E)   Narrative rhetoric

Passage 61

Question 153 is based on the following passage.

According to a recent study conducted at the University of Minnesota, men spend more money when there is a dearth of women in their locale. Researchers were able to determine that U.S. cities with a higher male to female ratio had correspondingly higher levels of male debt. Consequently, men are much more willing to take financial risks and engage their consumer habits in the aforementioned areas than men in regions with gender equilibrium.

Select only one answer choice.

153.   The author intends "a dearth of women" to be analogous to

   (A)   An abundance of women

   (B)   The rarity of women

   (C)   A surplus of men

   (D)   A total lack of women

   (E)   A paucity of women

Passage 62

Question 154 is based on the following passage.

Although professional women make up over 40% of the employees at organizations in the United States, they are still woefully underrepresented in the corporate upper echelons; only 21% of women serve among the ranks of business executives. However, in the post-feminism world this is not due to outright discrimination but rather covert bias. There is a strong pipeline of female talent that is fed into the corporate sphere, but women rarely make the executive suite due to high levels of attrition that typically occur after they have reached the management level. Many researchers claim that this is due to the fact that U.S. businesses make it extremely difficult for women to advance up the chain of command when they decide to have a family - U.S. businesses do not focus on maternity leave options for women that allow them to easily re-access the upper levels of the company.

Select only one answer choice.

154. According to the passage, in what clandestine way are U.S. businesses anti-female?

    Ⓐ U.S. businesses do not provide women with the professional development needed for career advancement

    Ⓑ U.S. businesses do not afford women the opportunity to the management level

    Ⓒ U.S. businesses do not provide women with maternity leave

    Ⓓ U.S. businesses do not equip themselves to deal with issues important to women in the work place

    Ⓔ U.S. businesses do not place emphasis on family friendly policies

Passage 63

Questions 155 to 157 are based on the following passage.

Social entrepreneurship has become a vitally important concept in the business world. Global attitudes increasingly desire the promotion of the unselfish concern for the common good. Social entrepreneurs believe that business emphasis should be placed on the creation of social capital and not the traditional goals and objectives of industry that revolve around profit and return. Social capital is the value of social relations. It is engendered when entrepreneurs identify a pressing social problem and then use the principles of business and management to erect ventures that address these issues by way of social dialogue and collaboration. Thus, cooperation and social relationships facilitate economic results.

For Questions 155 to 157, select only one answer choice.

155. Based on the information given in the passage, what main difference can be inferred between social entrepreneurs and conventional entrepreneurs?

    Ⓐ Social entrepreneurs build better relationships with clients than traditional entrepreneurs

    Ⓑ Social entrepreneurs don't rely on the axioms of business while traditional entrepreneurs do

    Ⓒ Social entrepreneurs are concerned with quality of life and traditional entrepreneurs are concerned with fiscal gain

    Ⓓ Social entrepreneurs are more concerned with climate change than traditional entrepreneurs

    Ⓔ Social entrepreneurs and traditional entrepreneurs are essentially the same

156. The author would agree with all of the following statements regarding social capital except

    Ⓐ Social capital is the product of collaborative problem solving

    Ⓑ Social capital is the salient feature of social entrepreneurship

    Ⓒ Social capital is a tangible feature of social entrepreneurship

    Ⓓ Business management principles support social capital

    Ⓔ Social capital has monetary value

157. According to the information given in the passage, what is meant by the term social capital?

    Ⓐ The author does not give enough information to define social capital.

    Ⓑ Social capital means building community.

    Ⓒ Social capital means building relationships.

    Ⓓ Social capital is synonymous with social problems.

    Ⓔ Social capital is money created by people sharing in a concerted effort towards a common goal.

Passage 64

Questions 158 and 159 are based on the following passage.

In the last twenty years trading on the stock market has gone from the stock room floors to computer screens. This has resulted in the rapid rise of high frequency trading, which researchers now believe leads to increased volatility in the stock market. High frequency trading makes it possible for large volumes of stocks to be traded in milliseconds, much faster than they can be tracked with the human eye. Multitudinous problems arise from high frequency trading, one of the most potent being the potential to disrupt the global economic balance more frequently and with little warning.

For Questions 158 and 159, select only one answer choice.

158. Based on the information given in the passage, how does the author intend to define high frequency trading?

    Ⓐ High frequency trading is when stocks are traded continuously

    Ⓑ High frequency trading is computer-generated stock trading on a grandiose scale

    Ⓒ High frequency trading is computer generated stock trading

    Ⓓ High frequency trading is stock trading that is done at a rapid pace

    Ⓔ High frequency trading is when large volumes of stock are traded on the stock room floor

159. Based the information given in the passage, what can be inferred about the global economic balance?

    Ⓐ The global economic balance cannot be sustained if high frequency trading is continued

    Ⓑ High frequency trading keeps the global economic balance at a healthy equilibrium

    Ⓒ High frequency trading makes rapid and unforeseen fluctuations in the global market more possible

    Ⓓ Nothing can be inferred about the global economic market based on the information given in the passage

    Ⓔ The global economic balance was more stable before the introduction of high frequency trading

Passage 65

Question 160 is based on the following passage.

The economic crisis that broke through the global floodgates in 2008 has placed the system of capitalism under attack from its opponents. Capitalism, however, has been under scrutiny since its inception, and thus this is not a new phenomenon. However, as society has evolved so have the criticisms launched against capitalism; imperialistic oppression, market failure and the wasteful and inefficient use of resources are all common gripes that constitute the anti-capitalism jeremiad. One of the prominent denunciations vaulted against capitalism over the course of the last fifteen years is its opposition to sustainability. Critics claim that capitalism promotes a milieu of exploitation because of its unbridled focus on consumption. Consequently, capitalism is a danger to a world that is increasingly strapped for natural resources, the foundation stones of capitalist enterprise.

Select only one answer choice.

160. According to the information given in the passage, why is consumption seen as a negative attribute of capitalism?

    Ⓐ Consumption led to the financial crisis in the late 2000s

    Ⓑ Consumption results in the overuse of natural resources that are currently in high demand globally

    Ⓒ Consumption contributes to the destabilization of the market in a capitalist economic system

    Ⓓ Consumption is the way in which proponents of capitalism distract people from the system's penchant for imperialistic oppression

    Ⓔ Consumption leads to an increase in wasteful consumer choices

Passage 66

Questions 161 to 163 are based on the following passage.

Sustainability has become a paragon virtue in business endeavors, an essential ingredient for corporate success at a time when social, economic, and environmental issues permeate the heart of public discourse, particularly in Western societies. However, civic pressure for companies to mold themselves based on the capacity to endure is not the only reason that businesses have homed in on sustainability; over the course of the last twenty years, research has shown that there is a widening chasm between organizations characterized as high-sustainability and companies deemed low-sustainability relative to accounting measures and stock market success. Thus, sustainability is just as much about success as it is about showing a good entrepreneurial face to the public. According to a study conducted by Dr. Robert G. Eccles of the Harvard Business School, several major factors show that long-term corporate success is determined by iterations of a rudimentary principle in business: meeting the expectations of both shareholders and stakeholders.

One factor in the success rate of high-sustainability companies is a three-pronged approach to business that involves placing equal value on the organization's social, environmental, and financial performance. Traditionally, low-sustainability companies focus solely on profit and turn a blind eye towards the wider ramifications of their business practices on society. This leads them to a kind of tunnel vision that misjudges the expectations of stakeholders; additionally, they undervalue the importance of building good relationships with employees, customers and members of civil society, causing their venture to stagnate. Conversely, high-sustainability companies make both fiscal and socio-environmental issues the crux of their corporate goals and objectives, facilitating their capacity to build meaningful relationships with stakeholders by taking their needs and opinions into account and finding a way to amalgamate them with business decisions that are financially sound. This is done by a process of active engagement and the creation of shareholder sub-committees focused on environmental, social, and financial issues.

Another contributing factor to the recent primacy of high-sustainability organizations is their propensity to be more forward thinking than their low-sustainability counterparts. High-sustainability companies have long-term communications strategies that render them more attractive to long-term investors and diverse stakeholders, something that all ambitious businesses crave as well as need to stay in top form.

Like all facets of life, the business world is an evolving world. It depends on foresight, creativity, and the ability to identify new ways of presenting and reinforcing the fundamentals of enterprise, in this case the way in which the mutual happiness of shareholders and stakeholders is propelled by a wider scope that includes social and environmental responsibility.

Select only one answer choice.

161. Given the information in the passage, it can be inferred that sustainability is a paragon virtue in the business world because

⊙Ⓐ Sustainability creates an atmosphere that is based on relationships and engagement between stakeholders and shareholders

Ⓑ Sustainability seeks to keep environmental concerns at the forefront of organizational practices, thus helping to mitigate the impact of climate change

Ⓒ Sustainability concerns itself with helping businesses maintain a high level of success in the face of the perpetually changing elements that constitute global society

Ⓓ Sustainability is about finding an adequate balance between social, economic, and environmental issues

Ⓔ Sustainability is in vogue in the realm of public discourse

Consider each of the three choices separately and select all that apply.

162. Corporate success can be seen as an iterative process because

☐A It relies on the repetition of business principles to find the right method of meeting the expectations of shareholders and stakeholders

☐B It is adaptive to social, fiscal and environmental changes

☐C It is a forward-thinking way of approaching business practices

163. Select the sentence that best illustrates the perils of fiscal aggrandizement within an organization.

Passage 67

Questions 164 and 165 are based on the following passage.

In recent years, American businesses have considered adoption of various business methods of Japanese companies. The most important of these methods, one that can influence the entire company is Just in Time. Just in Time (JIT), refers to the practice of having material delivered to the factory as it is needed, rather than having a quantity delivered and then stored in a warehouse. The practice greatly reduces overhead costs as there is no need for so much storage space. The practice calls for high coordination between suppliers and customers so that neither has to store material. JIT can lead to increases in quality, productivity, and adaptability to change. General Motors, for example, used JIT and was able to reduce its costs for inventory by 75%. The use of JIT creates the need for a number of other practices, among them is Strict Quality Control. Since the material arrives just as it is needed, there is no time for a complete inspection. The supplier has, therefore, to verify on its own the quality of the product sent to the customer. Supplier and customer have to work closely together. Another feature of JIT is single sourcing. Since JIT requires that buyer and customer work closely together, having many suppliers makes it difficult to work closely together with all of them. Companies using JIT, therefore, tend to have fewer suppliers than companies that do not rely on JIT. General Motors, for example, which does rely on JIT to some extent, uses 3,500 suppliers. Toyota, a company that completely relies on JIT, uses fewer than 250 suppliers.

Consider each of the three answer choices separately and select all that apply.

164. Based on the reading, advantages resulting from the use of Just in Time include

A   Less redundancy in the supply system, since there are fewer suppliers

B   No margin for error in the delivery of material

C   Buyer and customer work closely together

165. Select the sentence that best describes the general benefits of Just in Time (JIT).

Practice Set 4: Everyday Topics

Passage 68

Questions 166 to 171 are based on the following passage.

The English Cup is probably a bigger attraction to a footballer than any other. To a Scottish footballer his International cap against England is to achieve the height of his ambition, but somehow in England, to participate in the final at the Crystal Palace in April is the heart's desire of the average player. There is a glamour surrounding the English Cup Competition that nothing else can compare with.

I well remember when the Scottish clubs were entitled to enter into the arena, and great clubs such as Queen's Park, Glasgow Rangers, Cowlairs, Heart of Midlothian entered in the lists against the best clubs that prevailed at the time in England. Queen's Park, still the premier amateur club in Scotland, and the Heart of Midlothian, made history in this competition, but the first-named must be given the **laurels.**

There are still many old players in Scotland who maintain that in the first year, when they were beaten by Blackburn Rovers, the result should have gone the other way. As it was before my day I cannot, naturally, go into the matter as thoroughly as I should desire, but when such players as Messrs. Smellie and Campbell have assured me that they should have had the victory, I rather feel inclined to believe their statement. Queen's Park, as already stated, were for many years the greatest club in Scotland, and they played the game for the love of it; in the two finals which were played at the Oval most of their members had to travel overnight to play on the following day which shows their dedication. A great deal has been said, as well as written, about this matter, and it is often asked if the "Queens" deserved to win.

Perhaps the finest Cup-tie that has been seen at the Palace was the meeting of Everton and Aston Villa in 1897. I had thought at one time to participate in this final, but after playing three rounds I got knocked out, and was unable to play. I must say that my substitute at center forward did exceedingly well, and I could not grumble in any way at being left out. **The ordinary London man will always remember this match, when the Villa eventually finished winners by three goals to two.** I followed it very keenly, and in one way my sympathy went to the losers, because there was little or nothing to choose between them.

Select only one answer choice.

166. The underlined and bolded word "laurels" most nearly means in the context of the passage:

   (A) A plant-based wreath, given as a prize

   (B) A trophy given as a prize

   (C) A modern version of the original Greek prize wreath

   (D) First place ranking

   (E) A designation as a medal winner

Consider each of the three choices separately and select all that apply.

167. The passage discusses which of the following topics related to football?

   [A] Nationalistic viewers' support of football teams

   [B] The rivalry between teams from different countries, as compared to the rivalries of everyday citizens

   [C] A retrospective of a football career and memories made seeing games

Select only one answer choice.

168. The sentence in bold plays which of the following roles in the passage?

   (A) Conveying to the reader the sense of relief at the English victory

   (B) Emphasizing how important football is

   (C) Transitioning from a personal anecdote to the following paragraph

   (D) Revealing the match's outcome

   (E) Tying together the author's previous statements about the match

169.   Select the sentence that first shows a change in the author's style of writing.

Select only one answer choice.

170.   The author displays all of the following traits EXCEPT:

   Ⓐ   Personal bias in favor of English footballers

   Ⓑ   Regret at being unable to play in the final

   Ⓒ   Admiration for the English players

   Ⓓ   Appreciation for the sport of football

   Ⓔ   Attention to detail in matches

Consider each of the three choices separately and select all that apply.

171.   The author would probably agree with which of the following statements?

   [A]   It is acceptable to support teams of different nationalities, as long as you witness them play

   [B]   Playing a sport makes it easier to appreciate a sport

   [C]   The best way to watch a sport is in a stadium venue.

Passage 69

Questions 172 to 175 are based on the following passage.

New Urbanism is an urban design movement which promotes walkable neighborhoods containing a range of housing and job types. It arose in the United States in the early 1980s and has gradually permeated many aspects of real estate development and urban planning. New Urbanists support regional planning for open space, context-appropriate architecture and planning, and the balanced development of jobs and housing. They believe their strategies can reduce traffic congestion, increase the supply of affordable housing, and rein in suburban sprawl.

According to this model the neighborhood has a discernible center, often a square or a green, with a transit stop. Most of the dwellings, usually houses, row houses, and apartments, are within a five-minute walk of the center. At the edge of the neighborhood are shops and offices of sufficiently varied types to supply the weekly needs of a household. Elementary schools and playgrounds are close enough so that most children can walk from their home. Streets within the neighborhood, relatively narrow and shaded by rows of trees, form a connected network to disperse the traffic, and networked with pedestrian walkways. The neighborhood is organized to be self-governing where a formal association debates and decides matters of maintenance, security, and physical change. Taxation is the responsibility of the larger community.

For Questions 172 and 173, select only one answer choice.

172. All of the following could be found in a community that has embraced New Urbanism EXCEPT:

    Ⓐ Many parks and gardens

    Ⓑ Boarding schools

    Ⓒ Safe walkways

    Ⓓ Formal voting at community gatherings

    Ⓔ Increased taxes

173. Which of the following, if true, would most undermine the main point of the second paragraph?

    Ⓐ Some people protest New Urbanism

    Ⓑ The principles of New Urban social planning vary widely from region to region

    Ⓒ People in communities that have adopted New Urbanism have smaller social circles

    Ⓓ It is expensive to leave open spaces in construction

    Ⓔ Some buildings and open walkways look old-fashioned

Consider each of the three choices separately and select all that apply.

174. The author would most likely agree with which of the following?

    Ａ New Urbanism principles are hard to implement after construction is finished

    Ｂ New Urbanism should only be embraced in countries with lots of open space

    Ｃ People can begin small-scale New Urbanism practices on their own

175. Select the sentence that shows which members of the community bear responsibility for decisions.

Passage 70

Questions 176 to 179 are based on the following passage.

Coffee is a brewed beverage prepared from the roasted seeds of several species of an evergreen shrub of the genus Coffea. Coffee is one of the most consumed drinks in the world. The earliest evidence of coffee drinking appears in the middle of the 15th century in the Sufi monasteries in Yemen. From the Middle East coffee spread to different places around the world and gained popularity as a drink.

The primary psychoactive chemical in coffee is caffeine, an adenosine antagonist that is known for its stimulant effects. Coffee also contains the monoamine oxidase inhibitors β-carboline and harmane, which may contribute to its psychoactivity. Although recent research suggests that moderate coffee consumption is benign or mildly beneficial, coffee can worsen the symptoms of conditions like anxiety due to the caffeine and diterpenes it contains.

Polymorphisms in the CYP1A2 gene may lead to a slower metabolism of caffeine and in patients with a slow version of this enzyme the risk for myocardial infarction is increased by a third to two thirds, depending on the amount of coffee consumed (2–3 cups and >4 cups respectively). Interestingly, paper coffee filters bind to lipid-like compounds, removing most of the cafestol and kahweol found in coffee, and might present health benefits compared to boiled coffee or espresso.

For Questions 176 and 177, select only one answer choice.

176. The passage addresses which of the following issues revolving around caffeine use and coffee drinking?

     Ⓐ   The higher risk to geriatric patients leading from coffee consumption

     Ⓑ   The long-term risks of psychoactive chemicals

     Ⓒ   The side effects of psychoactive chemicals

     Ⓓ   The reasoning doctors have for suggesting a limited caffeine intake

     Ⓔ   The knowledge needed for patients to choose to abstain from caffeine

177. The passage explains or implies the potential physiological effects of ingesting all of the following EXCEPT:

     Ⓐ   harmane

     Ⓑ   caffeine

     Ⓒ   cafestol

     Ⓓ   diterpenes

     Ⓔ   monoamine oxidase inhibitors

Consider each of the three choices separately and select all that apply.

178. The author would most likely agree with which of the following?

     ☐A   Caffeine's stimulating effect is somewhat mitigated by potential side effects.

     ☐B   Caffeine has made itself indispensable to humans.

     ☐C   People should drink no more than 4 cups of coffee per day.

179.   Select the sentence that could be used as evidence in an argument for abstaining from coffee.

Passage 71

Questions 180 to 185 are based on the following passage.

Social media marketing refers to the process of gaining website traffic or attention through social media sites. Social media marketing programs usually center on efforts to create content that attracts attention and encourages readers to share it with their social networks. In the context of the social web, engagement means that customers and stakeholders are participants rather than viewers. Social media allows everyone to express and share an idea along a business's path to market. This engagement process is fundamental to successful social media marketing.

Availability of mobile phones has contributed significantly to social media marketing in recent times. They allow companies and advertisers to remind and update consumers about their capabilities and status of their products. Moreover, mobile phones help advertisers to identify specific habits of the consumers, and this data is invaluable to build statistics as well as to develop personalized advertisements. **Online advertising industry is repositioning itself to take advantage of the huge market that is offered by customers who are always online on their mobile phones.**

Emergence of social media marketing as a tool that can be analyzed to measure brand product performance and to obtain consumer information has led to its application in other areas of online activities as well. For example, social media optimization is becoming increasingly important for search engine optimization. Search engines are increasingly utilizing recommendations of users of social networks to rank pages in the search engine result pages. Consumer's online brand related activities (COBRAs) is one of the methods used by advertisers for identifying performance of products using social media. Monitoring the uploading of a photo of a branded product to your social networking site is an example for this. Another technique for social media marketing analysis is electronic word of mouth (eWOM), which are recommendations and appraisals promoted via "consumer-to-consumer" interactions. Companies and advertisers use these methods to gain insight into a brands' overall visibility. It can also be used to measure the social impact of advertising campaigns and to identify new opportunities for engagement or product development. Moreover, these techniques can help to identify emerging trends or impending crises.

However, privacy rights advocates warn users about intrusive monitoring of social media to gain information on their habits and preferences. This monitoring and data gathering is often made easier by uninformed users who make their personal information available online. These may be captured without the user's knowledge or consent, such as through electronic tracking and third-party application on social networks and used for personalized advertising. Such advertisements are often propagated throughout the networks of a person, often with specific pointers that help identification. Development of such techniques for analysis and personalized advertising shows that stringent laws are required for monitoring social media and its use as a marketing device.

For Questions 180 to 182, select only one answer choice.

180. The primary purpose of the passage is to:

Ⓐ Explicate the consumer benefits of social media marketing

Ⓑ Inform the reader that the risks of maintaining an online presence are acceptable

Ⓒ Question the risks of social media marketing compared to the payoff

Ⓓ Analyze the methods and downsides to social media marketing

Ⓔ Make the case that the invasion of privacy is necessary for ad targeting

181. Which of the following best summarizes the author's point in paragraph two?

Ⓐ The prevalence of mobile phones allows for more intensive marketing

Ⓑ Mobile phone use is linked to increased social media activity in users

Ⓒ Online advertising adapts to the latest technology, such as mobile phone use

Ⓓ Customers who use mobile phones can always have access to ads and videos

Ⓔ Frequent product updates and alerts sent via phone boost revenues

182. The sentences in bold play which of the following roles?

Ⓐ The first shows a new marketing frontier, the second presents a related concern.

Ⓑ The first highlights a commonly used tool, the second draws attention back to the thesis.

Ⓒ The first suggests a new approach, the second warns against that approach.

Ⓓ The first anticipates a new trend, the second suggests an alternative approach.

Ⓔ The first presents new evidence, the second returns to the passage's argument.

For Questions 183 to 184, consider each of the three choices separately and select all that apply.

183. The author would most likely support which of the following reforms to social media marketing?

☐A Changing targeted ads based on location, not gender or age

☐B Banning the use of a user's friends as potential advertising targets

☐C Limiting the number of ads per page

184. Which of the following could accurately describe the author's tone?

    [A] Anachronistic, because of the formal language

    [B] Imperious, because of the authoritative statements

    [C] Informed, because of the explanation of terms

185. Select the sentence recommending, as opposed to simply describing, a specific course of action.

Passage 72

Questions 186 to 189 are based on the following passage.

It is estimated that more than 1.1 billion people smoke tobacco as a daily habit. It is a major health hazard that causes reduction in life span and contributes to 500,000 deaths yearly in the United States. Smoking is a deep-rooted habit that developed in early human history and is widespread in societies and cultures. Some behavioral analysts state that peer pressure is a significant factor for initial tobacco use, while others stress that factors like family and education are also as important. Several health campaigns have reduced smoking habits in developed countries, but it is on a rise in developing countries, especially in young people who are influenced by advertisements and visual media.

Compounds like nicotine stimulate release of pleasure-associated neurotransmitters, like dopamine and endorphins, causing persistence of smoking. Tobacco smoke contains hundreds of chemicals, most of which are harmful to health. Polycyclic aromatic hydrocarbons like benzopyrene, for example, cause DNA damage and mutations. Even occasional smoking can lead to cancer and diseases of heart and lungs, like heart attacks and chronic obstructive pulmonary disease. Passive smoking is also harmful and causes medical complications. Smoking during pregnancy is harmful to the developing fetus. Cost to healthcare and loss of man power have major economic impact, but powerful lobbies often prevail over social movements, especially in developing countries.

For Questions 186 to 188, select only one answer choice.

186. Smoking harms all of the following people EXCEPT:

    (A) Geriatric smokers

    (B) Someone who smokes once a year

    (C) A pregnant, nonsmoking woman whose father quit smoking

    (D) Young (18-24 year-old) students who smoke on weekends

    (E) Someone living with a smoker

187. Which of the following is an assumption upon which the author's claim rests?

(A) Cigarettes and pipes are both deadly

(B) The reader is a smoker or knows a smoker

(C) The side effects of working in a tobacco factory are harmful

(D) Lobbyists sacrifice tax revenue to ensure that tobacco stays on the market

(E) Some cancers and lung diseases cannot be attributed to smoking

188. Which of the following would be the best example with which to continue the passage?

(A) Anecdotes about former smokers who have quit

(B) Scientific diagrams of the hydrocarbons mentioned

(C) History of tobacco lobbyists' actions

(D) Rising and falling taxes on tobacco over the last century

(E) Overview of the ban on flavored cigarettes

Consider each of the three choices separately and select all that apply.

189. The passage suggests which of the following views of smoking?

[A] Smoking can be a deeply ingrained cultural behavior, regardless of risk

[B] Younger smokers are more likely to contract disease than older smokers, as younger immune systems are weaker

[C] The risks of smoking are barely mitigated by quitting smoking

Passage 73

Questions 190 and 191 are based on the following passage.

The number of homeless female military veterans in the United States has intensified, with rates nearly doubling between 2006 and 2010 according to the most recent government surveys. While it is true that this increase can be attributed to an overall increase in female representation in the U.S. military, the trend is nonetheless deeply disturbing. Women are particularly vulnerable since many have to care for young children and a lack of access to veteran shelters that also provide family services only compounds the problem - more women and children have nowhere to go while many male veterans can still rely on traditional veteran shelters.

For Questions 190 and 191, select only one answer choice.

190. Rhetorically speaking, the author is appealing to the reader's

   Ⓐ Logos

   Ⓑ Pathos

   Ⓒ Metaphysical sensibilities

   Ⓓ Ethos

   Ⓔ Political sensibilities

191. The reader can most reasonably infer that

   Ⓐ The United States military does not take care of its veterans

   Ⓑ United States veterans are usually homeless

   Ⓒ Gender inequality is a problem among military veterans

   Ⓓ Women should not serve in the U.S. military

   Ⓔ Female veterans of the U.S. military have more children than male veterans

Passage 74

Question 192 is based on the following passage.

Lenny's Lemonade provides concession stands for large agricultural fairs throughout New England between the months of May and October each year. Lenny's Lemonade squeezes fresh organic lemons into filtered water and adds just the correct amount of organic cane sugar while the customer waits. Over the years, Lenny has developed a loyal following, and his lemonade is in great demand. In fact, last year, Lenny's sales increased twenty percent over the previous year. Lenny predicts that sales will continue to climb and has placed an order for twenty-five percent more lemons for the coming season.

Select only one answer choice.

192. Which of the following, if true, undermines Lenny's prediction?

      (A) The price of organic lemons has increased by twenty percent.

      (B) Last summer, almost all of New England experienced record high temperatures.

      (C) Sales of organic products have increased in stores across New England.

      (D) Fair organizers have announced a decrease in the entrance fee for attendees.

      (E) Fair organizers have increased the percentage of sales that concessionaires must pay to reserve their spaces

Passage 75

Question 193 is based on the following passage.

Realtors in Commonville have noticed a marked increase in home sales in the neighboring town of Placeton. Additionally, those houses are selling for 5 to 10 percent over the asking price, which, in turn, increases the realtors' commissions. Last year, a home staging company opened in Placeton, and several homeowners have used their services when putting their houses on the market. The realtors in Commonville have recommended that their clients use the staging company and predict that not only will their homes sell more quickly but for higher prices.

Select only one answer choice.

193. Which of the following conditions weakens the prediction made by the Commonville realtors?

      (A) Realtors in Commonville use a variety of media to market the houses they are selling.

      (B) Homes in Placeton have consistently been priced below market value.

      (C) A large employer in Commonville recently reduced its workforce by half.

      (D) A majority of the homes in Placeton are ranch style, while a majority of the homes in Commonville are Victorian style.

      (E) Thirty percent of Commonville homeowners are single parents.

Passage 76

Question 194 is based on the following passage.

Over the past few years, the deer population in northern Maine has declined significantly. Three years ago, a large landowner began clear cutting woodlands in areas of northern Maine, destroying underbrush that the deer feed on. Stopping the clear cutting will reestablish a healthy deer population.

Select only one answer choice.

194.   Which of the following, if true, weakens the argument?

    Ⓐ The large landowner has placed salt licks near the deer yards.

    Ⓑ Five years ago, the state issued a large number of doe permits to hunters in northern Maine.

    Ⓒ The landowner has plans to plant seedlings where it has clear cut.

    Ⓓ The clear cutting has led to erosion which has caused soil to wash into a nearby river.

    Ⓔ The state has employed more game wardens to curtail the illegal hunting of deer.

Passage 77

Question 195 is based on the following passage.

Robin has reduced her consumption of saturated fat and sugars by fifty percent. Her next blood test will reveal a significant decrease in her cholesterol levels.

Select only one answer choice.

195.   On which of the following assumptions does this argument depend?

    Ⓐ Reducing saturated fat and sugar intake is the only way to lower cholesterol.

    Ⓑ Reducing consumption of saturated fats alone will not lower cholesterol levels.

    Ⓒ Robin has increased her consumption of lean meat and fish.

    Ⓓ Six months will elapse between Robin's change in eating habits and the administering of the blood test.

    Ⓔ Robin is thirty pounds overweight.

Passage 78

Questions 196 to 199 are based on the following passage.

Then West leaned down and cleared a pebble from before his ball. It was the veriest atom of a pebble that ever showed on a putting green, but West was willing to take no chances beyond those that already confronted him. His mind was made up. Gripping his iron putter firmly rather low on the shaft and bending far over, West slowly, cautiously swung the club above the gutty, glancing once and only once as he did so at the distant goal. Then there was a pause. Whipple no longer studied his own play; his eyes were on that other sphere that nestled there so innocently against the grass. Joel leaned breathlessly forward. Professor

Beck muttered under his breath, and then cried "S--sh!" to himself in an angry whisper. And then West's club swung back gently, easily, paused an instant--and-- Forward sped the ball--on and on--slower--slower--but straight as an arrow--and then--Presto! it was gone from sight!

For Questions 196 to 198, select only one answer choice.

196. Which of the following is most correct about the ending of the passage?

    (A) Joel and Professor Beck distract West, and the ball vanishes from sight

    (B) West hits the ball expertly, but the grass slows it down too quickly

    (C) The golf club hits the ball, but the drive is evidently unsuccessful

    (D) The fate of the golf ball is not clear, but the ending has a positive tone

    (E) The ending leaves the reader in suspense

197. The themes of this passage include all of the following EXCEPT:

    (A) Golf's reliance on technology

    (B) Competition among men

    (C) Pressure in sporting events

    (D) The suspense and drama inherent in a single golf swing

    (E) The exhilaration of achieving a difficult task

198. The passage shows which character development over the course of the passage?

    (A) Professor Beck becomes angry at West, then calms himself

    (B) Joel waits in anticipation, and then is relieved

    (C) West prepares mentally, then relaxes

    (D) Joel waits for West to hit the ball, then sighs

    (E) West becomes stressed, and then succeeds

Consider each of the three choices separately and select all that apply.

199. The passage could be which of the following genres?

   A☐ Sports biography, because of the description of golfing and personal details

   B☐ Sports fiction, because of the setting of a golf game

   C☐ A bildungsroman, because of West's development

Passage 79

Questions 200 and 201 are based on the following passage.

A fourth approach advocates using the power of the free market to improve public education. Supporters assert that public schools don't improve because they have no real competition. By giving parents vouchers that could be used for students to attend either public or private schools, parents could choose the best school for their child, and public schools would be forced to improve to compete. "School choice" programs for public schools are now officially part of the No Child Left Behind Act, which permits parents in failing schools to transfer their children to another public school. Only a few communities, like Milwaukee, Cleveland, Dayton, Fla., and Washington D.C., have attempted to include private and religious schools in their voucher plans. That raises concerns about the separation of church and state, but the U.S. Supreme Court has upheld Cleveland's plan.

For Questions 200 and 201, select only one answer choice.

200. Which of the following attitudes is a likely result of the lack of competition to enroll students in public schools?

   Ⓐ Optimism

   Ⓑ Pessimism

   Ⓒ Complacency

   Ⓓ Defeatism

   Ⓔ Lethargy

201. In addition to concerns about separation of church and state, what other weakness lies in choosing a private or religious school in an effort to improve public education?

   Ⓐ Students may have to purchase their own books and uniforms

   Ⓑ Private schools do not have to comply with the No Child Left Behind act

   Ⓒ Private schools may not offer extracurricular activities

   Ⓓ Religion classes may be part of the curriculum

   Ⓔ Private schools might not offer transportation to school

Passage 80

Questions 202 to 204 are based on the following passage.

It is an even thing: New York society has not taken to our literature. New York publishes it, criticizes it, and circulates it, but I doubt if New York society much reads it or cares for it, and New York is therefore by no means the literary center that Boston once was, though a large number of our literary men live in or about New York. Boston, in my time at least, had distinctly a literary atmosphere, which more or less pervaded society; but New York has distinctly nothing of the kind, in any pervasive sense. It is a vast mart, and literature is one of the things marketed here; but our good society cares no more for it than for some other products bought and sold here; it does not care nearly so much for books as for horses or for stocks, and I suppose it is not unlike the good society of any other metropolis in this. To the general, here, journalism is a far more appreciable thing than literature, and has greater recognition, for some very good reasons; but in Boston literature had vastly more honor, and even more popular recognition, than journalism.

For Questions 202 to 204, select only one answer choice.

202. The author uses which of the following formats to achieve his purpose in this passage?

   Ⓐ Persuasive writing

   Ⓑ Logical appeal

   Ⓒ Narrative

   Ⓓ Symbolism

   Ⓔ Compare/contrast

203. According to this writer, in what way is New York similar to any other large city?

    Ⓐ It is home to many writers

    Ⓑ It treats literary work as a commodity

    Ⓒ It is a center of commerce

    Ⓓ It has great journalists

    Ⓔ It has a stock exchange

204. Consider the content of this passage as you select the pair of descriptors that contrast New York City and Boston

    Ⓐ Pragmatic versus aesthetic

    Ⓑ Industrial versus agrarian

    Ⓒ Competitive versus complacent

    Ⓓ Stereotypical versus unique

    Ⓔ Progressive versus stagnant

Passage 81

Question 205 is based on the following passage.

The rise in popularity of Oxycontin, an addictive prescription pain reliever, illustrates the challenge facing authorities trying to prevent drug use. The drug was first released in 1995, and its use has particularly spiked in the Appalachian states, which are more isolated from traditional illegal drug routes. Oxycontin is obtained through fake prescriptions, other people's legal prescriptions, theft, diversion from pharmacies and the practice of "doctor-shopping," in which people go from one doctor to another seeking multiple prescriptions. The problem for officials is how to separate legitimate users and legitimate prescription-writing doctors from addicts and dealers.

Select only one answer choice.

205. Which of the following, if true, might weaken the position that isolation from traditional illegal drug routes is the reason for increased use of OxyContin in Appalachian states?

    Ⓐ Residents of the Appalachian states, where coal mining is a common occupation, more commonly suffer from painful injuries

    Ⓑ There are fewer pharmacies per capita in the Appalachian states

    Ⓒ There are fewer doctors per capita in the Appalachian states

    Ⓓ The population density in the Appalachian states is lower than in other areas of the country

    Ⓔ OxyContin is more expensive than other prescription pain killers

Passage 82

Questions 206 and 207 are based on the following passage.

The year 1919 awarded coffee one of its brightest honors. An American general said that coffee shared with bread and bacon the distinction of being one of the three nutritive essentials that helped win the World War for the Allies. So, this symbol of human brotherhood has played a not inconspicuous part in "making the world safe for democracy." The new age, ushered in by the Peace of Versailles and the Washington Conference, has for its hand-maidens temperance and self-control. It is to be a world democracy of right-living and clear thinking; and among its most precious adjuncts are coffee, tea, and cocoa - because these beverages must always be associated with rational living, with greater comfort, and with better cheer.

Select only one answer choice.

206. If this paragraph were an introduction to a longer piece of writing, which of the following topics would logically be the focus of the next paragraph?

    Ⓐ How the properties of bacon sustained the soldiers during the war

    Ⓑ How bread served as the most important food item for the troops during the war

    Ⓒ How important right living and clear thinking are to democracy

    Ⓓ How coffee, tea, and cocoa are associated with rational living, greater comfort, and better cheer

    Ⓔ How coffee, tea, and cocoa might have deleterious effects on humans

Consider each of the three choices separately and select all that apply.

207. Which of the following is a possible topic for the longer piece of writing that contains this passage?

      Ⓐ   Coffee has accumulated a number of honors throughout history

      Ⓑ   Throughout history, a number of relatively commonplace commodities have helped to make the world safe for democracy

      Ⓑ   Coffee, tea, and cocoa are essential to a world democracy of right living and clear thinking

Passage 83

Questions 208 and 209 are based on the following passage.

The debate surrounding the Second Amendment to the United States Constitution has the ability to bring out the pugnacious nature of American politicians and civilians alike. Gun control discussions often raise pulses, but more importantly, they underscore the myopic nature of the American civic milieu. For example, the Virginia Tech University Massacre in 2007 engendered public and political outrage and gun control issues took center stage in American public discourse. At the time, many Americans believed that gun control laws were too lax and that stricter regulations needed to be put in place to protect the public from firearms. However, in just five short years the gun control tides have turned. Americans have relaxed their oppositions to and de-centered their focus from firearms control, likely resulting in the new laws that allow the carrying of concealed weapons in states like Wisconsin and even on university campuses, such as the University of Texas.

For Questions 208 and 209, select only one answer choice.

208. What overall message does the author intend to convey to the reader about American society?

      Ⓐ   America needs stricter gun control laws

      Ⓑ   Issues related to the Second Amendment typically do not concern Americans

      Ⓒ   American society is characterized by emotionally driven rhetoric

      Ⓓ   American public discourse is often short-sighted relative to civic issues

      Ⓔ   The Second Amendment is the cornerstone of American society

209. The author mentions "the pugnacious nature of American politicians and civilians alike" as

  Ⓐ A way to show how confused Americans are when it comes to the rules governing civil society

  Ⓑ A method of underscoring the belligerence of the American national character

  Ⓒ A means of capturing the reader's attention

  Ⓓ An argumentative strategy to convince the reader that Americans are aggressive by nature

  Ⓔ A narrative rhetorical strategy to convince the reader that Americans are short-sighted relative to civil issues

Passage 84

Questions 210 and 211 are based on the following passage.

The number of homeless female military veterans in the United States has intensified, with rates nearly doubling between 2006 and 2010 according to the most recent government surveys. While it is true that this increase can be attributed to an overall increase in female representation in the U.S. military, the trend is nonetheless deeply disturbing. Women are particularly vulnerable since many have or care for young children and a lack of access to veteran shelters that also provide family services only compounds the problem - more women and children have nowhere to go while many male veterans can still rely on traditional veteran shelters.

For Questions 210 and 211, select only one answer choice.

210. Rhetorically speaking, the author is appealing to the reader's

  Ⓐ Logos

  Ⓑ Pathos

  Ⓒ Metaphysical sensibilities

  Ⓓ Ethos

  Ⓔ Political sensibilities

211. The reader can most reasonably infer that

   Ⓐ The United States military does not take care of its veterans

   Ⓑ United States veterans are usually homeless

   Ⓒ Gender inequality is a problem among military veterans

   Ⓓ Women should not serve in the U.S. military

   Ⓔ Female veterans of the U.S. military have more children than male veterans

Passage 85

Question 212 is based on the following passage.

The term domestic violence generally conjures images of defenseless women being attacked by abusive and domineering men. However, statistics show that males account for 2 out of 5 cases of domestic violence; thus, men are frequently at the receiving end of abuse. Researchers also believe that these numbers could be misleading; in many Western societies, there is still a strong social stigma surrounding men being victims of abuse. Many men feel that it is socially unacceptable for them to display weakness or seek help in abusive situations. This may very well cause many cases of female on male domestic violence to go unreported.

Select only one answer choice.

212. The statistics relative to the domestic abuse of males are inaccurate because

   Ⓐ Women in Western society stigmatize abused men

   Ⓑ Researchers demonstrate a bias that supports the feminist agenda

   Ⓒ Men worry that reporting abuse will negatively impact their relationships with women

   Ⓓ Statistics in general can never be 100% accurate

   Ⓔ Men worry that reporting abuse will tarnish their image

Passage 86

Questions 213 to 215 are based on the following passage.

Debt is a hot topic and a major concern at all levels of American society and yet there is one group of Americans who are less troubled by the financial albatross that they bear than the rest: college students. Despite the high average student loan debt of $23,000 for graduating seniors, many students are not stressed about the money they owe - they in fact feel confident and empowered. Researchers attribute this response to student loan debt as atypical and evidence that college students see their education as an investment and feel that their level of debt indicates their commitment to opportunities for greater growth and later career advancement.

For Questions 213 to 215, select only one answer choice.

213. What can be inferred about American college students based on the information given in the passage?

Ⓐ American college students have high levels of student debt

Ⓑ American college students resent taking out student loans

Ⓒ American college students are not as heavily affected by debt as their older adult counterparts

Ⓓ American college students choose to view debt through a positive lens

Ⓔ American college students feel that debt is not an important issue

214. College students' attitude to student loan debt is best described as

Ⓐ Naive

Ⓑ Predictable

Ⓒ Preternatural

Ⓓ Banal

Ⓔ Unexceptional

215. The author intends the term "albatross" in the passage to be analogous to

Ⓐ The level of debt

Ⓑ The burden of debt

Ⓒ The stresses in American society

Ⓓ A bank account

Ⓔ Credit card debt

Passage 87

Questions 216 and 217 are based on the following passage.

One of the major roadblocks impeding equal opportunities for success in the United States is low literacy rates. While many people often lump low literacy and children together as one problem set, experts estimate that nearly 30 million American adults have literacy skills that are "below basic." This phenomenon is particularly harmful because low literacy among adults engenders a cycle of literacy problems; the children of adults with low literacy are more likely to struggle with school, drop out of school, and live in poverty. This is why literacy initiatives are such an important part of the fabric of American society: they help keep opportunities for success open to all individuals by fostering the development of critical language skills.

Select only one answer choice.

216.   The two parts in bold-face demonstrate how the author

ⓐ   Delineates the problems associated with low literacy

ⓑ   Appeals to the reader's emotional sensibilities relative to low literacy

ⓒ   Reinforces his or her beliefs as well as opposing beliefs relative to low literacy

ⓓ   Reaches a solution to the problem posed in his or her original claim

ⓔ   Makes use of paradox relative to low literacy

Consider each of the three choices separately and select all that apply.

217.   The author would agree with which of the following statements?

A   Low literacy is especially problematic in children

B   Low literacy stonewalls equal opportunities

C   Low literacy leads to higher crime rates

Practice Set 5: Physical Sciences

Passage 88

Questions 218 to 223 are based on the following passage.

The iron ores of the Lake Superior region are the result of the action of waters from the surface on so-called iron formations or jaspers. Here again it was at first supposed that the enrichment was related to the present erosion surface; but upon further studies the fact was disclosed that the concentration of the ores took place in the period between the deposition of Keweenawan and Cambrian rocks, and thus a new light was thrown on the possibilities as to depth and distribution of the ores. The old pre-Cambrian surface, with reference to which the concentration took place, can be followed with some precision beneath the present surface. This makes it possible to forecast a quite different depth and distribution of the ores from that which might be inferred from present surface conditions. Present surface conditions, of low relief, considerable humidity, and with the water table usually not more than 100 feet from the surface, do not promise ore deposits at great depth. The erosion which formed the old pre-Cambrian surface, however, started on a country of great relief and semi-arid climate, conditions which favored deep penetration of the surface waters which concentrated the ores.

The iron ores of eastern Cuba are formed by the weathering of a serpentine rock on an elevated plateau of low relief, where the sluggish streams are unable rapidly to carry off the products of weathering. Where streams have cut into this plateau and where the plateau breaks down with sharp slopes to the ocean, erosion has removed the products of weathering, and therefore the iron ore. An important element, then, in iron ore exploration in this country is the location of regions of slight erosion in the serpentine area. One of the largest discoveries was made purely on a topographic basis. It was inferred merely from a study of topography that a certain large unexplored area ought to carry iron ore. Subsequent work in the thick and almost impenetrable jungle disclosed it.

Bauxite deposits in several parts of the world require somewhat similar conditions of concentration, and a study of the physiographic features is an important factor in their location and interpretation.

A physiographic problem of another sort is the determination of the conditions surrounding the origin of sedimentary ores. Certain mineral deposits, like the "Clinton" iron ores, the copper ores in the "Red Beds" of southwestern United States and in the Mansfield slates of Germany, many salt deposits, and almost the entire group of placer deposits of gold, tin, and other metals, are the result of sedimentation, from waters which derived their materials from the erosion of the land surface. It is sometimes possible from the study of these deposits to discover the position and configuration of the shore line, the depth of water, and the probable continuity and extent of the deposits. Similar questions are met in the study of coal and oil.

218.   Select the sentence in the passage that reveals why it is less likely that the present erosion surface is the source of iron ore in the environment of the Lake Superior region.

For Questions 219 and 220, consider each of the three choices separately and select all that apply.

219.   In the context of this passage, which of the following is the best explanation of the relationship between weathering and erosion?

   [A]   Weathering weakens the surface, enabling erosion to occur.

   [B]   The same forces of nature that cause weathering also cause erosion.

   [C]   Weathering results from dry conditions, while erosion results from wet conditions.

220.   Which of the following statements most clearly expresses the advantage of following the pre-Cambrian surface instead of the existing surface when attempting to locate ore deposits?

   [A]   Following the pre-Cambrian surface leads to greater concentration of ore which is apt to produce greater income with lower associated costs and, eventually, higher profits.

   [B]   Enterprises involved in excavating and extracting the ores are able to predict the depth and distribution of those ores more accurately.

   [C]   Those with a financial interest in the ores can create a more effective hindrance to residential development in the area.

For Questions 221 to 223, select only one answer choice.

221. Why is it important to locate regions of slight erosion in the serpentine areas of eastern Cuba?

   Ⓐ The water table in these regions is closer to the surface.

   Ⓑ These regions are more likely to have retained deposits of iron ore.

   Ⓒ Familiarity with the techniques necessary to do so can help to locate bauxite deposits elsewhere.

   Ⓓ This information leads to a more complete understanding of sedimentation.

   Ⓔ It helps to form a hypothesis concerning the existence of place deposits.

222. Which of the following best identifies the writer's attitude toward his audience?

   Ⓐ Reverent

   Ⓑ Earnest

   Ⓒ Reflective

   Ⓓ Respectful

   Ⓔ Erudite

223. Which of the following is important to know about the author when considering the reliability of information presented in this passage?

   Ⓐ The length of time he has spent in each of the locations mentioned in the passage.

   Ⓑ His level of knowledge about the commercial applications of the ores and metals mentioned in the passage.

   Ⓒ The purpose for which he has written the passage.

   Ⓓ At which college or university he earned his degree in geology.

   Ⓔ Which aspect of geology he specialized in while in college.

Passage 89

Questions 224 and 225 are based on the following passage.

   After the first four, no more asteroids were found until 1845, when one was discovered; then, in 1847, three more were added to the list; and after that searchers began to pick them up with such rapidity that by the close of the century hundreds were known, and it had become almost impossible to keep track of them. It was long supposed that Vesta was the largest, because it shines more brightly than any of the others; but finally, in 1895, Barnard, with the Lick telescope, definitely measured their diameters, and proved to everybody's surprise that Ceres is really the chief, and Vesta only the third in rank. They differ greatly in the reflective power of their surfaces, a fact of much significance in connection with the question of their origin. Vesta is, surface for surface, rather more than three times as brilliant as Ceres, whence the original mistake about its magnitude.

For Questions 224 and 225, select only one answer choice.

224.   Which of the following statements is the most reasonable explanation for the increased frequency with which asteroids were discovered toward the end of the nineteenth century?

⒜ A shift in the jet stream created larger areas of cloudless skies, making the asteroids more visible

⒝ More colleges and universities offered courses in astronomy

⒞ A period of frequent volcanic activity had finally subsided, reducing the amount of particulate matter in the atmosphere

⒟ Advances in telescope technology made it possible to identify asteroids that had been previously overlooked

⒠ Astronomers had a better understanding of asteroids' identifying characteristics

225.   Which of the following predictions about the future of science is likely to be true based on your understanding of this passage?

⒜ New discoveries and accuracy will occur at an increasingly rapid pace

⒝ More asteroids will be discovered and correctly measured

⒞ Astronomers are likely to discover an asteroid larger than Ceres

⒟ Greater investment should be made in astronomical research

⒠ The origins of asteroids will continue to be identified

Passage 90

Questions 226 to 229 are based on the following passage.

A cross pole might also be set up, but most of the exercises for which this is used, may be performed by the triangle. On the parallel bars, several beneficial exercises may be done, and also on the bridge. This is a pole thick at one end, thin at the other, and supported at three or four feet from the ground by a post at one end and another in the middle, so that the thin end vibrates with the least touch. This, it will be evident, is an exercise for the organ of equilibrium, and exercises the muscles of the calf, of the neck, and anterior part of the neck, and those of the back, very gently. On this bridge a sort of combat may be instituted, two persons meeting each other, giving and parrying strokes with the open hands.

For Questions 226 and 227, select only one answer choice.

226. Which modern exercise would give benefits similar to the exercise that the author suggests?

     (A) Boxing with a partner

     (B) Raising one leg off the ground and holding it

     (C) Doing calf and shoulder raises

     (D) Drilling wrestling moves alone

     (E) Swinging on a trapeze

227. The passage would be improved by a paragraph on which of the following?

     (A) Evolution of exercise machines over time

     (B) Benefits of exercising alone or with or against another person

     (C) Advice on the implementation of the aforementioned exercise equipment

     (D) Differences in exercising for people of varying ages

     (E) Techniques and benefits of paired sparring

Consider each of the three choices separately and select all that apply.

228. Which of the following, if true, would most undermine the point of the passage?

     [A] The bridge is expensive and cumbersome to install

     [B] It is discovered that long balance exercises can damage the neck

     [C] Certain gyms decide to remove bridges from their facilities, making it difficult to practice balancing exercises

229. Select the sentence which describes the most thoroughly beneficial exercise one can do on the bridge.

Passage 91

Question 230 is based on the following passage.

As pitch depends upon the frequency at which sound waves strike the ear, an object may emit sound waves at a constant frequency yet may produce different pitches in ears differently situated. Such a case is not usual, but an example of it will serve a useful purpose in fixing certain facts as to pitch. Conceive two railroad trains to pass each other, running in opposite directions, the engine bells of both trains ringing. Passengers on each train will hear the bell of the other, first as a *rising* pitch, then as a *falling* one. Passengers on each train will hear the bell of their own train at a *constant* pitch.

Select only one answer choice.

230. Which of the following statements best describes the main discrepancy presented by this passage?

 (A) The continuity of sound waves emitted by an object varies in the unreliability of individual perceptions.

 (B) It is unusual for people to hear the same sounds in different ways

 (C) Two trains that are travelling in opposite directions meet at a common point at the moment that they pass each other.

 (D) Though theoretically two trains may emit identical sounds from their bells, the sound emitted is irrelevant to the sound that is heard.

 (E) The rate of change exhibited by a sound is in direct relation to the speed of the train.

Passage 92

Question 231 is based on the following passage.

The wear on a well-designed gas valve operating mechanism is practically nil; and even if there was wear, the effect would be to cause the valve to open a trifle later and close sooner than it would otherwise, i.e., it would remain open a shorter time during each charging stroke. This in turn (other conditions remaining the same) would give us a weaker mixture; and although too weak a mixture is preferable to a too rich one, we should have to adopt some means of increasing the richness of the mixture; otherwise the maximum power of the engine would soon be seen to diminish.

Select only one answer choice.

231. Choose the option that identifies a topic which, if added to the passage in more detail, would best strengthen the author's argument.

 (A) How to maintain the best overall function of an engine.

 (B) Whether the quality of a gas valve's design will adversely affect engine performance.

 (C) Whether a richer mixture is more detrimental to engine performance than a weaker one.

 (D) The destructive effects of wear on a gas-valve over time.

 (E) The numerous conditions that can affect an engine's maximum performance.

Passage 93

Question 232 is based on the following passage.

The process used to manufacture Biodiesel from pure vegetable oil is called ester interchange. In the process the vegetable oil is combined with a much smaller amount of Methanol. Methanol can be manufactured by the fermentation of starch or sugar and it can also be produced from natural gas. The vegetable oil and methanol are placed in a small quantity of an alkaline catalyst and it is in this process that the chemical makeup of the vegetable oil is altered. The result is a clean burning fuel with a viscosity (flow properties) approximating that of standard diesel fuel. During this process, approximately 90% of what is manufactured is Biodiesel fuel, while the remaining 10% is in the form of the glycerin that was broken down from the vegetable matter. This glycerin can also be used in other applications in the chemical industry, making the manufacture of Biodiesel practically waste-free.

232.   Select the sentence that reveals when ester interchange occurs.

Passage 94

Question 233 is based on the following passage.

Iron differs from the metals so far studied in that it is able to form two series of compounds in which the iron has two different valences. In the one series the iron is divalent and forms compounds which in formulas and many chemical properties are similar to the corresponding zinc compounds. It can also act as a trivalent metal, and in this condition forms salts similar to those of aluminum. Those compounds in which the iron is divalent are known as ferrous compounds, while those in which it is trivalent are known as ferric.

Consider each answer choice separately and select all that apply.

233.   Use the information in the passage to decide which of the following statements is accurate.

    [A]   Metals referred to as cuprous in a compound have a lower valence number as metals referred to as cupric in a compound

    [B]   The suffix, - ous, means full of or possessing a certain quality, and the suffix, - ic, means having some characteristics of

    [C]   Cuprous means possessing the qualities of copper and cupric means having some characteristics of copper

Passage 95

Question 234 is based on the following passage.

The reason for this peculiarity of mercury is that the pull between the particles of mercury themselves is stronger than the pull between them and your finger or handkerchief. In scientific language, the cohesion of the mercury is stronger than its adhesion to your finger or handkerchief. Although this seems unusual for a liquid, it is what we naturally expect of solid things; you would be amazed if part of the wood of your school seat stuck to you when you got up, for you expect the particles in solid things to cohere - to have cohesion - much more strongly than they adhere to something else. It is because solids have such strong cohesion that they are solids.

234.   Select the sentence in the passage which reveals that the writer's audience is most likely comprised of laymen.

Passage 96

Questions 235 to 237 are based on the following passage.

The difference between the ways in which snow and rain are formed is very slight. In both cases water evaporates, and its vapor mingles with the warm air. The warm air rises and expands. It cools as it expands, and when it gets cool enough the water vapor begins to condense. But if the air as it expands becomes very cold, so cold that the droplets of water freeze as they form and gather together to make delicate crystals of ice, snow is formed. The ice crystals found in snow are always six-sided or six-pointed, because, probably, the water or ice molecules pull from six directions and therefore gather each other together along the six lines of this pull. At any rate, the tiny crystals of frozen water are formed and come floating down to the ground; and we call them snowflakes. After the snow melts it goes through the same cycle as the rain, most of it finally getting back to the ocean through rivers, and there, in time, being evaporated once more.

For Questions 235 to 237, select only one answer choice.

235.   The use of the phrase, "at any rate" reveals which of the following about the sentence preceding it?

Ⓐ   That the information in that sentence is essential to understanding the passage

Ⓑ   That the information in that sentence cannot be scientifically proven

Ⓒ   That the information in that sentence is an unnecessary digression

Ⓓ   That the process described in that sentence is not true in every case

Ⓔ   That the information in that sentence is not very interesting

236. Consider the context of this passage to decide which of the following most accurately identifies the type of writing exhibited.

    (A) Narrative

    (B) Expository

    (C) Editorial

    (D) Persuasive

    (E) Compare/contrast

237. Based on the information in this passage, decide which of the following meteorological events is a result of the same process described here.

    (A) A rainbow

    (B) Fog

    (C) Wind chill

    (D) Degree days

    (E) Thunder

Passage 97

Questions 238 to 240 are based on the following passage.

Sound is the sensation peculiar to the ear. This sensation is caused by rapidly-succeeding to-and-fro motions of the air which touches the outside surface of the drum-skin of the ear. These to-and-fro motions may be given to the air by a distant body, like a string of a violin. The string moves to and fro, that is, it vibrates. These vibrations of the string act on the bridge of the violin, which rests on the belly or sounding-board of the instrument. The surface of the sounding-board is thus set trembling, and these tremors, or vibrations, spread through the air in all directions around the instrument, somewhat in the manner that water-waves spread around the place where a stone has been dropped into a quiet pond. These tremors of the air, however, are not sound, but the cause of sound. Sound, as we have said, is a sensation; but, as the cause of this sensation is always vibration, we call those vibrations which give this sensation, sonorous vibrations.

For Questions 238 and 239, select only one answer choice.

238. What is the correct definition of peculiar as it is used in the first sentence of this passage?

Ⓐ Odd

Ⓑ Uncommon

Ⓒ Distinctive in character or nature from others

Ⓓ Belonging characteristically

Ⓔ Belonging exclusively to some person, group, or thing

239. Consider the content of the passage and select the most likely audience for this information.

Ⓐ Musicians

Ⓑ Violin manufacturers

Ⓒ Students

Ⓓ Sonography technicians

Ⓔ Acoustics engineers

240. Select the sentence that a seismologist might find useful to describe the effect of an earthquake.

Passage 98

Questions 241 and 242 are based on the following passage.

Evapotranspiration is water transpired from plants and evaporated from the soil. *Rising* air currents take the vapor up into the atmosphere where cooler temperatures cause it to condense into clouds. Air currents move water vapor around the globe; cloud particles collide, grow, and fall out of the sky as precipitation. Some precipitation falls as snow or hail, and can accumulate as ice caps and glaciers, which can store frozen water for thousands of years.

For Questions 241 and 242, select only one answer choice.

241. Based on the information in the passage, which of the following would be an appropriate visual representation of the text.

Ⓐ A Venn diagram

Ⓑ A list

Ⓒ A flow chart

Ⓓ A time line

Ⓔ A T-chart

242. Based on the sequence of information in this passage, which of the topics listed below might logically be discussed in the paragraph immediately following this one?

Ⓐ Different cloud formations

Ⓑ Other forms of precipitation

Ⓒ Water evaporated from lakes and ponds

Ⓓ Glaciers and ice caps

Ⓔ The motion of air currents

Passage 99

Questions 243 to 245 are based on the following passage.

Lakes which fill rock-basins are such as are confined on all sides by the common rock of the country, so that in some cases a person can walk entirely around them without stepping off the solid rock; and in all cases they would be found to have a rocky rim inclosing them, were the superficial material removed. How such spoon-shaped depressions could be scooped out, was for a long time an enigma which eluded the search of the most painstaking observers.

As facts accumulated, however, it was noticed that the sides and bottoms of such lakes are smoothed, in many cases polished, and almost always covered with grooves and scratches; and also that in their vicinity beds of clay are usually found, intermixed with pebbles and large boulders which, like the rocky basins, are also smoothed and frequently scratched. It was noticed, too, that the rock from which these boulders and pebbles had been formed commonly differed from the rocks in place on the shores of the lakes. Thus, throughout New York and Ohio, huge boulders are common, composed of crystalline rock found in place nowhere nearer than the Canadian Highlands, a hundred miles to the northward; while the peculiar native copper of Northern Michigan is sometimes found mingled with the boulders and striated stones of the drift far southward in Ohio.

The problem now was to discover what forces in Nature could polish and scratch both rock-surfaces and detached stones, and could also transport masses of rock, tons in weight, far from their native home.

It is well known that the loose stones and pebbles along the sea-shore are made very smooth and round, and often polished, by the action of the waves. It might be thought from this that the pebbles found on the shores of the lakes, and imbedded in the clays, were fashioned in the same manner. On one occasion, at the Cape of Good Hope, the writer, after wandering for a time along the sloping sandy beach of Table Bay, came suddenly to a little rocky cove exposed to the full swell of the South Atlantic. As each wave broke on the steep, rocky beach and retreated, it was followed by a sharp, rattling sound that could be distinctly heard above the roar of the waves ; we noticed, too, that the stones all along the shore were in motion, rolling down the beach, only to be caught up by the next white-capped wave that came in from the ocean, and again carried up the beach, and rolled and pounded against each other by the untiring waters, that were fast reducing them to sand and dust. On examining these water-worn stones, we found them all smoothed and rounded, and often beautifully polished; but in no case could we discover, even with a magnifying-glass, any that were scratched, or in any way marked similarly to the stones which we have so often examined in the clays and hard-pans that cover so great a portion of our Northern States. From this fact, and also from watching the action of the waves on many other coasts, we conclude that the sea tends to smooth and wear away the stones and rocks along its shores, but has no power to cover them with grooves and scratches; and that, instead of wearing the coast into pockets and basins, it tends only to grind down the islands and continents to one uniform level.

243. Select the sentence in this passage that best conveys the initial step that a researcher would take in the scientific process.

Select only one answer choice.

244. In order to satisfy the writer's hypothesis that the action of the waves creates smooth surfaces on the stones on the shoreline, what additional steps should he take?

Ⓐ Collect and label samples from Table Bay

Ⓑ Create an experiment that tests the hypothesis

Ⓒ Do background research

Ⓓ Publish a report of the results

Ⓔ Seek others' perspectives

Consider each answer choice separately and select all that apply.

245.   Which of the following are obstacles for this writer in constructing a working hypothesis?

   [A]   The apparent migration of rocks from one location to another

   [B]   Seemingly contradictory evidence

   [C]   Erroneous prior information

Passage 100

Question 246 is based on the following passage.

When observed with astronomical instruments, or photographed, we discover that its surface is not smooth, as might be supposed, but granulated, presenting a number of luminous points dispersed over a more somber background. These granulations are somewhat like the pores of a fruit, e.g., a fine orange, the color of which recalls the hue of the Sun when it sinks in the evening and prepares to plunge us into darkness. At times these pores open under the influence of disturbances that arise upon the solar surface and give birth to a Sun-Spot. For centuries scientists and lay people alike refused to admit the existence of these spots, regarding them as so many blemishes upon the King of the Heavens. Was not the Sun the emblem of inviolable purity? To find any defect in him were to do him grievous injury. Since the orb of day was incorruptible, those who threw doubt on his immaculate splendor were fools and idiots.

Consider each answer choice separately and select all that apply.

246.   What purpose is served by the writer's use of euphemisms for the sun?

   [A]   They serve to illustrate the mythical significance attributed to the sun by humans prior to the invention of scientific instruments used to observe the sun

   [B]   They serve to demonstrate that early humans realized how important the sun was in providing heat and light to aid in their daily activities

   [C]   They serve to shed light on the disdain that common people had for anyone who challenged their beliefs

Passage 101

Question 247 is based on the following passage.

Since silver is not acted upon by water or air, and has a pleasing appearance, it is used to coat various articles made of cheaper metals. Such articles are said to be silver plated. The process by which this is done is called electroplating. It is carried on as follows: The object to be plated (such as a spoon) is attached to a wire and dipped into a solution of a silver salt. Electrical connection is made in such a way that the article to be plated serves as the cathode, while the anode is made up of one or more plates of silver. When a current is passed through the electrolyte silver dissolves from the anode plate and deposits on the cathode in the form of a closely adhering layer. By making the proper change in the electrolyte and anode plate objects may be plated with gold and other metals.

Select only one answer choice.

247.   Use the information in the passage to select what appears to be the main purpose of electroplating.

(A)   To fool consumers

(B)   To significantly increase the value of base metals

(C)   To add shine to otherwise dull objects

(D)   To make anodes and cathodes useful

(E)   To add aesthetic appeal to affordable, commonplace objects

Passage 102

Questions 248 and 249 are based on the following passage.

The article claims that Mr. Gary has made a discovery of a neutral line or surface, at which the polarity of an induced magnet, while moving in the field of the inducing pole, is changed. The alleged discovery appears to be an exaggerated statement of some curious facts, which, although not new, are not commonly recognized. If a bar of iron be brought up, end on, near a magnetic pole, the bar becomes an induced magnet, but an induced magnet quite different from what our elementary treatises seem to predict. On the first scrutiny it is a magnet without a neutral point, and only one kind of magnetism - namely, that of the inducing pole. Moreover, the single pole is pretty evenly distributed over the whole surface, so that if iron filings be sprinkled on the bar they will be attracted at all points and completely cover it. Now, if while the bar is covered by filings it be moved away from the inducing pole, the filings will gradually and progressively fall, beginning at the end nearest the inducing pole and continuing to some point near the middle of the bar; the filings at the remote end will generally be held permanently. When the bar is carried beyond the field of the inducing pole it is simply a weak magnet of ordinary properties - i. e., of two poles and a neutral point between them.

Consider each answer choice separately and select all that apply.

248. Based on your understanding of the information in the passage, select which of the following statements is likely to be true about induced magnets.

    A An induced magnet assumes the polarity possessed by the end of the existing magnet to which it is attached

    B The end of the induced magnet that is farthest from the original magnet retains its magnetism longer than the closer end when the induced magnet is removed from the original

    C The bar that becomes an induced magnet must be magnetized prior to placing it next to the magnet

Select only one answer choice.

249. What does the use of the words "alleged" and "exaggerated" imply about the writer's tone in this passage?

    Ⓐ He is skeptical

    Ⓑ He is reluctant

    Ⓒ He is expressing admiration

    Ⓓ He is convinced

    Ⓔ He is critical

Passage 103

Question 250 is based on the following passage.

Satellites can be placed in variations on geostationary orbits. The Japanese "Michibiki" satellite, launched in 2010, was intended to augment the American Global Positioning System (GPS) satellite navigation network. The GPS satellites provide coded timing signals that allow a receiver to determine its location on Earth, but GPS signals are not always easy to pick up in Japan's mountainous regions or skyscraper-studded cities like Tokyo. Michibiki was placed in an orbit that varied from above to below the geostationary distance, with the orbital plane at 45 degrees to the equator. Given this orbit, instead of hanging over the equator at a fixed location, it performed a daily figure-8 loop from Australia in the south to Japan in the north. The higher and smaller lobe of the figure-8 was over Japan, with the result that Michibiki remained high in the sky there for eight hours of its orbit, providing GPS augmentation signals to locations where GPS reception was otherwise spotty. Two more satellites were to be launched in the series to provide 24 hour a day coverage.

250. Select the sentence in the passage that leads the reader to conclude that an area's terrain should be used in calculating the orbits of GPS satellites.

Passage 104

Questions 251 to 253 are based on the following passage.

Our nuclear paranoia may be nowhere near as high as it was during the Cold War, but we still live in an age characterized by atomic energy. Hence the fears associated with the dangers of radiation still play a prominent role in public discourse. The recent meltdown at the Fukushima Daiichi nuclear power plant only serves to reinforce the fact that we cannot forget how high the risks really run vis-a-vis nuclear disaster. Science, however, claims to have found a method of assuaging our fears of both atomic disaster and atomic dependence. Researchers at the United States Department of Energy's Lawrence Berkeley National Laboratory are in the process of developing a method of decontaminating human bodies that have been exposed to high levels of radiation. As many people know, radiation contamination is the one of the most dangerous aspects of a nuclear meltdown, typically resulting in a slow and often painful degeneration of health in which sickness (sometimes for generations) and death are the common end results. **The Berkeley Lab researchers claim that they can treat the ravages of radiation orally with a pill; depending on how fast the medicine is administered, one pill could remove 90% of the actinide toxins in a mere 24 hours.** In 2 weeks, the body could be contaminant free.

While it is no doubt of the utmost importance to find a way to cure the effects of radiation, one must be skeptical of the treatment method proposed by the Berkeley Lab scientists because it is often times the case that things that sound too good to be true are, in fact, too good to be true. **A few pills over the course of a few weeks curing radiation exposure sounds a bit suspect and make one wonder what the side effects of such a treatment will be.** Such a fast cure to such a grave problem shines a light of doubt on the efficacy and safety of these anti-radiation drugs.

If our society is characterized by paranoia, then it is certainly also characterized by a need for quick fixes to problems. Until more proof can be shown, the radiation treatment proposed by the Berkeley Lab researchers sounds too much like a miracle cure in an age where we need everything to happen as fast as, well, a nuclear meltdown. Until this new treatment has the FDA stamp of approval (and even then, medications can remain suspect), the verdict will remain out as to whether or not science has found a viable cure for actinide contamination.

Select only one answer choice.

251. This passage can best be described as

   Ⓐ A narrative

   Ⓑ Objective prose

   Ⓒ A scientific theory

   Ⓓ Persuasive prose

   Ⓔ Comparative prose

Consider each of the three choices separately and select all that apply.

252.   The two sections highlighted in bold-face are related to each other in which of the following ways?

    A   The first section is an assertion, the second sections seeks to undermine that assertion

    B   The two bold-faced sections present assertions that are congruent with each other

    C   The first section is the scientist's main claim, the second section is the author's main claim

253.   Select the sentence that demonstrates the author's use of the concession and rebuttal rhetorical strategy.

Passage 105

Question 254 is based on the following passage.

Referring to the Higgs boson particle as the God particle is a bit of a misnomer; physicists agree that finding the Higgs boson will not prove or disprove the existence of spiritual beings. However, as gauche as it may be to say it, if physicists are able to finally locate the elusive elementary particle, then the scientific ramifications would be otherworldly indeed: the origins of particle mass in the universe would be explicated and physicists would know that their current hypotheses relative to string theory are on the right track.

Select only one answer choice.

254.   The Higgs boson particle is all of the following except

    Ⓐ   The God particle

    Ⓑ   The origin of particle mass in the universe

    Ⓒ   A hypothesis

    Ⓓ   An elementary particle

    Ⓔ   Scientific support for string theory

Passage 106

Questions 255 to 257 are based on the following passage.

Scientific progress is often measured in terms of medical progress; chemists, biologists, and even physicists work hard to find ways to keep humans healthy and whole and in doing so advance their respective scientific fields. **Furthermore, many of the medical discoveries engendered by the cooperation of doctors and scientists push the boundaries of our imaginations.** Recent developments within the field of chemistry have led to such a groundbreaking discovery: new "smart" material that could potentially help light be transmuted for medicinal purposes. Chemists report that their new polymer (plastic-like) material could help diagnose diseases and engineer new human tissues; whether or not these claims can be substantiated is another matter.

For Questions 255 and 256, select only one answer choice.

255.   According to the passage, what is so avant-garde about chemists' recent discoveries relative to the new "smart" polymer?

(A)   The "smart" polymer will lead to diagnosing more diseases and could even help scientists and doctors engineer new human tissues

(B)   The "smart" polymer will give chemistry a competitive edge among the other sciences represented in the medical community

(C)   The new polymer could help light be harnessed as a curative property

(D)   The "smart" polymer is the cooperative product of chemists, physicists, and biologists

(E)   There is nothing avant-garde about the new "smart" polymer

256.   The section highlighted in bold-face is intended to underscore

(A)   The fact that scientists and doctors often cooperate

(B)   The fact that scientists and doctors are creative

(C)   The fact that medicine evolves in unforeseen ways

(D)   The fact that medical discoveries could not occur without the cooperation of doctors and scientists

(E)   The fact that our imaginations are limited

257.   Select the sentence that belies the author's excitement vis-a-vis the new "smart" polymer.

Passage 107

Questions 258 and 259 are based on the following passage.

Star Wars showed us planets with more than one sun and now scientists are doing the same. The Earth only orbits one sun, but astrophysicists now believe in the ubiquity of other planets in the universe that orbit two stars. These so-called circumbinary planets possess rapidly changing flows of energy and wildly varying climates due to the orbital motion around two suns. Scientists believe that since the climate and seasonal change on such planets are in constant flux, the evolution of life in a circumbinary system would be vastly different than on earth. However, scientists can only speculate as to what this difference would entail; they are still unsure of how exactly life could manifest differently on different planets and in different solar systems.

Select only one answer choice.

258.   The author discusses Star Wars

Ⓐ   In order to draw a parallel between science and science fiction

Ⓑ   To show how science fiction films often predict scientific truths

Ⓒ   As a stylistic device to peak the reader's interest in the text

Ⓓ   As a narrative rhetorical strategy to peak the reader's interest in the text

Ⓔ   In order to promote the Star Wars films

Consider each of the three choices separately and select all that apply.

259.   Circumbinary planets can help us understand

Ⓐ   How life materializes and evolves on other planets

Ⓑ   Climate change on Earth

Ⓒ   The role of the sun(s) in climate control

Passage 108

Questions 260 to 262 are based on the following passage.

Chemists are one mind-blowing step closer than ever to building artificial life forms from scratch. Whether or not this is a good idea is another matter; we are faced here with the "just because we can doesn't mean we should" dilemma. Biochemical researchers have now been able to employ a novel chemical reaction that begets self-assembling cell membranes. Cell membranes are the structural foundation stones for life on Earth and scientists hope that this research break through will allow them to better understand the very origins of life on Earth; one of the great mysteries in science is how non-living matter transmuted to living matter and scientists argue that is important to unlock the secret to the basic chemical and biological principles necessary for the original formation of life. Such research would help us answer the fundamental questions as who we are, where we came from. However, some secrets are meant to stay hidden and the ability to create artificial life could open a Pandora's box with far reaching consequences from exploitation if the technology fell into the wrong hands to annihilation of natural life as we know it.

For Questions 260 to 262, select only one answer choice.

260. The author makes his or her point primarily by

Ⓐ Offering an objective evaluation of the facts

Ⓑ Dramatically appealing to the reader's fear of the unknown

Ⓒ Providing both a view and counterview

Ⓓ Castigating the mindset of the scientists

Ⓔ Using a specific source of authority to back up his or her claims

261. The author refers to a Pandora's Box in order to

Ⓐ Test the reader's intelligence

Ⓑ Highlight the fact that artificial life could never be controlled

Ⓒ Show that the creation of artificial life would be evil

Ⓓ Reinforce his point by way of a trope

Ⓔ Distract the reader with a red herring

262. In the last sentence the author apparently intends to

Ⓐ Explicate how non-living matter transformed into living matter

Ⓑ Underscore why the scientific research mentioned in the passage is important

Ⓒ Generalize an argument to make it more appealing to a wider audience

Ⓓ Give the reader more details related to the information previously discussed in the passage

Ⓔ Persuade the reader to believe an opinion by way of a rhetorical strategy

Passage 109

Question 263 is based on the following passage.

Dark matter is still a mysterious phenomenon to astrophysicists. There are large portions of the universe in which mass does not emit or scatter light or any other kind of electromagnetic radiation, so scientists deem these areas to be composed of dark matter. However, there is still no concrete evidence for the existence of dark matter; scientists can only infer that it exists based on the studied gravitational effects of visible matter and the discrepancies in mass that occur in calculations relative to the mass of galaxies and clusters of galaxies. Thus, dark matter provides a good example of how little we really know about the structures that compose our universe.

263.   Select the sentence that, according to the author, best describes the current state of astrophysics.

Passage 110

Question 264 is based on the following passage.

In physical geography, the earth can be divided into categories of climactic conditions, each with endemic communities of plants, animals, and soil organisms. These groups are known as biomes and it is critically important to understand and protect them because they play a vital role in sustaining the balance of life on the planet. There are four main types of biome: aquatic, forest, desert, and grassland. While each type of biome is different, all are equally important threads woven into the same tapestry: planet earth.

264.   Select the sentence that uses metaphor as a rhetorical strategy.

Passage 111

Question 265 is based on the following passage.

In the wake of global climate change hysteria, everyone is looking for reasons to explain fluctuating weather patterns, from lay people to meteorologists. Extremely hot summers have everyone convinced global warming is on the rampage and extremely cold winters have everyone convinced a new ice age is coming. Scientists, however, now believe that they have found a way to explain the recent phenomenon of extreme winters: harshly hot summers. Research suggests that hot summers contribute to the melting of ice in the world's Arctic regions, which in turn causes extreme cold and heavy snowfall in the winters of temperate climates. The exact cause of the harshly hot summers is still up for debate, but one thing is certain: Just as extreme behavior begets more extreme behavior in humans, so too does extreme weather beget extreme weather.

Consider each of the three answer choices separately and select all that apply.

265.   The author's attitude towards the public and scientific reaction to climate change can best be described as

   A   Petrified

   B   Incredulous

   C   Dubious

Passage 112

Question 266 is based on the following passage.

The origin of the universe is a hotly debated topic in the scientific community, but despite the fierce polemics, the Big Bang theory is still the prevailing explanation. Proponents of the Big Bang theory insist that the universe once existed in an incredibly dense and hot state until it exploded out and expanded rapidly, causing cooling and the formation of stars, galaxies, and eventually life. Most scientists estimate this event to have occurred around 14 billion years ago.

Consider each of the three answer choices separately and select all that apply.

266.   Which of the following are analogous to the term "polemic" in the passage?

   [A]   Contingency

   [B]   Brouhaha

   [C]   Argument

Passage 113

Questions 267 and 268 are based on the following passage.

In particle physics, antimatter is the inverse of matter; antimatter is composed of antiparticles while regular matter is comprised of particles. Antimatter was originally conceptualized in the late 1920s by physicist Paul Dirac as a means of better understanding the behavior of electrons and thus the behavior of our universe. Dirac theorized that nature's predisposition to binary pairs could help him explain the functioning of electrons. He hypothesized that electrons could only exist if there was an antielectron - the opposite of an electron with an opposite electrical charge, but proof of their existence wasn't possible until it could be tested in particle accelerators; a process that could not be undertaken until the 1960's. Today, most antimatter research is centered in Geneva, Switzerland at CERN, the European Organization for Nuclear Research.

For Questions 267 and 268, select only one answer choice.

267.   Dirac's antimatter hypothesis relies on the assumption that

   (A)   Scientific possibilities are never limited

   (B)   Electrons are the key to unlocking the structure of the universe

   (C)   Every extant thing has an inverse

   (D)   The universe can be fully delineated and understood

   (E)   Scientific ideas are sometimes ahead of their times in terms of technological capabilities

268. This passage can best be described as

   Ⓐ A narrative

   Ⓑ A testimony

   Ⓒ A scientific theory

   Ⓓ Persuasive prose

   Ⓔ Comparative prose

Passage 114

Questions 269 and 270 are based on the following passage.

For expeditions in the Antarctic, wind chill, the atmosphere's cooling power, is the most difficult weather issue facing explorers. Winds blow at high speeds in the coastal areas and, especially in East Antarctica, cold air flows down from the mountains. Called katabatic winds, they blow steadily, but can become almost chaotic, and when they reach a certain level of speed can pick up loose snow, causing a phenomenon known as an Antarctic Blizzard in which human movement is difficult. In such "blizzards" no snow actually falls and the sky above the "storm" can be clear. One year, at a camp known as Mirny Station, the katabatic winds reached speeds in excess of 110 miles per hour on seven different occasions. In the years from 1911 – 1914, during the expedition to Antarctica of the Australian Douglas Mawson, wind speed at his Adelie Coast camp averaged 40 miles per hour most of the time he was there. In 1960, winds thought to be between 140 and 155 miles an hour destroyed an airplane on the ground. Not all winds in Antarctica are so powerful. Near the South Pole, in fact, average speeds run from about nine miles an hour in the summer to about 17 miles per hour in the winter.

Consider each of the three answer choices separately and select all that apply.

269. Katabatic winds are probably caused at least in part by

   Ⓐ Atmospheric issues

   Ⓑ Terrain conditions

   Ⓒ The fact that the interior areas are cooler than the coastal areas

Select only one answer choice.

270. The sentence that best indicates the problems caused by winds in Antarctica begins

    Ⓐ For expeditions

    Ⓑ Winds blow

    Ⓒ Called katabatic

    Ⓓ In such blizzards

    Ⓔ In 1960

Practice Set 6: Social Sciences

Passage 115

Questions 271 to 274 are based on the following passage.

The study of the history of the Negroes of Cincinnati is unusually important for the reason that from no other annals do we get such striking evidence that the colored people generally thrive when encouraged by their white neighbors. This story is otherwise significant when we consider the fact that about a fourth of the persons of color settling in the State of Ohio during the first half of the last century made their homes in this city. Situated on a north bend of the Ohio where commerce breaks bulk, Cincinnati rapidly developed, attracting both foreigners and Americans, among whom were not a few Negroes.

For Questions 271 and 272, select only one answer choice.

271. The phrase "breaks bulk" most nearly means in the context of the passage:

    Ⓐ Loses size

    Ⓑ Stagnates

    Ⓒ Embraces diversity

    Ⓓ Disrupts tradition

    Ⓔ Unloads and disseminates

272. The passage implies that which of the following statements is true?

  Ⓐ African-Americans made up a smaller percentage of Cincinnati's population than foreign immigrants.

  Ⓑ Other locations might benefit from following Cincinnati's example.

  Ⓒ Cincinnati's geographic location caused 75% of African-American settlers in Ohio to avoid it.

  Ⓓ White citizens in Cincinnati accepted African-Americans as their equals.

  Ⓔ White foreign immigrants offered encouragement to their African-American neighbors because they sympathized with their plight.

Consider each of the three answer choices separately and select all that apply.

273. Which of the following is given as a reason for the large number of African-American settlers in 19th Century Cincinnati?

  Ａ Encouragement from white citizens

  Ｂ Economic opportunity

  Ｃ Geographic convenience

274. Choose the sentence which presents a specific example that illustrates a general principle.

Passage 116

Questions 275 to 278 are based on the following passage.

The emotions of the ignorant man are continuously kept at a pitch by the most blood-curdling stories about Anarchism. Not a thing too outrageous to be employed against this philosophy and its exponents. Therefore, Anarchism represents to the unthinking what the proverbial bad man does to the child, - a black monster bent on swallowing everything; in short, destruction and violence.

Destruction and violence! How is the ordinary man to know that the most violent element in society is ignorance; that its power of destruction is the very thing Anarchism is combating? **Nor is he aware that Anarchism, whose roots, as it were, are part of nature's forces, destroys, not healthful tissue, but parasitic growths that feed on the life's essence of society.** It is merely clearing the soil from weeds and sagebrush, that it may eventually bear healthy fruit.

Someone has said that it requires less mental effort to condemn than to think. The widespread mental indolence, so prevalent in society, proves this to be only too true. Rather than to go to the bottom of any given idea, to examine into its origin and meaning, most people will either condemn it altogether, or rely on some superficial or prejudicial definition of non–essentials.

For Questions 275 and 276, select only one answer choice.

275. The author's feelings towards anarchism could best be described by which of the following statements?

Ⓐ Anarchists are people who tend to act before they think which gives Anarchism a bad reputation despite its honorable intent.

Ⓑ Anarchists hinder progress in society by disrupting progressive thought patterns that would otherwise encourage people to think for themselves.

Ⓒ People who uphold anarchistic beliefs create the same type of fear amongst well-educated adults that imaginary monsters create in the minds of children.

Ⓓ Anarchism, though often associated with negative beliefs, creates a positive impact on society by doing away with the types of thoughts and actions that hold people back from reaching their full potential.

Ⓔ People who condemn anarchism are too afraid to rebel against the current order of society and therefore criticize others who are willing to take a stand against injustice.

276. What function do the sentences in boldface type serve in the passage?

Ⓐ The first sentence introduces the myth of anarchism that uninformed people believe; the second presents an explanation of another common misconception regarding anarchism and refutes it.

Ⓑ Both sentences express the ignorance that anarchism creates amongst rebellious groups of people who do not realize the destruction that they cause.

Ⓒ The first depicts the horror behind stories of anarchism, and the second explains the way that anarchism destroys combative forces in society.

Ⓓ The first sentence introduces the way that rumors about anarchism exacerbate common misconceptions, and the second sentence refutes the previous points about the problems that stem from ignorance.

Ⓔ Both sentences criticize the way that uneducated people base their decisions on hearsay rather than facts.

Consider each of the three choices separately and select all that apply.

277. What message does this passage primarily strive to impart?

    A   Anarchism causes fear and impedes progress in society, much like weeds in a garden delay healthy growth.

    B   Anarchism is a useful tool in encouraging social progress, yet uninformed people discourage such rebelliousness and by doing so impede the positive effects of anarchism.

    C   People who pass judgement on issues without investigating the root cause of their opinion tend to base their beliefs on unreliable facts.

278. Select the sentence in the passage that would, if true, most effectively support the idea that anarchism is an essential factor in strengthening society despite its seemingly destructive forces.

Passage 117

Questions 279 to 284 are based on the following passage.

"It ought to be matter of surprise how men live in the midst of marvels, without taking heed of their existence. The slightest derangement of their accustomed walks in political or social life shall excite all their wonder, and furnish themes for their discussions, for months; while the prodigies that come from above are presented daily to their eyes, and are received without surprise, as things of course. In a certain sense, this may be well enough, inasmuch as all which comes directly from the hands of the Creator may be said so far to exceed the power of human comprehension, as to be beyond comment; but the truth would show us that the cause of this neglect is rather a propensity to dwell on such interests as those over which we have a fancied control, than on those which confessedly transcend our understanding. Thus, is it ever with men. The wonders of creation meet them at every turn, without awakening reflection, while their minds labor on subjects that are not only ephemeral and illusory, but which never attain an elevation higher than that the most sordid interests can bestow.

For **ourselves, we** firmly believe that the finger of Providence is pointing the way to all races, and colors, and nations, along the path that is to lead the east and the west alike to the great goal of human wants. Demons infest that path, and numerous and unhappy are the wanderings of millions who stray from its course sometimes in reluctance to proceed; sometimes in an indiscreet haste to move faster than their fellows, and always in a forgetfulness of the great rules of conduct that have been handed down from above. Nevertheless, the main course is onward; and the day, in the sense of time, is not distant, when the whole earth is to be filled with the knowledge of the Lord, "as the waters cover the sea."

One of the great stumbling-blocks with a large class of well- meaning, but narrow-judging moralists, are the seeming wrongs that are permitted by Providence, in its control of human events. Such persons take a one-sided view of things and reduce all principles to the level of their own understandings. If we could comprehend the relations which the Deity bears to us, as well as we can comprehend the relations we bear to him, there might be a little seeming reason in these doubts; but when one of the parties in this mighty scheme of action is a profound mystery to the other, it is worse than idle, it is profane, to attempt to explain those things which our minds are not yet sufficiently cleared from the dross of earth to understand. Look at Italy, at this very moment. The darkness and depression from which that glorious peninsula is about to emerge are the fruits of long-continued dissensions and an iron despotism, which is at length broken by the impulses left behind him by a ruthless conqueror, who, under the appearance and the phrases of Liberty, contended only for himself. A more concentrated egotism than that of Napoleon probably never existed; yet has it left behind it seeds of personal rights that have sprung up by the wayside, and which are likely to take root with a force that will bid defiance to eradication. Thus, is it ever, with the progress of society. Good appears to arise out of evil, and the inscrutable ways of Providence are vindicated by general results, rather than by instances of particular care. We leave the application of these remarks to the intelligence of such of our readers as may have patience to peruse the work that will be found in the succeeding pages.

279. Select the sentence in the last paragraph that implies that the author believes that people should strive to understand Providence by its effect on the greater good instead of answering the prayers of the individual.

For Questions 280 and 281, consider each of the three choices separately and select all that apply.

280. What does the author supply as a reason for man's failure to contemplate the mysteries of the world?

   [A]   He lacks the ability to understand them.

   [B]   Man has no interest in events beyond his control.

   [C]   Man's propensity is to dwell on the mundane

281. What purpose is served by the author's including his comments about Napoleon's oppression of Italy?

   [A]   It prefaces the author's further discussion of despots and their legacies throughout history.

   [B]   It prefaces additional examples from history when political oppression led to increased determination on the part of the oppressed to secure individual rights.

   [C]   It serves as an introduction to a further discussion of the hand of Providence directing the lives of men.

For Questions 282 to 284, select only one answer choice.

282. Which of the following is the best description of the author's attitude toward his potential readers as expressed by the last sentence in the passage?

   Ⓐ Apathetic

   Ⓑ Sincere

   Ⓒ Obsequious

   Ⓓ Condescending

   Ⓔ Contemplative

283. Which of the following explains the relationship between Providence, the Creator, and the Diety as they are used in this passage?

   Ⓐ They represent the Holy Trinity in Christianity.

   Ⓑ The Creator and the Diety can be used interchangeably, and Providence is the result of the Diety's actions on behalf of mankind.

   Ⓒ They create a hierarchy with the Creator at the top followed by the Diety and then Providence.

   Ⓓ All three can be used interchangeably, as each is another term for God in the Christian belief system.

   Ⓔ They are metaphorical representations of predestination.

284. What do the underlined and bolded plural pronouns reveal about the author of this passage?

   Ⓐ He is a member of a group that presumes to be superior to the possible readers of the content to follow the passage provided here.

   Ⓑ He has written an introduction to an anthology in which various others with ideas similar to his own will address the failure of most men to acknowledge the wonders that Providence has provided.

   Ⓒ He is a member of a group that feels responsible for correcting the errors of mankind.

   Ⓓ He recognizes his own weaknesses and uses the pronouns to identify with his audience.

   Ⓔ He and other writers of the content that follows this passage hope that their readers will find some ideas that they can adapt for their own enlightenment.

Passage 118

Questions 285 to 290 are based on the following passage.

There is a saying of an ancient Sanskrit poet which, being translated into English, runs: "In a hundred ages of the gods I could not tell you of the glories of Himachal." This every writer on things Himalayan contrives to drag into his composition. Some begin with the quotation, while others reserve it for the last, and make it do duty for the epigram which stylists assure us should terminate every essay.

Some there are who quote the Indian sage only to mock him. Such assert that the beauties of the Himalayas have been greatly exaggerated—that, as regards grandeur, their scenery compares unfavorably with that of the Andes, while their beauty is surpassed by that of the Alps. Not having seen the Andes, I am unable to criticize the assertion regarding the grandeur of the Himalayas, but I find it difficult to imagine anything finer than their scenery.

As regards beauty, the Himalayas at their best surpass the Alps, because they exhibit far more variety, and present everything on a grander scale.

The Himalayas are a kind of Dr. Jekyll and Mr. Hyde. They have two faces—the fair and the plain. In May they are at their worst. Those of the hillsides which are not afforested are brown, arid, and desolate, and the valleys, in addition to being unpleasantly hot, are dry and dusty. The foliage of the trees lacks freshness, and everywhere there is a remarkable absence of water, save in the valleys through which the rivers flow. On the other hand, September is the month in which the Himalayas attain perfection or something approaching it. The eye is refreshed by the bright emerald garment which the hills have newly donned. The foliage is green and luxuriant. Waterfalls, cascades, mighty torrents and rivulets abound. Himachal has been converted into fairyland by the monsoon rains.

A remarkable feature of the Himalayas is the abruptness with which they rise from the plains in most places. In some parts there are low foothills; but speaking generally the mountains that rise from the plain attain a height of 4000 or 5000 feet.

It is difficult for any person who has not passed from the plains of India to the Himalayas to realize fully the vast difference between the two countries and the dramatic suddenness with which the change takes place.

The plains are as flat as the proverbial pancake—a dead monotony of cultivated alluvium, square mile upon square mile of wheat, rice, vetch, sugar-cane, and other crops, amidst which mango groves, bamboo clumps, palms, and hamlets are scattered promiscuously. In some places the hills rise sheer from this, in others they are separated from the alluvial plains by belts of country known as the Tarai and Bhabar. The Tarai is low-lying, marshy land covered with tall, feathery grass, beautifully monotonous. This is succeeded by a stretch of gently-*rising* ground, 10 or 20 miles in breadth, known as the Bhabar—a strip of forest composed mainly of tall evergreen sal trees (Shorea robusta). These trees grow so close together that the forest is difficult to penetrate, especially after the rains, when the undergrowth is dense and rank. Very beautiful is the Bhabar, and very stimulating to the imagination. One writer speaks of it as "a jungle rhapsody, an extravagant, impossible botanical tour de force, intensely modern in its Titanic, incoherent magnificence." It is the home of the elephant, the tiger, the panther, the wild boar, several species of deer, and of many strange and beautiful birds.

Whether from the flat plains or the gently-sloping Bhabar, the mountains rise with startling suddenness. The flora and fauna of the Himalayas differ from those of the neighboring plains as greatly as the trees and animals of England differ from those of Africa.

Of the common trees of the plains of India the nim, mango, babul, tamarind, shesham, palm, and plantain—not one is to be found growing on the hills. The lower slopes are covered with sal trees like the Bhabar. These cease to grow at elevations of 3000 feet above the sea-level, and, higher up, every rise of 1000 feet means a considerable change in the flora. Above the sal belt come several species of tropical evergreen trees, among the stems and branches of which great creepers entangle themselves in fantastic figures. At elevations of 4000 feet the long-leaved pine (Pinus longifolia) appears. From 5000 to 10,000 feet, several species of evergreen oaks abound. Above 6000 feet are to be seen the rhododendron, the deodar and other hill cypresses, and the beautiful horse-chestnut. On the lower slopes the undergrowth is composed largely of begonias and berberry. Higher up maidenhair and other ferns abound, and the trunks of the oaks and rhododendrons are festooned with hanging moss.

285. Select the sentence that implies that the contrast between the living aspects of the plains and the mountains is, despite their relative proximity to each other, surp*rising*ly greater than one might expect.

For Questions 286 and 287, consider each of the three choices separately and select all that apply.

286. The first paragraph, which includes the quote from the ancient Sanskrit poet, serves which of the following purposes?

   [A]   It shows contempt for writers who have overused the quote from the ancient Sanskrit poet.

   [B]   It demeans writers who contrive to follow formulaic style of writing.

   [C]   It serves as a contrast to the author's attitude toward the poet's words.

287. Based on the author's description of the seasons in the area of the Himalayas, which of the following might the reader infer about the climate?

   [A]   Periods of rain are followed by periods of drought.

   [B]   The climate is influenced by the great disparities in elevation of the area.

   [C]   The climate creates periods of scarcity and abundance.

For Questions 288 to 290, select only one answer choice.

288. Which of the following best identifies the organizational structure of this passage?

    Ⓐ Least important to most important

    Ⓑ Cause and effect

    Ⓒ Problem/ solution

    Ⓓ Specific to general

    Ⓔ Compare and contrast

289. Based on the progression of ideas in the passage, which of the following is most likely to be the author's next topic?

    Ⓐ The vegetation at elevations above 10,000 feet.

    Ⓑ The contrast between the cultures of the inhabitants of the plains and the inhabitants of the higher elevations.

    Ⓒ How the features of the Alps contrast with those of the Himalayas.

    Ⓓ The fauna that can be found at higher altitudes.

    Ⓔ The manner in which the inhabitants cultivate the alluvial plain.

290. Considering his choice of words, select the tone displayed by the author in the fourth paragraph.

    Ⓐ Quizzical

    Ⓑ Lyrical

    Ⓒ Fanciful

    Ⓓ Whimsical

    Ⓔ Intimate

Passage 119

Questions 291 and 292 are based on the following passage.

The Japanese remained almost entirely ignorant of these preparations. Many of the Japanese military command were suffering from "senshobyo (victory disease)". They had easily won almost every battle they had fought, and they had no reason to believe they would not win just as easily in the future. The defeat at Midway had not been made public and did not disturb this belief. Few senior military officers believed there would be a serious Allied counterstroke against Japan until well into 1943.

There were those among them who were more realistic in their thinking, including Lieutenant Commander Itoo Haruki of the Naval Intelligence Center in Tokyo. In late July, his unit identified two new Allied radio callsigns, both operating on the 4.205 megahertz band and communicating with Pearl Harbor. On 1 August, Japanese radio direction finders pinpointed the location of the stations as Melbourne and Noumea. Itoo correctly guessed these were headquarters for Allied operational forces, massing for an attack on New Guinea or the Solomons. He relayed an urgent warning to Truk, the main Japanese base in the central Pacific, and Rabaul. The warning was ignored.

For Questions 291 and 292, select only one answer choice.

291. Based on the information in the passage, select the most likely symptom of senshobyo from the following list.

   (A) Optimism

   (B) Courage

   (C) Overconfidence

   (D) Complacency

   (E) Satisfaction

292. What purpose is served by the writer's including the specific details of Lieutenant Commander Haruki's intelligence?

   (A) To show the level of efficiency in the Naval Intelligence Center in Tokyo

   (B) To establish a foundation for Haruki's warning

   (C) To provide information about the location of the Allies in the Pacific

   (D) To justify Haruki's rise to the level of Lieutenant Commander

   (E) To demonstrate the lack of preparedness on the part of the Japanese Navy

Passage 120

Questions 293 to 295 are based on the following passage.

This distinction must be borne in mind - that while the early chiefs were spokesmen and leaders in the simplest sense, possessing no real authority, those who headed their tribes during the transition period were more or less rulers and more or less politicians. It is a singular fact that many of the "chiefs", well known as such to the American public, were not chiefs at all according to the accepted usages of their tribesmen. Their prominence was simply the result of an abnormal situation, in which representatives of the United States Government made use of them for a definite purpose. In a few cases, where a chief met with a violent death, some ambitious man has taken advantage of the confusion to thrust himself upon the tribe and, perhaps with outside help, has succeeded in usurping the leadership.

For Questions 293 to 295, select only one answer choice.

293.   Which of the following terms describes tribal structure prior to interference by the American government?

   Ⓐ Matriarchal

   Ⓑ Patriarchal

   Ⓒ Oligarchal

   Ⓓ Egalitarian

   Ⓔ Tyrannical

294.   What question might be created in the mind of the reader after reading this passage?

   Ⓐ How did tribal chiefs get their names?

   Ⓑ How many tribes were negotiating with the American government?

   Ⓒ What other misconceptions about Native Americans have been perpetuated?

   Ⓓ Why did the chiefs meet with violent deaths?

   Ⓔ Did early politicians model their behavior after that of tribal chiefs?

295.   Which of the following is the best definition for the word "singular" in the context of this passage?

   Ⓐ Extraordinary

   Ⓑ Unusual or strange

   Ⓒ Distinctive; unique

   Ⓓ Separate; individual

   Ⓔ A form in the singular

Passage 121

Questions 296 to 299 are based on the following passage.

   The Baluch character is influenced by its environment as much as by its origin, so that it is impossible to select any one section of the general community as affording a satisfactory sample of popular Baluch idiosyncrasies. They are not a homogeneous race. Peoples of Arab extraction intermixed with people of Dravidian and Persian stock are all lumped together under the name of Baluch. The Marri and Bugti tribes, who occupy the most southern buttresses of the Suliman Mountains, are Sind Baluchis, almost certainly of Arab extraction. They came to Sind either with the Arab conquerors or after them and remained there mixed up with the original Hindu inhabitants. The Arab type of Baluch extends through the whole country at intervals and includes all the finest and best of Baluch humanity. Taking the Sind Baluch as the type opposed to the Afridi Pathan, the Baluch is easier to deal with and to control than the Pathan, owing to his tribal organization and his freedom from bigoted fanaticism or blind allegiance to his priest. The Baluch is less turbulent, less treacherous, less bloodthirsty and less fanatical than the Pathan. His frame is shorter and more spare and wiry than that of his neighbor to the north, though generations have given to him too a bold and manly bearing. It would be difficult to match the stately dignity and imposing presence of a Baluch chief of the Marri or Bugti clans. His Semitic features are those of the Bedouin and he carries himself as straight and as loftily as any Arab gentleman. Frank and open in his manners, fairly truthful, faithful to his word, temperate and enduring, and looking upon courage as the highest virtue, the true Baluch of the Derajat is a pleasant man to have dealings with. As a revenue payer he is not so satisfactory, his want of industry and the pride which looks upon manual labour as degrading making him but a poor husbandman. He is an expert rider; horse-racing is his national amusement, and the Baluch breed of horses is celebrated throughout northern India. Like the Pathan he is a bandit by tradition and descent and makes a first-rate fighting man, but he rarely enlists in the Indian army. He is nominally a Mahommedan but is neglectful of the practices of his religion.

296.   Select the sentence in the passage that explains why the Baluchi are not likely to be farmers.

Consider each of the three answer choices separately and select all that apply.

297.   Which of the following is the best explanation for the Baluch's reluctance to join the Indian army?

   A   They feel that their superior fighting skills make joining the Indian army beneath their dignity

   B   Their allegiance to their own tribes is stronger than their allegiance to India

   C   Their tendency to flout social expectations makes it difficult for them to develop a sense of patriotic duty

For Questions 298 and 299, select only one answer choice.

298. The writer's use of the phrase, influenced by its environment as much as by its origin, in the first line of the passage and the phrase, tradition and descent, in the next-to-last sentence allow the reader to reach which of the following conclusions about the Baluch?

    Ⓐ The Baluch scoff at the traditions of Indian culture

    Ⓑ Heredity has determined a greater portion of the Baluch character than environment has

    Ⓒ Environment has determined a greater portion of the Baluch character than heredity has

    Ⓓ The Baluch's behavior and character has been formed by both nature and nurture

    Ⓔ Their tribal organization is more tolerant of individual differences

299. In which of the following texts would you be likely to find this passage about the Baluch?

    Ⓐ A gazetteer

    Ⓑ An atlas

    Ⓒ An almanac

    Ⓓ A digest

    Ⓔ An anthology

Passage 122

Question 300 is based on the following passage.

Botel Tobago is an island in the South Seas which has lately been visited by a party of United States naval officers. They were surveying a rock east of the South Cape of Formosa and called at this island. They found a curious race of Malay stock. These aborigines did not know what money was good for. Nor had they ever used tobacco or rum. They gave the officers goats and pigs for tin pots and brass buttons and hung around the vessel all day in their canoes waiting for a chance to dive for something which might be thrown overboard. They wore clouts only, ate taro and yams, and had axes, spears, and knives made of common iron. Their canoes were made without nails and were ornamented with geometrical lines. They wore the beards of goats and small shells as ornaments.

Select only one answer choice.

300. Based on the information in this passage, select the list of adjectives that best describes the inhabitants of Botel Tobago.

(A) Aggressive, amenable, cunning

(B) Naive, narcissistic, opportunistic

(C) Vain, opportunistic, overt

(D) Herbivorous, humble, hardy

(E) Social, stoic, omnivorous

Passage 123

Question 301 is based on the following passage.

In this way will the whole problem of freedom be solved, that natural laws be ascertained by scientific discovery, and the knowledge of them be universally diffused among the masses. Natural laws being thus recognized by every man for himself, he cannot but obey them, for they are the laws also of his own nature; and the need for political organization, administration and legislation will at once disappear. Nor will he admit of any privileged position or class, for "it is the peculiarity of privilege and of every privileged position to kill the intellect and heart of man. The privileged man, whether he be privileged politically or economically, is a man depraved in intellect and heart." "In a word, we object to all legislation, all authority, and all influence, privileged, patented, official and legal, even when it has proceeded from universal suffrage, convinced that it must always turn to the profit of a dominating and exploiting minority, against the interests of the immense majority enslaved."

Select only one answer choice.

301. Based on your understanding of the purpose served by this passage, determine which of the following terms identifies its structure.

(A) Manifesto

(B) Proclamation

(C) Edict

(D) Fiat

(E) Mandate

Passage 124

Question 302 is based on the following passage.

Toch estimates that 50% of home-schooled children attend college, the same percentage as children educated in public schools. But are these students skilled enough to compete successfully with conventionally-schooled students in the college setting? Galloway concludes that home schoolers and traditionally educated students demonstrate similar academic preparedness for college and academic achievement. And according to Rudner, achievement test scores of home-schooled students are high. The students' average scores were typically in the 70th to 80th percentile, with 25% of home-schooled students enrolled one or more grades above their age-level peers in public and private schools. Christopher Klicka, Senior Counsel for the Home School Legal Defense Association, reports that home schoolers tend to score above the national average on both the SAT and ACT, the primary tests used by colleges in evaluating college applicants. A study of 2219 students who reported their home-schooled status on the SAT in 1999 showed that these students scored an average of 1083--67 points above the national average of 1016; similarly, the 3616 home schooled students who took the ACT scored an average of 22.7--1.7 points above the national average of 21.

Select only one answer choice.

302. What additional information is needed to support a conclusion that home-schooled students typically perform better on standardized college entrance exams than do traditionally educated students?

Ⓐ Socioeconomic statistics of the students

Ⓑ Student scores on other standardized tests

Ⓒ The curriculum of both home schoolers and traditional classroom teachers

Ⓓ At least two previous or subsequent years' SAT and ACT results

Ⓔ The colleges to which the students were accepted

Passage 125

Questions 303 and 304 are based on the following passage.

Total fertility rate is the average number of children that would be born per woman if all women lived to the end of their childbearing years and bore children according to a given fertility rate at each age. The total fertility rate (TFR) is a more direct measure of the level of fertility than the crude birth rate, since it refers to births per woman. This indicator shows the potential for population change in the country. A rate of two children per woman is considered the replacement rate for a population, resulting in relative stability in terms of total numbers. Rates above two children indicate populations growing in size and whose median age is declining. Higher rates may also indicate difficulties for families, in some situations, to feed and educate their children and for women to enter the labor force. Rates below two children indicate populations decreasing in size and growing older. Global fertility rates are in general decline and this trend is most pronounced in industrialized countries, especially Western Europe, where populations are projected to decline dramatically over the next 50 years.

For Questions 303 and 304, select only one answer choice.

303. Which of the following is a probable challenge for western European countries as their fertility rates decline over the next few decades?

   (A) Caring for the children who are born during this time

   (B) Rising unemployment

   (C) Providing for the elderly

   (D) Increased poverty

   (E) Reduced expenditures for education

304. What is a possible reason for higher fertility rates in non-industrialized countries?

   (A) Lower divorce rates

   (B) Fewer women in the workforce

   (C) More live births

   (D) Lower infant mortality

   (E) Higher number of extended families

Passage 126

Question 305 is based on the following passage.

   Malaysia is a destination and, to a lesser extent, a source and transit country for women and children trafficked for the purpose of commercial sexual exploitation, and men, women, and children for forced labor; Malaysia is mainly a destination country for men, women, and children who migrate willingly from South and Southeast Asia to work, some of whom are subjected to conditions of involuntary servitude by Malaysian employers in the domestic, agricultural, construction, plantation, and industrial sectors; to a lesser extent, some Malaysian women, primarily of Chinese ethnicity, are trafficked abroad for commercial sexual exploitation. Malaysia improved from Tier 3 to the Tier 2 Watch List for 2008 when it enacted comprehensive anti-trafficking legislation in July 2007; however, it did not take action against exploitative employers or labor traffickers in 2007; the government has not ratified the 2000 UN TIP Protocol (2008).

Select only one answer choice.

305. Which of the following statements most closely reflects the probable conditions that facilitate human trafficking and/or labor exploitation in Malaysia?

    (A) There is a lack of employment opportunities in South and Southeast Asia

    (B) Malaysia has fewer cultural taboos about sexual activity

    (C) The Southeast Asian and Malaysian cultures deem it acceptable for children to work in agriculture and industry

    (D) The 2000 UN TIP Protocol is too restrictive

    (E) Industrialized nations outsource much of their factory production to Malaysia

Passage 127

Question 306 is based on the following passage.

These caves were inhabited by man during an immense stretch of time, and, as you dig down, you light upon one layer after another of his leavings. But note in such a case as this how easily you may be baffled by someone having upset the heap of clothes, or, in a word, by rearrangement. Thus, the man whose leavings ought to form the layer half-way up may have seen fit to dig a deep hole in the cave-floor in order to bury a deceased friend, and with him, let us suppose, to bury also an assortment of articles likely to be useful in the life beyond the grave. Consequently, an implement of one age will be found lying cheek by jowl with the implement of a much earlier age, or even, it may be, some feet below it.

Select only one answer choice.

306. How do archaeologists reconcile apparent contradictions in the location and age of artifacts uncovered in a dig?

    (A) They examine written records of early inhabitants of the area

    (B) They interview current residents of the area

    (C) They create a scenario that explains the juxtaposition of artifacts from different time periods

    (D) They make note of the level of preservation of the artifacts

    (E) They sort the artifacts according to their function

Passage 128

Question 307 is based on the following passage.

Research into the eating habits of women shows that they are mimetic; women tend to want to mirror the way their fellow female diners enjoy their food. Psychologists theorize this has to do with the fact that women are more prone to same-gender imitation than their male counterparts - men seem to be oblivious to the behavior of other eaters in the dining group. Underpinning women's copycat eating habits is likely a stronger need to both belong to and be liked by the group, particularly the other females in the group.

Select only one answer choice.

307. All of the following can be inferred from the passage except

Ⓐ Same-gender conformity is a more feminine trait

Ⓑ Men are the less conventional gender

Ⓒ Women in a dining group tend to eat the same amount of food

Ⓓ Women value how they are perceived by others

Ⓔ Men in a dining group eat disparate amounts of food

Passage 129

Questions 308 to 310 are based on the following passage.

Although it seems hard to imagine, humans originated in one place and then spread across the globe to create the vast network of cultures and nations that constitute our modern world. This phenomenon fascinates many, including scientists who are deeply interested in the Diaspora of modern man from the Horn of Africa to the far-reaching corners of the globe. While it is no longer disputed that modern man originated in northern Africa, many anthropologists debate the area from which human settlers organized and then colonized the rest of the world. Recent research suggests that the first humans out of Africa settled in Arabia and from there staged the global dispersal of modern man. This conclusion was drawn based on DNA comparisons between populations in Europe, North Africa, and the Near East. Scientists were able to determine that all the populations were most closely related with the Arabians samples. Thus, the Arabian settlers are the common denominator in the dispersal of modern man.

For Questions 308 to 310, select only one answer choice.

308.   The primary purpose of this passage is to

   (A) Discuss the African Diaspora of early humans

   (B) Show how the interests of scientists and laymen intersect

   (C) Discuss the dissemination point of modern man

   (D) Show how DNA analysis can be used in anthropological research

   (E) Start a debate about man's origins in Africa

309.   The author's attitude towards DNA analysis as an anthropological research method can best be
       described as

   (A) Skeptical

   (B) Leery

   (C) Impartial

   (D) Favoring

   (E) Devoted

310.   According to the author, polemics surrounding the dispersal of early humans tend to focus on

   (A) Whether or not early humans originated in the Horn of Africa

   (B) Whether or not Europe or Arabia were the starting points of modern man's colonization of the
        globe

   (C) The Near East's role in the dispersal of humans throughout the world

   (D) The point of origin for organized human dispersal across the globe

   (E) Whether or not DNA analysis is an effective way of determining the point of origin of the
        organized human diaspora

Passage 130

Question 311 is based on the following passage.

According to recent psychological research published in the British Journal of Psychology, men are more
likely to display altruistic behavior in the presence of attractive women. Conversely, women's behavior
remains constant regardless of the attractiveness of their male company. Psychologists conclude that male
behavior is determined by the need to impress prospective mates, while female behavior is based less on the

need to impress and more on the need to be selective and receptive with respect to potential male partners.

Select only one answer choice.

311. The author primarily makes his or her point by

    Ⓐ Objectively evaluating the facts

    Ⓑ An emotional appeal to the reader

    Ⓒ Providing both a view and counterview

    Ⓓ Criticizing the opinions of the psychologists

    Ⓔ Offering a source of authority

Passage 131

Question 312 is based on the following passage.

It pays to work hard in college. Literally Researchers have concluded that slacker students in college are at the highest risk for credit card debt, unemployment, and hunkering down for a permanent stay in mom and dad's basement. Even more troubling is the fact that these students lack critical job skills - they run the highest risk of not improving their reasoning, writing, and critical thinking skills by the time they walk across the stage to accept their diploma. Many students believe college to be a time of fun and exploration, but if such experiences are not combined with hard work, future success is not a guarantee.

Select only one answer choice.

312. The author's claims about slacker students would be weakened by all of the following except

    Ⓐ Several examples of students who were slackers yet still succeeded after college

    Ⓑ Research that demonstrated slacker college students improving their academic skills despite low work ethics

    Ⓒ Evidence that slacker college students obtained post-graduation jobs as easily as their hard-working counterparts

    Ⓓ Evidence that slacker students do not struggle with financial issues any more than their hard-working counterparts

    Ⓔ Evidence that hardworking and slacker college students had similar post-graduation living conditions

Passage 132

Questions 313 and 314 are based on the following passage.

Many scholars hold Karl Marx to be one of the founding fathers of modern-day social science. Karl Marx is and always has been a polemical figure, but his conceptualization of the dialectic that shapes all societal conflicts, class struggle, has fundamentally changed the way that many politicians, academics, and lay people view and analyze global power relationships. The theories of Karl Marx, known as Marxism, are most often employed as methods of critiquing not only capitalism, but also the very political systems that they engendered: socialism and communism. Thus, Marxism can be a highly useful and self-reflexive analytical tool.

For Questions 313 and 314, select only one answer choice.

313.   According to the author, Marxism is a self-reflexive analytical tool because

(A)   It accurately deconstructs power structures within capitalistic societies

(B)   It can be used as a method of critically examining its own economic systems

(C)   It elucidates important issues related to class conflict

(D)   It helps academics set up a dialectical research framework

(E)   It enables free-thinking academic exchange

314.   The term "dialectic" in the passage is most analogous to

(A)   The scientific method

(B)   Reason engendered by discussion

(C)   Protest

(D)   Political dialogue

(E)   Exploitation of workers

Passage 133

Question 315 is based on the following passage.

Art is often considered a defining characteristic of civilization, but recent anthropological finds suggest otherwise. The oldest known painting kits were recently unearthed in a South African cave, and anthropologists estimate the artifacts are over 100,000 years old. The painting kits consisted of stone and bone tools for crushing, mixing, and applying paint to cave walls, animal skins and maybe even body parts. The paint was made from red and yellow ochres and housed in sea snail shells. Thus, art predates not only modern man, but also complex human societies.

Select only one answer choice.

315. The author suggests that the painting kits found in South Africa are important because

    Ⓐ They give us insight into the early humans

    Ⓑ They illuminate the kinds of tools available to early humans

    Ⓒ They give us information on the earliest forms of art as body decoration

    Ⓓ They show that art predates civilization

    Ⓔ They help us trace the development of artistic methods in human civilization

Passage 134

Questions 316 and 317 are based on the following passage.

Niccolo Machiavelli's seminal work, *The Prince*, is considered to be one of the first works of modern political philosophy; it is also one of the most controversial. Nonetheless, The Prince has influenced Western thought related to governance ever since its publication in 1532. Machiavelli uses his treatise to outline leadership and success relative to royal (or political) rule. **In today's world it is quite controversial as The Prince negates the importance of personal virtue in leaders and lofty political idealism - realism is the goal of the treatise and the reality of the world is that successful outcomes go to the strongest in the fight for survival and the battle of the wits.** Despite its controversial message, The Prince is written in eloquent, yet simple language that relays its message with surgical precision. **Nearly all English speakers are well-acquainted with the polemical aphorism that lies at the thematic heart of The Prince: The end justifies the means.**

For Questions 316 and 317, select only one answer choice.

316. The two portions in bold-face are related to each other in which of the following ways?

    Ⓐ The first bold-faced section undermines the conclusion drawn by the second bold-faced section

    Ⓑ The first bold-faced section is an extrapolation on the conclusion drawn by the second bold-faced section

    Ⓒ Both bold-faced sections challenge the author's position

    Ⓓ The first bold-faced section is a position that the author does not agree with; the second bold-faced section is a position that the author does agree with

    Ⓔ Both bold-faced sections undermine the goals and objectives of the modern-day political landscape

317.   The author most clearly makes a case for the fact that

   Ⓐ   Polemical books are often among the most influential

   Ⓑ   Leadership requires a combination of virtue and vice

   Ⓒ   Political ideas often evolve

   Ⓓ   Human nature remains the same as political systems change

   Ⓔ   Political goals are best achieved by way of a Machiavellian approach

Passage 135

Questions 318 to 321 are based on the following passage.

Millions of people across the globe struggle with depression, some for only days and some for a lifetime. It is a universal mental malaise that effects people from every socio-economic background in every country. Depression is defined by psychologists as a mood disorder characterized by sadness, low activity, apathy, and hopelessness. Since depression hinders sufferers from obtaining a good quality of life, researchers make it a priority to both understand the cause of the mood disorder and discover ways to treat it.
In the 1950s psychologists and neuroscientists teamed up to proclaim that depression was the result of a chemical imbalance, more specifically low levels of serotonin, and a milieu was born that sought to frame mental health issues as curable deficiencies. Medications like Prozac, more formally known as Selective Serotonin Reuptake Inhibitors, became the main method of treatment for depression and other mood disorders.

The belief that low serotonin levels cause depression is ubiquitous, but psychologists have begun to change their tune regarding the link between so-called chemical imbalances and mental health issues. New research shows that neurotransmitters such as serotonin control moods and mental health much less than previously thought.

A study conducted in the 1990s showed that depleting the serotonin levels of people without depression did not in turn cause them to become depressed; this action in fact had little effect on their mood and behavior. This information coupled with more insight into the nuances of genetics and how they affect mood and personality has led many psychologists and medical researchers to look for new treatment methods and possibilities. Although it is still widely acknowledged that depressed people do have some type of serotonin aberration, serotonin as the primary controller of human moods is a belief that is outmoded; pills as a means of solving mood problems may hopefully become a thing of the past (bad news for pharmaceutical companies).

Whether low serotonin levels, genes, or environment are the cause of depression, one thing is clear: scientists don't really know what causes mood disorders. While this may seem like a discomforting thought for those who suffer from depression or other mental health issues, the good news is that many treatment methods such as talk therapy still have high rates of success. Life can still be lived in a world of uncertainty.

For Questions 318 and 319, select only one answer choice.

318. The author's attitude towards Selective Serotonin Reuptake Inhibitors (SSRIs) can best be described as

   Ⓐ Candid

   Ⓑ Positive

   Ⓒ Castigating

   Ⓓ Leery

   Ⓔ Condescending

319. Given the information in the passage, all of the following can be inferred except

   Ⓐ SSRIs are not a good method for treating depression

   Ⓑ Genes determine whether or not a person will become depressed

   Ⓒ Serotonin does not directly affect a person's mood

   Ⓓ Talk therapy can help heal people from depression

   Ⓔ Depression is a phenomenon common to all humans regardless of culture or ethnicity

Consider each of the three choices separately and select all that apply.

320. Depression is likely caused by

   ☐A☐ Genes that contribute to a person's biological profile

   ☐B☐ Environmental factors that contribute to a person's mental health profile

   ☐C☐ The combination of past and present experiences, as well as biological factors

321. Select the sentence that best describes why Selective Serotonin Reuptake Inhibitors (SSRIs) have been promoted as a method of treating depression.

Passage 136

Questions 322 to 325 are based on the following passage.

No person shall be held to answer for a capital, or otherwise infamous crime, unless on a presentment or indictment of a Grand Jury, except in cases arising in the land or naval forces, or in the Militia, when in actual service in time of War or public danger; nor shall any person be subject for the same offense to be twice put in jeopardy of life or limb; nor shall be compelled in any criminal case to be a witness against himself, nor be deprived of life, liberty, or property, without due process of law; nor shall private property be taken for public use without just compensation.

For Questions 322 to 324, select only one answer choice.

322.   This passage specifically addresses which of the following?

    Ⓐ   The right of citizens accused of crimes to face an unbiased jury

    Ⓑ   The right of soldiers accused of crimes during war time to face a jury of their peers

    Ⓒ   The right of citizens accused of crimes to have an attorney

    Ⓓ   Exceptions to the right of just compensation for the seizure of property

    Ⓔ   The right of citizens to refuse to provide incriminating evidence against themselves

323.   In this passage, the phrase "due process of law" may be defined as which of the following?

    Ⓐ   Indictment of a grand jury

    Ⓑ   Just compensation

    Ⓒ   The phrase is compound in meaning, referring to all of the other legal requirements in the passage combined together.

    Ⓓ   The phrase is general in meaning, referring to whatever legal measures are appropriate in a given situation.

    Ⓔ   The phrase is archaic and its meaning cannot be determined by the context of its usage here.

324.   The word "infamous" is used in this passage in which of the following ways?

    Ⓐ   It is used to mean "serious."

    Ⓑ   It is used to mean "notorious."

    Ⓒ   It is used to mean "hidden or concealed."

    Ⓓ   It is used to mean "less serious."

    Ⓔ   It is used as a direct synonym for "capital."

Consider each of the three choices separately and select all that apply.

325. The exception for members of the military discussed in the passage applies explicitly to which of the following?

    A   The taking of private property for public use without just compensation

    B   A person being held to answer for a crime without the presentment of a grand jury

    C   A person being held to answer for a crime without an indictment by a grand jury

Explanatory Answers

Practice Set 1 - Arts and Humanities

Passage 1:

Answer to Question 1:

The correct answer is C. A is incorrect because the passage describes this view as that of the popular press, not as the author's assessment and not of Shostakovich. B is incorrect because the passage does not describe this as the Conference's purpose nor does it describe the controversy as having an adverse effect on the Conference. D is incorrect because Shostakovich is described as being far from the focus of attention of the Conference and the public is said to have been already aware of these matters. E is incorrect because the passage in no way suggests the composer's popularity was increased by the Conference. C is the correct answer. The passage lists several examples of the composer's experiences at the conference that contribute to the impression of a debut that was not particularly glorious. Shostakovich was one of five delegates. He played piano only once. He mumbled and listened passively to translators. Finally, he is depicted as concerned with stocking up on cigarettes.

Answer to Question 2:

The correct answer is A. B is incorrect because the sentence does not draw any connection between Shostakovich and the overall public reception of the Conference. C is incorrect because the sentence does not describe or imply the feelings of those aware of Shostakovich. D is incorrect because the sentence does not describe or imply any causality between the two things. E is incorrect for the same reason. A is the correct answer. The use of the word "however" indicates that the point stands in spite of the negative factors described in the rest of the passage.

Answer to Question 3:

A and C are correct. A is clearly implied by the passage by the statement that he played the piano only once and attended concerts by others. B is not justified. It is not clear whether the composer wanted to be there or not. C is implied by the passage. It is technically possible that the cigarettes were for others, but the passage clearly gives the impression he bought them for himself.

Answer to Question 4:

The correct answer is "Many Americans, however, were familiar with Shostakovich's music, and many knew about the recent banning of his works in the Soviet Union".

The passage does not give much information at all about the composer's works. The second sentence gives a great deal of information about his experience at the Conference, but none at all about his compositions. The final sentence, at least, tells us that they were banned in the Soviet Union and were known in America.

Passage 2:

Answer to Question 5:

D is correct. The passage traces several influences which led to Spanish domination of the natives. Paganism is mentioned as an initial excuse, but the passage then explains that attitudes about both gender and race gave significant support to the Spaniards' cultural domination of the natives. A is incorrect. The passage discusses race and gender even-handedly and does not suggest that either was more influential. B is incorrect. The passage discusses gender issues as a separate matter, not as a factor in conversion efforts. C is incorrect. The passage discusses race and gender separately and does not mention how one might affect the other. There may be an implication that gender ideology would have been different with more females, but not racial ideology. E is incorrect. The impulse toward conversion is presented as an initial excuse for Spanish dominance but is not presented as the origin of race and gender issues. Rather, they are said to have replaced religious attitudes once the conversion was successful.

Answer to Question 6:

B is correct. The beginning of the passage states that race replaced religious attitudes as a prime influence and the final sentence reinforces this. A is incorrect. The passage makes no statement about the effect of racial and gender attitudes upon one another. C is incorrect. The sentence "race and gender ideologies interacted to reinforce the political and cultural hegemony of the Spanish in the New World," is correctly parsed to mean both ideologies influenced both forms of hegemony. D is incorrect. The natives' racial attitudes are not discussed or implied in the passage. E is incorrect. Racial attitudes are said to have replaced religious attitudes, not to have been justified by them.

Answer to Question 7:

B is correct. The point of the passage is to explain the factors that influenced the Spaniards' domination of the natives. The term is used in the final sentence to summarize this thesis. A is incorrect. The passage discusses a few characteristics of the native and Spanish groups, but context makes clear that the passage is about domination, not distinguishing the two groups from one another. C is incorrect. The hegemony mentioned belonged to the Spanish and the passage is about their cultural ascendance, not their decline. D is incorrect. Race and gender traditions are cited as influences upon hegemony, not as synonyms for it. E is incorrect. Religious-inspired policy is discussed early in the passage, but only as a precursor to two other influences upon hegemony.

Answer to Question 8:

B and C are correct. The passage makes clear that both racial attitudes and the gender make-up of the Spanish populace influenced Spanish dominance. A is incorrect. Political hegemony refers to one of the modes of dominance that was influenced by race and gender.

Passage 3:

Answer to Question 9:

The correct answer is "C". This comment indicates that truth does not exist on a 100% basis. Truth varies according to experiences and needs. What is considered "true" may have tinges of dishonesty in it, changing the "color" from white to grey.

Incorrect responses:

"A" This passage refers to people's behavior most of the time. Just as a compass doesn't point true north,

neither are people entirely honest. The sentence just describes the unusual times.

"B" Again, the passage just speaks of usual behavior of people and of compasses. This sentence describes an unusual situation.

"D" While past experience does affect a person, it is only a small portion of what this article addresses. Therefore, this is not the best answer.

"E" This statement is too extreme for the passage. The passage didn't focus on extreme dishonesty and lack of trust worthiness. The passage just suggested that people have trouble being 100% honest, on account of other situations influencing them.

Passage 4:

Answer to Question 10:

The correct answer is (C). This question asks the reader to identify the author's main point, not the Idiot's; though the Idiot is the main character, his name implies the author's view of him as an unreliable source. Therefore, it can be inferred from the passage that the author's viewpoint of proverbs and maxims differs from the Idiot's view, and is best represented by the correct answer, "C", which states the idea that these popular sayings are indeed important.

"A" and "B" are incorrect as they state the Idiot's incorrect perspective, that these widely–used expressions are meaningless and ambiguous.

"D" is incorrect because this passage does not address the issue of why some people may not understand proverbs, as this option states. Though the passage depicts a character who does not see the meaning behind them, the passage does not delve into why that is so, other than the fact that these types of people may be categorized as 'idiots'.

"E" is also incorrect in stating that these sayings are to be taken literally. While the Idiot attempts to understand them in a literal sense, depicting the inaccuracy of the lane at his grandfather's farm in regard to the statement about "long lanes", it is clear from the author's satirical treatment of this character that such an approach to understanding these phrases misses the point of their metaphorical meaning.

Answer to Question 11:

The correct answer is (D). "D" is the correct answer as it is the only choice that is inconsistent with the information found in the passage. By stating that this sentence provides an alternate explanation, this option incorrectly identifies this sentence as an alternate explanation for the Idiot's opinion when in fact it is not an explanation of his opinion but rather an introduction of his perspective.

"B", "C", and "E" all correctly explain the function of this sentence by identifying how it encompasses the Idiot's opinion that popular phrases are useless. By stating that he agrees with this professor, the Idiot establishes consistency between his own opinion and that of the professor, thus summarizing his main point and presenting his argument. It also introduces his opinion by explaining how he feels about this topic in the beginning of the passage.

"A" is also correct, as the professor's statement is presented as a fact, which can function as evidence to further the Idiot's stance on the subject.

Answer to Question 12:

The correct answer is "There wasn't a turn nor a twist in it, and I know by actual measurement that it wasn't sixty feet long."

This sentence most accurately illustrates the Idiot's lack of understanding by demonstrating the way that he approaches proverbs literally, rather than figuratively, as they are meant to be analyzed. By referring to a specific lane and discussing the measurements in contrast to the information in the proverb, the Idiot makes it clear that he judges the accuracy of these statements on their literal details rather than their deeper potential meaning.

Answer to Question 13:

A and B are correct. Choices "A" and "B" both correctly reflect the author's apparent treatment of people who tend to misunderstand popular phrases. By calling the main character an 'idiot', the author clearly mocks these types of people, indicating a derisive attitude. Also, by identifying this character as an imbecile by assigning him the 'name' of Idiot rather than simply stating outright that he is idiotic, this passage takes on a satirical quality.

"C" is also a likely option; though the author is clearly insulting this character, the issues being discussed do not cross over into anything that is too serious or political.

Passage 5:

Answer to Question 14:

The correct answer is "The visual metaphors that evolve link these indigenous peoples through their ancestors and varied cultures to the beginnings of time forging identity and creating a sense of security and order."

The last part of this sentence informs the reader that the clothing helps to forge an identity and create a sense of security and order, all of which lead individuals to feel better about their place in society.

Passage 6:

Answer to Question 15:

The correct answer is "Team dances are common but there are also times when the dance involves 2-4 individuals taking turns on the dancing ring."

The other sentences in the passage describe the types of movement and props that the dancers incorporate. The statement "individuals taking turns on the dancing ring", suggests that some competition may have existed. The remaining sentences in the passage fail to mention individual dances. The previous sentence suggests that various body parts (e.g., legs, arms, and head) performed intricate motions but not necessarily by individuals in a competitive manner.

Passage 7:

Answer to Question 16:

A is correct. The passage describes, in a linear fashion, the two great periods of painting of this era, the lull between them and why the lull occurred. B is incorrect. Giotto is discussed as an important figure of the era, but his influence is not discussed. C is incorrect. The passage may imply that 14th century painting was technically superior but does little more than allude to a greater complexity of form. It certainly does not describe any specific superior elements in a manner that suggests this is the author's primary purpose. D is incorrect. The "lull" described in the passage is simply a lull in painting achievement. The passage notes that the Revival was still new and implies that it continued through the next century. E is incorrect. The passage does mention two important eras, but mainly in terms of chronological progression. There is no explicit qualitative comparison between the two, and not enough implied comparison to make it the author's main purpose.

Answer to Question 17:

The correct answer is C. The passage notes that after the first half of the 14th century, Medieval Italian culture had been thoroughly expressed artistically. The passage further notes that Revival culture had not had time to sink in and artists had not yet developed the technical skills needed to execute Revival-style paintings. Because the passage asserts that the next great era of painting began in1400, the implication is that the half-century gap provided time for Revival culture to become assimilated and for artists to sufficiently develop their skills for the next great period. A is incorrect. Giotto's achievement is presented as an endnote for the medieval period, not a starting point for the next period. B is incorrect. Giotto is presented as a key figure, not a limiting influence and the passage clearly states that Medieval Italian culture had been thoroughly explored artistically. D is incorrect. The passage clearly points to a lull between the two periods because artists were not yet ready to progress, despite having finished off the old period. E may be partially correct, but the passage notes that the artists had not yet mastered their craft to create complex works. New techniques may be part of the mastery, but E is definitely not the complete reason.

Answer to Question 18:

D is correct. The author distinguishes the two periods by noting that Medieval period painters had not mastered the technical skills necessary for complicated works, implying that Revival artists had done so. A is incorrect. The author does not compare the depiction of culture between the two periods. B is incorrect. The author does imply greater complexity of the Revival works but not an overall superiority. The passage states that while Revival culture existed in Italy during the 14th Century, it had not yet had enough influence for painters to express it. The same sentence states that the painters had not yet developed the technical skills necessary for more complex paintings. This implies that a comparative complexity of beauty was a feature of the later Revival period. The author does not assert or imply an aesthetic superiority between the two. C is incorrect. The lull described is a lull in "splendid" painting. A literal cessation of painting is unlikely and not justified by the passage. E is incorrect. The passage states simply that painters of the period had not yet mastered a complex style, not that they were uninterested in doing so.

Answer to Question 19:

A, B and C are correct. The passage states that Revival culture had not had enough influence on artists for them to have the ability to express it. It also states emphatically that the culture and perspective of Italy's Medieval period had been expressed thoroughly by artists, suggesting little further could be expressed. And finally, the passage notes that the artists of the early 14th century had not yet developed the technical skills necessary to create complex works. By noting the half-century gap before the commencement of the next period, the passage implies that the skillset took that long to develop.

Passage 8: Summary / Paraphrase

The passage tells the story of Sheddad. The main idea is that although Sheddad was very powerful, he was struck down by a divine force for his impurity. The major points are (a) that Sheddad used his power to construct a lavish garden and (b) that before he had the opportunity to enjoy his garden, he was struck dead for his "impure soul". The purpose of the passage is to warn the reader that no amount of worldly power and wealth can save a bad man.

Answer to Question 20:

The correct answer is E. Sheddad has built a garden to rival the beauty of heaven and has assembled his slaves and courtiers to view it. In the construction of this garden, Sheddad has angered God, who sends the angel of death to take Sheddad's life before he can see the fruits of his labor. Sheddad's pride has caused his downfall, making E the correct answer. There is no evidence in the story to suggest that others might steal the precious metals and jewels, so A is not correct. God and the angels have no need for a beautiful garden on earth, making B an incorrect choice. Based on the words of the angel of death, one cannot presume that the garden was hidden to prevent Sheddad's heirs from claiming it, eliminating C as a correct answer. It appears that Sheddad used the resources of other countries for hundreds of years; if preventing that were the object of the lesson, it likely would have happened before the construction had been completed. D is incorrect.

Passage 9: Summary / Paraphrase

The passage is about Social Darwinism. The main idea is that Social Darwinism was used to justify oppressive and racist views and policies. The major points are (a) that Social Darwinism is nothing more than the notion that "might makes right" dressed in a quasi-scientific guise and (b) Social Darwinism was used to justify segregation and a belief in a master race. The purpose of the passage is to explain Social Darwinism and how it was used to justify racist ideologies.

Answer to Question 21:

The correct answer is "In about two hours he sent a messenger with an order from the judge authorizing us to remove it."

That the colonel expedited a judicial decision in such a short period of time is likely an acknowledgement of his status in the community.

Answer to Question 22:

The correct answer is D, sanguine. The author is both cheerful and optimistic. His life is both active and enterprising. Answer choice A is incorrect because choleric is hot–tempered and easily angered. Even when obstacles present themselves, the author remains calm. Answer choice B is also incorrect. Earnest implies more seriousness than the author exhibits in his writing. To be objective is to remain impartial. If the author were objective, the reader would not get a sense of his enjoyment and excitement with his enterprises. Answer choice C, therefore, is incorrect. Sincerity is genuine. The author is genuinely happy with his life in California, but he's not attempting to convince the reader about the benefits of living there. Overall, his tone is happy and upbeat; sincere implies some level of seriousness. Answer choice E is also incorrect.

Answer to Question 23:

The correct answer is B. Having had his land poached, the author may feel it necessary to erect a structure on it to secure the property for himself and signal that it is not available. Answer choice A is incorrect because it goes beyond the author's personal narrative. The text here focuses on his own enterprises and not those of the city. Answer choice C is incorrect because it is too broad. The reader may discover the outcome of the author's enterprises after several more pages or chapters of his narrative, as his interests were many and varied. The author does not indicate when he expects his brig to arrive. It is difficult to imagine his interrupting his narrative to await its arrival before continuing. Answer choice D is incorrect. The reader may expect the author to reveal the result of his interest in the brewery, but that may not be his immediate concern. Its tale may appear later in the author's narrative. Answer choice E is also incorrect.

Answer to Question 24:

The best answer is A. Answer choice B is questionable. Although one might repeat the maxim that possession is nine-tenths of the law, there is no indication on the part of the author or the colonel that they might have to consider squatters rights in this case. The speed with which the colonel was able to get a judgment on the land supports this. Answer choice C is incorrect because Colton himself pretended to have a title, which implies that he was the only person involved in the land grab. He did not protest that someone had sold him the title. By process of elimination, answer A remains as the only logical choice. Colton obviously has a strong desire to reside in the area, and all choice pieces of real estate may already have been sold.

Passage 10: Summary / Paraphrase

The passage is about supernatural powers for humans. The main idea is that, since man is created in God's image, man too must possess supernatural abilities. The major point is that the work from which the passage is excerpted hopes to demonstrate that humans possess powers "not subject to the general laws of nature"; in other words, that humans have supernatural powers. The purpose of the passage is to serve as a primer for demonstrating that humans are capable of possessing magical abilities.

Answer to Question 25:

The correct answer is B. The author states his conviction that man is undoubtedly endowed with magic powers. This belief may lead him to make the facts fit his theory, which is contrary to objective, scientific research. B is the correct answer. His belief in God should not be an impediment, as many who conduct scientific research also believe in God, making A an incorrect answer choice. The reader cannot tell from the information presented here if there is little or no research on this topic, eliminating C as the correct answer choice. The reader cannot assume that the church will not cooperate, nor that the public will scoff at his ideas, making both D and E incorrect.

Passage 11: Summary / Paraphrase

The passage is about the author's fascination with books about WWI. The main idea is that although the author is aware that his fascination may seem horrific, he is nonetheless unable to resist it. The major point is that the author feels comfortable in the setting and characters of the war, however appalling the war itself may have been. The purpose of the passage is confessional: the author is admitting the oddities of his fascination while justifying and affirming it.

Answer to Question 26:

The correct answer is "I must confess, though, that I am a bibliophile with War books."

Confession is generally a form of catharsis. One may confess to a priest or someone he/she has harmed in the past. In this case, the author thinks that others may find his love of war books strange as the author; himself was most likely a witness to the horrors about which he reads. By revealing his love of these books, he has eliminated the necessity to keep it a secret and probably feels relieved.

Passage 12: Summary / Paraphrase

The passage is about morning as a metaphor for renewal. The main idea is that, although the author is apparently rather world weary, the beauty of the morning renews some sense of hope in the world. The major points contrast (a) the freshness and innocence of the morning to (b) the sense of the world as "trampled" and the characters as 'grey' and 'sated'. The purpose of the passage is to contrast the author's general state of mind with the symbolic purity of the morning.

Answer to Question 27:

The correct answer is B. The narrator is speaking about morning and the manner in which it is regarding this portion of the earth early in the day.

Answer to Question 28:

The correct answer is A. When the author says that this particular morning must have got lost in the year's progression, he implies that it should have occurred earlier in the year. Halcyon, when describing weather, means calm, or peaceful, or tranquil. A is the only answer that includes both of these descriptors of the day in question. There is no suggestion of a holiday celebration, making B an incorrect choice. The author mentions nothing about the emotions or attitudes of the "we" in the passage. He is describing the morning rather than people. C is not the correct choice.

Passage 13: Summary / Paraphrase

The passage is about the author's strategy for speaking to local populations. The main idea is that the author always attempts to learn some particulars about the place where he is going to speak before overlaying the particulars with a more general theme. The major points are (a) that the author speaks to various townsfolk to find out about their town, what they are proud of, and where they see failures and (b) that the author then modifies his speech with its general themes of civic pride with certain specific features. The purpose of the passage is to reveal the author's way of addressing each town. The rhetoric suggests that the author may be somewhat cynical about his vocation.

Answer to Question 29:

The correct answer is D. The purpose of his presentation is to help the residents realize their potential for improvement. He aims to motivate them, making D the best answer. The writer gathers information in order to confirm what he believes about the inhabitants of towns everywhere. He hopes that their behavior will become new or innovative. There is nothing in this passage that he attempts to intimidate them or cause fear. He desires to use what he knows to motivate them to realize their full potential. D is the correct answer.

Answer to Question 30:

The correct answer is B. The writer's basic assumption is that, although each town has its unique characteristics, they all fail in the same way. The last two sentences provide the general idea that he uses to illuminate the specific failure of the town he is visiting. B is the correct answer. A is incorrect because he uses those visits to tailor his presentation. There is no indication that he looks down on the people in positions of power in the town, making C incorrect as well. This passage is an overview of his process and reveals nothing specific about any town, eliminating D as a possible answer. The lecture focuses on possibilities, not failures. E is incorrect.

Passage 14: Summary / Paraphrase

The passage is about O. Henry. The main idea is that although O. Henry was a superb literary craftsman, his work is gimmicky and lacking in depth. The major points are (a) O. Henry was a unique and skillful writer (b) that his work favors sensation and surprise over genuine substance and (c) that he can be accused of lowering the overall standards of American literature. The main purpose of the passage is to severely critique O. Henry's works while giving some credit for certain topical skill.

Answer to Question 31:

The correct answer is C. The writer's use of words like caricature and cheapness describe the overall effect of O. Henry's writing, and they point to a lack of subtlety, making C the correct choice. The critic states that the reader can never be sure of himself, indicating that the stories do create tension, eliminating A as the correct answer. The writer of this passage deals with O. Henry's style extensively, so B is not the correct answer. The writer also provides information about plot elements, so it would be incorrect to assume that plot is a weakness; D is not correct. There is too little information here to select conflict resolution, answer E, as a weakness.

Answer to Question 32:

Both A and C are correct choices. The author of this passage implies that both writers entertain but fail to reach the level of important literature. Their writing lacks moral background. Answer B does not provide enough information to justify a change in the critics' opinions. One would need to know the reason for the authors' inclusion in those anthologies.

Passage 15: Summary / Paraphrase

The passage is a critique of the human race's self-importance. The main idea is that people have always tended to view the world with an erroneous belief in their own importance and that this way of looking at things continues to influence important aspects of our beliefs. The major points are (a) people hold on to old, outmoded beliefs for fear of the unknown (b) that out of ignorance, people formed all manner of wrong beliefs about the nature of their world, tending to privilege things relatively close at hand (c) that modern science has proven the bulk of our earlier beliefs wrong and destroyed our ability to hold ourselves above the rest of creation (d) our tendency to hold onto the old is the reason for our "crude religions, our crude laws, our crude ideas, and our exalted opinion of the human race." There is a minor point that uses the story of Jacob's ladder to illustrate our way of understanding the world according to our most current knowledge. The purpose of the passage is to give the author's view of why we maintain older beliefs in the face of countervailing evidence.

Answer to Question 33:

The best choice is A. B refers to resources in their natural state, such as crude oil. C could describe a creative product like an essay or a hand-made piece of furniture. D and E describe behavior rather than beliefs and ideas.

Answer to Question 34:

The correct answer is B. The writer is contrasting what man knew in the past with what he now knows to be true. B is the correct answer. The writer is not attempting to show off his own level of education or intelligence, nor is he touting the value of telescopes, eliminating both A and E as correct choices. Answer D is what he is telling the reader but not why. The figure does nothing to enhance the words surrounding it; C is incorrect.

Answer to Question 35:

The correct answer is C. The writer has a low regard for those who refuse to revise their opinions and ideas despite the availability of new information, making C the correct choice. There is nothing in the passage that leads the reader to believe that the writer has any optimism for the human race, so A is incorrect. He does not speculate about the future of the human race, nor reveal any fears about that future, making B the wrong answer. The writer does not tout his own beliefs, so does not express superiority over others, eliminating D as the correct answer. The writer may feel that humankind is hopeless in its desire to hold on to old ideas, but it is overshadowed by his contempt for them. E is not the best answer.

Answer to Question 36:

A, B and C are correct. All of the answers are acceptable choices based on the premise that the people in question were basing their statements or beliefs on what they had to go on. President Kennedy probably could not have imagined the day that scientists would say that human travel to Mars is likely. Until advances in astronomy and physics and mathematics evolved, it was reasonable to assume that everything revolved around the Earth. Columbus believed that he had found a shorter route to India and, logically, called the inhabitants of the New World Indians.

Answer to Question 37:

B is the best answer choice. The author suggests that, at each stage of history, men thought that they had discovered all of the answers only to be proven wrong by successive generations. The same is true for man today. The next best answer is just around the corner. The writer does not suggest that man has made no progress despite his fondness for old ideas. A is not a good answer choice. Although the author expresses contempt for those who cling to old ideas, he does mention the way in which new technology has created new, beneficial understanding, making C an incorrect choice.

Answer to Question 38:

The correct answer is "So to have the idea that all of this was made for man gives man a great deal of what Weber and Field used to call "Proud flesh."

Conceitedness comes from having a high opinion of oneself. The idea that the universe and everything in it was created for man's comfort and/or amusement is the height of conceitedness.

Passage 16: Summary / Paraphrase

The passage is about the political philosophy of Thomas Hobbes. The main idea is that Hobbes developed a theory in which humans are seen as naturally inclined to do evil and require a government to reign in their naturally evil tendencies. The main points are: (a) that Hobbes believes that in a state of nature, humans are engulfed in perpetual state of conflict (b) that Hobbes believes that only in civil society governed by a social contract are humans able to escape the evils of their "natural" condition. A minor point, the mention of the age-old debate between whether human nature is inherently good or bad, is used to introduce the discussion of Hobbes' ideas. The purpose of the passage is to briefly summarize Hobbes' political thought: although the passage presents a potentially controversial matter, the author avoids any indication of bias and merely presents the content.

Answer to Question 39:

The correct answer is "For Hobbes, society is what tames and controls the ultimately selfish and corrupt natural state of the human being."

Hobbes' view on human nature is clearly stated: it is corrupt and selfish.

Passage 17: Summary / Paraphrase

The passage is about the relation between Pop Art and capitalism. The main idea is that while Pop Art may appear trivial on the surface, it often has deeper and more serious ramifications. The main points are: (a) that Pop Art is an artistic development of the mass production and consumerism that are the hallmarks of capitalism and (b) that Pop Artists have used the medium to both mock and critique capitalist culture and represent and re-imagine familiar aspects of everyday life. A minor point that distinguishes British and American Pop Art develops the second major point more fully. The purpose of the passage is to inform: the author briefly summarizes several key points about the Pop Art movement. There is a slight indication that the author may be trying to convince the reader to take Pop Art seriously, as indicated by the phrase "While Pop Art seems superfluous at the surface level, it is actually produced with marked intentionality".

Answer to Question 40:

The correct answer is B.

A. Wrong. The passage clearly states that there is a difference between British and American Pop Art.

B. Correct. The passage states that British Pop artists mocked (lampooned) America's consumer culture while American Pop artists were more interested in representations of reality.

C. Wrong. Both American and British Pop Art is worthy of critique according to the passage.

D. Wrong. The passage does not discuss whether or not British or American Pop artists are more famous.

E. Wrong. The passage clearly states that British Pop Artists explored capitalism in their work since they were highly critical of American consumer culture.

Answer to Question 41:

The correct answer is A and B.

A. Correct. The passage lists consumerism as one of Pop Art's themes relative to its exploration of capitalism.

B. Correct The passage lists mass production as one of Pop Art's themes relative to its exploration of capitalism.

C. Wrong. The passage does not indicate that Pop Artists used free markets as a part of their artistic expression relative to capitalism.

Passage 18: Summary / Paraphrase

The passage is about the Art Nouveau movement. The main idea is that Art Nouveau developed art in directions that had never before been seen. There is a major point that Art Nouveau represents a conscious break from Neoclassicist attempts to mimic Greco-Roman aesthetics. A minor point develops the ways in which Art Nouveau differs from art based in classical aesthetics by discussing the use of asymmetry and unusual patterns. The purpose of the passage is to inform, which is reflected in the descriptive tone.

Answer to Question 42:

The correct answer is "Art Nouveau arose at the turn of the 20th century as a reaction against the Neoclassicist movement's propensity to simply mimic the style of the Greeks and Romans. "Art Nouveau artists wanted to find new ways of creating art because they were tired of forms that were constantly mimicking the past.

Passage 19: Summary / Paraphrase

The passage is about Jacques Derrida's critical theory. The main idea is that Derrida believed that the critical analysis of a literary work could only be done by thoroughly investigating its context. The major points are that (a) Derrida believed that there was no objective starting point to begin the analysis of a work and (b) analysis of narrative could only begin by deconstructing the assumptions underlying the interpretive process. The main purpose of the passage is to introduce the reader to Derrida's idea about critical theory.

Answer to Question 43:

The correct answer is B.

A. Wrong. While this statement is true according to the passage, it does not explicate why subjectivity is needed to deconstruct complex narratives.

B. Correct. The passage shows that Derrida insisted that textual analysis was ultimately dependent on understanding and interpreting the various contexts that inform the text, an act that is an exercise in subjectivity since subjectivity is concerned with engaging a diversity of perspectives.

C. Wrong. The passage does not give enough information about how readers read in order to make a judgment as to whether or not subjectivity accounts for the interpretive process of readers.

D. Wrong. The passage does not give enough specific information about readers to make the inference that the inner experience of the reader is what characterizes deconstructionist theory.

E. Wrong. The problem word here is interesting. While it may be true that subjectivity may allow for a wider array of textual interpretations, this does not necessarily mean that they would be more interesting than objective interpretations, or at least there is not enough information given in the passage for the reader to make such an inference.

Answer to Question 44:

The correct answer is A and B.

A. Correct. The passage states that Derrida' believed that the contexts informing a given text's content are not outside of but in relationship with the text.

B. Correct. Texts cannot be independent of contexts: they can never exist completely alone.

C. Wrong. The passage does not indicate that Derrida believed that the text was the only form of reality - reality can still exist without a text.

Passage 20: Summary / Paraphrase

The passage is about modernist literature. The main idea is that the events of the early to mid-20th century caused modernist writers to shift their tone from a relatively optimistic to a relatively pessimistic tone. The major points are that (a) writers such as Eliot and Pound celebrated the individualism and order of the modern age and (b) that the advent of the World Wars marked a shift to a more pessimistic tone about the same subjects. The main purpose of the passage is to describe an important aspect in the development of modern literature.

Answer to Question 45:

The correct answer is C.

A. Wrong. The passage states that modernist writing shifted towards a more cynical, introspective tone to reflect the realities surrounding the World Wars, thus is evolved to mirror cultural changes.

B. Wrong. The passage makes it clear that modernist writing is characterized by concise language and structure, thus the coherency of form is a highly esteemed feature of modernist writing.

C. Correct. While the passage states that modernist writing evolved to become more introspective in nature, introspection is not a hallmark feature of modernist writing - autonomy and the exactitude of form lie at the heart of modernist writing.

D. Wrong. Since precise language is a hallmark feature of modernist writing, modernist writers avoid florid or elaborate prose.

E. Wrong. Modernist writing has a very mechanistic quality since it is chiefly concerned with form, structure, and precision.

Passage 21: Summary / Paraphrase

The passage is about Sun Tzu's The Art of War. The main idea is that The Art of War is seminal text on military strategy that is familiar to a broad swath people. The major point is that The Art of War emphasizes the ability to be flexible and alter strategies as required by circumstances. The main purpose of the passage is to inform: the tone of the passage emphasizes summary facts about the work.

Answer to Question 46:

The correct answer is C.

A. Wrong. While the author clearly delineates that The Art of War is a seminal work on military strategy, the tone does not betray a sense of buoyancy or positivity and liveliness; the author is in fact quite neutral relative to Sun Tzu's work.

B. Wrong. While the author's personal opinion can be best described as dispassionate towards The Art of War, the tone is not cold. Aloof can also be a synonym for dispassionate, but in a way that is uppity or icy and thus it is not the accurate term to describe the author's personal attitude.

C. Correct. Unaligned is a synonym for dispassionate and detached, which are the characteristics of the author's personal opinion of The Art of War. Unaligned is also a synonym for dispassionate that does not come with any overly positive or negative connotations, so it is very much a good term to use to convey neutrality.

D. Wrong. The author's personal opinion of The Art of War is neutral because it is never directly expressed, but inert is too strong of a word to equate with neutrality; to be inert is to be apathetic, immobile or indolent.

E. Wrong. The author's personal opinion of The Art of War is neutral in that the author never explicitly conveys his or her opinion. Phlegmatic is a term more appropriate for describing a demeanor that is calm and collected but not necessarily neutral and thus it is not the best option for describing the author's personal opinion towards The Art of War.

Answer to Question 47:

The correct answer is C.

A. Wrong. Ambitious is not a synonym for efficacious as ambitious means the determination to succeed and efficacious means the power to produce a desired effect.

B. Wrong. Useful can be a synonym for efficacious but the author is making the point that Sun Tzu's strategy is more than just useful - it leads to military success which demands a stronger adjective.

C. Correct. Efficacious means the power to produce a desired effect and thus potent can be substituted here since potent can also mean the power to produce a desired effect and the author intends to show that Sun Tzu's military strategy is powerful and effective.

D. Wrong. Adequate can also be a synonym for efficacious, but again it does not properly describe, from the author's viewpoint, the power of Sun Tzu's military strategy.

E. Wrong. Unorganized is not a synonym for efficacious as it means not organized or incoherent and efficacious means the power to produce a desired effect.

Passage 22: Summary / Paraphrase

The passage is about a recent theoretical development in the humanities called postcolonial theory. The main idea is that later 20th century academics reacted to the dominant sociocentric paradigm with a more pluralistic theory. The main points are (a) that postcolonial theory attempts to give colonized peoples more of a voice in the humanities and (b) that postcolonial theory looks at the "cultural space" as a complex interaction of European and other cultures. The main purpose of the passage is to give a brief primer on what postcolonial theory is.

Answer to Question 48:

The correct answer is A.

A. Correct. The passage states that the main consequence of European Imperialism was that is shaped global society by exercising cultural dominance.

B. Wrong. It is true that diversity could not thrive under European Imperialism, but this is more of a byproduct of the fact that European cultural norms were dominant.

C. Wrong. The passage does not discuss whether or not the colonized participated in the colonial political process.

D. Wrong. The passage clearly states that global society was heavily influenced by colonialism.

E. Wrong. The passage clearly shows the culturally hegemonic nature of European Imperialism.

Passage 23: Summary / Paraphrase

The passage is about the debate in literary criticism over authorial intent. The main idea of the passage is that while there are two main schools of thought about authorial intent, one makes more sense than the other. There are several main points: (a) some critics believe that the author's intentions and ideologies form the content of the work where others take the view that the work is independent of external factors (b) that Kafka is an author whose work is exemplary for highlighting the points of the debate (c) that most critics tend to believe that Kafka's experiences and beliefs shaped the content of his work (d) the author believes that there is significant evidence for the received critical view and (e) a reaffirmation of the view that, in general it makes sense for authors' intentions and beliefs to strongly influence the content of their works. There are several minor points that underscore key issues raised by the major points: (a) that the often bizarre nature of Kafka's works makes them especially open to the interpretations of either school of criticism (b) that Kafka's legal training coupled with his fascination with the law in his literary works support the notion that his experiences and beliefs shaped his works. The main purpose of the passage is to describe two conflicting schools of literary criticism and use an example to demonstrate why one makes more sense than the other. The author's stance is made definitively clear in the final paragraph with the phrase "it is difficult to imagine that a writer can produce a text without having some kind of interpretive goal or objective in mind." The rhetorical bow to multiplicity of interpretive possibilities does not take away from the author's clear stance on the issue.

Answer to Question 49:

The correct answer is A.

A. Correct. Kafka's literature was critical of what he saw as the arbitrariness and tyranny of the legal system and thus it can be inferred that Kafka himself was anti-authoritarian.

B. Wrong. The passage does not provide any indication that Marxist literary criticism is the most efficient way of extracting meaning from a text or knowing with certainty the intent of the author of a fictional work.

C. Wrong. The passage does not indicate that Kafka's fictional representations of the law had any bearing on actual, real-world legal practices and policies.

D. Wrong. The passage in no way indicates that the intent of the author can ever be determined with certainty.

E. Wrong. The passage makes it clear that finding absolute truth in literature is neither the goal of literary criticism nor within the realm of possibility.

Answer to Question 50:

The correct answer is A.

A. Correct. According to the information given in the first paragraph, authorial intent can be defined as the intentions and ideological leanings of an author that have the potential to shape the meaning of his or her text.

B. Wrong. The passage does not indicate that authorial intent is the term for the catalyst behind an author's decision to write, rather that it is the conglomeration of an author's subjective thoughts and experiences that could influence the text.

C. Wrong. While it is true that authorial intent is the sum of an author's thoughts and experiences, the passage makes it clear that the literary community does not agree that they always shape the meaning of a text - they only have the potential to do so.

D. Wrong. Authorial intent is not shown to be a type of writing style and furthermore the New Critics rejected the concept of authorial intent all together.

E. Wrong. The first paragraph of the passage gives enough information for the reader to form a solid definition of authorial intent.

Answer to Question 51:

The correct answer is D.

A. Wrong. Methodological means relating to a type of discipline and hermeneutical means interpretive therefore the two terms are not analogous.

B. Wrong. Hermeneutical means interpretive and intentional is the expression of intention or purpose; therefore, the two terms are not analogous.

C. Wrong. Epistemological is related to the study of the nature of knowledge while hermeneutical is related to the interpretation of knowledge and therefore the two terms are not analogous.

D. Correct. Explicative is a synonym for interpretive and thus can also be a synonym for hermeneutical, which is also analogous to interpretive.

E. Wrong. Remedial means curative and hermeneutical means interpretive and thus both terms are not analogous.

Answer to Question 52:

The correct answer is A and B.

A. Correct. The passage indicates that, according to Kafka, both laymen and lawmen did not understand the law or legal process.

B. Correct. The passage indicates that Kafka's imagery representations of law and legality convey his opinion that the legal system was arbitrary and oppressive.

C. Wrong. The passage in no way indicates how Kafka felt about being a trained lawyer.

Answer to Question 53:

The correct answers are A, B and C.

A. Correct. The passage states that Kafka believed the legal system to be rigid and intransigent is a synonym for rigid, both meaning uncompromising.

B. Correct. The passage states that Kafka believed the legal system to be absurd and incongruous can be a synonym for absurd, both meaning senseless.

C. Correct. The passage states that Kafka believed the legal system to be absurd and inane can be a synonym for rigid, both meaning senseless.

Answer to Question 54:

The correct answer is "The images and metaphors that Kafka infuses his prose with regarding the law and the legal process are what constitute not only the meaning of his fiction but also his personal view on the law."

Tropes are rhetorical strategies that include metaphors and images and thus the sentence above both identifies and describes the tropes used by Kafka in his prose.

Practice Set 2 - Biological Sciences

Passage 24:

Answer to Question 55:

The correct answer is B. Choice A is incorrect, as nothing in the passage depends on the use of illicit substances. Choice C is incorrect. If the director is an unusual example, this would undermine the passage's point about people increasing muscle mass in different ways. Choice D is incorrect, as the passage makes no claims about the best way to be healthy. Choice E is incorrect, as this is true, but it is not the point of the passage. Choice B is correct, as the passage makes the general assertion that different people gain muscle and strength in different ways and gives the director as a specific example. This assumes that there are a significant number of people like the director.

Answer to Question 56:

The correct answer is D. The logic of the passage is that something that looks unimpressive can actually be quite strong. Choice A is incorrect, as the point of the passage is that people are not always as they appear to be. Choice B is almost correct, but the sentence should be flipped: appearance cannot prescribe activity. Choice C is incorrect, as this does not fit the point of the passage about appearances being deceiving. Choice E is incorrect, as the passage implies that appearance does not always show someone's true health. Choice D is correct, as the passage says that appearance does not always reflect health. Thus, it is true that physical activity will not always prescribe appearance.

Answer to Question 57:

The correct answer is B. Choice A is incorrect, as this represents something doing less than was expected (the expensive motor should work well, but it does not). Choice C is incorrect, as this shows that the tractor's appearance is deceiving, but in a negative sense (the large tractor should be powerful, but it is not powerful). Choice D is incorrect, as the passage is concerned more with power rather than capacity. Choice E is incorrect, as a cheap car coming with a warranty does not reveal something special about the car. Choice B most nearly captures the logic of the passage, as the unimpressive car is actually more than it seems in a positive sense, just as how the director looks thin, but is quite strong.

Answer to Question 58:

The correct answer is A. Choice B is incorrect, as the passage does not favor one type of exercise over another. Choice C is incorrect, as the passage notes that the traditional big muscle look is not necessary to fitness and strength but does not advocate any specific training practices. Choice A is correct, as the passage states that the gymnasium director has made a life-long study of himself, which implies that those who want to follow his example must also be capable of this kind of self-study.

Passage 25:

Answer to Question 59:

The correct answer is B. Choice A is incorrect, because the Danger theory states that DAMPs lead to activation of antigen preserving cells. Choice C is incorrect because the Danger theory states that innate immunity is essential for adaptive immunity. Choice D is incorrect because it is known that T cells can destroy non-self-tissue. Choice E is incorrect because the discovery of a new antigen would not affect the Danger theory. Choice B is correct because the Danger theory is based on the idea that tissues secrete danger associated molecular patterns.

Answer to Question 60:

The correct answer is B. Choice A is incorrect, because it is an accurate definition of the word, but it does not fit the sentence. Choice C is incorrect because it has nothing to do with expression. Choice D is incorrect because it has nothing to do with expression. Choice E is a semi-accurate definition of the word, but it does not fit the sentence. Choice B is the correct answer, because the sentence says that these cells lead to other molecules being created.

Answer to Question 61:

The correct answer is D. Choice A is incorrect, because the self and non-self are not identical. Choice B is incorrect, because the conventional view states that cells distinguish between self and non-self. Choice C is incorrect, because the Danger theory states that cells do not recognize the self. Choice E is incorrect, because the Danger theory states that cells do not recognize the self. Choice D is correct, as the Danger theory states that the self and non-self are indistinguishable, and the conventional views state that cells recognize the self and target the non-self.

Answer to Question 62:

The correct answer are A and C. Choice A is correct, because the Danger theory states that cells that are distressed begin secreting DAMPs, which are molecular patterns. Choice B is incorrect, because the passage says nothing about experiments. Choice C is correct, because Danger theory states that there is no adaptive immunity without innate immunity. Choices A and C are correct.

Passage 26: Summary / Paraphrase

The author provides an overview of the concept of mimicry, along with a real-world example of an organism using mimicry. The author does not present an argument or opposing views.

Answer to Question 63:

The correct answer is A. Choice B is incorrect, because evolutionary pathways are never mentioned in the passage. Choice C is incorrect because the author uses the ash borer as an example, but it is not the focus of the passage. Choice D is incorrect because the author mentions a specific observation from evolutionary biology but does not provide an overview of the field. Choice E is incorrect because the author never specifies which mutations help the butterflies adapt. Choice A is correct, because the passage provides general information about mimicry.

Answer to Question 64:

The correct answer is B. Choice A is incorrect, because the table would show the prevalence of mimicry in organisms. Choice C is incorrect, because avoiding predators is the goal of mimicry. Choice D is incorrect because mimicry is responsible for the decreasing numbers of moth ash borers caught. Choice E is incorrect because mimicry would boost the population of stick insects. Choice B is correct, because decreasing populations who adapted using mimicry would show that mimicry did not help them survive.

Answer to Question 65:

The correct answer is B. Choice A is incorrect because the passage never mentions reproductive rates. Choice C is incorrect because the passage mentions organisms developing closeness of resemblance, not speed. Choice B is correct because mimicry increases the chance that a predator will avoid a certain type of organism.

Answer to Question 66:

The correct answer is "In evolutionary biology, mimicry is the similarity of one species to another in characters like appearance, behavior, sound and scent which protects one or both the species involved."

The first sentence is the only sentence to explicitly list appearance, behavior, sound, and scent as ways in which an organism can adapt to better mimic another organism.

Passage 27:

Answer to Question 67:

The correct answer is (B). Choice A is incorrect, as a diagram would help show the cell structure. Choice C is incorrect, as the passage speculates about the development of the nucleolus but leaves open the questions of what it does and why it might not be absolutely essential. Choice D is incorrect, as comparing old and young cells would help the passage make its point. Choice E is incorrect, as the sentence provided gives just enough detail for the reader to understand the nucleus. Choice B is correct, as all technical and uncommon words are defined in the passage, with the possible exception of "morphological." But a full list would be unnecessary.

Passage 28: Summary / Paraphrase

The passage provides a general overview of phylogenetics and the methods used to determine evolutionary relationships. There is no argument present, and the author mentions no opposing views.

Answer to Question 68:

The correct answer is C. Choice A is incorrect because the passage explains what a phylogenetic tree is. Choice B is incorrect because the passage states that missing data makes phylogenetic trees less accurate. Choice D is incorrect because the passage states the phylogenetic methods depend on mathematical models. Choice E is incorrect because the passage states that populations can branch, hybridize, or terminate. Choice C is correct, because the passage mentions no significant drawbacks to phylogenetic methods.

Answer to Question 69:

The correct answer is D. Choice A is incorrect, because vibrant is a correct synonym for robust, but it does not fit the meaning of the sentence. Choice B is incorrect, because it does not fit the meaning of the sentence. Choice C is incorrect, because thriving is a correct synonym for robust, but it does not fit the meaning of the sentence. Choice E is incorrect, because blossoming is not a synonym for robust. Choice D is correct because it expresses the ideal state of a phylogenetic tree

Answer to Question 70:

The correct answer is A. Choice B is incorrect, because the passage states that one can only determine the accuracy of a hypothesis if one knows the true relationship among taxa. Choice C is incorrect because the passage states that more data makes results more accurate, but it never says complete data is necessary. Choice A is correct, because the passage explains that phylogenetics uses math to show the evolutionary relationships of organisms.

Answer to Question 71:

The correct answer is "Phylogenetic methods depend upon an implicit or explicit mathematical model describing the evolution of characters observed in the species included."

The fifth sentence is the only sentence to explicitly link phylogenetics to a mathematical model. While the first sentence is promising, it does not mention a specific technique, just sequencing data and matrix data. The correct answer is the fifth sentence.

Passage 29:

Answer to Question 72:

The correct answer is E. Choice A is incorrect because there are no complex scientific words in need of definition. Choice B is incorrect because the images would distract the reader, and because the robots and sensors are only mentioned briefly. Choice C is incorrect because computer use is not part of the main point of the passage. Choice D is incorrect because the passage is about systems biology, not its founder. Choice E is correct, because information on current research would show the reader how the field has evolved to be today.

Answer to Question 73:

The correct answer is A. Choice B is incorrect, because the passage does not go into detail about important discoveries. Choice C is incorrect because the passage does not mention recent advances. Choice D is incorrect because the passage's tone never praises technology. Choice E is incorrect because the passage never shows data that has been obtained. Choice A is correct, because the passage provides an overview of the field and its history.

Answer to Question 74:

The correct answer is B. Choice A is incorrect because confusing and complicated are similar words to perturbation, but it would make no sense to have confusing and complicated scientific methods. Choice C is incorrect because unclear and unfinished are not synonyms of perturbation. Choice D is incorrect because purposely difficult is not a synonym of perturbation, and because it would make no sense to have purposely difficult methods. Choice E is incorrect because lacking sense, direction, or reason does not make sense for a scientific technique. Choice B is correct, because it is the only choice that makes sense considering the context of a type of scientific method.

Answer to Question 75:

The correct answers are A and B. Choice C is incorrect because this is a short passage, while a treatise is an extensively researched academic work. Choice A is correct because the passage describes the beginning of the study of systems biology. Choice B is correct because the passage mentions recent advances due to technology. Choices A and B are correct.

Passage 30: Summary / Paraphrase

The passage is about basic locational terminology in anatomy. The main idea is that students of anatomy need to master a specialized lexicon of locational terms. The major point is the discussion of key locational terms used in anatomy. The major point is supported by (a) several examples of how to use the terms when discussing the anatomy of a rabbit and (b) a brief justification for why anatomists prefer a specialized locational terminology to more general terms. The purpose of the passage is to introduce the reader to anatomical terminology.

Answer to Question 76:

The correct answers are A, B and C. The passage emphasizes the importance of using correct and uniform terminology depending on the task or occupation. When sailing, for example, it is crucial to know the parts of a ship in relation to the bow. If one were to us the word left instead of port, the listener might think that the speaker is referring to his own left rather than the left side of the boat. When performing brain surgery, the terms front, back, top, or bottom can change depending on the patient's position. Medical terminology for the parts of the brain and their relative position in the cranium remain constant enabling everyone involved in the procedure to understand what is happening. In the same way, a mechanic must know and use the correct names for parts of an engine, especially if he is working with another mechanic or ordering parts.

Passage 31: Summary / Paraphrase

The passage is about strategies for dealing with insect pests. The main idea is that while an insect may do the most harm during one point in its lifecycle, it may be easier to destroy at another point in its cycle. The major point is that it may be easier to destroy a mature insect than its larvae even though the larvae may be more harmful. There is a minor point that underscores the potential harmfulness of larvae by explaining that larvae require a large food supply to furnish their tremendous growth rate. The purpose of the passage is to provide information on pest control. Although the passage features normative language such as "it is better to", it is mainly factual; the reader is not being told that they ought to kill pests, merely the most strategic approach to dealing with them should they desire pest control.

Answer to Question 77:

The best answer is E. The first words of this passage, "from this", indicates that an explanation or example has been given in the earlier portion of the text. The content of the text here presented reinforces it. There is too little information to assume that this is a conclusion. The writer may very well continue with the topic. Answer choice A is incorrect. The writer is really restating what he has said or shown in the previous text, rather than providing an example, so B is also incorrect. The writer presents the reader with alternatives rather than issuing a warning, making C incorrect as well. There is no indication that the writer is going to further develop an idea presented in this passage, so D is the wrong answer choice.

Passage 32: Summary / Paraphrase

The passage is about the mammalian skull. The main idea is that mammal skulls can be better understood in comparison to the skulls of lower life forms. The major point is that by comparing a mammal skull to a frog skull, one can see how they are similar, but also how the mammal skull is more developed and more complex. The purpose of the passage is to develop an illustration of the mammal skull.

Answer to Question 78:

The correct answer is E. Herpetologists study snakes and amphibians; even though the frog is an amphibian, it is not the focus of the information in this passage, so A is not the correct answer choice. Zoologists study animals. Since the apparent focus of the writer's words is the human skull, answer B is also incorrect. Endocrinologists study and treat malfunctions and disorders of the endocrine system, making C incorrect. Thoracic surgeons operate in the area of the chest, eliminating D as a correct answer choice. The correct answer is E, craniologists since they study the cranium, another word for skull.

Answer to Question 79:

The best definition is answer B. Primarily means first and does not fit in this context, so A is incorrect. In this case, answer C is also incorrect because fundamentally is not modifying the word similar in this way, nor does fundamentally mean originally similar, eliminating D as the correct choice. The structure is not indispensably similar; E is incorrect.

Answer to Question 80:

The correct answer is C. Because the author has mentioned the skull only in this passage, it would be incorrect to assume that other human anatomical structures have corresponding structures in lower life forms, making A an incorrect answer choice. The same reasoning may be applied to answer choice B. There is no indication that all of amphibian anatomy corresponds to human anatomy. Answer choice C is the best response. It may be that, because studying the frog's skull leads to a better understanding of the human skull, studying anatomical structures of other life forms leads to a better understanding of human anatomy in its various parts.

Passage 33: Summary / Paraphrase

The passage is about strategies for cotton growing. The main idea is that through a variety of methods, farmers have succeeded in generating cotton crops with higher yields than were possible historically. The major points are: (a) that using seed selection, special cultivation, and hybridization, cotton farmers have created new varieties of cotton that produce unprecedented yields and (b) that farmers need to carefully consider numerous factors in order to optimize their results when using one of these new varieties. The purpose of the passage is to inform the reader about how cotton varietals affect yields and advise on how to optimize them.

Answer to Question 81:

The correct answer is "Many of these attempts have succeeded, and there are now a large number of varieties which excel the older varieties in profitable yield."

The writer is advising farmers to select and plant hybrid cotton. His justification for this recommendation is the success that others have had doing so. The increasing popularity of the hybrids is evidence of their effectiveness.

Answer to Question 82:

The correct answer is D. The writer reveals that hybrids are grown in ideal conditions before being made available to farmers. For farmers to produce the best crop with the highest yields, they should mimic the conditions under which the hybrid was developed. Hybridization may be a long and costly process, but this passage does not reveal any information that would make this a reasonable conclusion. A is not correct. Contrary to the conclusion expressed in answer choice B, hybrids are developed for very specific soil and climate conditions. It is likely that all plants need fertilizer to increase their yields, but it is not the only factor in a plant's success, so C cannot be correct. The price of a harvested crop depends on factors that are sometimes beyond the control of the grower. He may have planted a pricey hybrid, but there may be no demand for it at the time of harvest. E is not the best answer choice.

Answer to Question 83:

The correct answer is A. Tillage most commonly means soil that has been plowed in preparation for planting. The writer implies that each hybrid has been raised in the best tillage, meaning the best-prepared soil. A farmer can apply fertilizer, water, pesticides, and mulch and still have a crop fail because the soil was not prepared correctly.

Passage 34: Summary / Paraphrase

The passage is about effective planting. The main idea is that true grasses thrive best with the addition of another type of plant, legumes. The major points are: (a) that true grasses will exhaust the nitrogen supply in soil because they can only get nitrogen from the soil (b) that legumes such as clover are able to extract free nitrogen from the air as well as from the soil and (c) that in order to optimize planting, farmers should add legume to grass seed in order to keep the grass from exhausting all the nitrogen in the soil. The main purpose of the passage is to inform and persuade by explaining to the reader why it is optimal to add in legume.

Answer to Question 84:

The correct answer is "Hence without cost to the farmer these clovers help the soil to feed their neighbors, the true grasses."

Adding fertilizer with the correct proportion of nitrogen is probably as effective as growing clover in tandem with the true grasses. The downside is the cost. Since the clover is perennial, it will grow every year without replanting, whereas chemical fertilizers must be added to the soil every year at great cost to the farmer.

Passage 35: Summary / Paraphrase

The passage is about stocking water with fish. The main idea is that despite it seeming obvious that it is necessary to provide feed for fish that are being stocked, the issue of feeding is often forgotten. There is a major point that stocking feed after the fish have been introduced is often a failure. The main purpose of the passage is to inform. The author leaves unstated the explanation of why introducing feed after the fish does not work.

Answer to Question 85:

The correct answer is "Small attempts at stocking with creatures suitable for food, particularly after the fish have been already introduced, are not at all likely to succeed."

Attempting to treat an illness is more time-consuming and expensive than taking steps to prevent the illness in the first place. One may succeed in curing the patient, but success is not guaranteed. In much the same way, stocking the body of water with food before introducing the fish is more likely to have a successful result than stocking the water with fish and, then, introducing the food. Many or all of the fish will have already died.

Answer to Question 86:

The correct answer is A. There is no evidence in the passage to suggest that the fish will migrate; a pond may not even provide an egress for that purpose. Answer choice E is not correct. Answer choice D is also incorrect based on the lack of evidence to suggest cannibalism. The writer says that an appropriate food source is necessary but does not say that fish will adapt to a new type of food, making answer choice C incorrect. Although one may stock a pond in order to catch the fish, no mention of this is made in the passage, eliminating B as the correct answer. The best answer choice is A and failing to provide food that the fish will eat insures their death.

Answer to Question 87:

The correct answer is C. The writer's use of the word "superfluous" should lead the reader to believe that he has already discussed the creatures that are suitable as food for the fish to be stocked in the pond. The writer is now admonishing his audience that neglecting to create a food supply before putting the fish in the pond will cause the fish to die. For this reason, C is the correct answer choice.

Passage 36: Summary / Paraphrase

The passage is about determining the age of trees. The main idea is that many methods of determining a tree's age are unreliable. The major points are that (a) scientifically rigorous measurement of growth rates has only existed since the 18th century and (b) that only the measurement of a tree's girth is reliable for telling its age. The main idea of the passage is primed by an extensive preamble that ponders questions of our knowledge of a tree's age. The purpose of the passage is to briefly discuss the longevity of trees and several methods for determining it.

Answer to Question 88:

The correct answer is "Is the period of one thousand years, the favorite figure of tradition, a common or probable period of arboreal longevity, or have our proudest forest giants attained their present size in half the time that is commonly claimed for them?"

The phrase "favorite figure of tradition" suggests that scientific methods were not used to determine the ages of old trees. It may be that the only way people could judge the age of an apparently antique specimen was through a family or village oral history. As in the popular childhood game, Telephone, the initial information can undergo several transformations before reaching the final participant, so exactly when a tree was planted may be impossible to determine.

Answer to Question 89:

The correct answer is E. The writer is not talking about something that amuses; therefore, A is not the correct choice. Pleasure and amusement have similar connotations, so, for the same reasons, answer choice B is also incorrect. Answer choice C may be the easiest to eliminate, as the author is clearly not describing a performance of any kind. To entertain an idea is to consider it; one may also do this with a question, which is why E is a better answer choice than D.

Answer to Question 90:

The correct answer is A. By the end of this passage, the writer has mentioned ways in which scientists have measured the ages of trees. It is logical to assume that he will continue in this vein. He does mention, at the beginning of this passage, that it would be proper to consider where trees grow and how that affects their chances of longevity, but he does not elaborate and moves on to other topics, eliminating B as the correct answer. This same reasoning can be used to claim that answer choice C is wrong. The purpose of this passage is not to persuade, so the writer's creating an argument is not logical. Answer choice D is not correct. To this point in the passage, the writer has made no mention of specific geography, nor is it likely to be the next topic, making E incorrect.

Passage 37: Summary / Paraphrase

The passage is about the effects that hormones have on behavior. The main idea is that hormone levels have a more significant effect on mating potential than other indicators such as attractiveness. There are two major points: (a) that the behavior observed in swallows correlates to other animal species, including humans and (b) that the increased confidence and higher testosterone levels affected mating outcomes as much as the changes to the vibrancy of the birds' coloring. The purpose of the passage is to inform the reader of the important role that hormones play in animal behavior

Answer to Question 91:

The correct answer is B.

A. Wrong. The passage lists confidence as one of two main factors involved in increasing male barn swallows' testosterone levels.

B. Correct. The passage claims that confidence is caused by an attractive physical appearance.

C. Wrong. The passage states beta males can turn into alpha males and thus have increased levels of testosterone, ruling out the idea that high levels of testosterone are inherent or unchangeable.

D. Wrong. The passage lists confidence as one of two main factors involved in increasing male barn swallows' testosterone levels.

E. Wrong. The passage does not attribute fluctuating levels solely to mating.

Passage 38: Summary / Paraphrase

The passage is about primate behavior. The main idea is that sharing among primates is often not strictly altruistic. The main points of the passage are (a) that anthropologists believe that chimpanzee behavior is analogous to the behavior of early humans and (b) that chimpanzees are mainly motivated to share food and tools in exchange for sex. Major point (b) is backed up by additional facts that male chimpanzees are most likely to share food and supplies with sexually receptive females. The purpose of the passage is to inform and to draw a comparison between human behavior and that of other primates.

Answer to Question 92:

The correct answer is A.

A. Correct. Since sexually receptive females in their reproductive years have a higher chance of receiving food and supplies, they have the highest chance for survival.

B. Wrong. The passage actually infers that male primates' motivation is to perpetuate the species since they are most likely to exchange food for sex with females in their reproductive years.

C. Wrong. Male primates trade food for sex as a means of survival not exploitation. Their ultimate goal is to perpetuate the species.

D. Wrong. The passage states that the food for sex process is not altruistically motivated therefore primates cannot possess a high level of magnanimity or selflessness.

E. Wrong. The passage does not infer that male primates are in any way lazy, in fact it infers the opposite: that male primates work to gather supplies to exchange.

Answer to Question 93:

The correct answer is B.

A. Wrong. The passage states that primate behavior likely mirrors that of early humans, but then goes on to make it clear that sharing is the primary reason anthropologists are interested in understanding group behavior in primates.

B. Correct. The passage explores gender relationships among primates and homes in on sharing as the central reason anthropologists want to study their behavior.

C. Wrong. Since the author makes it clear that the sharing among primates is not altruistically motivated, group behavior in primates cannot teach humans about the importance of altruism.

D. Wrong. The passage indicates that group behavior in primates can only be related to humans.

E. Wrong. The sexual behavior of primates (or humans for that matter) is not the primary focus of the passage; sex is mentioned as a byproduct of the main goal of anthropological studies on group behavior in primates: sharing.

Answer to Question 94:

The correct answer is "According to anthropologists, observing primates in Senegal is like opening a window to the world of understanding the behavior of early humans, particularly related to sharing."

One type of trope is a metaphor employed for rhetorical purposes - to either clarify or enhance a reader or listener's understanding of something. The first sentence uses a metaphor comparing anthropological research to a window that opens to knowledge and thus makes use of the trope rhetorical device.

Passage 39: Summary / Paraphrase

The passage is about bacterial resistance to antibiotics. The main idea is that even bacteria that are affected by antibiotics are capable of surviving an antibiotic onslaught. The main points are that (a) many antibiotic treatments work by targeting active bacteria, with the implication that they do so by cutting nutrients and (b) some bacteria are able to slow their growth rate into dormancy when their source of nutrients is threatened, thus rendering them immune to the antibiotic. The purpose of the passage is to explain how some bacteria resist antibiotics.

Answer to Question 95:

The correct answer is A and B.

A. Correct. Starvation causes the bacteria to stop growing and lie dormant.

B. Correct. The passage states that starving bacteria are immune to medications because they are dormant; most antibiotics are only effective against active bacteria.

C. Wrong. Starvation does not change bacteria's chemical composition according to the passage.

Passage 40: Summary / Paraphrase

The passage is about the phenomenon of ocean acidification. The main idea is that increasing acid levels in ocean waters are disrupting the growth of coral reefs that are vital to maintaining the diverse ecosystem of the ocean. There are several major points: (a) that increased levels of carbon dioxide in the atmosphere are leading to the acidification of the oceans due to the way the ocean absorbs atmospheric carbon dioxide (b) that increased acidification of ocean water prevents the proper growth of coral reefs and (c) the alteration of coral reefs could be disastrous for oceanic life, since coral reefs support a notable percentage of marine species. The main purpose of the passage is to explain and call to action; the process by which carbon dioxide affects the oceans is concisely explained and loaded rhetoric such as the use of terms like "threat" and "terrible catastrophe" indicates that there is an implied intention we take action on atmospheric carbon dioxide levels.

Answer to Question 96:

The correct answer is E.

A. Wrong. The ocean absorbs carbon from the atmosphere.

B. Wrong. While it is true that 25% of marine species depend on the coral reef ecosystem, low pH in the ocean does not mean they will all go extinct.

C. Wrong. The statement is correct except that low pH means high acidity and not low acidity and thus the answer is ultimately incorrect.

D. Wrong. While it is true that many types of coral reefs can grow in low pH environments, the passage nonetheless leads us to believe that the coral reef ecosystems are still in danger from acidification.

E. Correct. The information in the passage implies that since the base of the coral reefs cannot calcify in low pH environments the reefs as an aggregate will struggle to grow and this will harm the marine life they support.

Answer to Question 97:

The correct answer is E.

A. Wrong. While it is true that the passage delineates the dangers of carbon dioxide in the world's oceans, description is not a rhetorical strategy; the goal of rhetoric is always to persuade and not describe.

B. Wrong. While the information in the passage may stimulate an emotional response in the reader, the actual rhetorical goal of the passage is to persuade the reader of the harms of ocean acidification.

C. Wrong. Persuasion is always the goal of rhetoric and this passage seeks to persuade the reader that ocean acidification is harmful, but the answer needs to be more specific - the author ultimately wants to convey the danger that coral reefs are in as a result of ocean acidification.

D. Wrong. Again, a rhetorical goal must always be persuasive and not merely descriptive; therefore, explaining the specifics of pH levels' effect on coral reefs is not a rhetorical goal.

E. Correct. The rhetorical goal of the passage is to convince the reader that ocean acidification is harmful specifically because of the damage it does to coral reefs.

Answer to Question 98:

The correct answer is "This is an especially vital area of exploration since coral reefs are home to 25% of all marine species."

While the passage later goes on to describe how ocean acidification damages corals reefs, the primary importance of the coral reefs, from an ecological standpoint, is that they house 25% of the world's marine species.

Passage 41: Summary / Paraphrase

The passage is about the parasitic disease malaria. The main idea is that the pathology of malaria makes those affected by sickle-cell anemia immune. The main points are that (a) malaria requires access to the exterior of blood cells by using certain adhesive proteins and (b) that mutations to the hemoglobin of those affected by sickle cell anemia mean that they rarely, if ever, possess the adhesive proteins needed for the malaria parasite to establish itself. The purpose of the passage is to inform - the tone is mostly dry and factual.

Answer to Question 99:

The correct answers are A and C.

A. Correct. Sickle cell anemics are protected from malaria because of a hemoglobin mutation, but this mutation does not facilitate adhesin bonding, it impedes it. The author's contention is that sickle cell anemics are protected from malaria as a result of a hemoglobin mutation that impedes adhesin bonding and thus the author's contention would be incorrect if sickle cell anemic hemoglobin mutations facilitated adhesin bonding.

B. Wrong. Adhesins can sometimes attach to the blood cells of sickle cell anemics and therefore this statement merely reinforces the author's claim that adhesin adhesions occasionally occur in sickle cell anemics, but still not frequently enough to successfully transmit the malaria virus.

C. Correct. According to the information given in the passage, the malaria parasite is not able to infect the blood of sickle cell anemics; sickle cell anemics are immune to malaria and hence this statement would weaken the author's contention if true

Passage 42: Summary / Paraphrase

The passage is about how hormones influence primate behavior. The main idea is that exposure to oxytocin, known as the "love hormone", has been shown to increase altruistic behavior in monkeys. The main point is that since the monkeys are closely related to humans, study of the hormone's effects in the monkeys can help us better understand how it affects human behavior. There are minor points that underscore the effect of the hormone: (a) its effects on developing intimate relationships such as that between mother and child and (b) a specific instance of the prosocial behavior it helped to promote in the affected monkeys. The purpose of the passage is to explain and inform.

Answer to Question 100:

The correct answer is B.

A. Wrong. Humans may be closely related to the macaque but the passage does not indicate that oxytocin will affect humans in the exact same manner as the monkeys.

B. Correct. The information in the passage implies that studying oxytocin's effects on monkeys can be used to have deeper insight into human behavior related to the hormone.

C. Wrong. While oxytocin could theoretically be used for this purpose, the passage does not indicate that the information garnered from the study on the macaques will be used to create medication to treat antisocial behavior in humans.

D. Wrong. The passage actually infers that scientists have already produced oxytocin synthetically for research purposes.

E. Wrong. The passage makes it clear that studying macaques could have long-term benefits on understanding humans relative to oxytocin.

Answer to Question 101:

The correct answer is A.

A. Correct. The passage indicates that prosocial choices are about sharing, which clearly benefits the well-being of two parties, in this case the two macaques.

B. Wrong. The passage states that prosocial choices.

C. Wrong. The passage does not indicate that prosocial choices play a role in the creation of social hierarchies.

D. Wrong. According to the passage, prosocial choices are the result of changes in hormonal patterns and thus do not influence them.

E. Wrong. The passages states that prosocial choices are often made under the influence of oxytocin.

Answer to Question 102:

The correct answer is "Oxytocin, also known as the love hormone, bonds mothers to their children and promotes intimacy and relationships in various species including humans." This sentence explicates why oxytocin is vital to the forging of social connections among species.

Passage 43: Summary / Paraphrase

The passage is about the biological causes of psychiatric disorders. The main idea is that scientists hope to be able to combine their findings about the RNF123 gene with a holistic understanding of mental health. The main points are (a) that the RNF123 gene affects the hippocampus and (b) that the hippocampus is altered in people with depression and (c) that scientists are looking at this information along with the experiences of patients to form a fuller understanding of the issues affecting mental health. The purpose of the passage is to present an objective account of a current trend in the life sciences.

Answer to Question 103:

The correct answer is "Scientists have taken another step in the direction of better understanding the biological underpinnings of various psychiatric disorders."

While the passage ultimately indicates that scientists are interested in both genes and environment, at first their main interest is discerning the biological factors underlying mental health issues.

Passage 44: Summary / Paraphrase

The passage is about stem cell research. The main idea is that while some scientists have promoted stem cells as having "miracle cure" potential, there is considerable trepidation about using stem cells in both the scientific community and among laymen. The main points are (a) that stem cells have been posited as a potential treatment for a wide variety of diseases and conditions (b) that there is opposition to stem cell research from those who see it as a disruption of the natural order of life and (c) there is caution from some scientists who worry that stem cell research may not be as effective as some claim. The main purpose of the passage is to briefly summarize the chief arguments for and against the use of stem cell research.

Answer to Question 104:

The correct answer is C.

A. Wrong. The passage does not claim that mitosis is specifically useful because it allows scientists to use stem cells in abundance.

B. Wrong. The passage does not claim that stem cells are stronger after mitosis.

C. Correct. Diverse cells, the byproducts of mitosis, can be controlled by scientists and manipulated towards diverse medical outcomes, thus rendering mitosis a key factor in stem cell research.

D. Wrong. The passage makes it clear that mitosis is important to stem cell research because it engenders a diversity of cells.

E. Wrong. This answer is true but more information should be given to explain exactly why diversified cells are useful in stem cell research; the reason why and not just the fact that diverse cells are useful to stem cell therapy specifies the importance of mitosis.

Answer to Question 105:

The correct answer is D.

A. Wrong. The author agrees that stem cell therapy is a highly sensitive issue given that he or she highlights the fact that many people believe stem cell therapy exploits human life.

B. Wrong. The author states that many medical doctors believe that stem cell therapy can have adverse effects despite the fact that it is an extremely useful treatment method. Thus, the benefits of stem cell therapy are sometimes overshadowed by its pitfalls.

C. Wrong. The author would agree that the outcomes of scientific research do not always align with social mores since stem cell therapy is a successful treatment method that also causes social controversy.

D. Correct. For the author to believe that the exploitation of natural life was the elephant in the room of the stem cell therapy debate, he or she would have to be anti-stem cell therapy; "the white elephant in the room" is a metaphor in the English language that serves as a rhetorical strategy to underline a glaring truth that is being ignored. Since the author's tone is objective regarding stem cell therapy as a whole in the passage, the author would not agree with the elephant in the room idiom for stem cell therapy, in this case because that would mean the author also believes that stem cell therapy is the exploitation of life.

E. Wrong. The entire passage is about how stem cells regenerate and can be used to treat a diverse variety of medical conditions and thus the author would agree that stem cells underscore the regenerative nature of the human body.

Answer to Question 106:

The correct answers are A and C.

A. Correct. The passage states that some people believe that stem cell therapy exploits and interferes with natural life even though it is a very effective method of medical treatment.

B. Wrong. The passage does not explicitly state that those opposed to stem cell therapy believe it promotes a culture of death.

C. Correct. The passage states that scientists worry about the potential for stem cell therapy to worsen various medical conditions despite its ability to treat a wide array of medical issues.

Passage 45: Summary / Paraphrase

The passage is about human genetics. The main idea is that the long-held view that our DNA was immutable has been challenged by recent evidence that suggests our genetics can in fact change in response to environmental factors. The major points are: (a) that epigenetic has discovered that a stimulus can alter a gene after conception, and that through cell division, the alterations in the gene can be passed on to further generations (b) that experimental evidence suggests that when pregnant rats are subjected to negative stimulus, it will cause behavioral problems in the baby (c) by studying and testing the genetic code of identical twins, scientists can determine the extent of genetic alteration. The purpose of the passage is to inform the reader about a cutting-edge area of genetics, and also to invite some speculation in the implications of these discoveries. The tone is largely factual, showing no obvious bias.

Answer to Question 107:

D is correct. Nascent literally means, "beginning to exist" and therefore epigenetic "being in its early stages of development" is the only correct answer. No other answer given contains a synonym for nascent.

Answer to Question 108:

The correct answer is B.

A. Wrong. The passage makes it clear that the DNA methylation profiles of twins are important to epigenetic since they allow scientists to compare and understand epigenetic changes to identical DNA.

B. Correct. The main reason it is important to collect the DNA methylation profiles of identical twins is so that scientists can see the epigenetic changes that have occurred in identical DNA.

C. Wrong. While it is likely true that DNA methylation profiles gives scientists a better understanding of the process of cell division, this answer does not account for why it is specifically important for scientists to study the DNA methylation profiles of identical twins.

D. Wrong. The passage does not indicate that DNA methylation profiles help scientists understand how twins inherit their DNA; the passage places emphasis on scientists investigating what happens to the already inherited DNA in twins.

E. Wrong. This statement is correct given the information in the passage but it does not give enough information about why it is important to specifically study the DNA methylation profiles of identical twins.

Answer to Question 109:

The correct answers are A and B.

A. Correct. The passage states that identical twins' identical DNA can help scientists identify DNA methylation patterns.

B. Correct. The passage clearly states that scientists use twins to better understand the DNA methylation process.

C. Wrong. The passage does not mention anything about twins' looks and their relationship to phenotypic expressions.

Answer to Question 110:

The correct answer is "It throws a wrench into Darwin's theory of evolution since it demonstrates how evolutionary changes can occur within in one generation instead of spanning thousands of years."

Darwin's theory of evolution is one of the foundation stones of modern biology and since epigenetic calls this theory into question by calming that evolutionary changes can occur within only one generation, the entire field of biology may have to reevaluate the way it conceptualizes the history of life on the planet.

Practice Set 3 – Business

Passage 46:

Answer to Question 111:

The correct answer is "Thus, as I believe, natural selection will tend in the long run to reduce any part of the organization, as soon as it becomes, through changed habits, superfluous."

The author quotes Darwin's theory that natural selection is responsible for the reduction of a feature due to disuse. The author, on the other hand, suggests that an organism may select the most beneficial use of features it already has using the possibility of weak-winged birds' choice to live on an island where it is more likely to survive than if it had to fly great distances to seek food and shelter.

Answer to Question 112:

The correct answer is A. The author provides an example of birds with weak wings who may choose an island for their habitat. It is to their advantage to avoid long flights to obtain food and shelter. An island habitat would insure their survival. Answer choice B is incorrect because it is contrary to the theory of natural selection, which states that features that are not useful for survival in a particular habitat will eventually be diminished. Organisms, in their quest for survival, cannot afford to allocate nutrition to maintaining a feature that serves little or no purpose. Answer choice C is incorrect because the author speaks only of these parts becoming diminished. In fact, he suggests that these diminished features may serve as an impetus for the organization to seek a more favorable habitat.

Answer to Question 113:

The correct answer is D. In the fourth sentence of the passage, the author states that the reduction of less useful features is no more important than the development of positive features. As features become less useful, they are diminished, and those features that are useful become more developed. Answer choice A is incorrect because the author does not mention the extinction of entire organizations, only the diminishment or disappearance of features that become less useful. Answer choice B is incorrect because the author does not address evolution, per se, or mutation. Neither does he mention genetic influences or hereditary traits, so answer choice C is also incorrect. The author briefly mentions adaptation to an environment in the last sentence of the passage, but not as an aspect of economy in organizations. Answer choice E is incorrect.

Answer to Question 114:

The correct answer is B. The author asks the question to provoke consideration of other explanations beyond that of Darwin for the diminishing or strengthening of features of organizations. Answer choice A is incorrect, because the author is not criticizing Darwin's theory. He acknowledges the validity of Darwin's claim but thinks that other explanations for changes in an organization's features have merit as well. Answer choice C is incorrect because the author is not treating Darwin's theory with disrespect. Although the author believes that Darwin's theory may be valid in many regards, he does not display reverence for the man or his theory. He wishes to amend it. Reverence implies awe. Answer choice D is incorrect. The author does not display cynicism toward Darwin. He does not question Darwin's sincerity or his motives, so answer choice E is incorrect.

Passage 47: Summary / Paraphrase

The passage is about the importance of time management in business. The main idea is that inefficient time management among higher management may lead a business to stagnate. The major point is that in spite of many platitudes about the importance of effective time management, many business leaders actually use their time poorly. A minor point reinforces this notion by explaining how poor time management affects a business. The purpose of the passage is to raise awareness of the harmful effects of poor time management.

Answer to Question 115:

The correct answer is C.

A. Wrong. The passage pinpoints upper management as an area of a business where time is most often poorly managed, so the reader can infer that upper management in is in general disorganized because the ability to distribute time correctly is a feature of the ability to organize.

B. Wrong. The passage indicates that time management is a principle of business and thus it can be inferred that businesses struggle to implement their theoretical maxims in actuality.

C. Correct. While the author does draw attention to the fact that sayings like "time is money" highlight a link between time management and money, there is not enough information given to draw the conclusion that time management skills are analogous to money management skills.

D. Wrong. The passage claims that businesses lacking in time management skills also lack the ability to be self-evaluative which often leads to poor leadership, thus poor leadership is a major indicator that an organization is also time management deficient.

E. Wrong. The passage points out the fact that businesses stagnate when they lack organizational self-reflexivity and thus the reader can infer that businesses to better when they are able to critically evaluate their own methods and practices.

Answer to Question 116:

The correct answers are A and B.

A. Correct. People in upper management should be the most responsible and time conscious given their position of power, but according to the passage they are the party that lacks critical time management skills and hence the understanding of the principles of business management - a clear incongruence.

B. Correct. Despite the fact that people know how valuable time is, as evidenced by the aphorisms" time is money" and "time is of the essence", businesses still commit the crime of wasting time.

C. Wrong. While wasting time may indeed lead to making poor business decisions, this is not a paradox; poor time management would logically lead to poor decision making. A paradox would require that the result was in logical conflict with the original statement.

Passage 48:

Answer to Question 117:

The correct answer is E. The phrase, investments in human capital and financial capital, suggests more than one meaning for the word capital in this passage. The correct choice should include definitions of both human and financial capital as elements to invest in a business. Both definitions in the answer must be correct. In choice A, the second definition could be correct, but the first part is not correct. In choice B, the first definition could be correct in a broad sense if one considered humans as an asset to a business, but the second part, referring to shares in a business, is not correct. The first part of C defines capital as the money that is left after the bills have been paid not as something to invest, eliminating this as the correct answer. D is incorrect because it defines an investment that already exists. E is the best choice; wealth available for use in the production of further wealth implies investing it, and the abilities and skills of any individual define human capital.

Answer to Question 118:

The correct answer is C. The phrase, relatively inexperienced people with limited capital, supports choice C. Facebook is likely information-intensive, and it is a form of social media, but those ideas do not address the model of limited capital and inexperience leading to success. Value and salary are not synonymous; lower value of labor does not mean that the laborers are being paid low salaries, so E is incorrect. The reader is not given enough information to determine that Facebook is not productive, eliminating D as the correct choice.

Passage 49:

Answer to Question 119:

The correct answer is C. Choice A is incorrect, as the statement is not an insight; it is a way of conducting business. Choice B is incorrect, as this is not a trait of businessmen; it is a strategy for selling products.

Choice D is incorrect, as the sentence does not provide specific financial benefits. Choice E is incorrect, as the sentence does not provide a negation. Choice C is correct, as the sentence suggests that giving goods for a low sum (price) is a good strategy for businessmen, as this will result in the business succeeding long-term.

Answer to Question 120:

The correct answer is D. Choice A is incorrect, as this is a synonym for liberal, but it does not fit the meaning of the sentence. Choice B is incorrect, because larger than life has nothing to do with the word liberal. Choice C fits the meaning of the sentence, but it is not a synonym for liberal. Choice E is incorrect, as thoughtful is not a synonym for liberal. Choice D is correct, as generous is a synonym for liberal, and because generous fits the sentence.

Answer to Question 121:

The correct answer is C. Choice A is incorrect, as instituting a mediation department for the company would have no effect on the company's relationship with clients, which is the focus of the passage. Choice B is incorrect, as this may help employees, but the point of the passage is to run a business and treat customers well in order to succeed. Choice C is correct. The passage cautions against driving a sharp bargain and urges kindness and liberality when dealing with customers. A generous refund policy would be a practical example of this advice.

Answer to Question 122:

The correct answer is "The man who gives the greatest amount of goods of a corresponding quality for the least sum… will generally succeed best in the long run."

The first sentence is incorrect as it recommends only the abstract qualities of politeness and civility. Sentence 2 is incorrect. While it mentions several specific strategies, these are noted as much less essential than the somewhat vague instructions to not treat customers abruptly. Sentence 3 recommends the abstract qualities of kindness and liberality and is incorrect. Sentence 4 gives the most specific and concrete instructions to provide the most goods for the least sum and is correct. Sentence 5 presents the very general and non-specific "Golden Rule" and is incorrect. Sentence 6 advises against driving sharp bargains but is not very specific about what this entails and is thus incorrect.

Passage 50:

Answer to Question 123:

The correct answer is E. The passage uses first person, so the language is not formal enough for choices B, C, and D. Choice A is incorrect, both because of the first person use and because the passage contains too much specific data for a newspaper article. Choice E is correct, as this passage would suit a guide explaining land laws to new citizens.

Answer to Question 124:

The correct answer is C. Choice A is incorrect, as the reader must have a basic understanding of the concept of land titles to understand the passage. Choice B is incorrect, as the reader must be familiar with the law of inheritance to fully understand the passage. Choices D and E are incorrect, as the reader must be familiar with the relationship between trusts and trustees as well as the basic concept of land rights to fully understand the passage. Choice C is correct, as the passage does not discuss or pertain to selling shares of companies.

Answer to Question 125:

The correct answer is B. Choice A is incorrect, as the author states that it is lengthy, but moves past this fact. Choice C is incorrect, as the passage only discusses one type of law. Choice D is incorrect, as the passage mentions certain requirements, but they are not the main point of the passage. Choice E is incorrect, as the passage mentions no downsides to acting as trustee. Choice B is correct, as the passage summarizes the process for transferring land rights.

Answer to Question 126:

The correct answer is B. Choice A is incorrect, as the passage only mentions one country. Choice C is incorrect, as the passage never makes the point that it is too complicated to own land. Choice B is correct, as the land laws for England are presented as too extreme, so it is reasonable to think that they should be revised.

Passage 51:

Answer to Question 127:

The correct answer is B. Choices A, D, and E are incorrect, as the passage never actually mentions priests, scientists, or politicians, just religion, science, and politics. Choice C is incorrect, as the passage clearly states that misers are the worst kind of money-getters, because they hoard money instead of spending it. Choice B is correct, as money-getters are more important than laypeople, but misers are even worse than everyday people, because misers hoard money and fail to perform the tasks of money-getters.

Answer to Question 128:

The correct answer is A. Choice B is incorrect, as the author expresses two opinions based on his judgment of others. First, he thinks that misers are inferior to money-getters because misers hoard, showing that he does not respect hoarding. Second, the author mentions that different fields have hypocrites, which shows that the author does not approve of people who are hypocrites. Choice C is incorrect, as the author refers to arts and sciences as "noblest fruits;" since art and science are clearly not fruits, the author is speaking in a metaphor, which is figurative language. Choice D is incorrect, as the passage uses a formal, academic tone. Choice E is incorrect, as the passage does present an analogy comparing hypocrisy in religion and demagoguery in politics to miserly behavior among "money-getters". Choice A is correct, as the author does not draw on social standings or hierarchies to make his point: the passage never talks about class differences or social hierarchies in the context of money-getting.

Answer to Question 129:

The correct answer is B. Choice A is incorrect, as the passage does not suggest that arts and sciences are more important than money-getters. Choice C is incorrect, as the passage does not discuss the moral struggles that money-getters may have. Choice B is correct, as money-getters should be praised for benefiting society, but people should not approve of misers and their hoarding.

Answer to Question 130:

The correct answer is "To them, in a great measure, are we indebted for our institutions of learning and of art, our academies, colleges and churches."

Only the third sentence states that money-getters are responsible for bringing the arts and sciences into society, which money-getters have done by bringing more money into society, which can be used for things other than necessities. The third sentence is correct.

Passage 52: Summary / Paraphrase

The passage is about the effects of certain economic policies on particular types of economies. The main idea is that developing economies need to balance the potential risks and rewards of liberalizing their capital markets. There are three major points:

a) First, capital market liberalization carries the risk of capital flight and other potential economic problems

b) Second, failure to liberalize capital markets can leave developing countries behind

c) Third, in light of these risks and benefits, developing economies need to tread a careful line between too much and too little regulation

The passage seems mainly designed to inform rather than convince -although the author suggests that regulators must take care not to over- or under-regulate capital markets, the claim isn't presented as something that regulators should do, merely as something that economists suggest. Chile is discussed to provide a concrete example of the sorts of challenges that developing economies face when making decisions on regulating their capital markets.

Answer to Question 131:

The correct answer is D. Answering this question should be fairly straightforward, based on the passage. Skimming the passage should give you a clear sense that has to do with a very particular sort of economic policy for developing countries. Realizing that rules out A and B, which in turn rules out E. That leaves only C and D as potential answers. Although the passage mentions Chile, it is not specifically about Chile, ruling out C. This leaves D as the only option.

Answer to Question 132:

The correct answers are B and C. Although you might infer from the passage that free market capitalism is the best system, such a claim is far beyond the scope of the passage; therefore, A cannot be correct. At first glance, you might think that only one of B and C could be right, since they seem to be contradictory. However, the passage indicates that capital market liberalization has both positive and negative potential for developing economies. B and C suggest the respective risks and benefits that the passage indicates attend capital market liberalization - they are therefore the best choices to answer the question.

Answer to Question 133:

The correct answer is E. The first two options are absurd and obviously incorrect - the passage is clearly not mainly about Chile, and there is no mention of dictatorship anywhere in the passage. Option C is true, since the passage does mention that "Chile restricted borrowing from abroad in an attempt to prevent capital from flowing in and out of its economy too rapidly" suggesting that Chile faced some of the negative consequences of deregulating its capital markets, but glancing back at the paragraph where Chile is mentioned, you can note that Chile has also faced pressure to liberalize, so although true, option C in not clearly the right answer. There is some indication in the passage that D might be true, but it seems beyond the scope of the passage. Option E, however, accurately suggests that Chile is mentioned as an example of the sorts of challenges that developing nations face when trying to decide whether to liberalize their capital markets. Therefore, option E is the choice that fits most logically with the rest of the passage.

Answer to Question 134:

The correct answer is "By allowing foreign capital to flow into developing nations, capital market liberalization can help to finance foreign trade and domestic investment opportunities that would likely be impossible otherwise." and "Foreign capital can easily flow out of a country as fast as it flows in, putting the nation's financial sector under strain and adversely affecting foreign exchange rates."

The best options are found in the second paragraph: "By allowing foreign capital to flow into developing nations, capital market liberalization can help to finance foreign trade and domestic investment opportunities that would likely be impossible otherwise" gives an indication of what the positive consequences of liberalization can be while " Foreign capital can easily flow out of a country as fast as it flows in, putting the nation's financial sector under strain and adversely affecting foreign exchange rates" suggests the corresponding dangers. To find the correct sections to highlight, you will want to focus your attention on parts of the passage that discuss the issue in fairly general terms. The first paragraph is too general, and doesn't give any substantive explanation of the pros and cons. The third paragraph is a specific example of the dilemma, so it is not general enough. The last paragraph appears somewhat promising, and it does reiterate the positive and negative consequences of deregulation; however, the two sentences (listed above) from the second paragraph are better for actually explaining the potential benefits and risks and are thus the best choices to answer the question.

Answer to Question 135:

The correct answers are B and C. Remember, that the question asks you to identify the options that are NOT TRUE of the passage. Looking over the options, A seems likely to be true—the passage indicates that although there are accompanying risks, opening capital markets is crucial to economic development. This leaves B and C. B is obviously not true, as the general tenor of the passage and especially the points of the last paragraph make clear. C is a little less obvious; however, given the overall tone of the passage which suggests that an influx of foreign capital has both positive and negative aspects, it seems unlikely that it ALWAYS has a good effect. Therefore, C is also not true of the passage.

Passage 53: Summary / Paraphrase

The passage is about the aim of business. The main idea is that while a net profit can only come about after the original capital outlay is recovered, net profit can actually be viewed as the creation of new capital. The major points are: (a) that net profit is the share of revenue left over after expenses are covered (b) that even with the payment of dividends; net profit is often reinvested in the business as capital. The purpose of the passage is to demonstrate that the true aim of business is the creation of capital.

Answer to Question 136:

The correct answer is B. Answer choice A is incorrect. Gross profits lead to greater net profits only if money remains after all expenses are met. That same reasoning makes answer choice B correct. If a business has money left over after subtracting initial capital from gross profits, they have made a net profit. Investors may benefit from spending their dividends, but they may also benefit from reinvesting or saving their dividends. The word "most" makes answer choice C incorrect.

Answer to Question 137:

The correct answer is D. The only way to increase net profits is to reduce expenses. Freezing wages means that they stay the same, so this action cannot lead to greater net profit, making A an incorrect choice. Concealing losses is not effective, because the losses will show up in the inventory, so B is not correct. Purchasing less inventory simply means that a business will have less inventory at the end of the period but has no effect on net profit. Answer C is not correct. Staying open more hours may generate more sales, but it also generates more expenses in wages and utilities like heat and electricity, so E is the wrong answer. The best answer is D. Spending less on electricity affects the bottom line and increases the net profitability of a business.

Passage 54:

Answer to Question 138:

The correct answer is C. Choice A is incorrect, as the passage never mentions developing management strategies. Choice B is incorrect, as the passage says that men should be systematic, but retain balance. Choice D is incorrect, as this is true, but it is not the point of the passage. Choice E is incorrect, as the passage does not mention respect for others; it suggests that organized businessmen will be respected, but this is not the main point of the passage. Choice C is correct, as the passage mentions that people should be systematic, but also says that they must retain balance in their lives.

Answer to Question 139:

The correct answer is D. Choice A is incorrect, as bedraggled is not a synonym for slipshod. Choice B is incorrect, as slovenly is a synonym of slipshod, but it does not fit the meaning of the sentence. Choice C is incorrect, as it is not a synonym for slipshod. Choice E is incorrect, as painstakingly is an antonym of slipshod. Choice D is correct, as it is the closest in meaning to slipshod.

Answer to Question 140:

The correct answer is A. The author's claim is that being systematic and organized in moderation will help people become better businessmen and work most efficiently. Choice B is incorrect, as the author suggests that working on one task at a time is most efficient. The author does not say that taking breaks will help efficiency, so the validity of breaks increasing efficiency does not matter for this claim. Choice C is incorrect, as the passage does not depend on people learning to be organized early in life. Choice D is incorrect, as the author suggests that a routine and a way of organizing are both important. Choice E is incorrect, as while this might be true, the passage discusses being systematic as an individual, so working with others is not relevant to the author's point. Choice A is correct, as the passage assumes that being systematic will always help people work better.

Answer to Question 141:

The correct answer is A. Choice B is incorrect, as the passage says that productive people will work on one task at a time. Choice C is incorrect, as nothing in the passage says that one's organizational methods cannot change over time and the passage cautions against being too systematic. Choice A is correct, as the passage implies by noting that the organized businessman will not be at "loose ends" and will have time for leisure activities.

Passage 55: Summary / Paraphrase

The passage is about changing demographics in the workforce. The main idea is that people are staying more active in the workforce later into life than ever before. The major points are: (a) that adults at or near retirement age make up a significantly greater proportion of the workforce than they did a decade ago and (b) that even adults who have officially retired are more likely to remain actively engaged in paid or unpaid work than ever before. Two minor points explore the reasons behind the major points: (a) that a variety of practical concerns are keeping older workers in the workforce and (b) that shifting concepts of retirement and the desires of older adults are changing earlier notions of career. The main purpose of the passage is to inform the reader and explain some of the factors behind a demographic shift in the workforce.

Answer to Question 142:

The correct answer is D. It might be logical to conclude that older workers' remaining in the workforce for more years means that there are fewer job opportunities for younger workers or those trying to enter the workforce for the first time. If, however, the percentage of the total population represented by workers aged 55-64 is small, it should have little detrimental effect on younger workers' ability to obtain employment. The correct answer is D.

Passage 56: Summary / Paraphrase

The passage is about the way that countries are responding to the threat of global warming. The main idea is that the response has been mixed. The major points are: (a) the United States, historically the largest producer of greenhouse gases, has not acted aggressively on climate change because of fear of the economic consequences (b) other developed nations have been more successful in curbing emissions through the use of nuclear power and cleaner natural gas (c) developing economies such as China and India are poised to become major producers of greenhouse gases and also have the possibility of developing the infrastructure for cleaner energy. The main purpose of the passage is to give an overview of how different countries are responding to global warming.

Answer to Question 143:

The correct answer is A. A fiat is an order or a decree. A is the correct answer. Because the government has decreed it, the use of paper money is acceptable, or sanctioned. Most countries have their own national currency. These characteristics of currency result from the government's decree. Solvent refers to having enough money to satisfy one's creditors.

Answer to Question 144:

The correct answer is B. The writer says that gold has no innate quality that makes it more suitable than anything else as a foundation for a monetary system. It could just as easily be tin or copper or coal. The choice is arbitrary, answer B. This arbitrary choice makes both A and D incorrect answers. Answer choice A contradicts the writer's statement that a money system based on precious metals is not necessarily more stable than one based on paper. In the same vein, gold is no more or less unreliable than any other foundation of a monetary system, making answer choice D incorrect. There is nothing in the paragraph to suggest that Latin America has greater resources for gold than other areas in the world, making C incorrect. The paragraph implies that gold was highly valued in Europe before the Spaniards and Portuguese visited Latin America, so E is not correct.

Answer to Question 145:

The correct answer is B. The value of existing Van Gogh paintings is unlikely to fall or rise. Examples in the passage show how the value of precious metals can be manipulated by controlling the supply, but, because Van Gogh is dead and cannot create new paintings, all existing paintings and any newly discovered works would remain rare and very valuable. The paintings would be carefully examined to determine their authenticity; they would not necessarily be declared counterfeit. Donating the paintings would have tax advantages only after ownership is determined. The value of the paintings would be determined only after thorough examination, making B the correct answer.

Answer to Question 146:

The correct answers are B and C. Both B and C are acceptable choices because they cause inflation. Advanced Placement classes are generally worth more points toward a GPA than are regular classes. As a result, they devalue the high grades that students earn in regular classes. Colleges that award supplementary points to SAT scores earned by students from culturally deprived areas devalue the true scores of other students. Answer choice A is not correct; when items are put on sale, the value of a dollar actually increases. End-of-season sales are temporary, and their intention is to get rid of old merchandise to make room for new items.

Answer to Question 147:

The correct answer is C. A medium of exchange allows individuals, groups, businesses, etc., to engage in transactions. The most common transaction involves exchanging money for goods or services. In the example in answer C, the transaction involves an exchange of services making it the only correct answer. The coupon in answer A is a gift; nothing is expected in return. Answer B only benefits the student. There is no exchange, eliminating it as the correct answer.

Answer to Question 148:

The correct answer is "Even without such a monstrous kick in the teeth, the price of gold tends to fluctuate drastically, dropping or rising relative to relatively stable fiat currencies."

Because the price of gold fluctuates on a daily basis, currency values based on the gold standard would, in theory, also change daily. Businesses would be challenged to purchase inventory if they sold their goods at today's value and had to replace the goods after the price of gold had risen. Consumers would face uncertainty in their buying power from day to day.

Passage 57: Summary / Paraphrase

The passage is about changes to patent law. The main idea is that while the privatization of research was designed to promote innovation, it has had some adverse effects as well. The major points are: (a) the government allowed commercial interests and public institutions to collaborate and share revenues in order to foster innovation (b) firms now have the right to deny foreign competitors the right to produce generic versions of products for which they hold the patent (c) the exclusivity of the licensing process makes it difficult for poorer countries to produce generic drugs to combat diseases such as AIDS. The purpose of the passage is to raise awareness of a flaw in the way the patent process works.

Answer to Question 149:

The correct answer is D. To equivocate is to use ambiguous or unclear language. The context of the passage suggests that America has difficulty deciding between economic or humanitarian concerns. The best word to express that behavior is vacillate, answer D. Hesitate would be correct if they eventually made a decision. To prevaricate is to lie. Pontification is similar to preaching, and to abrogate is to abolish. None of these other words are suitable choices in this context, eliminating answer choices A, B, C, and E.

Passage 58: Summary / Paraphrase

The passage is about the way that countries are responding to the threat of global warming. The main idea is that the response has been mixed. The major points are: (a) the United States, historically the largest producer of greenhouse gases, has not acted aggressively on climate change because of fear of the economic consequences (b) other developed nations have been more successful in curbing emissions through the use of nuclear power and cleaner natural gas (c) developing economies such as China and India are poised to become major producers of greenhouse gases and also have the possibility of developing the infrastructure for cleaner energy. The main purpose of the passage is to give an overview of how different countries are responding to global warming.

Answer to Question 150:

The correct answer is D. Rapid growth is a challenge. It is easier to use the technologies that already exist to meet the demands of a growing economy. Stopping to install cleaner and more efficient means of production would slow the economy. The information in this passage makes no mention of the work force, so A is not the correct answer choice. There is no evidence that they are reluctant to use examples set by other countries or that they are unaware of more efficient technologies, eliminating B and C as correct answers. The passage does not reveal any ignorance about global warming on the parts of the emerging economies, eliminating E as a correct answer.

Passage 59: Summary / Paraphrase

The passage is about measuring GDP. The main idea is that although economists prefer to calculate GDP using purchasing power parity (PPP), doing so is difficult. The major points are (a) that computing a PPP exchange rate is difficult, since it is not always possible to find equivalent sets of goods and services to base the calculation off and (b) some countries do not provide data on PPP, making GDP calculations imprecise. The purpose of the passage is to explain the challenges economists face when calculating GDP.

Answer to Question 151:

The correct answer is E. Another way of stating the information in the last sentence of the passage is to say that the OER measure is a fraction of the PPP measure, which would make the difference between the OER- and PPP-denominated GDP values for developing countries generally much greater. This eliminates answer choice A as the correct one. The reader would expect different results for industrialized countries, so answer choice B cannot be correct. This difference cannot be calculated for countries who do not participate in the World Bank's PPP project, so both C and D can be eliminated as correct answer choices. Because wealthy industrialized nations have products similar to those in the United States, it is easier for economists to assign US-dollar values to their goods and services. As a result, the difference between OER- and PPP- denominated values is likely to be smaller. E is the correct answer choice.

Passage 60: Summary / Paraphrase

The passage is about employers' concern with their employees' emotional attitudes. The main idea is that certain leadership behaviors can contribute to making employees more efficient. The major points are that (a) research indicates that employees tend to be more productive and creative when their work experience is positive and (b) that leadership that develops the meaning of work tasks and invites active engagement with projects fosters a positive work environment. The purpose of the passage is to persuade the reader to adopt the leadership practices described by explaining the positive effects of those practices.

Answer to Question 152:

The correct answer is A.

A. Correct. The author uses deductive reasoning to underscore why improving the inner work lives of employees improves their performance in the work place.

B. Wrong. Pathos rhetoric is a persuasive strategy based on ethics and the character or reliability of the author. Since the reader has no information about the author to go on, and the author does not specifically make claims about improving the inner work life of the employee from a distinctly ethical dimension, the passage does not make use of pathos as a rhetorical strategy.

C. Wrong. The author uses both deductive reasoning and a dispassionate tone to appeal to the importance of improving inner work the work place environment. Since ethos is a rhetorical appeal to the emotions, it cannot be applied as the rhetorical strategy of the passage in question.

D. Wrong. The author does not make comparisons to illuminate the importance of improving workplace conditions for employees; the author only deductively deduces why it is important to improve the inner work life of the employee.

E. Wrong. The author does not use narrative, or a recounting, to shed light on why improving workplace conditions benefits the inner work life of the employee and thus does not make use of narrative rhetoric.

Passage 61: Summary / Paraphrase

The passage is about the spending habits of men. The main idea is that men tend to spend more liberally if they live in a region with a disproportionately high male population than if they live in a region with relative gender equilibrium. The main idea is supported by the mention of a relevant study. The purpose of the passage is to inform, as indicated by the dispassionate rhetoric and clear summary of research findings.

Answer to Question 153:

The correct answer is C.

A. Wrong. The word dearth is not synonymous with abundance under any circumstances, regardless of the author's intent.

B. Wrong. While rarity can be a synonym for dearth, in this context dearth is more indicative of a higher rate of men than women and not the fact that women are rare.

C. Correct. The author uses this passage to discuss the implications of higher ratios of men than women on debt, and thus a dearth of women can be a synonym for a surplus of men.

D. Wrong. A total lack of women would mean that there were no women at all and the author clearly states that there are women, just less women than men.

E. Wrong. Paucity is synonymous with scarcity and thus not an adequate synonym in terms of the author's intention for dearth of women to indicate a surplus of men.

Passage 62: Summary / Paraphrase

The passage is about gender disparity in upper management. The main idea is that while women play an increasing role in the corporate world, they are far less likely to be represented in higher management. There are two major points: (a) that the gender disparity is not the result of explicit discrimination and (b) that the relative lack of women in high management positions can be attributed to a "covert bias" that can discourage women from advancing. There is a minor point that specifies an example of "covert bias": corporate policies on maternity leave that force women to choose between their career and having a family. The purpose of the passage is to explain - the passage tackles a known phenomenon and offers an explanation of why it is the case.

Answer to Question 154:

The correct answer is E.

A. Wrong. The passage does not discuss professional development and in fact infers that women have adequate professional development based on their ability to rise to the management level.

B. Wrong. The passage states that the attrition of female employees occurs after they have reached the management level, and thus women have the ability to reach the management level but are typically unable to rise beyond it.

C. Wrong. The passage does not state that U.S. businesses do not provide maternity leave, just that the maternity leave options do not allow women to easily reintegrate into the company.

D. Wrong. The passage does not mention anything about women's issues.

E. Correct. The passage states that U.S. businesses do not provide adequate maternity leave that allows for the successful re-entry of women into the company after their time off. Thus, it is difficult for women with children to balance family with work obligations and this impedes their ability to rise to the upper echelons of business organizations.

Passage 63: Summary / Paraphrase

The passage is about social entrepreneurship. The main idea is that social entrepreneurship is a form of doing business that places a higher value on serving the common good than traditional business practices. The main points are that (a) attitudes have shifted so that people now demand businesses to conduct themselves in a more socially conscious fashion and (b) social entrepreneurship is a corollary of these shifts. There is a minor point that socially responsible business can have positive economic outcomes, although it is not developed. The purpose of the passage is to inform.

Answer to Question 155:

The correct answer is C.

A. Wrong. The passage does not suggest that social entrepreneurs build better client relationships than traditional entrepreneurs. While it is true that social entrepreneurs must be adept at building relationships as means of promoting social capital, traditional entrepreneurs can be just as adept at creating client relationships as a means to the end of profit

B. Wrong. The passage clearly states that social entrepreneurs rely on the traditional principles of business and in the case of the passage above, axiom is analogous to principle.

C. Correct. It can be inferred from the passage that social entrepreneurs are more concerned with quality of life than their traditional entrepreneur counterparts because their main objective is to use business as a method of addressing social problems.

D. Wrong. The passage does not suggest that social entrepreneurs are more concerned with climate change.

E. Wrong. The passage delineates clear differences between the two categories, particularly in their conceptions of capital.

Answer to Question 156:

The correct answer is C.

A. Wrong. The author states that social capital is engendered by social dialogue and collaboration and thus the author would agree that it is a product of collaborative problem solving.

B. Wrong. The author states that social capital is the prominent feature that distinguishes social entrepreneurship from other business ventures and entrepreneurs and would thus agree that social capital is the salient feature of social entrepreneurship.

C. Correct. While it is true that social capital is a feature of entrepreneurship, the author would not agree that social capital is concrete or tangible; he or she describes it as the value of social relations which in and of itself cannot be materially embodied.

D. Wrong. The passage states that the principles of business management are used to create social relations and social capital.

E. Wrong. Since the passages states that social capital facilitates economic results, the author would clearly agree that it has monetary value.

Answer to Question 157:

The correct answer is E.

A. Wrong. The author clearly gives enough information to define social capital in stating that cooperation and social relationships facilitate economic growth.

B. Wrong. The author intends social capital as capital in the traditional sense that it refers to financial assets and thus it does not mean community building.

C. Wrong. The author intends social capital as capital in the traditional sense that refers to financial assets and thus it does not mean relationship building.

D. Wrong. The author intends social capital as capital in the traditional sense that refers to financial assets and thus it does not mean social problems.

E. Correct. The passage indicates that social capital is the monetary result of people cooperating and building relationships in order to reach a goal.

Passage 64: Summary / Paraphrase

The passage is about changes in the way stock market trading is conducted. The main idea is that increased computerization in stock market trading has led to greater volatility in the global economy. The main points are (a) computerization has facilitated high frequency trades and (b) high frequency trading can disrupt global economic equilibrium without warning. The purpose of the passage is to inform and explain; the passage summarily informs the reader about the volatility caused by high frequency trading while explaining why this is the case.

Answer to Question 158:

The correct answer is B.

A. Wrong. Stocks being traded continuously does not account for the fact that a high volume of stocks are being traded digitally as is the case with high frequency trading per the information relayed by the author in the passage.

B. Correct. High frequency trading occurs rapidly and on a massive scale with the assistance of a computer program.

C. Wrong. While high frequency trading is computer generated, this answer does not account for the fact that the author makes it explicitly clear that high frequency trading entails the rapid transference of huge quantities of stocks.

D. Wrong. It is true that high frequency trading means that stocks are being traded rapidly but this does not account for the fact that stocks are also being traded digitally as is the case per the information relayed by the author in the passage.

E. Wrong. The passage makes it clear that high frequency trading is done by computers and not on the stock room floor.

Answer to Question 159:

The correct answer is C.

A. Wrong. The author does not indicate that the global market cannot be sustained if high frequency trading continues, just that high frequency trading is potentially dangerous to the global economic balance.

B. Wrong. The author makes it explicitly clear that high frequency trading has a negative impact on the global economic balance and thus it does not facilitate equilibrium, so this inference is not accurate.

C. Correct. The information in the passage indicates that the global economic balance can be affected quickly and in an unforeseen manner by high frequency trading, thus it can be inferred this will lead to trends of irregularity.

D. Wrong. The author gives plenty of information for the reader to make inferences regarding the global economic balance.

E. Wrong. The passage does not give indications regarding the state of the global economic balance before high frequency trading was introduced as a method on the stock market.

Passage 65: Summary / Paraphrase

The passage is about the evolution of criticisms leveled against capitalism. The main idea is that critiques of capitalism tend to evolve to match the concerns of the day. The major points are (a) that critics of capitalism carry over many older complaints and (b) in light of current concerns about the environment and resource depletion, current critiques of capitalism claim that it is a danger to the world itself as well as its social structures. The main purpose of the passage is to inform the reader about the history of the ways in which capitalism has been attacked. The tone of the passage suggests that the author may be trying to undermine current critiques of capitalism by lumping them with earlier critiques - the phrase "this is not a new phenomenon" seems dismissive in the context.

Answer to Question 160:

The correct answer is B.

A. Wrong. The passage does not in any way discuss consumption leading to the financial crisis of the late 2000s.

B. Correct. The passage states that consumption leads to the exploitation of natural resources that are in high demand and since the passage states that consumption is a main focus of capitalism it is thus also a negative attribute of capitalism.

C. Wrong. While the passage does mention that market failure (a result of destabilized markets) is often seen as a negative attribute of capitalism, it does not directly link consumption with this specific issue.

D. Wrong. The passage makes no claims directly linking imperialistic oppression and consumption within the paradigm of capitalism.

E. Wrong. While it is true that consumption leads to the overuse (and waste) of natural resources, the passage does not explicitly state that consumption leads directly to wasteful consumer choices, even if the reader can make this inference based on the information given in the text.

Passage 66: Summary / Paraphrase

The passage is about sustainability in business practice. The main idea is that businesses that show a robust concern for sustainability tend to outperform those that do not along a variety of metrics. The major points are: (a) sustainable business practice has become important for the public image of many firms, especially those in the West (b) that there is strong evidence to suggest that high-sustainability businesses tend to outperform low-sustainability businesses along traditional measures of profitability. Several minor points support the major points: (a) a Harvard study indicates that business success is determined by repeatedly meeting the expectations of both shareholders and stakeholders (b) that high-sustainability businesses are better at consistently meeting shareholder and stakeholder expectations over the long-run by being able to assimilate those needs into fiscally sound practices and (c) that due to their already-progressive practices, high-sustainability businesses are often more forward-thinking, and thus better able to attract long-term investment. The main purpose of the passage is to persuade the reader that sustainable business practices are better than non-sustainable practices by explaining why high-sustainability businesses tend to do better than low-sustainability businesses. While the rhetoric of the passage does not show overt bias, the fact that such strong emphasis is placed on the benefits of sustainability gives away the intent.

Answer to Question 161:

The correct answer is B.

A. Wrong. While this statement is true, it does not account for what the passage suggests: That sustainability is such a vital factor in business because it facilitates both relationships and success by executing a forward-thinking, integrative approach to enterprise.

B. Wrong. The passage claims that environmental issues are a component of business sustainability, but it does not suggest that sustainability relative to corporations will assuage the problems associated with climate change.

C. Correct. The passage suggests that sustainability is of paramount importance in business because it will keep businesses enduring and successful despite the fact that the environmental, economic, and social milieu is in a constant state of flux.

D. Wrong. While it is true that sustainability is primarily concerned with helping businesses balance social, economic, and environmental factors related to organizational success, this answer does not specifically account for why the passage suggests that sustainability itself is vitally important: its ability to keep a company healthy and at the cutting edge despite the fact that global social, economic and environmental issues are in a constant state of flux. Sustainability is fosters adaptability, which keeps companies successful.

E. Wrong. The passage claims that sustainability is a popular topic in public discourse but again this does not account for why sustainability is crucial to the success of business endeavors.

Answer to Question 162:

The correct answer is A.

A. Correct. The first paragraph in the passage states that long-term business success is determined by iterations or repetitions on business principles to meet the needs to both shareholders and stakeholders; thus an iterative process is also a repetitive process.

B. Wrong. While it is true that sustainable businesses are adaptable to social, fiscal and environmental changes, this answer does not relate to the iterative process since it does not mention iteration or repetition.

C. Wrong. The passage does not give any indication that an iterative process is a forward-thinking process; an iterative process is defined by the repetition of business principles to meet shareholder and stakeholder demands.

Answer to Question 163:

The correct answer is "This leads them to a kind of tunnel vision that misjudges the expectations of stakeholders; additionally, they undervalue the importance of building good relationships with employees, customers and members of civil society, causing their venture to stagnate."

This sentence explicates how low-sustainability organizations' over-focus on the financial aspects of enterprise contributes to their inability to perform as successfully as high-sustainability companies; their overemphasis on the fiscal side of enterprise causes their ventures to stagnate.

Passage 67: Summary / Paraphrase

The passage is about Just In Time (JIT) method. The main idea is that JIT method is adopted by many American businesses due to its various benefits. The purpose of the passage is to elaborate on the advantages of using JIT method.

Answer to Question 164:

The correct answer is A. B is not an advantage and C having buyer and customer work together is not necessarily an advantage.

Answer to Question 165:

The correct answer is "JIT can lead to increases in quality, productivity, and adaptability to change."

It lists general advantages of Just in Time. The other options present specific advantages which may not necessarily be applicable to other manufacturers.

Practice Set 4 - Everyday Topics

Passage 68: Summary / Paraphrase

The author speaks about the difference between Scottish and English soccer players and their respective prestige. The author clearly recognizes the English teams as carrying more prestige, but he still appreciates Scottish soccer. He does not present opposing views.

Answer to Question 166:

The correct answer is D. Choice A is incorrect, as this is the literal meaning of "laurels," but it does not fit the meaning of the sentence, because the football club was not given a wreath of vines. Choice B is incorrect, as this is not the correct meaning of laurel. Choice C is incorrect, as again, the author does not mean that the football club was given a wreath of vines. Choice E is incorrect, as the author does not mean that the football club has won a medal. Choice D is correct, as laurels are given to the winners of competitions, so it is acceptable to use laurels to refer to first place.

Answer to Question 167:

The correct answer is B. Choice A is incorrect, as he clearly states that the English clubs are superior. Choice C is incorrect, as he appears to appreciate the skill of football players. Choice D is incorrect, as the author clearly enjoys watching football and knows much about it. Choice E is incorrect, as the author remembers the scores of games that happened years ago. Choice B is correct, as the author says that he could not "grumble" at being replaced.

Answer to Question 168:

The correct answer is B. Choice A is incorrect, as the author did not leave the reader in suspense, so the sentence does not convey a sense of relief. Choice C is incorrect, as the sentence does not function as a transition, that is, a sentence connecting one paragraph to the following paragraph. Choice D is incorrect, as while the sentence shows the outcome, the sentence does more than just this: the point is to show that it will never be forgotten. Choice E is incorrect, as the sentence does not tie together the author's previous opinions about football; the sentence states the end result of a football game. Choice B is correct, as saying that ordinary men remember it emphasizes football's importance.

Answer to Question 169:

The correct answer is "I well remember when the Scottish clubs were entitled to enter into the arena, and great clubs such as Queen's Park, Glasgow Rangers, Cowlairs, Heart of Midlothian entered in the lists against the best clubs that prevailed at the time in England."

The first paragraph is written entirely without using the first person. The first sentence of the second paragraph shows the author using first person, which is new to the passage. This shift shows a change in style from more formal writing (not using first person) to slightly less formal writing (using "I.") This less formal tone continues throughout the rest of the passage.

Answer to Question 170:

The correct answer is B. Choice A is incorrect, as he clearly states that the English clubs are superior. Choice C is incorrect, as he appears to appreciate the skill of football players. Choice D is incorrect, as the author clearly enjoys watching football and knows much about it. Choice E is incorrect, as the author remembers the scores of games that happened years ago. Choice B is correct, as the author says that he could not "grumble" at being replaced.

Answer to Question 171:

The correct answer is B. Choice A is incorrect, as the author would not require that someone watch a team play to appreciate them. Choice C is incorrect, as the author makes no such statement about only watching sports in stadiums. Choice B is correct, as the author mentions playing football himself, and then discusses his appreciation for the sport.

Passage 69:

Answer to Question 172:

The correct answer is B. Choice A is incorrect, as New Urbanism embraces more outdoor spaces. Choice C is incorrect, as people need to have a safe place to walk. Choice D is incorrect, as the passage states that the community votes on matters. Choice E is incorrect, as the passage does not state whether taxes are high or low. Choice B is correct, as there is no need for boarding schools in such a small community.

Answer to Question 173:

The correct answer is B. The main point of the second paragraph is to set out the structure of a society using New Urbanism principles. Choice A is incorrect, as some people may not like New Urbanism, but this does not affect the structure of a New Urbanism society. Choice C is incorrect, as the passage is not concerned with the size of social circles within New Urban communities. Choice D is incorrect, as the passage focuses on describing the precepts of New Urbanism, not advocating it or supporting its viability. Choice E is incorrect, as creating old-fashioned buildings is a design choice; this assessment could be correct, but this is irrelevant to the passage's effort to describe New Urbanism. Choice B is correct, since the main point of the passage is to describe these principles and the fact that the principles are not firm or generally adhered to would undermine the reliability of the passage.

Answer to Question 174:

The correct answer is A. Choice B is incorrect, as the passage does not state or imply the necessity of a great deal of open space for New Urbanism. Choice A is correct, as New Urbanism consists of maintaining open spaces and planning the layout of buildings; this would be difficult to do after construction is already finished. Choice C is correct, as anyone can walk more frequently, which is a key component of New Urbanism.

Answer to Question 175:

The correct answer is "The neighborhood is organized to be self-governing where a formal association debates and decides matters of maintenance, security, and physical change "

The second-to-last sentence explains that each community is self-governing, meaning that its citizens collect taxes and vote on community matters, so it is the correct sentence.

Passage 70:

Answer to Question 176:

The correct answer is C. Choice A is incorrect, as the passage does not focus on older patients. Choice B is incorrect, as the passage does not mention long-term risks. Choice D is incorrect, as the passage does not say anything about doctors' suggestions to drink coffee or not to drink coffee. Choice E is incorrect, as the passage does not advocate abstaining from caffeine. Choice C is correct, as the passage mentions side effects such as anxiety.

Answer to Question 177:

The correct answer is C. Choice A is incorrect, as the passage mentions that harmane may be psychoactive. Choice B is incorrect, as the passage suggests caffeine may worsen anxiety. Choice C is correct; the passage implies that there may be some benefit to removing cafestol, but does not suggest or imply the physiological effects of this compound. Choice D is incorrect, as the passage mentions that diterpenes may worsen anxiety. Choice E is incorrect. Monoamine oxidase inhibitors are the general class of potentially psychoactive compounds to which harmane belongs.

Answer to Question 178:

The correct answer is A. Choice B is incorrect, as while the drink may be the most popular drink worldwide, it is not a necessity. Choice C is incorrect, as four or more cups can lead to a risk for only certain people and the author stops short of actually recommending this limit. Choice A is correct, as the passage describes the general popularity of coffee but then notes some possible undesirable side-effects.

Answer to Question 179:

The correct answer is "Although recent research suggests that moderate coffee consumption is benign or mildly beneficial, coffee can worsen the symptoms of conditions like anxiety due to the caffeine and diterpenes it contains."

Sentence seven correctly states how caffeine can exacerbate existing conditions like anxiety. While the last paragraph does mention risks to people with mutations of the CYP1A2 gene, the rest of the population will experience minimal risk.

Passage 71: Summary / Paraphrase

The passage describes the process of marketing using social media and the prevalence of such marketing. The author does not present an argument, but the author raises the question of the safety of such practices.

Answer to Question 180:

The correct answer is D. Choice A is incorrect, as the passage does not mention benefits to the consumer of social media marketing. Choice B is incorrect, as the passage does not focus on the nature of the risks of an online presence. Choice C is incorrect, as the passage does not question social media marketing; it questions the abuse of privacy that monitoring consumers' actions online and data collection may bring about. Further, it does not suggest social media marketing, but describes how it works. Choice E is incorrect, as the passage does not argue for using personal information and data collection to make social media marketing succeed. Choice D is correct, as the passage sets out methods and drawbacks (data collection and monitoring consumers' actions that may lead to invasion of privacy) that play important roles in social media marketing.

Answer to Question 181:

The correct answer is A. Choice B is incorrect; it may be true that consumers who use phones spend more time on social media, but the paragraph does not continue to argue this point. Choice C is incorrect, as online advertising may adapt to suit new technology, but the point of the paragraph is discussing media marketing on mobile phones. Choice D is incorrect, as this is not the main point of the paragraph. Choice E is incorrect, as the paragraph does not explicitly say that revenues increase. Choice A is correct; the paragraph focuses on how many people have mobile phones, which shows how advertising has adapted to suit the new, prevalent technology that consumers depend on.

Answer to Question 182:

The correct answer is A. Choice B is incorrect; while the first sentence does highlight the commonly used tool of social media marketing via phones, the second sentence introduces a negative consequence; it does not return to the argument of the thesis. Choice C is incorrect; the first sentence describes a new approach but does not actually suggest it. Also, the second sentence mentions a negative consequence, but does not specifically caution against social media marketing on cell phones. Choice D is incorrect; while the first sentence may anticipate a new trend, the second does not suggest any alternative. Choice E is incorrect. The first sentence asserts a fact without providing evidence and the second sentence does not return to the passage's argument. Choice A is correct, as the first sentence states that phones may be an important place for social media marketing to take place, and the second sentence mentions a drawback of social media marketing in general.

Answer to Question 183:

The correct answer is B. Choice A is incorrect, as targeting ads based on location is still using someone's personal information. Choice C is incorrect, as the author does not care as much about the number of ads, it is the way the ads are targeted that is unacceptable. Choice B is correct, as the author would probably support making it more difficult for companies to use personal information.

Answer to Question 184:

The correct answer is C. Choice A is incorrect, because nothing in the passage suggests an anachronism (something out of chronological order.) Choice B is incorrect, because the passage is not commanding the reader to do anything. Choice C is correct, because the author appears to know what he is writing about, and the passage seems like a reliable source of information.

Answer to Question 185:

The correct answer is "Development of such techniques for analysis and personalized advertising shows that stringent laws are required for monitoring social media and its use as a marketing device."

The last sentence recommends that legislation be passed. All other sentences are assertions of fact or general marketing principles.

Passage 72:

Answer to Question 186:

The correct answer is C. Choice A is incorrect, as older people who smoke are still at risk. Choice B is incorrect, as even occasional smoking is harmful. Choice D is incorrect, as moderate smoking is still harmful. Choice E is incorrect, as the nonsmoker will still suffer secondhand smoke effects. Choice C is correct, as a nonsmoking pregnant woman whose father stopped smoking will not carry any health risks to her fetus.

Answer to Question 187:

The correct answer is A. Choice B is incorrect, because it is not important for the reader to smoke or know a smoker to understand the risks of tobacco. Choice C is incorrect, as nothing about tobacco factories is in the passage. Choice D is incorrect, as lobbyists make more tax revenue when tobacco is on the market. Choice E is incorrect, as this would only prove that people can contract diseases in several ways. Choice A is correct, as the passage mentions the adverse effects of tobacco, but does not specify what kind of smoking is done.

Answer to Question 188:

The correct answer is C. Choice A is incorrect, as anecdotes would not match the formal tone of the passage. Choice B is incorrect, as the passage would become more confusing with the addition of diagrams. Choice D is incorrect, as the passage never mentions changing tax rates. Choice E is incorrect, as the passage never mentions flavored cigarettes. Choice C is correct, as continuing the passage with this information would show the influence of tobacco companies on everyday people.

Answer to Question 189:

The correct answer is A. Choice B is incorrect, as the passage mentions nothing about immune systems. Choice C is incorrect, as the passage clearly argues that smoking is unhealthy, so the reader can assume that quitting smoking is better to continuing to smoke. Choice A is correct, as the passage states that it is a cultural behavior.

Passage 73: Summary / Paraphrase

The passage is about homelessness among female veterans in the United States. The main idea is that homelessness among female veterans can be attributed to a combination of increased female participation in the military and a lack of veterans' services targeted specifically at women. The major point of the passage is the problematic increase in homelessness among female veterans. There are two minor points: (a) that the increase in homelessness is partly attributable to an increase in female enlistment and (b) that traditional veterans' shelters do not provide enough appropriate services for female veterans. The purpose of the passage is to inform the reader of a problem. The tone of the passage suggests that problem of homelessness among female veterans needs to be addressed. The passage implies that increasing veterans' services targeted specifically at females is a remedy for the problem.

Answer to Question 190:

The correct answer is B.

A. Wrong. The passage does not appeal to the logos, or logical reason, to make his or her argument regarding the increase of homeless female veterans. The author appeals to the emotional sensibilities of the reader by showing that this homelessness is a problem through the example that homeless female veterans cannot care for their children - an emotional appeal.

B. Correct. The author uses the example of homeless female veterans not being able to care for their children to underscore the problem of homelessness among female veterans, which is a classic emotional (pathos) appeal that plays on the needs, values and emotional sensibilities of the reader.

C. Wrong. The passage in no way addresses metaphysical concerns (the fundamental question of being in the world according to philosophy) and thus does not appeal to the metaphysical sensibilities of the reader.

D. Wrong. Since the reader does not have any knowledge of which the author is, ethos does not apply here since ethos is an ethical appeal based on the reputation of the author.

E. Wrong. The political level is not addressed directly in this passage and thus the author is not appealing to the reader's political sensibilities.

Answer to Question 191:

The correct answer is C.

A. Wrong. The passage does not suggest that the U.S military offers its veterans no services, just that these services are lacking particularly when it comes to helping female veterans and their children.

B. Wrong. The passage does not suggest that all U.S. military veterans are homeless, just that the homeless phenomenon is increasing among female veterans.

C. Correct. It can be inferred from the information given in the passage that gender inequality exists among U.S. military veterans because veteran services are not inclusive of women and their children, thus leaving them more vulnerable.

D. Wrong. The passage in no way indicates that women should not serve in the U.S. military, just the fact that female veterans need more assistance.

E. Wrong. Based on the information given in the passage it cannot be inferred that more female veterans have children than male veterans overall, but it can be inferred that more female veterans are responsible for their children than male veterans.

Passage 74:

Answer to Question 192:

The correct answer is B. Higher temperatures can explain the increase in lemonade sales. Record high temperatures occur infrequently, and expecting to sustain high sales numbers during an average summer may be too optimistic. Answer choice A is incorrect because it is outside of the scope of the argument. It is impossible to say if this factor would have any impact on sales. Answer choice C is incorrect because the general increase in the sale of all organic products does not necessarily affect lemonade sales at seasonal events. In fact, it could make Lenny's lemonade more attractive to a number of fair attendees. Answer choice D may encourage higher attendance numbers at the fairs. They will have more money to spend on food and entertainment, so Lenny might sell more lemonade as a result. Answer choice E also has no predictive value concerning lemonade sales. Increased rent may force Lenny to raise his lemonade price, but the argument does not indicate that customers either choose or ignore Lenny's product because of price.

Passage 75:

Answer to Question 193:

The correct answer is C. The economy of Commonville has suffered a serious blow. It is not likely that any type of marketing, including home staging, will help homeowners sell their homes more quickly and for higher prices. Answer choice A is incorrect because using a variety of media makes real estate inventory more visible to the public. If sellers use the staging service, they will want the results to be visible in every medium used by the realtors. Answer choice B is incorrect because it does not address the advantages or disadvantages of home staging and does not relate to results that Commonville residents can expect from staging their homes. Answer choice D is incorrect because the argument does not reveal what style of home the staging company provides its services to. If staging is the difference between a quick sale or having a home sit on the market for several months, the style of home is irrelevant. Answer choice E is incorrect because it doesn't provide enough information. Without knowing the incomes of the single parents or how many children are in their care, the reader cannot discount them as potential buyers.

Passage 76:

Answer to Question 194:

The correct answer is B. Hunters' having been given more permits to hunt does five years ago would have had an effect on the number of fawns born in the following spring. It would take a few years to return the deer population to numbers that existed before the doe permits were issued. The argument does not provide enough information to conclude that the landowner clear cut woodlands near the deer yards or interfered with the deer's ability to find enough food. Answer A is incorrect because it is outside the scope of the argument. Salt licks cannot replace a main source of food for the deer. Answer C is incorrect because it does not address the issue of clear cutting. There is not enough information in the passage to indicate that the clear cutting occurred where the deer seek food. Answer D is incorrect because the erosion of soil into a nearby river does not address the availability of food for the deer herds. Answer E is incorrect. The passage does not address illegal hunting of deer, nor does the answer choice specify where the game wardens will watch for illegal hunting.

Passage 77:

Answer to Question 195:

The correct answer is D. Of the answer choices available, this one makes the clearest connection between her change in eating habits and a lower cholesterol level. After six months of a diet change, she is likely to see improved blood test results. Answer choice A is incorrect because a restrictive diet may not be the only way to lower cholesterol levels. Answer choice B is incorrect because some people may lower their cholesterol level by following this diet regimen and doing nothing else. Answer choices with restrictive words like "only" and "alone" must always be examined carefully. Answer choice C is incorrect because it restates the first part of the argument but fails to reveal how her diet leads to lower cholesterol levels. Answer choice E is incorrect because Robin's weight may have no effect on her cholesterol levels. It is not an assumption that ties the two statements in the argument together.

Passage 78:

Answer to Question 196:

The correct answer is D. Choice A is incorrect, as the passage does not suggest that the people distracted West. Choice B is incorrect, as the passage describes a strong forward momentum for the ball and does not describe the grass impeding its movement. Choice C is incorrect, as the results of the swing are not absolutely clear but nothing firmly indicates that it is unsuccessful. Choice E is incorrect, as the passage is a bit suspenseful, but the reader can infer the results from the generally positive tone of the ending, connoted by words such as "presto". Choice D is correct, as even though the ending does not state the exact result of hitting the ball, the happy tone makes it clear that the outcome is good.

Answer to Question 197:

The correct answer is A. Choice B is incorrect, as the passage has elements of competition among men on the putting range. Choice C is incorrect, as West is clearly under pressure in the passage. Choice D is incorrect, as the passage clearly details the suspense and drama of this moment in time. Choice E is incorrect, as the ending of the passage clearly conveys a sense of emotional exhilaration with its rhythm and word choice. Choice A is correct, as the passage does not focus on any characteristics or description of the golf clubs or other equipment.

Answer to Question 198:

The correct answer is C. Choice A is incorrect, as it is more likely that the professor is annoyed at Joel for blocking his view. Choice B is incorrect, as the passage never shows Joel's reaction. Choice D is incorrect, as the passage does not show Joel's reaction. Choice E is incorrect, as West never seems to lose control. Choice C is correct, as West is composed, and then he relaxes after he's hit the ball.

Answer to Question 199:

The correct answer is A. Choice B is correct, as the passage focuses on the drama of a game of golf. Choice C is incorrect, as a bildungsroman would show a character growing up, and the reader only sees West for a few moments. Choice A is correct, because the passage could indeed be a detailed, non-fictional account of an important golf game.

Passage 79: Summary / Paraphrase

The passage is about methods for improving outcomes in primary education. The main idea is that introducing a market system to primary education might be one way to improve outcomes. The main points: (a) that a voucher system will make primary education a free market and (b) that market forces will pressure underperforming public schools to improve their performance vis a vis their better-performing peers in order to compete. There is a minor point that some districts have tried to include private and even parochial schools, in their voucher program, raising a potential constitutional issue regarding separation of church and state. The main purpose of the passage is to inform the reader about an approach to improving outcomes in primary education: while the issue is often a charged one, the passage presents relevant information without clearly espousing a position.

Answer to Question 200:

The correct answer is C. When there is no sense of urgency to improve the way a business or school, etc. does business, that institution may suffer from complacency. When schools have a captive student body that has nowhere else to go, there is the temptation to think, "We're doing all right." It is easy to become complacent, or satisfied with the status quo. C is the best answer. Only when a school is striving to improve and is seeing some progress is there a reason to feel optimistic. Conversely, a school that is trying to improve and failing has reason to feel pessimistic or defeated. Lack of competition does not lead to A, B, or D. Lethargy implies a lack of energy, which can result from complacency. E is not the best choice.

Answer to Question 201:

The correct answer is B. If the purpose of the voucher system is to ensure that students get the best educational opportunities, then private schools who attract students under this system should have to conform to the guidelines set by the No Child Left Behind act. There is no oversight to ensure that private schools offer a curriculum that is any better than that of a public school. The best answer is B. Answer A is not correct; parents do not have to select a private school and may choose not to do so because of the added expense of books and uniforms. Extracurricular activities are not a measure of excellence of education offered by a school, so C is not correct. Again, parents would be aware of religion courses offered at religious schools, and can choose to send their children elsewhere. The same reasoning applies to answer E.

Passage 80: Summary / Paraphrase

The passage is about differences in attitudes toward literature in New York and Boston. The main idea is that although New York is a literary center, Boston society appreciates literature more than New York society. The major points are (a) New York is a center for writers and publishing and (b) New York society values commerce more than literature, while Boston society esteems literature. The purpose of the passage is to compare the attitudes of two major eastern cities toward literature. The author makes a latent assumption that his experience accurately reflects wider attitudes.

Answer to Question 202:

The correct answer is E. The writer is comparing and contrasting the attitudes of New York City's and Boston's regard for literary endeavors. The repetitive use of the word but is a standard tool for this purpose. The writer may be making a case for his point of view, but he is not asking the reader to take some action, which is the point of persuasive writing; A is not the correct answer choice. A logical appeal is a technique used in persuasive writing and not a format in itself, making B incorrect a well. A narrative is simply a story and does not describe the author's purpose here. C is incorrect. He writer has not employed symbolism to achieve his purpose here, eliminating D as a correct answer.

Answer to Question 203:

The correct answer is B. The writer claims that New York cares more for horse and stocks than it does for books and supposes that this attitude exists in other large cities. The writer tells the reader that New York is the home of many writers but does not say this about other cities, making A the wrong choice. It would be correct to say that New York City is a center of commerce and that it has great journalists, but that does not fulfill the purpose of comparison to other cities, eliminating both C and D as correct answers.

Answer to Question 204:

The correct answer is A. New York City has a more pragmatic or practical attitude toward the literary world; it cares more for the factual reporting of journalism than it does for the aesthetics of great literature. Boston, on the other hand is more enamored of literature than journalism, preferring its aesthetic sensibilities. The reader may conclude that New York is industrial in focus, but there is no evidence that Boston is an agrarian, or agricultural, city, so B cannot be correct. There is also no evidence that New York is more competitive than Boston in any sense, so answer choice C cannot be correct. Although the author reveals contrasts between the two cities, he makes no mention of New York's being a stereotypical American city or that Boston is one of a kind. D is the wrong answer. Boston is not described as being less progressive than New York, simply different from New York, making answer choice E also incorrect.

Passage 81: Summary / Paraphrase

The passage is about prescription drug abuse. The main idea is that the difficulty of determining legitimate drug use from abuse makes the prevention of prescription drug abuse difficult. The major point is that prescription drug abusers can obtain the drug in a variety of ways, many of them difficult to distinguish from proper use. The purpose of the passage is to illustrate the difficulties authorities face in preventing prescription drug abuse.

Answer to Question 205:

The correct answer is A. Fewer pharmacies and doctors might result in a lower use of all prescription drugs, including OxyContin, so neither B nor C is correct. Population density has nothing to do with the rate of drug use; that rate would be determined per capita, regardless of how those individuals are scattered in a geographic area; D is incorrect. Because OxyContin is expensive does not make it unlikely to be abused. The cost of a particular drug has little to do with its being abused by the public, so E is also incorrect. A spike in the use of OxyContin in Appalachian states may not indicate abuse of the painkiller. Its arrival on the scene may simply mean that residents of this area finally have a more effective drug for injuries or conditions that are painful.

Passage 82: Summary / Paraphrase

The passage is about public perceptions of coffee. The main idea is that coffee is a symbol of American values. The major points are (a) that an American general remarked that coffee helped the allies win WWI and (b) that coffee is associated with temperance and rationality, qualities needed for the functioning of democracy. The purpose of the passage is to celebrate coffee, and to associate coffee with what the author thinks are essential values of democracy.

Answer to Question 206:

The correct answer is D. It is typical of good writing that the last sentence of a paragraph previews the content of the subsequent paragraph. That being the case, it is correct to assume that the next paragraph will provide an explanation for or examples of the benefits of coffee, tea, and cocoa. D is the best answer choice. Answer choice A is incorrect; bacon is mentioned briefly in the second sentence of the passage, and the writer provides no reason to suspect that he will return to that subject. The same can be said for bread as a topic, eliminating B as a correct answer. It would be more correct to assume that coffee, tea, and cocoa contribute to clear thinking and right living than vice versa, so it is incorrect to assume that answer choice C is the best one. This writer extols the benefits of the three beverages rather than any harm they might cause; E is the wrong answer choice.

Answer to Question 207:

The correct answers are A, B and C. An argument can be made to support all three choices. Because the writer uses the word "one" in the first sentence, it is logical to expect a listing of the other awards that coffee has garnered. It could be that the writer wants to identify other everyday items that have had a greater impact on world democracy than their intrinsic value would lead one to believe. Finally, the writer might expand on the ideas about coffee, tea and cocoa that he has introduced in this passage.

Passage 83: Summary / Paraphrase

The passage is focused on the gun control debate in the United States. The main idea of the passage is that the debate over gun control is a good example of the short-sighted nature of American civic discourse. The major point of the passage is that the reversal of the dominant public opinion on gun control within a 5-year span is a prime example of how short-sighted American public policy debates can be. There is a minor point that Americans are often aggressive in their views on topics such as gun control. The purpose of the passage is to illustrate a point about the nature of civic discourse in the United States. There is an underlying assumption that the legislative initiatives mentioned toward the end of the passage are an accurate reflection of current overall public opinion.

Answer to Question 208:

The correct answer is D.

A. Wrong. The author does not clearly indicate his or her personal opinion on the state of gun control in American society, just that it is a hot-button issue that serves as a good example of rapidly fluctuating public opinions within the context of American public discourse.

B. Wrong. The author makes it very clear that gun control issues are an important aspect of American public discourse.

C. Wrong. While the passage states that American society can be very combative and intense in its debates, this is not the author's primary message since what the author really wants to convey is the fact that issues in American public discourse change rapidly - gun control can go from center stage to the periphery in a few short years.

D. Correct. The author states that the gun control debate demonstrates how myopic (short-sighted) American public discourse can be and then uses the remainder of the passage to provide an example that supports this claim.

E. Wrong. This answer cannot be inferred given the information provided by the author in the passage. The author claims that gun control issues play an important role in American society but not the central role.

Answer to Question 209:

The correct answer is B.

A. Wrong. The passage does not indicate that Americans are confused by the rules governing civil society - on the contrary their knowledge of the Second Amendment illustrates that they at least have some understanding of the law. The author's primary goal in the passage is to draw attention to the short-sighted nature of civil society, not the confused nature of it.

B. Correct. The author wants the reader to understand the short-sighted nature of American civic debate by way of a belligerent character - that is anger and aggression are easily triggered when the issue of gun control comes up.

C. Wrong. While this phrase may very well capture the reader's attention, there is more to its significance: it serves to highlight the fact that American civic debate is not only myopic but also aggressive.

D. Wrong. An argumentative strategy requires that the author convince the audience of his claim through reasoning and since the author in the passage above only convinces the reader that American civic society is myopic by way of reason, the phrase in question cannot be an argumentative strategy to convince the reader of American aggression.

E. Wrong. It is correct that the author wants to convince the reader that American civil debate is short-sighted, but the phrase in question is not an example of a narrative rhetorical strategy. A narrative rhetorical strategy would require the recounting of an event, the telling of a story.

Passage 84: Summary / Paraphrase

The passage is about homelessness among female veterans in the United States. The main idea is that homelessness among female veterans can be attributed to a combination of increased female participation in the military and a lack of veterans' services targeted specifically at women. The major point of the passage is the problematic increase in homelessness among female veterans. There are two minor points: (a) that the increase in homelessness is partly attributable to an increase in female enlistment and (b) that traditional veterans' shelters do not provide enough appropriate services for female veterans. The purpose of the passage is to inform the reader of a problem. The tone of the passage suggests that problem of homelessness among female veterans needs to be addressed. The passage implies that increasing veterans' services targeted specifically at females is a remedy for the problem.

Answer to Question 210:

The correct answer is B.

A. Wrong. The passage does not appeal to the logos, or logical reason, to make his or her argument regarding the increase of homeless female veterans. The author appeals to the emotional sensibilities of the reader by showing that this homelessness is a problem through the example that homeless female veterans cannot care for their children - an emotional appeal.

B. Correct. The author uses the example of homeless female veterans not being able to care for their children to underscore the problem of homelessness among female veterans, which is a classic emotional (pathos) appeal that plays on the needs, values and emotional sensibilities of the reader.

C. Wrong. The passage in no way addresses metaphysical concerns (the fundamental question of being in the world according to philosophy) and thus does not appeal to the metaphysical sensibilities of the reader.

D. Wrong. Since the reader does not have any knowledge of which the author is, ethos does not apply here since ethos is an ethical appeal based on the reputation of the author.

E. Wrong. The political level is not addressed directly in this passage and thus the author is not appealing to the reader's political sensibilities.

Answer to Question 211:

The correct answer is C.

A. Wrong. The passage does not suggest that the U.S military offers its veterans no services, just that these services are lacking particularly when it comes to helping female veterans and their children.

B. Wrong. The passage does not suggest that all U.S. military veterans are homeless, just that the homeless phenomenon is increasing among female veterans.

C. Correct. It can be inferred from the information given in the passage that gender inequality exists among U.S. military veterans because veteran services are not inclusive of women and their children, thus leaving them more vulnerable.

D. Wrong. The passage in no way indicates that women should not serve in the U.S. military, just the fact that female veterans need more assistance.

E. Wrong. Based on the information given in the passage it cannot be inferred that more female veterans have children than male veterans overall, but it can be inferred that more female veterans are responsible for their children than male veterans.

Passage 85: Summary / Paraphrase

The passage is about domestic violence. The main idea is that, contrary to popular belief, men are quite often the target of domestic violence. There are two major points: (a) 40% of domestic violence victims are male and (b) due to societal attitudes toward male weakness, domestic violence incidents involving men may be underreported. The main purpose of the passage is to (a) debunk the myth that men are rarely the victims of domestic violence and (b) give one potential reason that domestic violence against men may be underreported.

Answer to Question 212:

The correct answer is E.

A. Wrong. The passage does not suggest women stigmatize abused men, it suggests that Western society as a whole stigmatizes abused men.

B. Wrong. The passage does not suggest that researchers of the domestic abuse of males harbor any pro or anti female bias.

C. Wrong. The passage does not indicate that reporting domestic abuse harms the overall quality of the male victim's relationships with women.

D. Wrong. The passage does not give general drawbacks of statistical methodology as a reason for faulty statistics relative to male domestic abuse.

E. Correct. The passage states that men face social stigma if they admit to being victims of domestic abuse; society equates this with male weakness. Hence, male domestic abuse is underreported.

Passage 86: Summary / Paraphrase

The passage is about college students' attitudes toward their student loan debt. The main idea is that college students have an unusual attitude about their debt burden. There are two major points: (a) students are optimistic about their ability to use their education to succeed, and thus inclined to take a positive view of their debt. There is also an implied point (b) that most other Americans who are in debt do not share this positive view of their debt. There is a minor point that student views on empowerment through education are a key influence on their feelings about their debt burden. The main purpose of the passage is to point out an atypical attitude within the broader context of how people respond to being in debt.

Answer to Question 213:

The correct answer is D.

A. Wrong. This answer is not an inference about American college students given that it is a fact taken directly from the passage.

B. Wrong. The passage indicates that American college students feel that debt is a positive thing as it is evidence of their commitment to the future and a wider array of opportunities.

C. Wrong. The passage does not provide enough information about other adult debt levels to infer this comparison; additionally, the passage states that American college students are heavily affected by high levels of student loan debt.

D. Correct. The passage states that American college students see student loan debt as a way of advancing their careers and opportunities and thus it can be inferred that they are choosing to view debt through a positive lens.

E. Wrong. The passage states that American college students don't view student loan debt as a negative thing, which does not indicate that American college students feel that debt as an issue lacks importance - it is just not a negative issue for them.

Answer to Question 214:

The correct answer is C.

A. Wrong. The passage states that researchers see students' reaction to their debt level as atypical or unusual and since naïve means child-like; naïve is not a term that accurately reflects the attitude of college students.

B. Wrong. The passage states that researchers see students' reaction to their debt level as atypical or unusual and since predictable means reliable or typical; predictable is not a term that accurately reflects the attitude of college students.

C. Correct. The passage states that researchers see students' reaction to their debt level as atypical or unusual and since preternatural means unusual and is thus a synonym for atypical; preternatural is a term that accurately reflects the attitude of college students.

D. Wrong. The passage states that researchers see students' reaction to their debt level as atypical or unusual and since banal means trite or commonplace; banal is not a term that accurately reflects the attitude of college students.

E. Wrong. The passage states that researchers see students' reaction to their debt level as atypical or unusual and since unexceptional means typical or usual; unexceptional is not a term that accurately reflects the attitude of college students.

Answer to Question 215:

The correct answer is B.

A. Wrong. An albatross is a figure of speech for a burden and so it cannot be synonymous with the level of debt because that would require albatross to refer to an actual number.

B. Correct. An albatross is a figure of speech for a burden and in the passage, it is used to indicate the burden of debt.

C. Wrong. An albatross is a figure of speech for a burden and thus it cannot be used as a figure of speech that represents the stresses in American society.

D. Wrong. An albatross is a figure of speech for a burden does not indicate anything about a bank account; furthermore, substituting bank account for albatross in the passage would be illogical syntactically and semantically.

E. Wrong. An albatross is a figure of speech for a burden and credit card debt is a debt and thus a burden. However, the passage does not mention credit card debt specifically and thus credit card debt cannot be substituted for albatross.

Passage 87: Summary / Paraphrase

The passage is about the difficulty of achieving equal educational opportunities in the United States. The main idea is that while there is a tendency to focus on literacy rates and children, the problem of low literacy has broader implications. There is an explicitly stated major point that low literacy among adults engenders poor educational results in the children of the affected population. In addition, there is an implied major point that literacy is crucial to equal opportunity. The purpose of the passage is to rally support for literacy initiatives by explaining why they are important. Rhetorical cues such as the use of the word 'harmful' and the discussion of adverse outcomes indicate that the passage is a call to action.

Answer to Question 216:

The correct answer is D.

A. Wrong. The author actually delineates or describes the problems associated with low literacy in the section of the passage not in bold-face; the sections in bold-face demonstrate how the author finds a solution to his or her claim.

B. Wrong. The author actually appeals to the reader's emotional sensibilities in the part of the passage that are not highlighted in bold-face by invoking the problems children face when they struggle with low literacy.

C. Wrong. The author's beliefs are congruent and the author only discusses one belief and no opposing beliefs relative to low literacy: it obstructs equal opportunities.

D. Correct. The two-bold face parts demonstrate how the author presents his or her claim that low literacy obstructs access to equal opportunities and then reaches the solution to the problem: literacy initiatives.

E. Wrong. Since the two bold-face parts are congruent and serve to illustrate the author's contention that low literacy impedes equal opportunities in society; thus, they are not paradoxical.

Answer to Question 217:

The correct answer is B.

A. Wrong. The author spends the majority of the passage highlighting why low literacy is a major problem among adults, which leads to a cycle of low literacy perpetuated by the children of low literacy adults.

B. Correct. The passage discusses how low literacy rates in American adults impede equal opportunities.

C. Wrong. The passage does not indicate the effect of low literacy in American adults on crime rates.

Practice Set 5 - Physical Sciences

Passage 88:

Answer to Question 218:

The correct answer is "Present surface conditions, of low relief, considerable humidity, and with the water table usually not more than 100 feet from the surface, do not promise ore deposits at great depth."
The weather conditions and surface features, such as high humidity and low relief, are not conducive to the formation of large deposits of iron ore. In contrast, earlier conditions, which included low humidity and great relief, were favorable for creating these deposits.

Answer to Question 219:

Both A and B are correct answers. The second paragraph states that, under specific conditions, erosion carries away weathered surface material. The term weathering implies the effect of weather such as sun, wind, or water on a surface. Erosion, as described in the passage, also results from weather conditions, especially, rain. Answer choice C is incorrect because wet conditions can lead to weathering or erosion.

Answer to Question 220:

The best answer is B. A clearer picture of the actual depth and distribution of ores is beneficial for enterprises that seek to extract the ores. They can spend their time and resources more economically when they know more precise locations of the deposits. Using present surface conditions yield less precise results. Answer A is incorrect because, even though pre-Cambrian surfaces may more accurately predict the location, depth, and distribution of ore deposits, they cannot predict how large the deposits are. Without first uncovering the deposits, exploration cannot be assumed to yield amounts of ore to insure great profits. There is no indication in the passage that these new methods of locating ore deposits will have any effect on residential development or be used to either encourage or discourage development of any type. Therefore, choice C is incorrect.

Answer to Question 221:

The correct answer is B. The author states that, in areas of heavy erosion, the ores have been removed. The author states in the third sentence of the second paragraph that it is important to know the location of slight erosion because deposits of ore are more likely to occur in these areas. Answer choice A is incorrect because ore deposits are more likely to occur where the water has deeply penetrated the surface as the author states in the first paragraph. Answer C is incorrect because the author provides too little information about bauxite deposits. He does not mention their occurring in serpentine areas. Sedimentation is the result of erosion. The author touches briefly on sedimentation but does not suggest that locating regions of light erosion in Cuba leads to a better understanding of it. So, answer choice D is incorrect. Answer choice E is incorrect, again, because these placer deposits appear to arise from sedimentation and not light erosion.

Answer to Question 222:

The best choice is D, respectful. He is presenting specific and specialized information without dumbing down the content. The writer, thus, demonstrates respect for his audience by assuming that they have the requisite knowledge to understand his presentation. Answer choice A is incorrect because there is no evidence that the author feels reverence or awe for his audience. Earnest suggests some intensity which might be necessary if he were attempting to get his audience to take some action or he were warning them about some inherent or imminent danger. Since that is not the case, answer choice B is incorrect. An author would use a reflective tone to examine his feelings or motives, an unlikely event in scientific writing. Answer choice C is incorrect. The writer of this passage may, indeed, be erudite or learned and scholarly, but his tone is more informative than scholarly. Answer choice E is not correct.

Answer to Question 223:

The correct answer is C. If he has written the passage as part of an entry in a scholarly journal, he has likely remained objective. If he has been commissioned to compile this information for a mining company that is seeking investors, he may have applied some bias in order to appeal to prospective investors. In that case, reliability may suffer. The author need not have spent any time in the areas he mentions in the passage in order to collect and compile reliable information, so answer choice A is incorrect. The author gives the reader no indications that commercial applications have anything to do with the information in the passage, making answer choice B incorrect. The reader does not know that the writer is a geologist, so identifying the university where he earned his degree is a moot point. Answer choice D is the wrong one. For the same reason, answer choice E is incorrect. The reader does not know that the writer is a geologist. He is just as likely to have researched this topic for a college paper.

Passage 89: Summary / Paraphrase

The passage is about asteroids. The main idea is that astronomers originally had little knowledge of asteroids. The main idea is developed by two major points: (a) until the mid-19th century, astronomers had little accurate notion of how many asteroids there were and (b) astronomers mistakenly believed that Vesta was the largest asteroid due to its relative brightness, whereas the largest asteroid is in fact Ceres. A minor point explains that the mistake in determining the relative size of the asteroids stemmed from differences in the reflectivity of Ceres and Vesta. The purpose of the passage is to inform the reader about the history of our knowledge of asteroids.

Answer to Question 224:

The correct answer is D. Answer choice D is the most reasonable explanation. When one considers that several years passed between sightings before spotters began seeing them with increasing regularity, the logical conclusion is that, in some way, the spotters were better able to see the asteroids. The writer makes no mention of weather affecting the spotters' ability to identify more asteroids, so answer choice A is not the most reasonable. Offering more courses in astronomy does not inevitably lead to more astronomers; B is also incorrect. There is nothing in this passage to suggest that there had been a period of volcanic activity, the ash from which may have blocked the view of the sky, so C is incorrect. It is not clear in this passage that astronomers were confused about the characteristics of asteroids, eliminating E as the most reasonable explanation.

Answer to Question 225:

The correct answer is A. After periods of relatively slow advances in the discovery and accurate measurement of asteroids, the pace of both increased rapidly. It would be fair to predict that this pace would continue or increase. An important idea in this passage is the revision of current or previous understanding about objects in the universe. Regardless of the scientific field, ideas and theories are under continuing scrutiny as the ability to examine objects becomes more advanced. After all, humans for centuries believed that the Earth was the center of the universe. Although the other 4 answer choices are likely true, their truth doesn't have an impact on the entirety of science.

Passage 90: Summary / Paraphrase

The passage describes an old-fashioned piece of exercise equipment and the ways one can use it to practice balancing. The author does not present an argument or an opposing view.

Answer to Question 226:

The correct answer is B. The passage mainly focuses on balancing. Choice A is incorrect, as the balancing is more important than the combat in the context of the passage. Choice C is incorrect, as the passage suggests that these muscles will be involved, but does not specifically focus upon them. Choice D is incorrect, as nothing in the passage mentions wrestling. Choice E is incorrect, as there is nothing in the passage about swinging from a hanging crossbar. Choice B is correct, as this would test balance.

Answer to Question 227:

The correct answer is C. Choice A is incorrect, as the passage is focused on contemporary use of such machines, not their history. Choice B is incorrect, as the passage is concerned with various balancing exercises and equipment and a general discussion of exercising with partners would not be a natural extension of the topic. Choice C is correct, as the passage could be improved with more specific instructions for putting its general principles into practice. Choice D is incorrect, as age does not seem to be particularly relevant to the point of the passage. Choice E is incorrect, because the passage is focused more on the equipment and its uses than the general benefits of sparring.

Answer to Question 228:

The correct answer is B. The point of the passage is that several types of beneficial exercise may be performed on the equipment described. Choice A is incorrect, as the cost of the bridge has nothing to do with its effectiveness. Choice C is incorrect, as the availability of bridges does not diminish their effectiveness as exercise equipment. Choice B is correct, as this discovery would undermine the benefits of using the equipment.

Answer to Question 229:

The correct answer is "This, it will be evident, is an exercise for the organ of equilibrium, and exercises the muscles of the calf, of the neck, and anterior part of the neck, and those of the back, very gently."
The fourth sentence shows that balancing acts involve the whole body and are the most thorough exercise for which the bridge may be used. The fifth sentence does suggest other ways to exercise, but they do not necessarily work the entire body.

Passage 91:

Answer to Question 230:

The correct answer is A.

A is the correct answer; it explains that although identical sounds may be emitted by an object, the way that these sounds are heard varies based on several factors, such as a person's location in relation to that object. The paradox is created by the reliability of the sound emitted versus the unreliability of how those same sounds will be heard.

B is a true statement, though it does not present a paradox. It mentions more the unusual nature of this hypothetical situation rather than contrasting two ideas.

C is irrelevant; though the passage mentions two trains passing each other, the point at which they meet is a fact rather than a paradox.

D is incorrect because the sound emitted by these trains is not in fact irrelevant to this argument, and even if it were true, this statement still fails to present a paradox.

E can be supported by the text yet similarly to other incorrect choices does not identify two conflicting ideas.

Passage 92:

Answer to Question 231:

The correct answer is B.

This passage focuses on how wear affects a gas valve, namely one that is 'well-designed'. B is the correct answer; it identifies the main argument of this passage by designating the topic of how an engine's performance is affected not only by wear over time but more importantly by how well the gas valve is designed. If more reason why a gas valve's design impacts overall engine performance was added to this passage, the author's argument would have further evidence to support the idea that gas valve quality matters.

D is irrelevant because this passage states that there are few destructive effects of wear on a gas valve, especially one that has been well-designed. Therefore, adding evidence of ways that gas valves deteriorate over time would weaken the author's point that quality matters more than the age of the gas valve.

A is incorrect because this passage does not supply instructions for how to maintain overall engine function as it discusses the gas valve in particular rather than the entire engine. Thus, adding more information about the overall function of an engine would weaken the author's focus on gas valves.

C makes an accurate statement but does not relate to the passage's main concern. Though this information is relevant in determining the quality of performance in a gas valve, it does not target the reasons behind why a gas valve may or may not function optimally and thus delineates from the author's main point.

E is incorrect because it mentions several factors which the passage does not discuss and thus focuses on irrelevant information; by assuming that, for the sake of argument, "other conditions [remain] the same" the author is able to focus on just one topic of engine performance rather than other various causes that could affect the engine overall.

Passage 93:

Answer to Question 232:

The correct answer is "The vegetable oil and methanol are placed in a small quantity of an alkaline catalyst and it is in this process that the chemical makeup of the vegetable oil is altered."

Prior to the addition of the catalyst, the mixture of vegetable oil and methanol has no ability to be used as fuel. They cannot complete the ester interchange by simply being combined. The information following the highlighted sentence details the byproducts of the ester interchange.

Passage 94: Summary / Paraphrase

The passage is about the chemical properties of iron. The main idea is that iron can form two chemically distinct series of compounds. The major points are that: (a) iron can form a series of compounds with chemical similarities to zinc compounds and (b) that iron can also form a series of compounds that are chemically similar to aluminum compounds. The primary purpose of the passage is to inform the reader about the chemical properties of iron compounds.

Answer to Question 233:

The correct answers are A, B and C. All three statemens are accurate. The prefix di- means two, and the prefix tri- means three. It logically follows that the suffix -ous is used with metals that have a lower valence number than those with the suffix -ic. Using the knowledge of common words, the reader can agree that the definitions of the two suffixes are correct. For example, beauteous means possessing beauty. If B is correct, then C must also be correct.

Passage 95: Summary / Paraphrase

The passage is about the way that particle structure affects how matter interacts with matter. The main idea is that mercury is unusual in that it behaves like a solid even in a liquid state. The major points are: (a) that particles in solids cohere to each other more strongly than they adhere to the particles in other objects (b) that liquid mercury particles also cohere to one another more strongly than they adhere to the particles in other objects. The main purpose of the passage is to inform.

Answer to Question 234:

The correct answer is "In scientific language, the cohesion of the mercury is stronger than its adhesion to your finger or handkerchief."

The writer's use of the phrase "in scientific language" implies that the text before this is not written in scientific language. The writer also follows this sentence with an example that uses a common object to illustrate the topic of the passage. This indicates that the intended audience is not other scientists.

Passage 96: Summary / Paraphrase

The passage is about how snowflakes and raindrops form. The main idea is that snowflakes and raindrops form through a very similar process. The major points are: (a) raindrops form when water vapor reaches cooler temperatures and begins to condense to form droplets and (b) that snowflakes form in almost the exact same conditions except that it is cold enough to freeze the newly condensed water. There is a minor point that speculates on why snowflakes have the crystalline structure they have, and another that mentions that snow and rain are both part of the water cycle. The purpose of the passage is to inform.

Answer to Question 235:

The correct answer is C. The writer has wandered away from the topic of how rain and snow are formed in the upper atmosphere. He uses the phrase, in any case, to let the reader or audience know that he is returning to the original topic. Answer A is incorrect because the information is not essential to the main topic of the effect of cooling air on water vapor. Although the writer appears to be speculating about the manner in which snowflakes develop six points, the phrase, in any case, does not address that, making B incorrect. Answer D is incorrect for the same reason. There is no evidence that the writer does not find the information interesting, eliminating E as the correct answer.

Answer to Question 236:

The correct answer is E. The writer in this passage reveals how rain and snow are formed in the same manner although temperatures in the upper atmosphere determine whether raindrops or snowflakes are formed. His is mentioning both similarities and differences, therefore, the passage compares and contrasts, answer E. A narrative tells a story which is not the writer's goal here, making A an incorrect choice. Expository writing reveals, usually information about setting or characters. B is not the correct answer choice. Both editorials and persuasive writing present a point of view and support for that point of view, and this passage does not attempt to persuade, so neither C nor D are correct choices.

Answer to Question 237:

The correct answer is B, fog. Fog forms when cool air on the surface comes in contact with warm air vapor and small droplets of water form. A rainbow forms when light passes through water droplets in the air; A is incorrect. Wind chill is a measure of the effect of wind on the ambient air temperature, so C cannot be correct. A degree day is a measure of heating or cooling and not a weather event at all, making D incorrect. Thunder is, essentially, the sound made by lightning. Answer E is also incorrect.

Passage 97: Summary / Paraphrase

The passage is about sound. The main idea is that sound is a sensation caused by clearly delineated physical phenomena. The major points are: (a) that sound is a sensation rather than a physical phenomenon (b) that the sensation of sound is caused by a physical phenomenon known as "sonorous vibration" and (c) the sonorous vibrations cause the sensation of sound by reaching the skin of the ear. A minor point that compares sonorous vibrations to ripples in water serves to illustrate the phenomenon. The main purpose of the passage is to clarify and explain the link between a physical phenomenon and a bodily sensation.

Answer to Question 238:

The correct answer is D. Sound is neither odd nor uncommon to the ear; it is the exact opposite. Neither A nor B is the correct answer. The definition in C means unusual; it is not the correct choice. Answer E would be correct if the author had written that the peculiar ability of the ear is to hear sound. In this case, if the reader were to replace peculiar with belonging characteristically in the sentence, the meaning would remain the same.

Answer to Question 239:

The best answer is C, students. The passage is about the sensation of sound and is not related to any particular field of interest. The writer uses the violin as an example of an object that vibrates when a bow is applied, but he is not addressing musicians specifically, making A an incorrect choice. The content is not an instruction manual for manufacturers of violins as it doesn't deal with the specific measurements or materials needed to build the instrument, eliminating B as a correct answer. Sonography technicians administer sonograms to diagnose medical issues or to provide pictures of a fetus in utero. The passage has nothing to do with this procedure, so D is incorrect. Acoustics engineers design buildings or rooms to make sound in the rooms as clear as possible. Answer choice E is also not correct. The use of the violin as an example of how vibrations affect the eardrum would be appropriate for students, making C the best answer.

Answer to Question 240:

The correct answer is "The surface of the sounding-board is thus set trembling, and these tremors, or vibrations, spread through the air in all directions around the instrument, somewhat in the manner that water-waves spread around the place where a stone has been dropped into a quiet pond."

This sentence, in fact, uses some of the same language that is used to report earthquakes such as tremors and trembling. The effects of an earthquake are similar in that the movement of the earth radiates out from the epicenter.

Passage 98:

Answer to Question 241:

The correct answer is C. Both Venn diagrams and T-charts are used for comparison and contrast which is not the purpose of this passage. Neither A nor E are the correct choices. A list doesn't necessarily require an organizational pattern and would not fit the purpose of the information in this passage, eliminating B as the correct choice. A time line generally puts events in a chronological order and would include dates or times of the day. D is not the best choice. The passage describes a cycle; therefore, C is the best choice as a means for creating a visual of the information in the passage.

Answer to Question 242:

The correct answer is D. The passage reveals the process by which precipitation is formed and leads to a description of how ice caps and glaciers are formed by a particular type of precipitation. The paragraph can be assumed to be an introduction to a discussion of ice caps and glaciers. The correct answer is D. Clouds and air currents are mentioned in the paragraph but not with any specificity. If the passage were an introduction to a longer piece about precipitation, the topic sentence should include more forms of precipitation. The passage does not appear to be about all of the sources of water vapor that rise and form clouds, so it is unlikely that a subsequent paragraph would be about lakes and ponds.

Passage 99: Summary / Paraphrase

The passage is about the geology of a certain region. The main idea is that the author is unable to find a geologic explanation for the rock-basin lakes discussed in the first paragraph. The major points are (a) that some lakes are formed in a basin scooped out of solid rock (b) that the lake bottoms are often scratched or grooved apparently by rocks or boulders that are sometimes found nearby (c) that erosion by the ocean was ruled out as a possible cause for these lakes due to dissimilarities in the geology. Two minor points serve to develop two of the major points: (a) the rock-basin lakes are described as "spoon-shaped" in order to give the reader a clearer impression of the phenomenon and (b) the effects of tidal erosion are discussed prior to being ultimately dismissed. The purpose of the passage is to discuss a geological mystery and rule out one possible solution.

Answer to Question 243:

The correct answer is "The problem now was to discover what forces in Nature could polish and scratch both rock-surfaces and detached stones, and could also transport masses of rock, tons in weight, far from their native home."

In the first paragraph of the passage, the writer reveals observations that he has made. These observations lead him to state the problem, which, in turn, leads him to investigate in order to find a solution to the problem or to answer a question. Without clearly stating the problem, the writer would have no direction for his investigation, and the scientific process would not continue.

Answer to Question 244:

The correct answer is B. The writer's hypothesis appears to be based on his observations at Table Bay. At the very least, he should visit several other locations to discover if the conditions at Table Bay are typical. Ideally, the writer should conduct a series of experiments to test his hypothesis. The writer should collect and label samples from Table Bay, but that is not sufficient to prove his hypothesis. The comment, "as facts accumulate", leads the reader to believe that background research has already been done and should be done before developing a hypothesis, so C is not the correct answer choice. Scientists should never publish the results of their research before testing the hypothesis, making answer choice D incorrect as well. Seeking the perspectives of other scientists might be helpful in formulating a hypothesis, perhaps in order to create an experiment, but it is not a step that would prove the hypothesis to be correct. E is not the correct answer.

Answer to Question 245:

The correct answers are A and B. Both A and B are acceptable choices. How to explain the appearance of boulders in New York and Ohio that seem to have their origins in regions to the north plays a role in the writer's question about the condition of the rocks in and around lakes. The bottoms of the lakes and boulders in the vicinity have scratches in their otherwise smooth surfaces while rocks on the edges of the lakes are smooth without scratches. How can these two conditions occur in the same location? There is no evidence that the writer is testing the veracity of previous conclusions, making choice C incorrect.

Passage 100: Summary / Paraphrase

The passage is about sun spots. The main idea is that although the surface of the sun appears to be perfectly placid, it is actually covered with potential sun spots. The major points are (a) that observing the sun with a telescope, one can see that it is covered with "pores" (b) the pores open during times of solar disturbance, giving rise to a sun spot. There is a minor point that people refused to admit the existence of sun spots for many centuries because the sun was seen as a symbol of purity. The purpose of the passage is to briefly inform the reader about sun spots, and the history of human response to them.

Answer to Question 246:

The correct answers are A, B and C. Support exists for all three statements. Humans considered the sun to be the symbol of purity, a mythological concept. The name, King of the Heavens, denotes the sun's importance in the lives of humans. Humans thought of scientists as fools and idiots because of their attempts to demystify the sun and its power.

Passage 101: Summary / Paraphrase

The passage is about silver plating. The main idea is that silver plating is done using a process known as electroplating. The major points explain the process of electroplating: (a) the object to be plated is dipped in silver salt (b) an electrical connection is made with the object serving as the cathode and the silver solution serving as the anode (c) a current is passed through, and the silver dissolves and deposits on the cathode. There is a minor point that minor alterations to the process allow it to be applied to gold and other metals as well. The purpose of the passage is to explain the process of silver plating.

Answer to Question 247:

The correct answer is E. The writer states that silver has a pleasing appearance. A pleasing appearance would add aesthetic appeal to an object, making answer choice E the best choice. There is no mention of planting's being done to either fool consumers or to add value to an object, eliminating A and B as correct answers. The author fails to say that electroplating makes objects shiny, so C is also incorrect. Anodes and cathodes are the poles of a battery and have plenty of uses other than electroplating, making D the wrong choice. Answer E is the best choice.

Passage 102: Summary / Paraphrase

The passage is about induced magnets. The main idea is that induced magnets have some unusual properties that are unlike other magnets. The major points are (a) that induced magnets are caused when an ordinary magnet is brought near a magnetic pole (b) that induced magnets have a single pole evenly distributed over their surface and (c) that induced magnets become weak ordinary magnets when they are moved beyond the field of the inducing pole. A minor point details the way that iron filings behave on an induced magnet. The purpose of the passage is to inform the reader about an unusual form of magnetism.

Answer to Question 248:

Both A and B are correct. The conclusion in answer B can be derived from the next-to-last sentence in the passage, "the filings at the remote end will generally be held permanently". Answer choice A is confirmed in the fifth sentence of the passage, "the single pole is pretty evenly distributed over the whole surface." The writer reveals that a bar of iron is used in the experiment, but there is nothing to indicate that it must first be magnetized, so C is not a correct choice.

Answer to Question 249:

The correct answer is A. Alleged is not proven, and exaggerated is beyond what is provable. The writer is expressing skepticism; he needs proof. A is the correct answer. He is not expressing reluctance to believe; in fact, he wants to believe the claim. There are no words that express admiration. The passage is a fairly straightforward narrative. Neither B nor C is correct. Convinced is the opposite of skeptical. If the writer were convinced, he would not use words like Alleged and exaggeration. If the writer were being critical, he would reveal weaknesses and/or mistakes. D and E are not acceptable choices

Passage 103: Summary / Paraphrase

The passage is about GPS satellites. The main idea is that by exploiting new orbital patterns, GPS satellites can perfect their coverage. The major points are (a) that signals from GPS satellites were not always easy to pick up due to blockages from building or landforms (b) that by sending satellites into irregular orbits, the problem areas could be covered. The purpose of the passage is to briefly explain a problem with GPS coverage and how it was solved.

Answer to Question 250:

The correct answer is "The GPS satellites provide coded timing signals that allow a receiver to determine its location on Earth, but GPS signals are not always easy to pick up in Japan's mountainous regions or skyscraper-studded cities like Tokyo."

One of the difficulties with traditional GPS in Japan occurred as a result its being a mountainous country. The reader can assume that the same difficulties would arise in other areas of the world where mountains are a dominant feature of the geography.

Passage 104: Summary / Paraphrase

The passage is about a "miracle drug" that is being developed to treat radiation sickness. The main idea is that although scientists claim to have found a simple pill that can decontaminate a human body within two weeks, we should be guarded and skeptical of these claims. The major points are: (a) the most dangerous effect of a nuclear disaster is long-term radiation contamination, which leads to grave illness and death in those affected (b) that scientists working on decontaminating victims of radiation poisoning have discovered a pill that claims to quickly cure radiation sickness (c) that this "miracle cure" is almost undoubtedly too good to be true because (1) if a claim is too good to be true, it usually is (2) the pill may have untold side effects. The discussion is framed by a minor point that discusses our current and historic concern with fallout from nuclear disasters. The main purpose of the passage is to question the trustworthiness of the claim that a pill can rapidly cure radiation sickness. The tone is highly skeptical and shows a strong bias against the idea that the proposed miracle cure is really a cure. The author also assumes that past instances of things being too good to be true is evidence enough that the proposed cure is too good to be true, without citing any evidence against it.

Answer to Question 251:

The correct answer is D.

A. Wrong. The author is not recounting the story of scientific research relative to radiation treatment, rather using this passage to persuade the reader that the anti-radiation treatments are likely ineffective and unhealthy.

B. Wrong. There is absolutely nothing objective or unbiased about this passage; it is driven by the author's personal opinions in an attempt to persuade the reader that anti-radiation drug treatments are likely ineffective and potentially harmful.

C. Wrong. The passage itself is not a scientific theory, it is a piece of persuasive prose that the author is using to try to convince the reader that the radiation treatment being developed at the Berkeley Lab is likely ineffective and predicated on a false promise: the quick fix.

D. Correct. The author uses this piece as a platform to persuade the reader to believe his or her opinion that the effectiveness and safety of the radiation treatment being developed at the Berkeley Lab is unproven and likely a false promise.

E. Wrong. The author does not draw any comparisons relative to the research and development of radiation treatment, rather uses this piece as a platform to persuade the reader to believe his or her personal opinion on the matter: the effectiveness of the radiation treatment is likely a false promise.

Answer to Question 252:

The correct answer is A.

A. Correct. The first section is the claim of the Berkeley Lab scientists, which is that they can cure radiation exposure with a pill. The second section demonstrates that the author is trying to undermine the claim of the scientists by stating that their assertion is suspect and drawing attention to the fact that the side effects of the radiation treatment are still unknown.

B. Wrong. Only the first bold-faced section is an assertion; the second bold-faced section is the author's attempt to undermine the Berkeley's scientists claim that they can cure radiation exposure with a pill - it is a demonstration of the author's personal opinion. The second section is not in itself a claim and hence both sections cannot be congruent assertions.

C. Wrong. While the first section is correctly identified as the scientist's claim, the second section is not the author's main claim; it is the author's attitude or position towards the main claim of the scientists. The author's main claim is that the assertions of the scientists should not be believed until more proof can be given relative to the effectiveness of their radiation treatment.

Answer to Question 253:

The correct answer is "While it is no doubt of the utmost importance to find a way to cure the effects of radiation, one must be skeptical of the treatment method proposed by the Berkeley Lab scientists because things that sound too good to be true are good to be true."

In this sentence the author acknowledges the efforts of the Berkeley Lab scientists (concession), but ultimately, he or she uses the remainder of the sentence to demonstrate that their claims "sound too good to be true" (rebuttal).

Passage 105: Summary / Paraphrase

The passage is about the hypothetical Higgs boson. The main idea is that while calling the Higgs boson "the God particle" may be misleading, actually finding the particle would unlock some of the profoundest mysteries of modern physics. There are two main points: (a) discovery of the Higgs boson would not have any bearing on the existence of spiritual beings (b) discovery of the Higgs boson would explain the origins of particle mass, and would indicate that string theory is on the right track. The main purpose of the passage is to clarify and inform. The author wants to debunk the notion of the Higgs boson having supernatural implications, while affirming its profound implications.

Answer to Question 254:

The correct answer is B.

A. Wrong. The passage indicates that the God particle is another name for the Higgs boson particle.

B. Correct. The passage does not claim that the Higgs boson itself is the origin of particle mass in the universe, just that its discovery could potentially explain the origins of particle mass in the universe.

C. Wrong. Since the passage makes it clear that there is no proof of the Higgs boson then it is still just a hypothesis.

D. Wrong. The passage states that the Higgs boson is an elementary particle in physics.

E. Wrong. The passage states that finding the Higgs boson particle would reinforce the hypothesis of string theory.

Passage 106: Summary / Paraphrase

The passage is about the impact of scientific progress on health. The main idea is that developments in all scientific fields can have an impact on medical progress. The main idea is supported by a major point: that chemist have recently discovered new materials that could potentially be used for a variety of medical diagnoses and treatments. The purpose of the passage is to inform the reader about the extent to which medical progress draws on broader scientific progress.

Answer to Question 255:

The correct answer is C.

A. Wrong. The passage indicates that disease diagnostics and the engineering of new human tissues are indeed a byproduct of the new "smart" polymer, but since avant-garde is analogous to groundbreaking; the real merit in the new scientific discovery is the fact that the "smart" polymer could assist light in being used as a medicine.

B. Wrong. The passage does not discuss and does not give any information from which one could infer as to whether or not the development of the "smart" polymer will give chemists a competitive edge in the medical field.

C. Correct. The passage states that the new "smart" polymer is groundbreaking, which can be a synonym for avant-garde, and it specifically points out that this is true because the "smart" polymer would allow light to be transformed into a medicine.

D. Wrong. The passage does not indicate that the "smart" polymer was a product of scientific interdisciplinary cooperation.

E. Wrong. The passage makes it very clear that the "smart" polymer is special, specifically because it could facilitate the use of light for medicinal purposes.

Answer to Question 256:

The correct answer is C.

A. Wrong. While it is true that the section in bold-face shows that scientists and doctors cooperate, it is primarily intended to draw attention to the fact that our medicine develops in ways we never think of or expect.

B. Wrong. The primary purpose of the section in bold-face is to draw attention to the fact that medical advances are often beyond the grasp of our imaginations, not to merely show us those doctors and scientists are creative.

C. Correct. The section in bold-face draws special attention to the fact that we cannot imagine the various ways in which medicine will evolve.

D. Wrong. The section in bold-face does not indicate that medical advances could not occur without the cooperation of scientists and doctors, rather draws attention to the fact that their cooperation creates medical advances that are hard to imagine.

E. While the section in bold-face draws attention to the fact that we cannot always imagine the medical developments, this does not mean that our imaginations in and of themselves are limited.

Answer to Question 257:

The correct answer is "Chemists report that their new polymer (plastic-like) material could help diagnose diseases and engineer new human tissues; whether or not these claims can be substantiated is another matter."

For the majority of the passage the author's tone towards the new "smart" polymer is one of excitement and intrigue. However, the last sentence demonstrates that the author is actually skeptical as to whether or not the new "smart" polymer can live up to the promises of the scientists.

Passage 107: Summary / Paraphrase

The passage is about astrophysics. The main idea is that astrophysics now believes that it is not uncommon for planets in other solar systems to orbit more than one star, a notion that was once largely relegated to the realm of science fiction. The major points are (a) that the climate on a planet orbiting two stars would be quite unstable (b) that scientists are unsure of how or if life would come to be on such planets. The main purpose of the passage is to inform the reader about a recent development in astrophysics.

Answer to Question 258:

The correct answer is C.

A. Wrong. The author does draw a comparison between circumbinary planets in both Star Wars and now in scientific reality, but this does not mean that the author is drawing a parallel between science fiction and science overall, not enough information is given by the author to support such a broad, sweeping claim.

B. Wrong. This is a far-fetched inference that the reader could draw from the author's mention of Star Wars, but it is not the intent of the author to invoke Star Wars as a commentary how science fiction precedes scientific knowledge.

C. Correct. The author's use of Star Wars is a stylistic device used to peak the readers interest in a scientific text by relating the content of the passage to a common cultural reference.

D. Wrong. While the author does invoke Star Wars to peak the reader's interest in the text, this is a stylistic strategy rather than a rhetorical strategy: the author is not using Star Wars as a means of persuading the reader to adhere to a particular viewpoint. Furthermore, the narrative rhetorical strategy requires a recounting of events which clearly does not take place with reference to Star Wars.

E. Wrong. The author is in no way advocating or advertising for Star Wars, merely introducing it as a stylistic strategy to peak the reader's interest.

Answer to Question 259:

The correct answer is C.

A. Wrong. The passage indicates that scientists are unsure how life manifests and evolves on other planets, so circumbinary planets cannot help us better understand the way life materializes or evolves on other planets.

B. Wrong. The passage does not give enough information to indicate that researching circumbinary planets will help scientists understand climate change on Earth.

C. Correct. The passage only gives us enough information to let us know that circumbinary planets can help us better understand the way the sun controls planetary climates.

Passage 108: Summary / Paraphrase

The passage is about advances in biotechnology. The main idea is that while biochemical research is coming ever closer to creating life, actually doing so could have severely adverse consequences. The major points are that (a) biochemists are using a new chemical reaction to create self-assembling cell membranes (b) scientists hope the understanding cell-membranes, which are one of the basic building blocks of life, will lead to insights into how non-living matter becomes life and (c) in the author's view, some questions are best left unanswered, especially in view of the potentially destructive potential of such breakthroughs. The main purpose of the passage is to caution against research that digs too deeply into the origins of life. Rhetorical devices such as the mention of Pandora's Box and the vague danger of total annihilation indicate that the author has a strong bias against the research under discussion.

Answer to Question 260:

The correct answer is C.

A. Wrong. The author does provide the facts related to the potential creation of artificial life forms, but the entire passage is infused with the author's bias against this line of scientific inquiry; there is no purely objective evaluation of the facts.

B. Wrong. While the last line of the passage is certainly a dramatic way of driving home the author's point about the dangers of the creation of artificial life, the author primarily reinforces his or her claim by providing a counterview to the argument in delineating what scientists think about the matter.

C. Correct. The author's point that the creation of artificial life is problematic is driven home by the fact that the author also provides a counterview to his point, showing that the author is willing to both understand the other side and yet still maintain his or her own viewpoint.

D. Wrong. The author does not directly and harshly criticize the opinions of the scientists, just disputes them.

E. Wrong. The author provides no specific authority who agrees with his or her claims; the author's authority in this passage is merely his or her own opinions.

Answer to Question 261:

The correct answer is D.

A. Wrong. Whether or not the reader understands the meaning of the Pandora's box metaphor, the author still clearly delineates what it means in the same sentence by saying that creating artificial life would engender a situation in which scientists could not undo the consequences. The author's strategy is double-layered and provides both the metaphor and its literal meaning simultaneously, showing that the Pandora's box trope is not used to test the reader's intelligence.

B. Wrong. Pandora's Box is a metaphor for an action with consequences that cannot be undone and its use does not necessitate that the consequences can never be controlled.

C. Wrong. Pandora's Box is a metaphor for an action whose consequences can never be undone and but this does not mean that the consequences are evil. Hence, invoking Pandora's Box does not show that the creation of artificial life is evil.

D. Correct. The author is making the point that the creation of artificial life may have far reaching consequences that can never be undone and uses the trope or metaphor of Pandora's Box as a rhetorical device to reinforce this point.

E. Wrong. Pandora's Box is not a red herring since it is a metaphor that reinforces the author's main claim and not a rhetorical device that distracts the reader from the issue at hand.

Answer to Question 262:

The correct answer is E.

A. Wrong. The last sentence of the passage is meant to persuade the reader to believe in the author's opinion by way of a rhetorical appeal to the reader's emotions or sense of values (pathos).

B. Wrong. The author does not believe that the scientific research mentioned in the passage is important, rather that it is dangerous.

C. Wrong. The author does not generalize a specific argument in the last sentence of the passage, but instead uses the end of the passage to appeal to the sensibilities of the reader as a means of persuading the reader to agree with his or her viewpoint.

D. Wrong. The last sentence does not lay out more details related to self-assembling membranes; it actually seeks to convince the reader that scientific research vis-a-vis self-assembling membranes is dangerous.

E. Correct. The author uses the last sentence to appeal to the reader's sense of values or emotions (pathos).

Passage 109: Summary / Paraphrase

The passage is about our understanding of the universe. The main idea is that physicists' lack of clear understanding of dark matter is a good example of how little we really understand the universe. The major points are (a) that scientists posit dark matter to explain sizable stretches of the universe that emit no light or electromagnetic radiation and (b) that there is no definite evidence that dark matter exists. The main purpose of the passage is to use dark matter to illustrate a point about the limits of human knowledge.

Answer to Question 263:

The correct answer is "Thus, dark matter provides a good example of how little we really know about the structures that compose our universe."

In the last sentence of the passage, the author makes it clear that he or she believe that astrophysics still has a long way to go in fully elucidating the structure and functioning of the universe.

Passage 110: Summary / Paraphrase

The passage is about the way physical geography divides up the earth by climate zones. The main idea is that climactic zones, known as biomes, are crucial to understanding the balance of life on earth. The major points are (a) that biomes support a rich variety of plant and animal life and (b) the diversity of biomes is vital to sustaining the balance of life. A minor point specifies the major types of biome. The purpose of the passage is to raise awareness of biomes and their importance.

Answer to Question 264:

The correct answer is "There are four main types of biome: aquatic, forest, desert, and grassland and while all are different, all equally important because they are like threads in woven into the same tapestry: planet earth."

The last sentence creates a metaphor that likens the earth and its biomes to a tapestry and the author does this to underscore the fact that each part of the biome is unique but all are equally important.

Passage 111: Summary / Paraphrase

The passage is about climate change. The main idea is that although people are prone to jump to conclusions about the climate based off transitory trends in the weather, the real picture is more complex. The major points are (a) that people tend to see extreme temperatures, depending on the nature of the extreme, as either a confirmation or a refutation of global warming and (b) research suggests that factors associated with extreme high temperatures can also be used to explain severe winters. The purpose of the passage is to caution the reader from drawing glib solutions about the phenomenon about climate change by showing at least one way in which doing so has been demonstrated to be wrong.

Answer to Question 265:

The correct answers are B and C.

A. Wrong. The author is skeptical of public and scientific reaction to climate change but there is no indication that he or she is afraid of it.

B. Correct. Incredulous means skeptical or suspicious and since the author seems to be wary of the climate change hysteria permeating public and scientific discourse, incredulous is a good way to characterize the author's attitude.

C. Correct. Dubious means to be wary or suspicious of something and given the author's introductory sentence, it is clear that the author is skeptical of the climate change hysteria permeating public and scientific discourse.

Passage 112: Summary / Paraphrase

The passage is about the Big Bang theory. The main idea is that while the origins of the universe are still controversial, the Big Bang theory is the most widely accepted explanation. There are two major points that briefly sketch the basics of the theory: (a) that universe existed in an extremely hot and dense microcosm of itself and then exploded outward and created stars and galaxies in the process and (b) that the Big Bang is estimated to have occurred roughly 14 billion years ago. The main purpose of the passage is to give a brief, factual summary of the current position of science on the origins of the universe without commenting on whether that position is or is not correct.

Answer to Question 266:

The correct answers are B and C.

A. Wrong. Contingency means chance or possibility and polemic means dispute so the two terms are not analogous.

B. Correct. Both brouhaha and polemic are synonyms for dispute and thus the two terms are analogous.

C. Correct. Both argument and polemic are synonyms for dispute and thus the two terms are analogous.

Passage 113: Summary / Paraphrase

The passage is about antimatter. The main idea is that antimatter was posited as a way of understanding the behavior of electrons, but deeper understanding was not possible until the development of particle accelerators. The main points are that (a) antimatter is composed of antiparticles, just as matter is composed of particles (b) Dirac hypothesized the existence of antimatter as a way of better understanding electrons and (c) that the existence of antimatter was only proven by particle accelerators. There is a minor point that most current research on antimatter is at CERN, in Geneva. The main purpose of the passage is to familiarize the reader with some very basic points about antimatter, and give a brief, factual account of how it was initially posited.

Answer to Question 267:

The correct answer is C.

A. Wrong. While this may be the case, the author does not point to this line of thinking as the impetus behind Dirac's investigations into antimatter.

B. Wrong. The author does not claim that understanding electrons is the key to unlocking the universe, nor does the author show this to be the reasoning behind Dirac's hypothesis.

C. Correct. Dirac's antimatter hypothesis is founded on the presupposition that everything has an opposite.

D. Wrong. The passage does not indicate that Dirac believed in the idea that the universe could be fully delineated or he used such thinking to formulate his antimatter hypothesis.

E. Wrong. The passage discusses that Dirac conceptualized antimatter in the late 1920s but that it couldn't be tested until at least the 1960s, so it can be reasonably inferred that technological capabilities and scientific ideas do not always align.

Answer to Question 268:

The correct answer is A.

A. Correct. The author is recounting the conceptualization of the anti-matter hypothesis.

B. Wrong. A testimony relays a truth or conviction that something is true; this passage is merely recounting the development of the antimatter hypothesis.

C. Wrong. The passage itself is not a scientific theory, it is a recounting of the development of a scientific hypothesis.

D. Wrong. The author is not directly trying to persuade the reader to believe in the antimatter hypothesis.

E. Wrong. The author does not draw any comparisons relative to the development of the antimatter hypothesis.

Passage 114: Summary / Paraphrase

The passage highlights the issues faced by explorers in Antarctica due to the cold winds. The author starts by explaining how the katabatic winds are formed and proceeds to warn that these winds though steady can turn wild at times. He gives two examples to support his statement. He concludes by saying that not all winds in the Antarctic are so chaotic.

Answer to Question 269:

The correct answer is B and C. The reading makes no mention of atmospheric issues such as storm fronts. It does point out that the winds come off of the cold air from the mountains, implying that the coastal areas are warmer, thus B and C are correct.

Answer to Question 270:

The correct answer is C. The correct answer has a generality that the other options lack. Further, the correct answer actually indicates problems. The other sentences either indicate no actual problems or refer to specific events, not general problems.

Practice Set 6 - Social Sciences

Passage 115:

Answer to Question 271:

The correct answer is E. Commerce breaking bulk at this particular location is noted as a reason for the city's rapid development. This definition provides a practical explanation for the influx of people from different areas into the city. The unloading and dissemination of cargo and its accompanying commerce would clearly provide a motivation for those seeking work to settle in Cincinnati. This definition is also consistent with the wording of the phrase. "To break bulk" can be expanded to mean "to break out of bulk form and distribute." A is incorrect. It would not make sense for a city to grow where commerce shrinks. B is incorrect because stagnation would also not explain Cincinnati's development. C is incorrect. The term is used to explain the relationship between geography and commerce and does not justify this interpretation. D is incorrect for the same reason.

Answer to Question 272:

The correct answer is B. The passage declares that Cincinnati's history is important to study because African Americans benefit greatly when they have the support of white citizens. This is presented as a general principle to emulate. A is incorrect. The passage does not specify the relative sizes of the two demographics. C is incorrect. The passage implies that 25% of settlers ending up in one city is unusually high. It does not suggest that other settlers actively avoided it or why they would do so. Cincinnati's geography is mentioned to partially explain its economic growth. D is incorrect. The passage states that white citizens offered encouragement but in no way implies that Black citizens were accepted as equals. E is incorrect. The passage makes a general statement about "white neighbors." Nothing implies that these neighbors were exclusively foreign or why encouragement was offered.

Answer to Question 273:

The correct answer is B. The paragraph mentions that Cincinnati's economic expansion attracted African-American settlers. A is incorrect. The "encouragement" mentioned occurred between "neighbors" within the city; it is not suggested that it was an encouragement to African American immigration to the city. C is incorrect. The city's location is mentioned as an explanation for its economic growth, not as a matter of convenience for Black immigrants.

Answer to Question 274:

The correct answer is "The study of the history of the Negroes of Cincinnati is unusually important for the reason that from no other annals do we get such striking evidence that the colored people generally thrive when encouraged by their white neighbours."

This sentence contains the specific example of the history of African Americans in Cincinnati that illustrates a general principle about what happens when white citizens encourage their black neighbors. The other sentences contain only specific facts about Cincinnati racial history.

Passage 116:

Answer to Question 275:

The correct answer is (D).

"D" is the correct answer; though the author focuses on and describes the negative associations that many people have with anarchism, the main idea of the passage focuses on the benefits of anarchism. The author explains that the positive effects of anarchism outweigh the negative effects; though anarchism may be destructive, it only destroys negative forces—"parasitic growths that feed on the life's essence of society".

"A" touches upon one of the misconceptions of anarchism as stated in the passage, though the people who 'act before they think' are the uneducated people who think that anarchism is wrong, not the anarchists themselves, as this answer incorrectly states.

"B" is incorrect because this passage does not imply that anarchism hinders societal progress; rather, it argues that anarchism is only thought to be negative by people who do not think about it enough.

"C" is almost correct, yet incorrectly states that people who are afraid of anarchism are well–educated; the passage states that the people who fear anarchism are in fact not well-informed.

"E" is incorrect because the passage does not touch upon the idea of why non-anarchists do not rebel. The passage also does not say that their unwillingness to take action is the reason for their criticism; rather, the passage states that their criticism of anarchists stems more from a lack of information than laziness.

Answer to Question 276:

The correct answer is (A).

"A" is correct; the first sentence introduces the notion that people who lack knowledge about anarchism base their beliefs on stories and rumors, and the second explains another reason that the uninformed people who fear anarchism believe it to be bad, though they are wrong.

"B" is incorrect because these sentences do not infer that anarchism creates ignorance; rather, they explain that ignorance creates a negative view of anarchism.

"C" is partially correct; the first sentence does touch upon the scary or 'blood-curdling' stories that circulate about anarchism, but there is no mention in the second sentence of 'combative' forces.

"D" is incorrect in its claim that the second sentence refutes the problems that stem from ignorance, because to do so would go against the argument of the whole passage.

"E" is almost correct; in regard to the first sentence, it is accurate to say that uneducated people are being criticized for basing their opinions on hearsay, but the second sentence has nothing to do with such rumors and stories.

Answer to Question 277:

The correct answers are (B) and (C).

"B" and "C" are correct in reiterating the argument of this passage, which states both the opinions that anarchism is useful and that only ignorant, uninformed people disagree with the benefits of anarchism.

"A" is incorrect because it states that anarchism is detrimental to society, which is the opposite of what the author believes.

Answer to Question 278:

The correct answer is "It is merely clearing the soil from weeds and sagebrush, that it may eventually bear healthy fruit."

This sentence depicts the reality of the destruction that anarchism may cause, but compares it to destroying weeds in a garden to demonstrate the necessity of doing away with certain negative forces in order to clear the way for progress.

Passage 117:

Answer to Question 279:

The correct answer is "Good appears to arise out of evil, and the inscrutable ways of Providence are vindicated by general results, rather than by instances of particular care."

The phrase "instances of particular care" contrasts with the phrase "by general results". This implies that Providence sees to the needs of individuals by making situations better for a larger group. For example, if one were to pray for world peace and it comes to pass, everyone benefits, and the results are obvious, creating a visible demonstration of the ways of Providence. On the other hand, if one prays for his own benefit, the effect is minimal on a larger group and likely to go unnoticed.

Answer to Question 280:

The correct answers are A, B and C. All three are suitable responses. The author says, "our minds are not yet sufficiently cleared from the dross of earth to understand" the mysteries of Providence. In other words, man concerns himself with worthless matters and events rather than elevating his thoughts to consider the mysteries of Providence. In the first paragraph, he says that man is more likely to pay attention to the event over which he thinks he has some control. In the same paragraph, he claims that man is more interested in the sordid events of life rather than the "wonders of creation." The sordid events of life could include those that are self-serving, morally ignoble or vile. Those pique man's interest more readily than the natural wonders surrounding him.

Answer to Question 281:

Both answers B and C are reasonable choices His use of the phrase "good rises out of evil" can reasonably lead the reader to expect further examples from history to support this premise. The example of Napoleon appears before the author's final remarks when he tells the reader that they may apply this example and its significance in a way that suits them as they read further. The author's having used this example may lead the reader to infer that similar examples of oppression will follow; he says, "Thus it is ever, with the progress of society." In addition, the author mentions the inscrutable ways of Providence, likely to inform the reader that he will demonstrate how these ways also play a part in the triumph of good over evil, even though man may not understand why or how Providence has played a part in these outcomes. The focus of the writing is how the hand of Providence has had an effect on the lives of humans rather than the legacies or effects that despotic rulers have had on mankind. Therefore, it is unlikely that the author will focus specifically on despotic rulers, so answer A is incorrect.

Answer to Question 282:

The best answer is B, sincere. Sincere means genuine. The author's attitude displays sincere belief in his reader's ability to apply his ideas to their own ways of thinking or living if they are willing to take the time to read and think about them. The author may let his readers make their own decisions, but that does not indicate a lack of interest or concern on his part. He is not apathetic toward his readers, so answer A is incorrect. Neither is the writer being obsequious, which is being polite in order to gain something or an advantage. Answer choice C is incorrect. At first glance, the author's words may seem condescending. The reader may think he is saying that only the intelligent or patient reader will understand what he has written, so the rest should just forget about it. However, the words display confidence in his readers, so answer choice D is wrong. Contemplative would be an appropriate description of the author's attitude toward his topic rather than his readers. Answer choice E is also incorrect.

Answer to Question 283:

The correct answer is D. The author uses them to replace the word God throughout the passage. The Holy Trinity in Christianity consists of the Father, Son, and Holy Ghost, so answer choice A is incorrect. Answer choice B suggests a meaning for Providence apart from the meanings of Creator and Deity. Replacing Providence in any place in the paragraph with the definition provided here would change the meaning of the sentence, so answer choice B is the wrong choice. Answer choice C is incorrect because the author does not suggest that Creator, Deity, and Providence are separate from each other or that one is superior to the others. The author does say that any of these three have control over the events that affect humanity, but does not mention predestination, so answer choice E is incorrect.

Answer to Question 284:

The correct answer is E. The author says "application of these remarks" by which he means that the readers of them will find some truth in them that they can use in their own lives. Peruse means to read carefully, and he hopes that his readers will approach the material in this way in order to grasp the important ideas within. Answer choice A is incorrect because the author, although pointing out the shortcomings of most men, does not claim that they are inferior beings as a result. Answer choice B does not satisfy the meaning of the final words of the passage. It is too limited. He mentions other ideas in addition to the wonders that men take for granted. Answer choice C suggests that his goal is to make mankind see the errors of its ways and believe as he and the other writers do. The final sentence of the passage leaves room for men to form their own ideas. Answer choice C is incorrect. Answer choice D is incorrect because he does not include himself in the segment of humankind that he is addressing in the passage.

Passage 118:

Answer to Question 285:

The correct answer is "The flora and fauna of the Himalayas differ from those of the neighboring plains as greatly as the trees and animals of England differ from those of Africa."

The reader would expect that the flora and fauna of England would be vastly different from that of Africa given the differences in climate and the thousands of miles between them. The author uses this contrast to illustrate that, although the plains and mountains lie in close proximity to each other, their features display as great a contrast as places that are separated by thousands of miles.

Answer to Question 286:

The correct answer is C. Although the author believes that the quote has been overused and, in some cases, in service to a stylistic formula, he does not show contempt for those writers nor does he demean their efforts. He uses this paragraph as a point of contrast to his own inclusion of the quote and his support of the poet's declaration about the beauty of the Himachal, which he praises in the following paragraphs of the piece.

Answer to Question 287:

The correct answer is C. In the fourth paragraph, the author uses detailed description to paint a picture of the desolation present in May followed by a similarly detailed description of the abundance in September. According to the author, the monsoon rains are responsible for the transformation. Answer choice A is incorrect. The author does not describe the months between September and May, which may experience sufficient rain to prevent drought during several of those months. He describes the great contrast in the landscape which occurs between the months of May and September as a result of the monsoon rains, but fails to reveal how the landscape appears in the later months of the year and how the climate affects it. Answer choice B is incorrect. Although the author mentions the startling contrast in the elevation from the plains to the mountains, he does not reveal whether or not this change has any effect on the climate.

Answer to Question 288:

The correct answer is E, compare and contrast. The author begins by lauding the beauty of the Himalayas and proceeds to provide specific details about the flora that exists at each level of altitude, beginning at the lowest and moving to the higher elevations. These details enable the reader to visualize the contrast in conditions from one level to the next. He also provides stark visual images of the contrast between the seasons. Answer choice A is incorrect because the author provides no opinion about the value of any feature of the Himalayas as they relate to each other. Although the reader may infer that flooding - cause- makes it possible for the vegetation to exist - effect- on the plains, the author's intention is informative. Answer choice B is, therefore, incorrect. Answer choice C is incorrect because the author does not introduce a problem or dilemma nor their solutions. Answer choice D is also incorrect. The author does not list specific details in order to make general comments about the area. In fact, he does the opposite. For example, he makes the general comment that the plains are as flat as a pancake and follows it with specific details about the features of the plains.

Answer to Question 289:

The correct answer is A. There is no reason to assume that the author will change topics. The final sentences of the passage reveal the flora at increasing altitudes, and it is likely that the author will continue in this vein. That the author has omitted any reference to the culture of either area should make it unlikely that he will do so now, so answer choice B is incorrect. Answer choice C is incorrect because the author has made no comparison between the two mountain ranges to this point, so he is not apt to do so now. Although the author lists in detail the trees and crops that grow in the alluvial plain, he does not reveal anything about the cultivation of these or any other crops, so it is unlikely that he will proceed to do so in the next paragraph. Answer choice E is incorrect because it does not proceed logically from the last paragraph present here.

Answer to Question 290:

The correct answer is C, fanciful. He has piqued the reader's imagination, first by his allusion to Jekyll and Hyde to introduce the two faces of the Himalayas and ending with the image of a fairyland. Answer A is incorrect because quizzical means odd or eccentric. The author's detailed description, though imaginative, is not eccentric. Answer B is incorrect because his language does not reach the level of being song-like or emotional. The author does not display whimsy in this passage, as whimsical suggests that the writing is odd or strange. As a result, answer choice D is incorrect. Although the author appears to have intimate knowledge of the Himalayas, his words do not evoke a feeling of intimacy, so answer choice E is incorrect.

Passage 119: Summary / Paraphrase

The passage is about the attitude of Japanese officers during World War II. The main idea is that Japanese officers were underprepared for an allied counterattack. There are two main ideas: (a) that many Japanese commanders were overconfident due to the ease of early victories and (b) even those who were more alert to the possibility of an allied counterstrike tended to be ignored by the prevailing opinion. Two minor points amplify and develop the major points: (a) that the Japanese defeat at Midway had gone unpublicized and (b) that Lt. Commander I too had specific intelligence that was ignored. The primary purpose of the passage is to give insight into the prevalent attitudes in the Japanese military that led to their lack of preparedness.

Answer to Question 291:

The correct answer is A. The Japanese were probably optimistic about winning the war, but optimism is not likely to be considered a symptom of disease. Based on previous battle victories, they would feel optimistic when going into battle. Answer A is correct. Courage is a positive emotion and, like optimism, not symptomatic of disease, so B is not correct. Complacency and satisfaction are similar in meaning; it is doubtful that the Japanese would be satisfied until the war ended with their ultimate victory. D and E are incorrect choices. In this context, overconfidence is the best choice. Their overconfidence made them overlook warnings that could have changed the outcome of the war.

Answer to Question 292:

The correct answer is B. The writer includes these details to let the reader know that Haruki had not made a rush to judgment in warning the Japanese command, answer B. One example of work by the Naval Intelligence Center is insufficient to determine its level of efficiency of that group; A is not the correct answer. The passage is not about the location of the Allies in the Pacific; the fact that the positions were discovered is the salient information here, making C an incorrect answer. One might use this investigation by Haruki in conjunction with other actions he has taken to justify his position in the Japanese military, but one action in not enough for that conclusion, eliminating D as a correct answer. To this point in the war, the Japanese had won several naval battles, so their lack of preparedness is not a factor in their ignoring the warning. E is also incorrect.

Passage 120: Summary / Paraphrase

The passage is about American Indian chiefs. The main idea is that the popular understanding of the role of a chief in tribal affairs did not always reflect the actual role of the individuals designated as chiefs. The mains ideas are: (a) while chiefs had traditionally been figureheads with little actual power, they were often political leaders during a key transitional period and (b) the political power of chiefs during this transitional period was due to either backing from the US government or power-plays by ambitious tribesmen. The primary purpose of the passage is to disabuse the reader of a widely-held but not entirely correct belief, and to more accurately inform the reader about the facts.

Answer to Question 293:

The correct answer is D. The writer of this passage is careful to downplay the role of so-called chiefs in the tribal structure prior to interference by the American government. They had no real power or authority. Based on the absence of other information, the reader can conclude that the tribal structure was egalitarian, that all members had the opportunity to express their opinions and that all were listened to. Answer D is the best choice. There is no evidence that the structure was matriarchal - ruled by adult women - or patriarchal - ruled by adult males - so neither A nor B is correct. An oligarchy is ruled by a small select group, which does not appear to be the case here, eliminating C as a correct choice. A tyrant rules by fear, again, not the case with native tribes. E is also incorrect.

Answer to Question 294:

The correct answer is C. Any time that a popularly held belief is shown to be even partially incorrect, one should ask how he/she came to believe it in the first place. The writer of this passage states that the American public's understanding of a tribal chief's function is not correct according to the tribesmen. Now that the reader has a better understanding of the meaning of the title, chief, he or she may wonder what other commonly held ideas about the natives may also be incorrect or inaccurate. Answer C is the best choice. There is no mention in the passage of any specific chiefs, so curiosity about their names would not arise in this context, making A an incorrect answer choice. The purpose of the passage is to clarify the position of the chief in a tribe and not about the actual negotiations that took place between tribes and the American government, so it is not likely that the reader would have questions about the number of tribes involved in the negotiations, making B an incorrect answer choice. The violent deaths of chiefs is mentioned as an event that led to Americans taking advantage of the tribes, and the reason for their deaths is not important in this case. D is not the best answer choice. Although the writer mentions that chiefs served "more or less" as politicians, he does so to clarify their positions in the tribes. There is no evidence that the chiefs' behavior influenced the behavior of the Americans, eliminating E as a correct answer.

Answer to Question 295:

The correct answer is C. Extraordinary would be used in the sense of an achievement or accomplishment and does not apply in this context, so A is not the correct choice. Answer E refers to the use of the word in grammar, so it is not the correct choice. It is not a separate or individual idea, either, eliminating D as the correct answer. Distinctive or unique means that it stands alone as an example; there is no other like it. Answer C is to the best choice. Answer B is not the best choice in this case because this "singular" fact is neither unusual nor strange.

Passage 121: Summary / Paraphrase

The passage is about the Baluch tribes. The main idea is to explain that the Baluch are not a single homogeneous population. The major points (a) characterize Baluch tribesmen along ethnic lines explaining that the Balcuh draw from Arab, Persian and Dravidian stock and (b) characterize the Baluch in terms of stereotypical character and bearing. There is an extensive discussion of stereotypical attributes of a variety of different Baluch tribesmen. The main purpose of the passage is to characterize the Baluch people. The rhetoric of the passage is fairly chatty and anecdotal, suggesting that it is likely an ethnographic piece from an earlier time when stereotypical observations were favored over scientific rigor.

Answer to Question 296:

The correct answer is "As a revenue payer he is not so satisfactory, his want of industry and the pride which looks upon manual labor as degrading making him but a poor husbandman."

A Husbandman is a farmer; the Baluch's disdain for manual labor, a requirement for farming, makes it unlikely that they would be farmers.

Answer to Question 297:

Both B and C are reasonable choices. Because they are tribal by nature, the Baluchi are most likely to feel little connection to the interests of India. They have little in common with the native people of India. Their predilection to banditry along with their reluctance to contribute financially to society makes them unlikely to observe the strict standards required by military service. There is nothing in the passage to suggest that they feel superior to soldiers in the Indian army, eliminating A as a correct answer choice.

Answer to Question 298:

The best answer choice is D. Environment and tradition would nurture the character of the Baluch, while origin and descent would determine the nature of the Baluch. The author's use of these terms suggests that both nature and nurture have had equal influences on the resulting character of the Baluch. Answer choices B and C claim that either nature or nurture has had a greater effect on their resulting character, eliminating them as reasonable answer choices. There is nothing in the passage to suggest that the Baluch scoff at the traditions of Indian culture, making A incorrect. Answer choice E may be a correct inference on the part of the reader, it does not respond to the phrases used in the question, making it incorrect also.

Answer to Question 299:

The correct answer is D, digest. A gazetteer includes only geographical information, so A is incorrect. An atlas also deals with geography, making answer B incorrect. An almanac, published annually, includes a calendar, information about weather, when to plant a garden, etc. It is not the most likely place to find the passage above; C is incorrect. An anthology is a collection of writings by the same author or writings by different authors in the same genre, such as a poetry anthology. E is not the correct choice.

Passage 122: Summary / Paraphrase

The passage is about a previously unknown tribe of indigenous islanders. The main idea of the passage is to summarily characterize the islanders. There are no major points, merely a list of information of the islanders that indicates that they had little exposure to modern life. The purpose of the passage is to describe a previously unknown tribe.

Answer to Question 300:

The correct answer is C. The writer explicitly reveals that the natives eat taro and yams, both vegetables. Because the natives have spears and knives and trade goats and pigs, the reader may conclude that they also kill and eat meat. It would be difficult, with the limited information in this passage, to believe that their diet is either restrictive or inclusive, so answer choices D and E must be eliminated. There is nothing in the passage to suggest that the natives are aggressive, so A is also incorrect. Narcissism is also not evident here, making answer choice B incorrect. Opportunistic describes people who recognize and take advantage of an opportunity, much as these natives do when they paddle around the ship waiting to dive for objects that are thrown overboard. Overt means open or obvious. It was obvious to those on the ship that the natives waited openly for items to be thrown overboard. That the natives exhibit some vanity is revealed by the writer's description of the designs on their canoes and the body ornamentation in the form of goats' beards and shells worn by the natives. Answer C is the best choice.

Passage 123: Summary / Paraphrase

The passage is about political philosophy. The main idea is that any form of government that privileges one person over another is patently corrupt and oppressive. The major points are: (a) that once people recognize the natural laws that govern them, they will necessarily obey them, obviating the need for government and (b) that any form of government is oppressive because it will always privilege a governing minority at the expense the majority. The main purpose of the passage is to provide a rationale for anarchy.

Answer to Question 301:

The correct answer is A, manifesto. A manifesto is a declaration of intentions, opinions, or objectives; this passage is clearly a declaration of an opinion. A proclamation, edict, fiat, or mandate is an official declaration or instruction and is backed up by some form of authority. This fact of authority eliminates all of the other answer choices.

Passage 124: Summary / Paraphrase

The passage is about the performance of homeschooled students. The main idea is that despite concerns about their ability to compete with those educated in public schools, they actually perform slightly better than their peers according to some measures. The major point is that homeschooled students tend to perform noticeably better on achievement tests and college entrance exams than their peers. The purpose of the passage is to debunk the common perception that homeschooled students are under-prepared for college. The rhetorical question "But are these students skilled enough to compete successfully with conventionally-schooled students in the college setting?" frames the debate

Answer to Question 302:

The correct answer is D. Typical performance cannot be determined from one set of score. Each year's testing cohort can vary considerably. Without at least three years of results, one cannot determine a trend. Home schooled students would have to perform better over time to establish a pattern of higher achievement. Socioeconomic status and curriculum can affect scores on standardized tests, but those variables can vary for each cohort as well, which further supports including several years' test results in determining a trend. Other standardized tests may measure abilities very different from those measured by the SAT or ACT, so the score have no correlation, eliminating B as the correct answer. The colleges to which the students were accepted do not determine SAT or ACT scores, so E is also incorrect.

Passage 125: Summary / Paraphrase

The passage is about fertility rates. The main idea is that the total fertility rate is a more direct measure than the birth rate for determining a nation's potential for population change. The major points are (a) the total fertility rate measures the average number of children per woman (b) the total fertility rate tells demographers whether population is growing, declining, or holding steady (c) fertility rates are generally declining, especially in industrialized nations. The purpose of the passage is to explain a method for demographers to determine rates of population growth.

Answer to Question 303:

The best answer choice is C. As population growth declines, the median age of the population rises, eventually leading to a disproportionately large number of older people who will require more health care and/or long-term care. A is not the correct choice because fewer children will be born, decreasing the demand for child care. With fewer people competing for available jobs, it is more likely that unemployment will decline, making B incorrect. A reduction in population means that fewer people share in the wealth of the country, causing a decline in poverty. D is not the best answer. Having to spend less on education frees up budget dollars for other societal needs. E is not the correct response.

Answer to Question 304:

The correct answer is B. Non-industrialized countries likely have fewer career opportunities for women, so they are less likely to postpone having children. There is not enough information in this passage to infer that divorce rates have any effect on fertility rates, so A cannot be the correct answer. Neither the number of live births nor infant mortality has an impact on fertility rates, eliminating both C and D as correct answers. The presence of an extended family may contribute to child care, but may not have an effect on fertility rates, so E is incorrect. The correct answer is B.

Passage 126: Summary / Paraphrase

The passage is about human rights in Malaysia. The main idea is that Malaysia is a notorious hub of human trafficking. The major points are that (a) Malaysia is a destination for people trafficked for both sexual exploitation and for forced labor and (b) that while Malaysia took action to improve its anti-trafficking laws, it has yet to tackle exploitative labor practices. The purpose of the passage is to inform the reader about the status of human trafficking in Malaysia.

Answer to Question 305:

The correct answer is A. The passage reveals that men, women and children from South and Southeast Asia willingly migrate to Malaysia to work. One can infer that jobs are in short supply in the countries that they have left. Answer A is the correct answer. There is no information in the passage about the cultural beliefs in Malaysia, so answer B cannot be correct. We also cannot infer that the Malaysian culture is more accepting of child labor, eliminating C as the correct answer. There are no details about the 2000 UN TIP Protocol and its restrictions, so D must be eliminated as an answer. Finally, the passage does not reveal that industrialized nations outsource their labor to Malaysia; E is not correct.

Passage 127: Summary / Paraphrase

The passage is about the archaeology of cave dwellings. The main idea is that the distribution of finds is often counterintuitive. The major points are (a) over centuries of occupation, cave dwellers left behind many layers of leavings (b) the leavings are sometimes found in unexpected layers (c) the occupants of the caves may themselves dug into the layers and buried bodies and implements in a way that disturbed the layering process. The purpose of the passage is to explain how objects from a much older age can often be found alongside much newer objects in archaeological sites.

Answer to Question 306:

The correct answer is C. Depending on the age of the artifacts, there may be no written records or residents left in the area who can, through memory or oral tradition, identify the function or relative age of the artifacts, making A and B incorrect choices. The level or degree of preservation can depend on a variety of factors, including weather over time or the type of soil in which they were found, so it is not a reliable means of dating artifacts. D is not the correct answer choice. Sorting the artifacts according to their function will only make collections of artifacts that serve a similar function. Using earlier discoveries or prior knowledge about human artifacts is the most logical place to begin dating what has been found.

Passage 128: Summary / Paraphrase

The passage is about gender differences in imitation of behaviors. The main idea is that women tend to imitate the way other women behave more than men tend to imitate the way other men behave. The main point is that studies show that women tend to imitate other women in their eating habits, where men do not exhibit a similar pattern, lending credence to an existing hypothesis that women exhibit more same-sex imitation than men. There is a minor point that speculates that the reason for this phenomenon is that women have a greater need to fit in to and be liked by groups. The purpose of the passage is to inform and explain, which is indicated by the straightforward and factual language.

Answer to Question 307:

The correct answer is B.

A. Wrong. It can be inferred from the information given in the passage that women have a greater tendency to conform to their same-gender counterparts because they have a stronger need to be liked by other females.

B. Correct. Just because men are not as keen as females are to follow group behavior at the dining table does not mean that men are the less conventional gender as a whole; the passage does not allude to the fact that men are never conventional, just vis-a-vis the eating habits of their same-gender counterparts.

C. Wrong. Since the passage states that women copy each other's eating habits in a group, it can be inferred that women would then eat generally the same amount of food during a meal together.

D. Wrong. The passage states that women find it important to be liked and accepted by a group and thus the inference can be made that they value how other perceive or see and understand them.

E. Wrong. Since men who dine together do not pay attention to the eating habits of the men around them, it can be inferred that the amount of food consumed by each male in a given dining group will be different.

Passage 129: Summary / Paraphrase

The passage is about the spread of human-kind. The main idea is that while there is a consensus among specialists that humans originated in Africa before spreading outward, there is still debate as to exactly where early humans settled first as they dispersed from northern Africa. The main point is that recent evidence suggests that the initial point of colonization was the Arabian Peninsula. There is a minor point about DNA evidence suggesting genetic similarities between relevant populations that support the major point. The purpose of the passage is to inform and persuade: much of the tone is factual, but the final sentence suggests that the author is trying to get the reader to accept the conclusion that Arabia was the first area of human colonization. The author seems to assume that the evidence cited is conclusive.

Answer to Question 308:

The correct answer is C.

A. Wrong. While the African Diaspora is an important aspect of the passage, the primary purpose of the passage is to show that scientists have determined the location of modern man's dissemination (Arabia)

B. Wrong. The author mentions that many are fascinated by the spread of human culture across the globe, and this "many" includes scientists and the inference can be made that this "many" also includes laymen. However, this statement is never developed and the author never directly references laymen and thus the primary purpose of the passage could not be to discuss the ways in which the interests of scientists and laymen intersect.

C. Correct. The primary purpose of the passage is to discuss the point of origin from which modern man disseminated across the globe; this point was determined to be Arabia by way of DNA analysis.

D. Wrong. The primary goal of the passage is to discuss the point of origin for the dispersal of modern man. DNA analysis helps scientists to determine this point, Arabia, but discussing the use of DNA analysis in anthropological research is not the main purpose of the passage.

E. Wrong. There is nothing polemical about the passage; the author does not use the information relayed in the passage relative to the dispersal of modern man across the globe to instigate a debate.

Answer to Question 309:

The correct answer is C.

A. Wrong. The author's tone and style do not indicate that he or she doubts the validity of DNA as an anthropological research method. The author in fact seems to be neutral towards this practice and thus is not skeptical.

B. Wrong. The author's tone and style do not indicate disbelief relative to anthropological DNA analysis; the author demonstrates candid detachment from the topic and thus is not leery.

C. Correct. The author makes use of a tone and style that do not betray any judgments towards the validity of DNA analysis as an anthropological research method; the author's attitude appears cool and detached thus impartial.

D. Wrong. The author's tone does not suggest that he or she finds DNA analysis a good or favorable anthropological research method, the author's attitude is much more detached and candid.

E. Wrong. The author in no ways exhibits an attitude of devotion or dedication to anthropological DNA analysis; the author is much more detached and observational.

Answer to Question 310:

The correct answer is D.

A. Wrong. The author states that anthropologists are no longer debating whether or not early humans originated in the Horn of Africa, thus the scientific polemics do not focus on this issue.

B. Wrong. The author discusses how DNA samples of Europeans and Arabians were compared to determine the origin of the organized human Diaspora, but the author does not give information to suggest that these two specific places are the focus of scientific debate.

C. Wrong. The author names the Near East as a region subjected to DNA testing but does not give any information about the Near East's specific role in the human Diaspora and definitely does not suggest that the Near East lies at the nexus of scientific debate relative to the dispersal of modern man.

D. Correct. The author indicates that the focus point of scientific debate is the point of origin of modern man's organized dispersal across the globe.

E. Wrong. The author does not say that scientists debate the use of DNA analysis in the study of the dispersal of modern man.

Passage 130: Summary / Paraphrase

The passage is about gender differences in altruistic behaviors. The main idea is that men are more likely than women to change their behavior based on the presence of attractive members of the opposite sex. The two main points are (a) that men are more likely to perform altruistic acts in the presence of attractive women and (b) that this behavior is caused by a need to impress potential mates. The purpose of the passage is to explain gender differences in a particular type of behavior.

Answer to Question 311:

The correct answer is E.

A. Wrong. While the author does objectively evaluate the facts vis-a-vis altruistic behavior in males and females, his or her point is made most compelling by the use of a source of authority, the British Journal of Psychology.

B. Wrong. The author's approach to making his or her claim is deductive and objective and thus not rhetoric aimed at invoking an emotional response.

C. Wrong. The author does not provide a counterview to his or her claim.

D. Wrong. The author does not criticize the opinions of other psychologists.

E. Correct. The author offers a source of authority to back-up his or her claims, the best method of making a claim convincing and believable.

Passage 131: Summary / Paraphrase

The passage is about the longer-term benefits of working hard in college. The main idea is that lazier college students tend to fare significantly worse along several measures than their more industrious peers. There are two main points: (a) that slacker students are at a higher risk of poor economic outcomes and (b) that slacker students often do not improve vital skills such as critical reasoning. The purpose of the passage is to caution students to take college seriously - rhetorical flourishes such as "even more troubling" indicate that the author has a clear bias toward what outcomes are better.

Answer to Question 312:

The correct answer is A.

A. Correct. This option would not weaken the author's claims because several slacker college students who are still able to achieve success are within the margin of error; there are always a few exceptions to every rule.

B. Wrong. The authors maintain that slacker college students suffer from low academic skills like critical reasoning and this hinders their ability to succeed in the future; evidence to the contrary, such as academic skills improvement despite a low work ethic, would definitely undermine the author's claims.

C. Wrong. The author claims that one of the main problems with slacking in college is that it makes it more difficult for students with low work ethics to obtain jobs after graduation; research pointing to a different conclusion, such as there being no marked difference between low and high work ethic students obtaining jobs, would undermine the author's claims.

D. Wrong. If the financial situation of both the hardworking and slacker college students was the same, then the author's claim that it pays to work hard in college would be undermined.

E. Wrong. If the living situation of both the hardworking and slacker college students was the same, then the author's claim that slacker students suffer the consequences of living with their parents post-graduation due to their lack of academic effort would be undermined.

Passage 132: Summary / Paraphrase

The passage is about the political philosophy of Karl Marx. The main idea is that Marxist analysis is a highly useful tool in analyzing a variety of social and political systems. There are two major points: (a) that Marxist analysis has changed the way people think about socio-political systems and (b) that while Marxist theories are often used to critique capitalism, they can also be used to critique socialism and communism, systems that are themselves based in Marxism. The purpose of the passage is to inform the reader of an under-publicized aspect of Marxism, namely its usefulness in critiquing its own systems.

Answer to Question 313:

The correct answer is B.

A. Wrong. Self-reflexivity means the ability of a person (or in this case a theory) to accurately see and assess its own artificialities and contradictions and thus merely saying that Marxism deconstructs capitalistic power structures does not account for self-reflexivity at all.

B. Correct. Since self-reflexivity means the ability to self-critique and find contradictions and artificialities, it is true that, according to the passage, Marxism is self-reflexive because it critically analyzes its own theories.

C. Wrong. Self-reflexivity is the ability to self-critique or analyze and thus it is not a way of delineating the specifics of class conflict in general.

D. Wrong. While it may be true that self-reflexivity, the ability to self-analyze and critique, helps academics set up research frameworks, the passages states that self-reflexivity in Marxism is a particularly valuable feature because it allows for Marxism to critique its own economic theories.

E. Wrong. The passage does not indicate that self-reflexivity or engaging in self-critique creates an environment of free-thinking academic exchange.

Answer to Question 314:

The correct answer is B.

A. Wrong. Dialectic means the method of inquiry that uses discussion as a means of eliciting reason and intellectual discovery and it stands in opposition to the scientific method which gathers information using empirical methods.

B. Correct. Dialectic means to gather intellectual information or reason by way of discussion and debate.

C. Wrong. Dialectic is a method of academic inquiry powered by discussion and protest means to express and objection to words, thoughts, or policies and thus the two terms are not analogous.

D. Wrong. Dialectic is certainly dialogue but it is not limited to the political arena.

E. Wrong. Dialectic is a method of eliciting reason via discussion not the process of worker exploitation.

Passage 133: Summary / Paraphrase

The passage is about how art relates to civilization. The main idea is that, contrary to popular belief, art predates complex human civilizations. There are two main points: (a) that art is often considered constitutive of civilization and (b) recent archaeological finds suggest that art significantly predates civilization. The purpose of the passage is to debunk a commonly held view that the author views as false. The author of the passage makes an implicit assumption that art is well-defined, and that primitive painting is in fact art.

Answer to Question 315:

The correct answer is D.

A. Wrong. The author suggests that the painting kits are an important find because they show that art was practice among the earliest human ancestors, not just one of the characteristics of human civilization.

B. Wrong. The author does discuss the specific tools that were used by the early humans, but the main importance of the tools is that they predate human civilization.

C. Wrong. The author suggests that art was used for body decoration among the early humans, but again the main importance of the findings was the fact that they are evidence that artistic practices predate civilization.

D. Correct. According to the author, the importance of the anthropological discovery of early human painting kits is that they are a sign that artistic practices predate human civilization even though art is typically seen as a marker of human civilization.

E. Wrong. While this statement may be true, the author is more intent on getting the message across that the painting kits are an important find because they show that art predates human civilization.

Passage 134: Summary / Paraphrase

The passage is about Machiavelli's The Prince and its influence. The main idea is that The Prince has been both highly controversial and very influential on political thought. There are two main points: (a) that The Prince has been controversial for its cynical view of political life and (b) that its message of "the end justifies the means" has made a lasting impression on many readers. There is minor point that specifies some of the ways in which The Prince runs contrary to many cherished political ideals contrasting the work's brazen realism with belief in political ideals. The main purpose of the passage is to inform and briefly familiarize the reader with the work and surrounding controversy. The tone is largely factual, and while the author mentions the controversial nature of the work, they do not express an opinion on the controversy.

Answer to Question 316:

The correct answer is B.

A. Wrong. Both bold-faced sections highlight how The Prince promotes political theories that are controversial in the modern political landscape and thus the first section cannot undermine the second.

B. Correct. The second bold-faced section concludes that the statement "the end justifies the means" at the heart of The Prince is well-known and controversial; the first bold-faced section outlines in more detail why The Prince is controversial.

C. Wrong. The author's position is that the Prince is a poignant yet controversial book and both of these bold-faced sections in fact support this claim.

D. Wrong. Both bold-faced sections reinforce the author's position that The Prince is a controversial yet poignant book.

E. Wrong. Both bold-face sections discuss how The Prince undermines many of the ideas relative to modern political practices, but the bold-faced sections do not undermine modern political practices themselves.

Answer to Question 317:

The correct answer is A.

A. Correct. The author spends the duration of the passage discussing how The Prince was and has remained a book that is highly influential despite the fact that it is equally controversial; thus, a clear case is made for the fact that polemical books are the most influential.

B. Wrong. The author never discusses leadership in terms of combining virtue and vice, just the fact that The Prince negates the importance of personal vice in leaders. Thus, a case is not made for the concept that leadership requires a combination of virtue and vice.

C. Wrong. It can be inferred that political ideas evolve since the author points out the fact that modern political ideas clash with Machiavellian political ideas, but this is still an inference and not a clear case or argument for a specific fact.

D. Wrong. The author does not directly discuss human nature even though it does show how political systems change and evolve.

E. Wrong. The author does not make a case for how the Machiavellian approach works when it moves from the realm of theory to the practical world of practice and thus this does not make a case for the Machiavellian approach as the best political method.

Passage 135: Summary / Paraphrase

The passage is about the causes of depression. The main idea is that after years of scientific consensus that depression is caused by low serotonin levels, there has been recent support for the idea that depression may not correlate as clearly with chemical imbalance as was previously thought. The main points are: (a) starting in the 1950s, scientists studying behavior and the brain agreed that depression was caused by serotonin deficiency (b) the notion that chemical imbalance caused depression let mental health professionals treat depression using pharmaceuticals (c) recent research has suggested that depleted levels of serotonin are not the sole factor in depression, opening the door to different treatment possibilities. A minor point that genetics, and more subtle views about mood and personality, develops the main points. The purpose of the passage is polemical: the author has a clear bias against the notion that mental disorders can be treated pharmaceutically as evidenced by the phrase "pills as a means of solving mood problems may hopefully become a thing of the past" and by the tone of the final paragraph.

Answer to Question 318:

The correct answer is D.

A. Wrong. Candid means impartial and since the author believes that serotonin as a cause of depression is outmoded, he or she is at least slightly skeptical of SSRI's as a treatment method for depression and thus is not rendered impartial or unprejudiced.

B. Wrong. The author is critical of SSRIs believes them to be outmoded and thus does not have a positive or affirmative attitude towards them.

C. Wrong. While the author is critical of SSRIs (calling them outmoded), castigating is too harsh of a term to describe the author's attitude as castigating means to chastise or criticize severely.

D. Correct. Leery is a synonym for skeptical and the author is clearly skeptical of SSRIs since he or she believes it is outmoded to regard serotonin as the main cause of depression.

E. Wrong. The author's tone and word choice relative to SSRIs do not indicate snobbery (condescension) but rather skeptical disbelief.

Answer to Question 319:

The correct answer is B.

A. Wrong. Since the passage states that SSRIs are an outmoded, the reader can infer that they are not a good way of treating mood disorders.

B. Correct. The passage states that scientists see genes as a potential cause of depression and thus inferring that they are the definite cause of depression is incorrect.

C. Wrong. The passage discusses a study that concluded that decreased serotonin levels in healthy people did not affect their mood so the reader can infer that serotonin does not play a direct role in affecting a person's mood in general.

D. Wrong. The passage lists talk therapy as one of the successful methods of treating depression

E. Wrong. The beginning of the passage discusses how depression is a universal, global phenomenon so the reader can infer that it affects all humans regardless of culture or ethnicity.

Answer to Question 320:

The correct answers are A and B.

A. Correct. The author makes it clear that genes contribute to a person's biological profile and thus genes could engender depression in an individual.

B. Correct. The author also makes it clear that environmental factors can contribute to a person's mood and hence could engender depression.

C. Wrong. The author does not mention past and present experiences in conjunction with biological factors as a cause of depression.

Answer to Question 321:

The correct answer is "In the 1950s psychologists and neuroscientists teamed up to proclaim that depression was the result of a chemical imbalance, more specifically low levels of serotonin, and a milieu was born that sought to frame mental health issues as curable deficiencies."

This sentence underscores the fact that a treatment framework was erected around depression characterizing it as a curable deficiency. The mentality of mental health practitioners thus became SSRI based, as those were pills that could be used to treat depression.

Passage 136:

Answer to Question 322:

The correct answer is E. A is incorrect because the passage does not discuss jury trials. While military personnel are mentioned in relation to an exception to the requirement for Grand Juries, a right to a jury of peers is not discussed. Thus, B is not correct. The right to an attorney is also not discussed here, therefore C is not correct. The passage requires just compensation for property seizures but mentions no exceptions, so D is not correct. While A, B and C may be rights guaranteed by the Constitution or legal precedent, they are not addressed in this passage. D is not mentioned at all. E is the correct answer. The passage specifically mentions that a citizen cannot be compelled "to be a witness against himself."

Answer to Question 323:

The correct answer is D. A is incorrect because "indictment of a grand jury" has been discussed elsewhere in the passage using just those words. B is incorrect for several reasons. For one deprivation of life with just compensation seems nonsensical. Also, the term "just compensation" is used in the same sentence with regard to property. To use it here, also in regard to property, would be redundant. C is not justified or implied. Some of the requirements in the passage contradict one another, such as the exceptions to the Grand Jury rule. Also, the few specific rules discussed in this passage would not likely be the only ones in force when depriving someone of life, liberty or property. E is out because the terms "due" and "process" are still in usage and their present-day definitions, even in combination make sense in this context. D is correct because the simple definitions of the words "due" "process" and "law", as used contemporarily, can be combined to mean "required legal steps" in a general sense.

Answer to Question 324:

The correct answer is A. B is the common modern definition of the term, but notoriety does not seem relevant here. C refers to a common misunderstanding of the term as the opposite of "famous." D implies that the word is the opposite of "capital," but this is contradicted by the use of the word "otherwise." E might make sense but this would make the passage needlessly redundant. The modifier "otherwise" makes it clear that "infamous" is used to expand the protection to a broader class not limited to capital crimes. The answer is A.

Answer to Question 325:

The correct answers are B and C. Parsing the structure of the first sentence shows that the military exemption applies only to B and C through the connector "unless." A is presented as a separate clause. B and C are correct

Chapter **5**

Introduction to Text Completion

Text Completion questions are designed to further test your ability to understand what you read. They will also test your vocabulary, particularly your ability to apply sophisticated vocabulary in context. You will be asked to read a short passage of 1-5 sentences. There will be 1-3 blanks in the passage where a crucial word is missing. You will need to fill in each blank using several options provided.

The passages used for Text Completion questions will be drawn from a variety of topics, including the physical, biological and social sciences, the arts and the humanities, business and everyday life. As with Reading Comprehension questions you do not need to be an expert on the topic covered, you only need to read the passage attentively enough to be able to pick the right word for the blank.

All Text Completion questions will be in a multiple-choice format. Each passage will have 1-3 blanks, and you will be given several options to choose from to fill in the blanks. Generally, passages with only one blank will have five options to choose from, while those with 2-3 blanks will have only three options per blank.

What does a Text Completion question look like?

Text Completion questions will always be based off a short passage of one or more sentences. The passage will have 1-3 blanks. You will be asked to read the passage and get a feel of what words will best complete it using several options given. Below are examples of what Text Completion questions will look like on the GRE General Test:

For each blank select one entry from the corresponding column of choices. Fill all blanks in the way that best completes the text.

1.   The later Roman Empire was continually (i) _____ invasions of nomadic and semi-nomadic peoples who were often themselves (ii) _____ by marauding tribes from the Central Asian steppes.

Blank (i)
delighted
threatened
enthralled

Blank (ii)
displaced
dismissed
averred

2. Harry's _____ performance on the project both failed to impress his superiors and helped to lose the company an important client.

rapacious
desultory
indomitable
arcane
indefatigable

Answer Key

The correct answers are:

1. (i) threatened   (ii) displaced

2. desultory

What skills do Text Completion questions test?

Text Completion questions test your ability to understand complex sentences and passages. They also test your ability to use sophisticated vocabulary in context and your ability to use reasoning to complete an idea based on incomplete information. Some key skills that are tested include your ability to

- understand a text holistically and be able to determine the meaning of individual components

- use reasoning to fill in important gaps in information

- understand high level vocabulary

- apply vocabulary in context

Key facts about Text Completion questions

- Questions will be based off short passages 1-5 sentences long

- For each passage, you will need to fill in 1-3 blanks using 3-5 options provided

- Passages will be on a variety of topics including the physical, biological and social sciences, the arts and the humanities, business and everyday life

- Questions will be answerable based on the information in the passage alone and your ability to apply vocabulary

Strategies for Text Completion Questions

Depending on what version of the GRE you are taking, you will have 30 or 35 minutes to complete each Verbal Reasoning section. While budgeting your time is important, Text Completion questions are different than Reading Comprehension questions and require you to alter your strategies accordingly. In the first place, the passages used for Text Completion questions will generally be much shorter than those used for Reading Comprehension questions. This means that it will take you less time to carefully read a passage for a Text Completion question than it would for you to carefully read a Reading Comprehension passage. Moreover, Text Completion questions are much more focused, and to answer them effectively, you may need to grasp subtle aspects of sentence structure. While you will not want to get hung up on a single Text Completion question, you will generally want to read the passages with more care than those used for Reading Comprehension questions. Do not try to skim through Text Completion questions. If you feel that you are taking too much time on a single question, either make an educated guess or bookmark it in case you have time later and then move on.

As with Reading Comprehension, do not let the subject matter of the passage throw you off -your ability to correctly answer these questions will not rely on your expertise in any particular area. When answering Text Completion questions, one of the key skills you will need is the ability to grasp the overall meaning of the passage even with certain words missing. You will then need to apply your understanding of the passage, coupled with your grasp of key transitional words in the passage, to correctly choose the word that best fits with the overall meaning of the passage. Where Reading Comprehension questions test your ability to grasp general meanings, Text Completion tests your ability to read carefully and understand more subtle cues about the meaning of specific sections of text.

The key skills for Text Completion are reading closely and applying vocabulary in context. You'll need to get a quick idea of what the passage is about, and the general tone, but beyond that, you need to be able to see how specific words fit into the whole passage. Focus most of your attention on the individual meanings of different components of the passage. Often there are overt indications of which words will best complete the passage; either the word you need to complete the passage will be essentially defined in another clause, or the context will strongly suggest that you use a word with the opposite meaning to what has already been said. These contextual indicators are quite valuable, so keep a close eye out for them. Also, because vocabulary is a more important part of Text Completion questions, anything you can do to review or improve your vocabulary will probably be helpful.

- Read the passage carefully - do not skim

- Focus on significant words to help you grasp precise meanings

- Keep an eye out for sections of the passage that either closely match or negate the definition of one of the word options

- Apply vocabulary in context

What follows are some more specific strategies for answering Text Completion questions. In the next chapter, you'll have a chance to put your skills to the test through several practice questions and learn how to hone them in the answers and explanations that follow.

Review Vocabulary

Anything that you can do to strengthen your vocabulary prior to the test will be helpful. Although the GRE General Test does not feature any section that is strictly designed to test vocabulary, the Verbal Reasoning section assumes a fairly high-level vocabulary. Your command of sophisticated vocabulary is especially important for the Text Completion and Sentence Equivalence sections, since you will need to identify the right word to fill in a blank. If you are not confident of your vocabulary, do what you can to improve it as preparation for the test (this will serve you well in graduate school as well). Note that in many cases you will not need to know a precise definition of a word, but you do need to have a general sense of what it means. There are several things you can do to improve your vocabulary for the test:

- Review lists of common "GRE words" such as the one included in this book

- Use a vocabulary builder

- Get a sense of key Greek or Latin root words and what they mean - many words in English are based on Greek or Latin words, and knowing the meaning of a few key Greek or Latin words can help you figure out the meanings of numerous English words

Get a General Feel of the Passage

Before you try to fill in any blanks, get a general sense of what the passage says, and the tone. Doing this will help you get a general feel whether a particular word fits or not. As you read the passage, pay close attention to words that may signal a shift in tone or perspective. Such words give insight into the meaning of the passage as a whole, and can also tell you something about the particular phrase that you'll need to complete.

Pay Special Attention to Significant Words

Certain key words can give tremendous insight into the meaning of a passage or phrase. Many times, your ability to correctly answer Text Completion questions will hinge on whether you are able to detect qualifying words in a passage. Be especially alert for words like "although" and "despite", which suggests that the what has been said so far is about to be qualified. Also keep an eye out for words like "therefore", "moreover" and "thus" which suggest summation or additional support for points that have already been made.

Don't Assume That You Should Always Fill In the First Blank First

Sometimes the order in which you fill in the blanks won't matter. For some questions, however, it will be difficult to fill in one blank without first correctly filling in another blank. The first blank won't always be the one you should try to fill in first - sometimes you will need to reason backwards through the passage. Keep in mind that some Text Completion questions are very straightforward - others are designed to test your reasoning, so be prepared to use more than just vocabulary to find the correct answer.

Come up With Your Own Words to Fill in the Blanks

As you read through the passage, try to think of words that would fill in the blanks; then, compare the answer options given to the words you have thought of and try to select similar words from among the options. If you are unsure of what some of the words mean and cannot identify similar words, try to eliminate words with opposite meanings to the words you picked.

Check Your Work

Always re-read the passage with the answer(s) you have selected and filled in to see whether the passage is grammatical and makes sense with the options you have chosen. Even if your choice seemed right, if it does not produce a coherent, grammatically correct passage, it isn't the correct answer.

Use Process of Elimination

You can apply process of elimination to Text Completion questions as well. Sometimes, you may quickly identify the correct answer or answers, but other times you may be uncertain. In cases where you don't find the right answer to be immediately obvious, use process of elimination to narrow the options. Many times, a word with the opposite meaning from the correct answer will appear among the choices - you can immediately dismiss such words. Other times you will find words that simply have nothing to do with the context, and these can be dismissed as well. As with any other multiple-choice question, eliminating obviously wrong answers will always increase your odds of getting the right answer.

Chapter **6**

Practice Questions for Text Completion

1.   Although he took great pains as an educator to (i) _____ a love of reasoning and virtue in his students, Athenian (ii) _____ of the day considered Socrates to be a/an (iii) _____, intent on destroying their authority and subverting the youth of Athens.

Blank (i)	Blank (ii)	Blank (iii)
ingurgitate	portents	centurion
importune	potentates	iconoclast
inculcate	profligates	neophyte

2.   Stephens professes to have no bias, but a discerning analysis of his article "Our Youth Must Work" reveals that the author employs (i) _____ to create an ingenious yet invalid argument aimed at misleading readers into agreeing with a youth service program that penalizes students from the lower socio-economic echelons in favor of their (ii) _____ peers who will simply be able to buy their way out of the proposed two years of community or military service.

Blank (i)	Blank (ii)
dissimulation	erudite
hubris	ostentatious
sophistry	patrician

3.   Because of crime distribution data, criminologists can add to their qualitative analysis a quantitative dynamic; this _____ of approaches allows for greater insight.

confluence
reduction
petulance
reluctance
diaspora

4. While the original conception of rhetoric confined its uses to political discourse, many people now agree that the art of debate _____ every field of study.

permits
permeates
aggrandizes
aggravates
rectifies

5. The crude tools of human civilizations leave a trail throughout time that _____ even when the written records of events become unclear or seem to be in direct contradiction to one another.

discontinue
perdures
excavates
derides
beguiles

6. The various psychosocial variables that constitute the human mind cannot be understood through strict experimentation without also considering the _____ such experiments inherently introduce in the subject.

prejudices
pellucidity
impartiality
riposte
plutocracy

7. Competition is highly desirable in a free market economy – the concentration of market capital in relatively few enterprises can _____ economic health by forcing customers to pay prices they can barely afford.

attenuate
consecrate
commiserate
alleviate
fulminate

8. Looking back, he was amazed by his own (i) _____. His experienced friends told him that there was no fast way to learn guitar. They said that he would just have to accept a slow progression of skill. But he (ii) _____ this advice every step of the way, pushing his hands as hard as he could. Now that he was staring down the harsh reality of carpal tunnel syndrome, he wished that he had taken their advice.

Blank (i)	Blank (ii)
pensiveness	articulated
reticence	flouted
obstinacy	expounded

9. Gary always resented the way people (i) _____ television. If he ever mentioned a program he had recently watched he was always met with reprimands from others. They told him how television was a waste, how it rotted his brain. The (ii) _____ was staggering. Gary knew that these same people also watched television; they just denied it in public in order to put on airs. And what was so sacrosanct about the other forms of media? There were trashy novels, just like there were trashy television programs.

Blank (i)	Blank (ii)
derided	equanimity
bolstered	duplicity
protracted	sublimity

10. He had never ridden a motorcycle before but the notion (i) _____ him. The idea of cruising across the country instilled him with a feeling a freedom he had never experienced before. He had always been (ii) _____, preferring the safety of an office environment to anything else.

Blank (i)	Blank (ii)
vetoed	obdurate
exhilarated	milquetoast
censured	contrarian

11. The newfound money couldn't (i) _____ the sorrow. Tiffany had inherited more money than she would ever be able to spend, but she would rather have had her parents back. She couldn't help but (ii) _____ the comments that her friends made about her situation. They reprimanded her for her sullenness, told her that she was lucky to be in the situation that she was.

Blank (i)	Blank (ii)
masticate	lionize
interpolate	oblige
alleviate	begrudge

12. Howard knew that the story of the musician who trades integrity for money was (i) _____, but it felt new to him. He was being offered the chance to sign a recording contract, but a quick glance at the fine print told him that he would be signing away his dignity. The contract would guarantee him fame and fortune, but it would license his music to the highest bidder and charge (ii) _____ prices to his loyal fans.

Blank (i)	Blank (ii)
cliché	inconsequential
facetious	judicious
metaphorical	appalling

13. Horoscopes are somewhat like fortune cookie fortunes - they sound true, because they are based on human nature and human behavior, both of which are homogenous and therefore fairly predictable. Furthermore, horoscopes are highly generic or shrouded in metaphor whose (i) _____ can easily be changed to meet the (ii) _____ of our lives and can be applied to almost everyone almost anytime.

Blank (i)
palpability
elucidation
omnipotence

Blank (ii)
exigencies
generalizations
generalities

14. The flu of 1918 infected an estimated 500 million people worldwide, killing 3 to 5 percent of the world's population within two years. Although the (i) _____ was entirely unpreventable and particularly deadly, it galvanized leaders world-wide to develop a (ii) _____ strategy for dealing with mass infections, leading ultimately, to the creation of the World Health Organization.

Blank (i)
endemic
pandemic
epidemic

Blank (ii)
congruous
germane
refractory

15. The combined _____ of scientists present at the time of the launch could not have enabled them to predict the unanticipated events predicated by what should have been a routine display of military prowess.

demeanor
heresy
efficacy
acumen
callosity

16. At a loss to explain the overwhelming popularity of today's insipid TV reality shows, critics have come to the conclusion that viewers who are obsessed with reality programs are drawn to the _____ lifestyles depicted and allow the radiance of the stars' lives override the spurious dilemmas and dubious coping skills of the so-called stars.

refulgent
austere
laudable
monotonous
sanctimonious

17. The more loudly and adamantly he denied any involvement with the crime, the less the jury believed him. Clearly his _____ would not pass muster with them, and he had no doubt their deliberations would be short and to the point. guilty!

dyspepsia
harangue
approbation
peregrination
gaucherie

18. Strict laws prohibiting dog fighting aim to reduce the number of dogs injured or killed each year in this heinous but lucrative industry by targeting those truly responsible, not the dogs who are bred and forced to fight, but the depraved owners who perpetuate this _____ of sport for personal glory and financial gain.

tirade
artifice
debauch
travesty
apparition

19. Perhaps the most _____ of any play ever performed, James Carthwaite's rendition of "Born to be Wilde," based on the art and antics of the late Oscar Wilde, took eight hours to perform and was executed over two consecutive nights - or would have been had it not closed down halfway through the first night.

pedantic
odious
onerous
moribund
prolix

20. A few of us watched in awe from the (i) _____ above town as the last of our makeshift barriers (ii) _____ and Cowtown, built on the shifting alluvial soils of the Temash Delta, crumbled and was swept away like so much (iii) _____ being sucked down a drain.

Blank (i)	Blank (ii)	Blank (iii)
estuary	capitulated	calumny
ravine	countenanced	aspersion
butte	assuaged	detritus

21. More people living longer lives due to worldwide improvements in health care and nutrition translates to the need for nursing homes across the country to develop their _____ care capacity to attend to the needs of an aging population over the long run.

ameliorative
palliative
regressive
salubrious
proprietary

22. Henry VIII may have been the most powerful man in the world in his time, but as a monarch he
     certainly was not fortuitous when it came to producing a male heir to ascend to the throne. His
     _____ included Prince Edward who died in childhood and the Princesses, Mary and Elizabeth.

progenitors
scions
devisees
lineage
promulgations

23. Though its name would suggest it is (i) _____, the Kiss-Kiss, a leech with a predilection for human
     blood, (ii) _____ infiltrates homes and ensconce themselves among the bedding to ambush its
     prey - us! Once thought to be rare, recent Kiss-Kiss inventories confirm of the kiss-kiss bug, a vector of
     Chagras Disease, is (iii) _____ in the southwestern US, Mexico, and most parts of Central-America.

Blank (i)	Blank (ii)	Blank (iii)
innocuous	surreptitiously	ubiquitous
portentous	precipitously	exiguous
accumbent	quintessentially	anomalous

24. _____, once thought to be the result of poor motivation or bad genetics and the fault of
     the released prisoners rather than the institutions that released them, has institutional and social
     dimensions that are far beyond the control of the ex-offender, and, that unabated, virtually enslave
     ex-offenders to criminal lifestyles ensuring that they become permanent residents of our penal
     institutions.

Gasconade
Recidivism
Exfiltration
Chicanery
Attenuation

25. In the story the "Confessions of Felix Krull, Confidence Man," the young protagonist, Felix feigns
     a serious illness to (i) _____ both his mother and the family physician who is also her lover, that
     he is indeed very sick. Felix describes the almost intolerable pleasure that his performance brings
     him, saying, "I was beyond beatific, absolutely (ii) _____ with the alternate tension and relaxation
     necessary to give reality, in my own eyes and others, to a condition that did not exist."

Blank (i)	Blank (ii)
suborn	desultory
cajole	rapturous
inveigh	aberrant

26. In light of his many (i) _____ with the ladies and his illicit dealings in pornography, the pastor's
     comments on the on the aberrations of deviate behavior among parishioners was viewed as
     sanctimonious (ii) _____ and readily dismissed.

Blank (i)	Blank (ii)
adumbrations	chit-chat
dilettantes	invective
peccadilloes	cant

27. Although the problems identified with the SR7 (i) _____ Rover, designed to collect data and soil
     samples from the surface of Mars have been publicized extensively over the past few weeks, they are
     not of much consequence when considered individually. However, the cumulative effect of the myriad
     of (ii) _____ must be factored into scientists' decision to launch the Rover or (iii) _____.

Blank (i)	Blank (ii)	Blank (iii)
Canard	gimmicks	take the bull by the horns
Reconnaissance	gimcracks	throw the baby out with the bath water
Alliance	glitches	go back to the drawing board

28. Although Aristotle did not have a high opinion of octopi, calling them "stupid creatures," their reputation as problem solvers and critical thinkers has recently been _____, largely due to the antics of a Delhi zoo octopus named Andy who selects what he wants to eat from a menu of 28 fresh fish choices, regularly ambushes his fellow tank mates just for fun, and has to be kept in a specialized tank because he has learned to pick all traditional tank locks.

ruminated
bifurcated
expedited
ameliorated
scintillated

29. Growing a vegetable garden may seem difficult, but anyone can do it. Home-grown (i) _____ is tastier, healthier, and cheaper than what you find in grocery stores. It is important to plan out your (ii) _____ – research what plants grow best in your region, find out how much sun the plants require, and make sure you have the tools you need. After planting your vegetables, tend them daily. Watering and weeding are a must. Once your (iii) _____ is ripe, harvest and enjoy the fruits of your labor!

Blank (i)	Blank (ii)	Blank (iii)
calumny	acreage	concurrence
produce	nadir	fruitage
morasses	quagmire	exculpation

30. (i) _____ criminals are an increasing threat to both private companies and the world economic system. Not only were five computer programmers recently arrested for hacking into the servers of several American companies and stealing 160,000,000 credit card numbers, but their leader was also caught hacking into the Nasdaq stock exchange. The America's stock exchange is far from alone in its (ii) _____. 53 percent of the world's exchanges have fallen victim to the (iii) _____ of hackers in the last year.

Blank (i)	Blank (ii)	Blank (iii)
Cyber	aversion	puissance
Cryptic	perfidy	nostrum
Captious	vulnerability	cynosure

31.   General Motors saw a 19 percent fall in net income due to a (i) _____ drop in profits in Asia. Recently poor economic conditions have made Europe the largest trouble spot for the company, but GM narrowed losses in Europe while registering higher than normal losses in Asia. A rise in (ii) _____ from the Japanese, Korean, and Australian automobile markets contributed to losses in the region. Despite a 4 percent gain in North America, GM is in trouble if it does not come up with strategies to perform more (iii) _____.

Blank (i)	Blank (ii)	Blank (iii)
propitious	competitors	erratically
precipitous	assailant	consistently
promontory	hindrances	pedantically

32.   To combat the fears of Russification, Christianization, and general assimilation, Tatar reformers had to (i) _____ the importance of strengthening Tatar cultural identity. This, along with a more flexible (and therefore in many ways more durable) (ii) _____ of Islam, helped the Tatar community retain their ethnic identity while developing a modernized secular relationship with Russia. To this end, writers like Amirkhan highlighted the capability of Tatars to embrace reforms and secular education while still (iii) _____ their Tatar identity.

Blank (i)	Blank (ii)	Blank (iii)
desiccate	aesthetic	abdicating
accentuate	indoctrination	perpetuating
abrogate	apperception	gainsaying

33.   Proposed solutions to the conflict take the form of the packaged and phased approaches – addressing all the (i) _____ of the conflict in one fell swoop versus creating a schedule to deal with each question one at a time. The first allows for resolution in a single document and enables everyone to focus immediately on (ii) _____ action. Unfortunately, it is less politically viable and less flexible. The second (iii) _____ immediate pressures making leadership able to engage in substantive conversation, but risks derailing due to changes in external circumstance and inertia.

Blank (i)	Blank (ii)	Blank (iii)
inaccuracies	tangible	alleviates
perquisites	ephemeral	exterminating
components	amorphous	implicates

34. The Abkhazian uprisings against the Russian Empire were unsuccessful, but had a lasting impact on the (i) _____ of the region. Some Abkhaz fled of their own accord – mostly those who were (ii) _____ to the anti-Russian revolts. Others left involuntarily, as victims of the ethnic cleansings in the North Caucasus. During the late 1800s the Russian Army forced the Abkhaz, Adyghe, Ubykh, and Abaza peoples from their homelands. The majority of these (iii) _____ populations settled in the Ottoman Empire.

Blank (i)	Blank (ii)	Blank (iii)
demographics	copasetic	complacent
recidivism	sympathetic	appeased
raiment	phlegmatic	dispossessed

35. Wildflowers are faithful to their bumblebee "sweethearts." In a recent study, (i) _____ found that wildflowers produce fewer seeds when a single bumblebee species is removed. Apparently, the plant/pollinator relationship is (ii) _____. Each bee species focuses on a single plant variety until it finishes blooming, thus increasing the fidelity of the species. The result is a rise in seed production. The study underlined the importance of (iii) _____ in the conservation of ecosystems as the removal of a bee species resulted in decreased plant reproduction.

Blank (i)	Blank (ii)	Blank (iii)
cryptologists	monogamous	anathemas
geologists	polygamous	surfeit
ecologists	hypergamous	biodiversity

36. Researchers have discovered (i) _____ method for targeting and manipulating any gene in the human genome. An RNA-guided enzyme found in the Streptococcus bacteria could (ii) _____ be used to cure many genetic diseases as well as to reprogram stem and adult cells. The (iii) _____ of this discovery are far-reaching, but scientists are not yet sure what all the possibilities are. Using the RNA-guided enzyme is relatively simple, which makes the scientific community hopeful in regard to its real-world applications.

Blank (i)	Blank (ii)	Blank (iii)
a superfluous	abstractly	impositions
an expedient	presumptively	implications
an imprudent	dubiously	inhibitions

37.   Scientists have long been fascinated by superfluids, such as liquid helium, since they seem to defy the laws of (i) _____. Moving without the (ii) _____ of gravity or surface tension, superfluids have zero viscosity and can squeeze through holes the size of a molecule or climb up the side of a glass. They have been (iii) _____ to remain in motion for years after the centrifuge containing them has stopped spinning.

Blank (i)	Blank (ii)	Blank (iii)
geology	opprobrium	observed
physics	celerity	obliterated
biology	interference	envisioned

38.   A series of intense storms and rising water levels over the last several years has resulted in (i) _____ in erosion on beaches across the country. As a result, many states are considering beach nourishment projects: replacing the large amounts of lost sediment with similar material either transported from other locations or manufactured. This new sand is usually (ii) _____ as a result of the processing methods used to manufacture it and therefore erodes faster, creating (iii) _____ cycle of erosion and replacement.

Blank (i)	Blank (ii)	Blank (iii)
an escalation	darker	an accelerated and expensive
a depletion	smaller-grained	an ineffective and unhygienic
an altercation	foul-smelling	a never-ending and inexplicable

39.   The human ability to recognize that the size of an object is _____, even as the distance between the person and object makes it appear to change in size, is called size constancy.

immutable
flexible
stable
abiding
uniform

40. Perception differs from sensation and refers not just to the reception of stimuli, but the _____ of those stimuli to determine what information can be gathered and how the information should be used.

insight
interpretation
translation
elucidation
adaptation

41. An example of operant conditioning is a commuter who _____, after several experiences, which route to his or her job takes the least amount of time, and adopts that route as a result of this learning.

assumes
theorizes
ascertains
disputes
validates

42. Psychologists refer to the ability to determine what information is important and what is background noise as signal detection, as it is the act of detecting what signals require or deserve focus and which can be _____.

unheeded
rejected
considered
abandoned
underestimated

43. Sensory adaptation occurs when a stimulus that is _____ .When a subject first encounters it, eventually fades from notice, such as the sound of a ticking clock, or cooking smells in a room.

| negligible |
| pronounced |
| significant |
| imperceptible |
| appreciable |

44. All vertebrate cardiovascular systems include a heart, a muscular pump that contracts to (i) _____.blood through the blood vessels. The upper chamber of the heart is the atrium, and is where blood enters the muscle. The lower chamber is the ventricle. When the ventricle (ii) _____, blood is forced from the heart via an artery. The aorta is the main artery leaving the heart and bringing nutrients and oxygen out to the other organs. The pulmonary artery returns the oxygen-(iii) _____.blood to the heart so that it can be enriched with nutrients and sent back out into the body.

Blank (i)	Blank (ii)	Blank (iii)
pitch	constricts	squandered
propel	compresses	augmented
project	cinches	depleted

45. While single celled organisms use the cell surface to (i) _____.nutrients from the world outside the system, and to release waste from the organism, multi-celled organisms require a circulatory system and medium of transport for nutrients. Sea-sponges, among the most (ii) _____.animals, take advantage of sea-water as a medium of transport, as the sea water flows in and out of the organism it delivers nutrients and removes waste.

Blank (i)	Blank (ii)
annex	primitive
procure	vestigial
relinquish	rudimentary

46. Diabetes results from inadequate levels of insulin in the body. When not enough insulin is produced many physiological functions are compromised. The results include vision (i) _____, decreased circulatory function, failures in the nervous system and kidney failure. The second most common cause of blindness in the United States is diabetes, which demonstrates how serious and (ii) _____.this condition is in the U.S.

Blank (i)	Blank (ii)
diminishing	pervasive
stagnation	circumscribed
impairment	capacious

47. In the human body two systems manage hormone release. The endocrine system is a (i) _____ of glands each of which (ii) _____ different hormones into the blood stream. Hormones pass through the blood to bring "messages" to different organs, which have hormone-receptors. The exocrine system, which is distinct from the endocrine system, an internal system, releases products outside of the body, including sweat and saliva.

Blank (i)	Blank (ii)
force	disperse
crux	secrete
cadre	beget

48. While single-celled organisms can (i) _____ nutrients directly from the environment, multicellular organisms have specialized structures for obtaining and breaking down the food that is the source of necessary nutrients. These digestive systems are composed of multiple functions that (ii) _____ food sources into processable liquid and extract nutrients. The process results in waste, which is expelled from the organism via another, related system.

Blank (i)	Blank (ii)
osmose	flux
exude	deliquesce
cull	coagulate

49. An Augustinian monk, Gregor Mendel, studied genetics by conducting experiments on garden peas, and in 1865 was the first scientist to propose the concept of _____ traits and the science of genetics.

bequeathed
inbred
maternal
acquired
heritable

50. Robert Remark, a Polish embryologist, discovered that cells originated from the division of _____ cells and did not spontaneously appear.

inanimate
extant
living
surviving
mortal

51. In 1665, Robert Hooke discovered the cell and established the _____ for the development of cell theory, and based on his discoveries, other scientists were able to develop new theories.

infrastructure
innovation
consequence
foundation
production

52.   It is not just the existence of multiple types of cells, but the _____ between these cells that allow a multi-cellular organism to function.

communion
accord
synergy
intimacy
contention

53.   Rather than operate independently, cells in a multi-cellular organism are arranged into complex _____ of specialized cells that work together to complete complex functions.

cooperatives
aggregates
collectives
division
unanimity

54.   In 1915 Niels Bohr proposed a model of an atom that modified an earlier model. Based on quantum mechanics, the Bohr model is called a planetary model, as it shows electrons with a negative charge (i) _____ a nucleus, which has a positive charge. Bohr suggested a(n) (ii) _____ relationship between gravitational forces in the solar system and the electrical force between positively charged nucleus and negatively charged electrons.

Blank (i)		Blank (ii)
envelops		analogous
converges		homologous
orbits		retrogression

55.   An element is a(n) (i) _____ substance. It cannot be broken into other elements and has no component elements. There are 92 elements that occur in nature. When different elements are connected to create a new substance, the result is a compound, which is made of multiple, sometimes (ii) _____ elements, that are otherwise unrelated. Pure elements are rare as most matter exists in the form of compounds.

Blank (i)	Blank (ii)
unalloyed	multifarious
adulterated	homogenous
veritable	conglomerate

56.   In a(n) (i) _____ relationship, when one variable increases, the other decreases. The most (ii) _____ obvious example of this involves heating water. When a pan of water is placed over a heat source, as the temperature rises, liquid water begins to vaporize, thus reducing the mass of the water in the pan. In this case, as the variable temperature increases, the variable, mass, decreases.

Blank (i)	Blank (ii)
contradictory	familiar
conforming	proverbial
inverse	mundane

57.   While the consequences of criminal law cases may exceed those of civil law, especially in terms of financial reparations, the two function _____ to maintain social order.

perniciously
superciliously
redundantly
intractably
conjunctly

58. The meteorologists of the world have recently found themselves working under the (i) _____ of political discourse. With environmental concerns suddenly on everybody's mind, these (ii) _____ scientists have been thrust into the vicious world of political partisanship. Although many of them have stepped up to the challenge admirably, it seems unfair to suddenly demand political insight from people previously focused exclusively on scientific pursuits.

Blank (i)
encumbrance
auspices
insight

Blank (ii)
reticent
ostentatious
conspiratorial

59. In spite of the immense intellect, and sometimes outright genius, of the people working within it, the field of physics still faces many factors (i) _____ to its growth. As it turns out, the difficulty of accepting new ideas does not exist solely among the working-class population, but can be found in academia as well. Entrenched logic, petty careerism, and just plain (ii) _____ are all as prevalent in the field of physics as they are in the conventional, nine-to-five world.

Blank (i)
correlated
antagonistic
supplanted

Blank (ii)
eminence
acquiescence
inscience

60. Fiona was simultaneously (i) _____ by the magic of dreams and turned off by their potential to turn into nightmares. She wondered what they revealed about the human psyche. They were so (ii) _____, yet there had to be some logical impetus for their genesis. She often read books on dream analysis in order to better understand this topic, but the more she read the more she suspected that the purported "experts" in the field were merely (iii) _____.

Blank (i)
enraptured
vindicated
denounced

Blank (ii)
debonair
abstruse
gentile

Blank (iii)
charlatans
solemn
guileless

61. Locating the (i) _____ organisms of the ocean has proven a daunting task. The ocean has more than 250 times the habitable volume as the land, leaving (ii) _____ amounts of space to cover. Even being able to locate viruses and phytoplankton, let alone being able to study their relationship to the environment, is a tremendous undertaking. But (iii) _____ understanding of marine life cannot be attained without knowing the role that microscopic organisms play in it.

Blank (i)	Blank (ii)	Blank (iii)
haughty	exorbitant	exhaustive
vituperative	coquettish	diminutive
enigmatic	ardent	reticent

62. Just the name "Biotechnology" evokes powerful images: the use of recombinant genes in genetic sequencing, applied immunology to fight diseases, and so on. But the lofty heading of "Biogerontology" includes many (i) _____ that one wouldn't typically associate with advanced medicine. Both the brewing of alcohol and the development of agriculture involve manipulating biological systems to make products. Therefore, even without the scientific (ii) _____ of medical techniques, these "rough-and-tumble" jobs also fall under the heading of "Biotechnology."

Blank (i)	Blank (ii)
verisimilitudes	exactitude
denigrations	unsophistication
vocations	fallacy

63. Although its desolate landscapes and small population may make South Dakota seem a (i) _____ locale, it is actually one of the best places to start a business. High taxes in eastern states like New York and New Jersey can (ii) _____ even well-planned ventures. In contrast, South Dakota has some of the lowest taxes in the country.

Blank (i)	Blank (ii)
morbid	foil
inhospitable	obviate
germane	lampoon

64. Ghengis Khan is remembered as one of history's most _____ leaders; as founder of the Mongol Empire, he initiated the invasions that would ultimately lead to Mongol control of most of Eurasia.

rancorous
timorous
disingenuous
erratic
belligerent

65. Women, though not (i) _____ genetic disorders generally, are far less likely than men to display symptoms of an X-linked hereditary disease such as hemophilia. In the case of hemophilia, for example, the woman's second, X chromosome acts as a kind of buffer; the normal gene is typically able to produce enough clotting factors to (ii) _____ any life-threatening bleeds.

Blank (i)
inclined to
intransigent towards
impervious to

Blank (ii)
mollify
forestall
engender

66. If the candidate's speech was intended to stir up (i) _____ feeling, he must have been sorely disappointed by the almost (ii) _____ effect it had on the audience. Although it was refreshing to see a politician (iii) _____ inflammatory taglines in favor of reasoned argument, his speech was simply too long to hold the audience's attention.

Blank (i)	Blank (ii)	Blank (iii)
rancorous	incendiary	eschew
partisan	noxious	preclude
indigenous	soporific	abhor

67. The findings of multiple social psychology studies suggest that humans are much more (i) _____ than we like to admit. Although we tend to think of our opinions and beliefs as highly personal and deeply-rooted, the truth is that they are greatly influenced by our surroundings. In some cases, we are even willing to (ii) _____ the evidence of our own senses in the interests of conformity; in the Asch experiments, participants routinely misjudged the length of a line in order to (iii) _____ the majority judgment.

Blank (i)	Blank (ii)	Blank (iii)
tractable	vituperate	abide by
fatuous	repudiate	preclude
dogmatic	garner	quibble with

68. No doubt because of its potential hazards, we tend to think of radiation as something out of the ordinary; in truth, however, radiation is essentially _____, and it is therefore impossible to avoid low-level exposure.

ineffable
ubiquitous
nebulous
quiescent
foolproof

69. Invasive species constitute a serious threat to (i) _____ plants and animals, whether by preying on them directly or competing with them for resources. The emerald ash borer has had a particularly (ii) _____ effect on the environment; as its name implies, it attacks and kills all varieties of ash trees, and it is spreading throughout the United States at an alarming rate.

Blank (i)	Blank (ii)
inveterate	deleterious
pugnacious	covert
indigenous	perfidious

70. The English teacher was impressed by his newest student's _____ observations; on her first day in class, she commented on several aspects of the novel that her classmates had overlooked.

urbane
pedantic
trenchant
equivocal
loquacious

71. The death of Hu Yaobang, a Party leader committed to economic and social reforms, was the (i) _____ that caused the now famous Tiananmen Square protests. The demonstrations, which lasted seven weeks and were primarily non-violent, culminated in the government's brutal massacre of hundreds, if not thousands, of protestors - a (ii) _____ abuse of government power that resulted in widespread (iii) _____.

Blank (i)	Blank (ii)	Blank (iii)
catalyst	redoubtable	encomium
imbroglio	heinous	sanctimony
antidote	dubious	opprobrium

72. Prior to the nineteenth century, female ballet dancers were effectively barred from lead roles due to their (i) _____ corsets, hoops, and high heels. With the invention of the pointed shoe, however, all of this changed; ballet dancers came to be seen as ethereal creatures capable of floating effortlessly across the stage. Ballets consequently began to feature stories of nymphs and spirits that showcased the (ii) _____ costumes and (iii) _____ bodies of nineteenth-century ballerinas.

Blank (i)	Blank (ii)	Blank (iii)
cumbersome	dulcet	brittle
maladroit	meretricious	supine
disheveled	diaphanous	lithe

73.   Perhaps not surprisingly, a recent study suggests that teens in the United States spend a _____ amount of money on clothes; in fact, apparel accounts for roughly 20 percent of all teen spending.

conspicuous
temperate
nebulous
ignominious
impecunious

74.   Although folklore regards a green sky as a (i) _____ of tornadoes, the belief is not backed by scientific evidence. In fact, tornadoes are one of the more unpredictable forms of severe weather; although radar can detect signs indicating a possible tornado, such data generally requires eyewitness (ii) _____.

Blank (i)	Blank (ii)
propagation	reciprocity
incursion	approbation
harbinger	corroboration

75.   Those who are familiar with Shakespeare's plays no doubt see Richard III as a murderous (i) _____ who killed his two young nephews in order to claim the throne for himself. Some modern historians, however, believe that the evidence against Richard is (ii) _____ at best, and suggest that Shakespeare may have had politically compelling reasons for (iii) _____ his character.

Blank (i)	Blank (ii)	Blank (iii)
iconoclast	quotidian	renovating
mendicant	tenuous	commemorating
reprobate	whimsical	maligning

76.   The children grew _____ when cold temperatures forced them to remain inside.

| boorish |
| phlegmatic |
| gregarious |
| restive |
| feckless |

77.   The most successful companies can have humble – even (i) _____ - beginnings; that Sony's first product was an ineffective rice cooker surely proves that (ii) _____ is nearly as important as vision when trying to get a business off the ground.

| Blank (i) |
| mundane |
| frugal |
| bogus |

| Blank (ii) |
| tenacity |
| presumption |
| sophistry |

78.   Victimology at times ventures into highly (i) _____ areas, such as victim precipitation, which occurs when a victim attracts the attention of an attacker through (ii) _____ behavior of some sort. Although studies that center on the victim's identity and habits ultimately aim to reduce crime, to some, the terminology used in such research does little besides blame the victim and implicitly (iii) _____ the crime.

| Blank (i) |
| salacious |
| propitious |
| contentious |

| Blank (ii) |
| timorous |
| brash |
| fulsome |

| Blank (iii) |
| condone |
| provoke |
| rescind |

79.   Monteverdi's L'Orfeo enjoys its (i) _____ reputation in part because it is regarded as the first fully developed opera. Yet due credit must also be given to both the score and the libretto, which retells the (ii) _____ tale of Orpheus's journey to the underworld to restore his beloved Eurydice to life.

Blank (i)
renowned
incongruous
unscathed

Blank (ii)
droll
poignant
maudlin

80.   The (i) _____ nature of the sloth is well documented; its very name is a reference to the Biblical sin of spiritual and physical apathy. Unlike the average (ii) _____, however, the sloth has a compelling reason to (iii) _____ physical activity; the sloth's diet consists almost entirely of leaves, which provide little in the way of energy or nutrition, forcing the sloth to conserve its strength.

Blank (i)
fulsome
lugubrious
phlegmatic

Blank (ii)
virago
libertine
sluggard

Blank (iii)
abstain from
inveigh against
wean themselves off

81.   Though we were charmed by the (i) _____ waters of the Mediterranean, the highlight of our trip to Greece was undoubtedly the chance to visit the Parthenon. Photos cannot adequately capture the grandeur of this (ii) _____ relic from ancient times, so we found ourselves stunned into silence when confronted by its stately columns and imposing pediments.

Blank (i)
pellucid
turbid
quiescent

Blank (ii)
portentous
august
irrevocable

82. It is hardly surprising that questions concerning the nature and behavior of light have _____ some of the most brilliant thinkers throughout history; depending on how it is studied, light exhibits the properties of either a wave or a particle.

| placated |
| confounded |
| fettered |
| implicated |
| enervated |

83. An eye for seemingly (i) _____ details can make all the difference in marketing a product. Color, for example, can have (ii) _____ but powerful effects on a person's mood if not used carefully. Yellow runs the risk of being overpowering, but its undeniably eye-catching intensity can be an effective tool for a (iii) _____ businessman; Harry N. Allan, who first brought the taxicab to the United States, painted his cars yellow for precisely this reason.

Blank (i)	Blank (ii)	Blank (iii)
disparate	inadvertent	sagacious
spurious	nugatory	impecunious
trifling	salutary	officious

84. The _____ with which he ate appalled the other guests, who prided themselves on their impeccable table manners.

| efficacy |
| decorum |
| adroitness |
| temperance |
| alacrity |

85.   Petra's one-time importance as a key stop on a trade route is reflected in its unique and beautiful architecture; although the so-called "Great Temple "was" almost certainly built by an Arab tribe known as the Nabataeans, its style reveals a _____ of cultural influences - its columns, for example, draw on both the Corinthian and Suleiman styles.

travesty
dearth
adulteration
plethora
imprecation

86.   In order to _____ the hypothesized age of a given fossil, scientists rely on their knowledge of the radioactive decay rates of various isotopes.

correlate
discern
substantiate
gainsay
palliate

87.   While the study of viruses is important in and of itself, it must be noted that it also has potential (i) _____ for other areas of medicine. For example, a handful of otherwise innocuous viruses may (ii) _____ the development of certain forms of cancer; the Epstein-Barr virus has so far been linked to Hodgkin's lymphoma, Burkitt's lymphoma, nasopharyngeal carcinoma, and central nervous system lymphomas associated with HIV.

Blank (i)	Blank (ii)
proscriptions	precipitate
exigencies	attenuate
ramifications	truncate

88.   Although incest is now (i) _____ to many, if not most, societies, a surprisingly large number of cultures have at one time or another permitted it. Indeed, brother-sister marriage was virtually (ii) _____ within the ancient Egyptian royal family, where it was used to ensure that the bloodline remained (iii) _____.

Blank (i)	Blank (ii)	Blank (iii)
venial	condoned	omnipotent
abhorred	mandated	immaculate
ancillary	rectified	empyreal

89.   While most people are aware of the existence of vestigial structures like the appendix, far fewer realize that humans also retain some reflexes and behaviors that, though (i) _____ now, would have proven valuable to the organisms from which we evolved. Goose bumps, for example, cause whatever fur an animal has to stand on end, thereby making it appear larger and a more (ii) _____ opponent when faced with a potential predator.

Blank (i)	Blank (ii)
superfluous	impassive
apocryphal	formidable
exiguous	obsequious

90.   Although The Picture of Dorian Gray was (i) _____ at the time of its publication as a (ii) _____ account of a man's descent into moral depravity, it is now regarded as a classic work of English literature. In fact, the book's history underscores how the current social climate can (iii) _____ the true value of a piece of art.

Blank (i)	Blank (ii)	Blank (iii)
vaunted	histrionic	obfuscate
reviled	insipid	emblazon
expunged	lurid	atrophy

91. Contrary to a popular myth, the _____ pinks and oranges of a sunset are at their most brilliant in areas with relatively unpolluted air.

fervid
plangent
crepuscular
lambent
winsome

92. The governor signed the bill into law despite widespread and (i) _____ objections, leading some to question whether he truly had the people's best interests at heart. In response to such criticisms, the governor merely stated that the new laws, however (ii) _____ in the short term, were ultimately necessary.

Blank (i)	Blank (ii)
bombastic	unpalatable
moribund	imminent
vociferous	execrable

93. In 2010, California approved a cap-and-trade program that aims to reduce the greenhouse gas emissions of California-based businesses. But while most people agree that action must be taken to (i) _____ the worst effects of climate change, some companies feel these particular demands are too (ii) _____ to meet. Makers of concrete are particularly (iii) _____ of the new regulations; because the release of carbon dioxide is central to the production of concrete, the new law could have devastating effects for businesses that specialize in this.

Blank (i)	Blank (ii)	Blank (iii)
forestall	onerous	cognizant
descry	meretricious	wary
propitiate	amorphous	devoid

94.   The Romantic notion of "the sublime" has its origins in the eighteenth-century fascination with the natural world in all its forms; the term was used to describe landscapes so awe-inspiring that they simultaneously terrified and _____ those who saw them.

perturbed
eviscerated
transcended
galvanized
beguiled

95.   Although we tend to think of our judgments of others as (i) _____ observations, the reality is that a variety of unconscious beliefs and biases affect our opinions. For example, we so expect a person's physical appearance to (ii) _____ his overall intelligence and morality that attractive people are more likely to receive good grades in school and land a well-paying job.

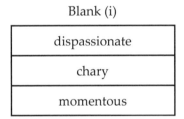

Blank (i)
dispassionate
chary
momentous

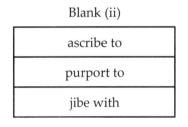

Blank (ii)
ascribe to
purport to
jibe with

96.   The average person is likely familiar with only three phases of matter - solid, liquid, and gas - and would no doubt be _____ to learn of the bizarre states of matter, such as super fluids and Bose-Einstein condensates, that can occur at extremely low temperatures.

contrite
saturnine
nonplussed
dispirited
livid

97. It did not take the new members long to see that the group was (i) _____ its leadership was disorganized and (ii) _____ and virtually all efforts at community outreach had ceased. They hoped, however, that their own enthusiasm would not only revive the organization but also (iii) _____ renewed outside interest in its cause.

Blank (i)	Blank (ii)	Blank (iii)
chimerical	frowzy	perpetrate
superannuated	torpid	foster
moribund	stringent	convoke

98. Even the most (i) _____ of glances at one of Vincent van Gogh's paintings will give the viewer some idea of his highly distinctive style. His use of bold brushstrokes and (ii) _____ colors give his art an unusual emotional intensity - an intensity that can be somewhat disconcerting when one remembers his (iii) _____ struggle with mental illness.

Blank (i)	Blank (ii)	Blank (iii)
cursory	incarnadine	iniquitous
jaundiced	funereal	harrowing
perspicacious	dynamic	affected

99. The jagged peaks and _____ drops of the Himalayas are signs of their relative youth; older mountains tend to be smaller and more rounded as a result of erosion.

overweening
notorious
surreptitious
precipitous
nascent

100. Although their (i) _____ beauty suggests extreme fragility, butterflies have developed a number of practical defenses against predators and other dangers. Some species advertise their (ii) _____ taste with bright colors and memorable patterns in the hopes that a predator will not make the same mistake twice, while others attempt to (iii) _____ their enemies with misleading eye-shaped spots on their wings.

Blank (i)	Blank (ii)	Blank (iii)
tremulous	insidious	maim
inordinate	elusive	placate
mincing	fulsome	confound

101. Although the (i) _____ against murder is universal, the definition of the crime is highly (ii) _____. A strict adherence to Buddhist teachings, for example, would most likely lead one to condemn even killing in self-defense, which is generally tolerated in modern society.

Blank (i)	Blank (ii)
litigation	contentious
vituperation	fallacious
proscription	inclusive

102. Although all parents expect some degree of (i) _____ obedience, those that carry their demands may inadvertently hinder their child's development. Children who grow up in a household where absolute (ii) _____ parental authority is the norm are often not given a chance to exercise their own judgment, and may therefore have low-self-esteem and a (iii) _____ sense of self.

Blank (i)	Blank (ii)	Blank (iii)
filial	propensity for	tenuous
reciprocal	intransigence towards	mercurial
scrupulous	deference to	dissolute

103. Although the majority of urban legends are no doubt _____ their doubtful origins do not seem to have any effect on their ability to captivate listeners.

hyperbolic
ephemeral
judicious
prurient
apocryphal

104. Much to the (i) _____ of consumers, modern technology has allowed businesses to advertise more effectively - and more (ii) _____ than ever; the average city-dweller is now exposed to somewhere between 3,000 and 5,000 ads every day. The constant (iii) _____ of marketing is so frustrating that 43 percent of cell phone users say they would willingly pay more for a cell phone service that blocks such messages.

Blank (i)	Blank (ii)	Blank (iii)
edification	consummately	dearth
trepidation	obtrusively	parlance
disgruntlement	nefariously	barrage

105. Cirrus clouds, which form high in the atmosphere and are known for their wispy, _____ appearance, are actually composed of ice crystals rather than water droplets.

halcyon
sinuous
gossamer
variegated
lambent

106. Those unfamiliar with her (i) _____ sense of humor tended to take her words at face value, and were sometimes repelled by her apparent inability to speak seriously of any subject. For those in the know, however, her (ii) _____ remarks were endlessly entertaining.

Blank (i)
flippant
raucous
erudite

Blank (ii)
jocular
iconoclastic
equivocal

107. According to the theory of natural selection, traits that prove particularly _____ have a greater chance of being passed on to future generations, because the individuals that possess these traits are more likely to survive long enough to mate.

innocuous
expedient
salient
titillating
prolific

108. Although the Salem witch trials remain a (i) _____ passage of American history, there is no shortage of speculation as to their cause. Although the hallucinations purportedly experienced by the victims may have resulted from something as simple as moldy bread, it seems likely that socio-economic tensions and the (ii) _____ religious climate created an atmosphere in which mass hysteria could (iii) _____.

Blank (i)
clandestine
enigmatic
infamous

Blank (ii)
austere
vitriolic
pristine

Blank (iii)
convene
fester
languish

109.   Cyrano de Bergerac, as he is portrayed in Rostand's play, is something of a (i) _____. For all his swagger and (ii) _____ words, he remains a deeply sympathetic character, no doubt because at heart he is simply an insecure man tormented by unrequited love.

Blank (i)	Blank (ii)
archetype	licentious
paradox	iconoclastic
cliché	bombastic

110.   His decision to become a middle-school drama teacher surprised those who were familiar with his considerable talent and (i) _____ interest in performing. In response to the queries of his friends, he said that felt it was (ii) _____ him to do something about the (iii) _____ state of arts education in the public schools.

Blank (i)	Blank (ii)	Blank (iii)
manifest	inimical to	banal
inordinate	munificent of	abysmal
perfunctory	incumbent upon	odious

111.   Although the differences are no doubt (i) _____ to the casual listener, various studies have that men and women do not use language in precisely the same way. Men, for example, are far more likely to compliment women than vice versa, perhaps due to deeply ingrained cultural attitudes that condemn as (ii) _____ any romantically assertive woman.

Blank (i)	Blank (ii)
pertinent	garish
blatant	brazen
indiscernible	capricious

112. 3M is an extremely diversified company, with businesses dealing in health care, office supplies, display and graphics, electronics and communications, industry and transportation, and security and personal protection all falling under its _____.

aegis
vagaries
covenant
opus
tutelage

113. When thinking about the vast (i) _____ of the universe, it is hard to (ii) _____ that there could be more than one galaxy like the Milky Way, which is home to millions of stars, but according to scientists there are an untold number of galaxies, all moving through the universe at different (iii) _____.

Blank (i)	Blank (ii)	Blank (iii)
length	fathom	velocities and trajectories
darkness	explain	ways and means
reaches	measure	angles and dimensions

114. Some scholars (i) _____ that the works of William Shakespeare were in fact written by a(n) (ii) _____ of authors, rather than a single man. But, they have a difficult time identifying any possible suspects, figuring out how many there were or explaining how so many people could write in such a(n) (iii) _____.

Blank (i)	Blank (ii)	Blank (iii)
declaim	coterie	cohesive style
assume	menagerie	flamboyant manner
contend	gild	complicated time

115. Automobiles sold in the United States have either a manual or automatic transmission. If the car is a manual, that means the driver has to shift through a (i) _____ of gears to accelerate, while an automatic car will shift on its own with no (ii) _____ from the driver. It is fair to say driving an automatic takes (iii) _____, but most people can learn to drive a manual with little trouble.

Blank (i)	Blank (ii)	Blank (iii)
gamut	contrivance	less coordination
sequence	assistance	a long time
filigree	reliance	more stability

116. Gazelles are known to be fast as well as (i) _____; this often leads people to (ii) _____ dance and ballet performers with these graceful creatures of the savanna.

Blank (i)	Blank (ii)
erratic	associate
lithe	trivialize
diaphanous	defer

117. Good financial (i) _____ is required to run a small business, and if you are not (ii) _____ in the ways of accounting, you should consider hiring a professional.

Blank (i)	Blank (ii)
vitiate	pliant
acumen	learned
credence	frenetic

118. The study of metallurgy involves the mining and processing of metal (i) _____, as well as the mixing of different types of metals to form (ii) _____.

Blank (i)	Blank (ii)
magma	composites
ore	deposits
treacle	striates

119. Blinking is an involuntary movement that occurs many times a day, and most times people are not even _____ of the fact that they do it so often.

reticent
foretold
cognizant
belied
unctuous

120. Monarch butterflies have a very long and often (i) _____ migration route that can often take them several months depending on their (ii) _____ in North America.

Blank (i)
vicarious
fractious
precarious

Blank (ii)
volition
origin
polarity

121. Most people in North America are more familiar with grey squirrels, but in some regions and smaller, _____ areas, black squirrels thrive in abundance.

variegated
razed
homogenized
localized
denigrated

122. "Shooting stars" are meteors, hunks of rocks that (i) _____ through space, that burn up in the Earth's atmosphere in a streak that can often be seen by the naked eye; meteorites are pieces of meteors that aren't completely (ii) _____, and fall all the way to the ground.

Blank (i)
hurtle
waft
droll

Blank (ii)
collated
extirpated
serrated

123.   The people's (i) _____ toward their repressive government increased when they heard that a
       series of long-promised reforms were (ii) _____. The parliament had been suspended indefinitely,
       meaning that no changes would be made for the foreseeable future.

Blank (i)
revulsion
fidelity
rancor

Blank (ii)
saprophagous
moribund
nascent

124.   The former dictator's (i) _____ was legendary, although it was only after he was deposed, the full
       extent of his wealth became known - huge mansions spread across the country, and a (ii) _____ of
       luxury goods.

Blank (i)
prowess
cupidity
prudishness

Blank (ii)
paucity
surfeit
postulate

125.   Judge Gordon was known for his _____ in upholding the law; although his rulings sometimes went
       against his personal preferences, they were always in keeping with legal precedent.

turpitude
probity
speciousness
torpor
urbanity

126.   Our group worked _____ on the account; for months many of us got to work early and left late, and
       some even took work home.

ambiguously
exultantly
formidably
imperturbably
assiduously

127. We were appalled by the waiter's _____; when we complained that our food came cold, he told us that it was our fault for ordering an unusual dish.

effrontery
pusillanimity
dexterity
circumspection
asperity

128. My seat mate was so _____ that I could neither sleep nor read through the entire flight.

lethargic
rapacious
irascible
loquacious
indigent

129. Medieval European rulers often tried to legitimize their rule by (i) _____ ties to the ancient Roman Empire. Although actual ties were tenuous, this strategy engendered the German emperor adopting the (ii) _____ title of "Holy Roman Emperor".

Blank (i)	Blank (ii)
rending	ludicrous
alleviating	grandiose
espousing	gregarious

130. Walt's presentation was very _____; it helped clarify some difficult aspects of our group's goals for the remainder of the project.

lucid
malevolent
meretricious
obscure
bewildering

Explanatory Answers

Answer to Question 1:

inculcate, potentates and iconoclast

We can teach logic, but values such as the love or reason and virtue must be instilled. Clearly Socrates did not ingurgitate (A) or gulp his students, or importune (B), meaning inconvenience, them with a love of reasoning and virtue. The love of reasoning and virtue is an abstract quality and something we attempt to inculcate (C) in students, making C the correct answer.

Those who have authority are not portents (D), as portents are omens or premonitions. They can, however, be referred to as potentates (E) or autocratic rulers. They would not be profligates (F), or recklessly wasteful individuals. Option E is the correct answer.

Socrates cannot be considered a centurion (G) or leader of a unit of 100 soldiers, but Athenian potents may well have perceived him as an iconoclast (H). Iconoclasts attack or otherwise undermine cherished ideas and institutions including social structures and authorities of the day. Neophyte (I) must be eliminated as neophyte means novice and implies inchoate knowledge and skills; this certainly would not describe a teacher charged with educating the patrician Athenian youth. H is the correct answer.

Answer to Question 2:

sophistry and patrician

An ingenious yet invalid argument would amount to a dissimulation of the truth, but simple dissimulation, or deceiving, would not lead to the very specific aims Stephens has "to create an ingenious yet invalid argument." Option A, then, can be eliminated. Option B can also be eliminated as it is unlikely Stephens employs hubris or pride to create an ingenious yet invalid argument. Sophistry (C), however, has been employed since the time of the ancient Greek sophists whose specialty was creating ingenious yet invalid arguments aimed at getting readers or listeners to agree with them. Option C, then, is the correct answer.

If students from the lower socio-economic echelons are penalized, and their peers who don't have to serve can buy their way out of the proposed youth service program, we can safely assume that the latter are affluent youth from socio-economically advantaged families. Erudite (D) can be eliminated as erudite means learned, not socio-economically advantaged. These peers, furthermore, may or may not show off their wealth; the passage does not tell us if they are ostentatious (E). These peers, however, could be described as patrician (F) or deriving from the refined or wealthier class, making F the correct answer.

Answer to Question 3:

confluence

This sentence is saying that criminologists use both qualitative and quantitative approaches to yield greater insight in their work. They have combined the two approaches. "Reduction" means "decrease." The passage clearly states that criminologists have added to their analysis. "Petulance" means "sullenness." There is no reason to believe that combining qualitative and quantitative measures is "sullen." "Reluctance" means "hesitancy." There is no evidence in the sentence to suggest that the combination of qualitative and quantitative analyses was done hesitantly. "Diaspora" means "migration." This answer makes no sense in the context of the question "Confluence" means "union." The combining of qualitative and quantitative measures can accurately be described as a "union" of measures.

Answer to Question 4:

permeates

This sentence is saying that rhetoric used to be confined to a field, but now it is not. We want a word to express this idea of rhetoric's newfound ubiquity. "Permits" means "allows." There is no indication given in the passage that rhetoric now "allows" other fields of study to do anything.

"Aggrandizes" means "glorifies." Again, the passage is stressing that rhetoric used to be confined, but now it is not. Rhetoric may very well aggrandize every field of study but it is not indicated in the shortcomings as "Aggrandizes" – it's possible, but there's no specific reference in the passage. "Rectifies" means "fixes." This answer, once again, is given no reference in the passage. We are left with "Permeates." This word means "pervades." This makes sense. If rhetoric used to be confined to political discourse, but is now more widespread, then it would indeed pervade other areas of study.

Answer to Question 5:

perdures

This sentence is saying that when one thing (written records) fails, another (crude tools) does not. Therefore, we want a word to express this enduring quality. "Discontinue" means to "abandon." This is not a word that expresses an enduring quality. "Excavates" means "exhumes." This answer does not make any sense in the context of the question. "Derides" means "scorns." There is no indication given that crude tools "scorn" anything when the written record fails. "Beguiles" means "charms." Again, there is no indication that crude tools "charm" anything when the written record fails. "Perdures" means "continues to exist." This is the exact action that would cause crude tools to "leave a trail throughout time" even when "the written records of events become unclear."

Answer to Question 6:

prejudices

This sentence is saying how "strict experimentation" introduces something into the human mind, and this "something" makes understanding the results of an experiment more difficult. We want to choose as our answer something that would undermine "strict experimentation." "Pellucidity" means "clarity." Clarity would not undermine strict experimentation. "Impartiality" means "objectivity." Objectivity would not undermine strict experimentation, either. "Riposte" means "comeback." This answer does not make sense in the context of the question. A "Plutocracy" is a type of government, and therefore does not make sense as an answer. "Prejudices" means "biases." The prejudices of the human mind would be able to undermine "strict experimentation."

Answer to Question 7:

attenuate

This sentence is saying that market competition is good, and then gives an example of the opposite situation. Therefore, the opposite situation (the concentration of market capital in few enterprises) must be bad for the economy. "Consecrate" means "bless." "Blessed" economic health is not a bad thing. "Commiserate" means "empathize." This answer does not make sense in the context of the question. "Alleviate" means "improve." The sentence clearly implies that concentration of market capital in few enterprises is a bad thing, so it will not improve the economy. "Fulminate" means "criticize." There is no evidence given that the concentration of market capital in relatively few enterprises will criticize the economy. "Attenuate" means "lessen," or "weaken." This is the correct answer. This continues the idea of concentrated market capital being bad for an economy.

Answer to Question 8:

obstinacy and flouted

This passage is stating that the man was too stubborn to listen to his friends' advice about learning guitar. "Pensiveness" means "thoughtfulness." The man would not be amazed by his own thoughtfulness, because he did not act very thoughtful in ignoring his friends' advice. "Reticence" means "reserve." He would not be surprised by his own reserve, either, because he wasn't reserved: he pushed ahead and ignored everyone's advice. We are left with "Obstinacy." This word means "stubbornness." This makes sense. The man would be amazed at his own stubbornness because he ignored all of his friends' advice.

For the next blank, the passage is stating that the man continued to push his hands hard even though his friends told him to accept a slow progression of skill. "Articulated" means "expressed." The man obviously did not "express" his friends' advice if he continued to push himself hard. "Expounded" means "explained." The man did not explain his friends' advice if he was ignoring it. We are left with "Flouted." This word means "disobeyed." This makes sense. If the man ignores his friends' advice every step of the way then he would be disobeying it.

Answer to Question 9:

derided and duplicity

The passage is stating that Gary often receives criticism for watching television. "Bolstered" means "reinforced." If the people in his life are criticizing television then they are not "reinforcing" it. "Protracted" means "prolonged." Nobody in Gary's life seems to be trying to "prolong" television. "Derided" means "ridiculed." If the people in Gary's life are reprimanding him for watching television, then they are deriding television as a waste of time.

For the second blank, Gary notices that the same people that deride television often watch it themselves. "Equanimity" means "composure." Gary is not commenting on any sense of composure from the people that deride television, he is criticizing them for deriding television while also watching it. "Sublimity" means "state of high spiritual value." Gary is not commenting on the high spiritual values of these people, he is criticizing them for being dishonest. "Duplicity" means "deceitfulness." If Gary knows that the same people who criticize him for watching television also watch it themselves, he would consider them very deceitful.

Answer to Question 10:

exhilarated and milquetoast

This passage is stating that the idea of riding a motorcycle helps the man break away from his boring existence. "Vetoed" means "prevented." The notion of riding a motorcycle does not prevent the man from doing anything. The passage clearly shows it exciting him and empowering him. "Censured" means "reprimanded." Again, the passage does not show the man being "reprimanded" for wanting to ride a motorcycle. "Exhilarated" means "excited." Riding a motorcycle would cause the man to feel excitement because the rest of his existence is "the safety of an office environment."

For the second blank, the passage is talking about the type of person the man has always been – very meek. "Obdurate" means "stubborn." Nothing about the description of the man's life describes him as being "stubborn." "Contrarian" means "going against popular opinion." Again, nothing in the passage shows the man contrarian in his life before discovering motorcycles. "Milquetoast" means "meek." One who prefers the "safety of an office environment to anything else" can accurately be described as "milquetoast."

Answer to Question 11:

alleviate and begrudge

This passage is saying that Tiffany has received lots of money, but she knows it will never help her stop missing her parents. "Masticate" means "chew." This obviously makes no sense in the context of the question. "Interpolate" means "include." It doesn't make any sense that Tiffany would want to "include" sorrow in her money. "Alleviate" means "ease." The line "she would rather have had her parents back" shows that money cannot ease Tiffany's pain.

For the second blank, the passage is saying that Tiffany doesn't appreciate the comments that her friends are making. "Lionize" means "idolize." If Tiffany does not like the comments that her friends are making then she would not be idolizing them. "Oblige" means "accommodate." Again, if Tiffany doesn't appreciate her friends' comments then she would not try to accommodate them. "Begrudge" means "resent." If Tiffany didn't appreciate the advice her friends are giving her, then she would "resent" the comments.

Answer to Question 12:

cliche and appalling

The passage is stating that Howard feels like his experience is unique, even though he apparently knows that it is not. "Facetious" means "foolish." Howard does not seem to find his story foolish, because it is causing him much consternation. "Metaphorical" means "symbolic." This situation is really happening to Howard, so it is not symbolic. "Cliche" means "overused." This answer works. The first sentence implies that even though Howard feels like his situation is new, it might not be. "Cliche" opposes the word "new," so this is the correct answer.

For the second blank, the passage is talking about all of the bad side effects Howard will face after signing his record contract. "Inconsequential" means "unimportant." If what Howard was doing to the prices that his fans pay was "unimportant" then it would not be giving him so much pause. "Judicious" means "sensible." If Howard was charging sensible prices to his fans then he would not be so concerned. "Appalling" means "dreadful." Howard would feel bad if the prices he was charging to his "loyal fans" were "dreadful."

Answer to Question 13:

elucidation and generalities

From the passage, readers can tell that the predictions made by horoscopes are generic and manipulable and their comprehension, explication and application can be easily changed to fit almost any situation. We are looking for a synonym for "understanding" or "interpretation" to complete the first blank. Palpability (A) means touchable and implies a sense of reality that is not present in generic horoscopes. Elucidation (B), meaning explanation or explication, however, fits and is the correct answer. If we can explain something, we understand it. Option C can be eliminated as omnipotence refers to the quality of being all powerful and does not fit in the context of this sentence. Option B is the correct answer.

Horoscopes are better applied to the general aspects than to the specific details of our lives. Clearly, we are looking for the correct synonym for "generic details "to complete Blank (ii). Exigencies, or extreme moments that demand attention, vary from person to person and are not the domain of horoscopes. They tend to be anything but generic, so Option D, then, can be eliminated. We must distinguish between shades of meaning to choose between options E and F. Generalizations (E) are generalities that are stated audibly or in print, and E must consequently be eliminated. The passage, however, refers to the generalities (F), or general/generic aspects of our lives, making F the correct answer.

Answer to Question 14:

endemic and congruous

An endemic disease is one that is constantly present, as in "malnutrition is endemic to certain impoverished regions of Africa." Option A, then, does not actually describe the world-wide flu of 1918 and must be eliminated. An epidemic (C) is a widespread outbreak of infectious disease making epidemic (C) a strong contender for correct answer. However, before selecting C, we must consider option B, pandemic. A pandemic is an epidemic that occurs throughout a large region or, as in the passage above, throughout the entire world. Clearly, option B, is the word that actually describes the flu that ravaged the entire world in 1918 and the correct answer.

The fact that world leaders came together to develop a single strategy for dealing with mass infections suggests that said strategy is comprehensive and homogenous. Option D, congruous, means harmonious/homogenous and reflects the homogeneity of a single worldwide strategy for addressing pandemics. Option E, germane means relevant or appropriate, and does not reflect the singleness of purpose of a single worldwide approach. Option F, refractory, meaning difficult to manage does not fit the context of the sentence and must be eliminated, making D, congruous, the correct answer.

Answer to Question 15:

acumen

Although the scientists may have all carried themselves in the same way, thus affecting a "combined demeanor" such a demeanor (A) would have no bearing on the scientists' predictions and makes little sense in the context of the sentence. The sentence, furthermore, gives us no reason to suspect the scientists of heresy (B). Even if they were all heretics, their heresy would have no bearing on their predictions or the events that followed the launch. Option C can be eliminated because it takes knowledge and critical thinking, not efficacy or efficiency, to predict events. The combined acumen (D), or expertise, of the scientists, however, should have enabled them to foresee problems and predict what came to pass, making D the correct answer. The callousness (E) of the scientists is not relevant to the remainder of the sentence. As we do not rely on callousness, but acumen, to make predictions, E must also be eliminated. Option D is the correct answer.

Answer to Question 16:

refulgent

The lifestyles described here are clearly ostentatious, though that is not one of the options. We must look, then, for a synonym for ostentatious. Refulgent (A), meaning gleaming or radiant is a good match for ostentatious as both denote notable radiance or opulence. Austere (B), on the other hand, means severe, somber, self-disciplined and is clearly the antithesis of the word needed here. Laudable (C) can hardly apply as the passage makes clear that the lives depicted are not laudable or praiseworthy. Monotonous (D) must be eliminated because there is no indication that the stars' lifestyles are repetitive and boring. Option E must be eliminated as the passage does not support the idea that the stars' lives are sanctimonious or hypocritically pious. Option A, refulgent, is the correct answer.

Answer to Question 17:

harangue

Here we are looking for a word that describes the loud and adamant denial the defendant is making. Option A can be eliminated as dyspepsia means indigestion and has no application here. Option B, harangue, on the other hand, means a loud or bombastic declamation and makes sense in the context of the sentence. Option C, approbation, meaning praise can also be eliminated as it makes no sense in the context of the sentence. Peregrination, option D, can be eliminated as a period of wandering or travels, does not make sense here.

Finally, option E, gaucherie, must be eliminated as the defendant's denial is not a case of tactless and socially awkward behavior but a harangue. Option B is the correct answer.

Answer to Question 18:

travesty

We can use tone and syntax to arrive at the right answer to this question. Words like "heinous industry" and "depraved owners" tell us that the author adamantly disapproves of dog fighting and those who fight dogs. Furthermore, the sentence structure and particularly the word "of" that occurs after the blank require that we find a word that works within this structure. A tirade (D) is a prolonged period of bitter denunciation or criticism and does not make sense within the sentence. Furthermore, we would not say a "tirade of justice." Artifice (B), meaning a hoax, can be eliminated as can debauch, meaning to corrupt through sensual pleasures (C); they do not make sense in the context of the sentence. Travesty (D), when used with the word "of" as in "a travesty of justice" means a debased imitation. Option D makes sense and is consistent with the syntax of the sentence. Certainly, the author of this passage would agree that dog fighting is a debased imitation of a sport. Apparition (E) must be eliminated as apparition means ghost, and would make little sense here. Dog fighting is not a ghost of sport but a travesty of sport, making option D the correct answer.

Answer to Question 19:

prolix

Any play that is eight hours long and takes two nights to be executed is bound to be tedious. It cannot be pedantic, as this is a word reserved for people who are ostentatious about their leaning. And though the play might well be odious (B) odious simply means hateful and does not reflect the excessive length of the play. Onerous (C), meaning difficult, can also be eliminated as onerous means difficult but does not speak to the length of the play, and moribund (D), meaning being on the point of death could describe play-goers but cannot describe a play that can close but cannot literally die. Prolix (F) means excessively long and tedious and this word effectively describes the world most tedious play. Option F is the correct answer.

Answer to Question 20:

butte, capitulated and detritus

The speaker cannot be watching his town wash away from an estuary (A) or river, or he would have washed away as well. Neither can he be watching from a ravine (B), as being in a narrow steep-walled canyon would not place him above the town or afford him a vista. He could, however, watch the town below being swept away from a butte (C) or hill rising abruptly from the surrounding, flat landscape.

The barriers did not countenance (E), meaning placate or pacify as this would make no sense in the context of the sentence. Neither did they assuage (F) or soothe the flood waters. The makeshift barriers obviously gave in or capitulated (D) to the rising flood waters.

Neither calumny (G) nor aspersion (H) make sense in the context of the sentence. Both refer to verbal attacks meant to destroy reputations or friendships (calumny) or disparaging remarks (aspersions) that cast doubt. Aspersion, furthermore, is almost invariably used in the plural with the word "cast" as in "cast aspersions." The town washed away like so much debris or detritus (J), for it is indeed the detritus that gets sucked down the drain.

Answer to Question 21:

palliative

The words "care," "aging" and the phrase "over the long run" are the keys to answering this question. As there is no cure for aging, the focus here is very clearly on providing long-term care aimed at assuaging the pain and discomforts of the geriatric patients referred to rather than care aimed at achieving a cure. Ameliorative (A) care, however, would be any care that meliorates or makes better. That could include improving to the point of recovery, in which case we would no longer be talking about the long-term care that is the focus of this sentence. Palliative (B) care is provided to people when there is no hope for cure, the aim being to alleviate their suffering or symptoms as they degrade. It is the kind of care that nursing homes traditionally provide elderly clients, making patients comfortable until they "pass." Exogenous (C) must be eliminated as it means "deriving from "without;" it sounds good, but is irrelevant to the sentence. Salubrious (D), meaning healthy, must be eliminated as it does not make sense in the context of the sentence. Proprietary (F), pertaining to property or proprietorship must also be eliminated as it does not logically complete the sentence or have a match. Palliative care is long-term alleviative care making option B the correct answer.

Answer to Question 22:

scions

The list of Henry's children's names following the blank in the second sentence strongly suggests that we are looking for a word that means the equivalent of offspring. We are not looking for the word "heir" from sentence 1, as there can only be one heir to the throne. Progenitors (A), means ancestors, not offspring and must consequently be eliminated. Scions, however, not only means offspring, it means elite or royal offspring from noble or noteworthy families. Clearly option B fits in the context of the sentence. Devisees (C), on the other hand, may include offspring, but may also refer to anyone to whom property is devised by means of a will, related or not." Lineage (D) is related to ancestry, but refers specifically to one's line of descent back from, not forward to, from a common ancestor. Promulgations (F) refer to bulletins or announcements, not offspring and must be eliminated. Henry's offspring would be scions (B).

Answer to Question 23:

innocuous, surreptitiously and ubiquitous

The word "although" is critical to this sentence, suggesting that the name belies the true nature of the Kiss-Kiss beetle. The passage tells us the Kiss-Kiss beetle is a dangerous and prevalent pest vector of Chagras Disease. If its name suggests it is the opposite of its true nature, we can assume that its name suggests it is innocuous, option A. The name is suggestive but not foreboding or portentous (B), and the name is not accumbent (C), or reclined, as this would make little sense in the passage. The name of the Kiss-Kiss beetle hides its true nature suggesting it is innocuous (A).

Based on the description of how the Kiss-Kiss beetle enters homes, including words like "infiltrates" and "ensconce" we can safely infer that the bug enters homes surreptitiously (D). Precipitously (E), or abruptly, does not account for the secretive qualities of the beetle and must consequently be eliminated as an option. Finally, quintessentially can be eliminated as it means representing the ultimate or perfect example, leaving us to wonder, "example of what?" As the Kiss-Kiss beetle enters furtively and hides itself, surreptitiously (D) is the correct answer.

The phrase, "Once thought to be rare" that opens the second sentence suggests that it is now known that the Kiss-Kiss beetle is the opposite of rare, or highly prevalent. We must consequently look for a synonym for "highly prevalent." Ubiquitous (G) means everywhere, and if the beetle is highly prevalent it is everywhere. Option G, then, is the correct answer. The beetle is not exiguous (H), meaning scanty, nor is it anomalous, meaning atypical. The Kiss-Kiss beetle is what it is, and what it is, in this instance, is ubiquitous (G).

Answer to Question 24:

Recidivism

When faced with a passage without a topic, focus on what, specifically the passage is about. In this case, the passage is about prisoners, but more specifically, it is about ex-offenders and reoffending. The passage does not deal with the topic of gasconade (A) as this refers to sessions or incidents of extravagant boasting, and gasconade has no relevance to the passage. The passage does, however, address the matter of recidivism (B), or in simple terms, reoffending. It does not deal with exfiltration (C), or clandestine rescues, or with chicanery (D), trickery and deception. Attenuation (E) must also be eliminated as the passage is not about weakening or reducing but about recidivism.

Answer to Question 25:

inveigh and rapturous

To suborn (A) involves secretly deceiving someone and, very significantly, includes tricking that person into committing a crime. Although Felix is clearly tricking his mother and her lover, there is no indication he is inducing them to commit a crime, and option A must consequently be eliminated. Cajole (B), meaning to persuade by means of flattery or promises, does not relate as Felix does not make use of either. Felix inveighs (C), meaning that he entices and manipulates his mother and her lover into believing in a complete fabrication, making option C correct.

If Felix refers to himself as "beyond beatific," or beyond blissful, we can safely say he was rapturous (E). Felix cannot be described as desultory (D) as this means unfocused or jumpy, and Felix is clearly focused on his performance and the pleasure he derives from it. Option D must be eliminated. Felix's behavior is certainly a departure from the normal or right path, psychologically speaking, but he does not feel and would not describe how he felt as aberrant (F). He feels absolutely rapturous as stated in option E

Answer to Question 26:

peccadilloes and cant

As adumbrations are faint images, real or metaphorical, option A does not really fit in the context of this sentence. Option B refers to lovers or patrons of the arts and does not fit into the existing structure of the sentence either and so must be eliminated. Peccadilloes (C) or minor infractions on the slightly depraved side, would, however, give parishioners good reason to let the pastor's comments on their shortcomings go in one ear and out the other without going so far as to galvanizing them to leave the church.

Chit-chat (D) refers to idle conversation among a few individuals, but here we have a pastor addressing his congregation, regaling rather than chatting with them. There is no indication from the passage that the pastor is guilty of invective or rough or crude speech, so option E must be eliminated. Invective (E) would not, at any rate, fit grammatically within the existing sentence. Cant (F), or overstated and somewhat hypocritical statements supporting morality and piety does fit the context of the passage and is the correct answer.

Answer to Question 27:

Reconnaissance, glitches and go back to the drawing board

In all probability the SR7 Rover, designed to go out into space and gather intelligence, would not be named a Canard (A) Rover as canard means a derogatory story, report or rumor. Option A certainly does not imply the exploratory nature of the mission but rather raises questions about its legitimacy. Neither would the Rover be named Alliance (C) as that would imply a pact between organizations or nations that is not supported by the passage. The SR7 is going out on a reconnaissance (B) mission to conduct an on-the-ground search/ investigation with the aim of bringing back information for the superiors, in this case, the scientists.

Clearly the SR7 suffers from a number of small problems or glitches (F) that are not significant on their own, but when taken together have the potential to delay the launch of the Rover. If the project were merely riddled (loaded) with gimmicks (D), or ingenious and novel stratagems to attract attention and increase appeal, there probably would be no threat to the launch. Furthermore, gimcracks (E) being showy, insignificant trifles such as one might pick up at a country fair, are not the issue here, and option E must be eliminated. F, glitches, or small, or idiosyncratic problems, is the correct answer.

Taking the bull by the horns is synonymous with taking action, and taking action, in this case amounts to launching the SR7. Option H must be eliminated as it would make the sentence repetitive and nonsensical, suggesting that scientists "...launch the SR7 or launch the SR7." Scientists should not throw the baby out with the bathwater (I), or scrap the entire SR7 because of a few glitches, but should "launch the SR7 or go back to the drawing board" to redesign it as stated in option J.

Answer to Question 28:

ameliorated

Clearly Aristotle damaged the reputation of octopi by calling them stupid, and clearly their reputation has been restored by the clever antics of Andy the octopus. With that in mind, we can eliminate option A, as their reputation has not been ruminated, meaning chewed or pondered, by Andy. Their reputation can be described as bifurcated, or divided into two branches (stupid and brilliant in this case) but note that it was not Andy who bifurcated it. Andy has not expedited (C), or sped up the reputation of octopi, but has ameliorated (D), or improved their reputations. Option E can be eliminated as Andy has not scintillated or caused the reputation of octopi to glow or burst forth in flames. Scintillated, furthermore, has no match among the options given. Andy has ameliorated or improved the reputation of octopi, making D the correct answer.

Answer to Question 29:

produce, acreage and fruitage

Calumny is a misrepresentation or slander, produce (as a noun) is a product, usually agricultural, and a morass is a marsh or a confusing and difficult situation. Since the text is discussing growing vegetables, the only possible answer for Blank (i) is *produce.*

For the second blank, *acreage* means an amount of land, a nadir is the lowest point, and a quagmire is a situation that is difficult to extract *oneself* from. In the context of planning your garden, only *acreage* makes logical sense.

The last blank needs a word that means the vegetables that have grown. *Concurrence* is a convergence or simultaneous occurrence; *fruitage* is the harvest or yield, usually from an agricultural endeavor, and *exculpation* an acquittal. Again the correct answer should be obvious – *fruitage* is the only word that fits.

Answer to Question 30:

Cyber, vulnerability and puissance

After reading the entire text, it should be easy to tell that the answer for Blank (i) is A. The passage is talking about hackers and computer programmers and *cyber* criminals work online and with technology.

The Nasdaq is an American stock exchange and it was hacked, so the second blank must mean something similar to being open to an attack by hackers. *Vulnerability* (how capable something is of being attacked or how susceptible it is to danger) means exactly that.

Puissance means force or strength, and thus makes it the best choice for the third blank, rather than *nostrum* (a panacea or a sham cure) or *cynosure* (a thing that attracts notice because of its beauty or brilliance).

Answer to Question 31:

precipitous, competitors and consistently

The options for the first blank are *propitious* (favorable or auspicious), *precipitous* (steep), or *promontory* (an outcropping or peninsula). We can immediately cross off *promontory* as it does not fit logically or grammatically. A drop-in profits is rarely a positive thing, and 19 percent is rather high, so the only reasonable choice is B.

The second blank could be filled with a variety of words. However, an *assailant* is an attacker, and *hindrances* is vague, so the best and most logical choice is *competitors* – in Asia it makes sense for these other countries to have companies competing for the same business.

The last sentence logically must be making the point that GM will be in trouble if it does not perform better. *Erratically*, or unstable and unpredictable, is not a positive thing when talking about a business's performance, and *pedantically*, didactically and pompously, does not make sense in this context either. Performing *consistently*, steadily or evenly, is a positive thing that GM would want to do.

Answer to Question 32:

accentuate, apperception and perpetuating

The text is about the attempt to both embrace modernizing reforms and maintain a Tatar identity, so the first blank must be *accentuate* (give importance to or stress), rather than *desiccate* (to dry out or dehydrate) or *abrogate* (to revoke or annul).

If the Tatars are developing a secular approach, then they must find a new *apperception*, or understanding, of Islam.

Since the entire passage has been about how Tatars continued to maintain, or perpetuated, their identity, H is the only reasonable choice for the third blank.

Answer to Question 33:

components, tangible and alleviates

The first blank is part of a comparison. The second half – dealing with each question one at a time – tells us that the first half must mean the opposite of that, or dealing with all the parts at once. *Components* means pieces or parts, and therefore is the only acceptable choice.

The second blank is also a comparison. *Ephemeral* and *amorphous* mean not concrete or lacking form, while *tangible* means the opposite. In this comparison concrete action is the more logical opposition to continued negotiations, so *tangible* is the best choice. Both *alleviate* and *exterminate* could work logically in the last sentence – the phased approach could lessen *(alleviate)* or destroy/get rid of *(exterminate)* the immediate pressures. However, grammatically and stylistically only *alleviate* fits.

Answer to Question 34:

demographics, sympathetic and dispossessed

The first blank can only be filled in after reading the entire passage, which is about migration of ethnic groups. Thus we know that the first blank is about the changing ethnic make-up of Abkhazia, or its *demographics*.

If the Abkhazians were leaving after revolts against the Russians failed, then they probably were also somewhat anti-Russian, or at least were *sympathetic* to (agreed with, looked on with favor) anti-Russian activity.

For the last blank, we know that the groups, or peoples, were moved from their homes – they were expelled, kicked out, which is what *dispossessed* means. The phrase "ethnic cleansing" makes it doubtful that they were mollified and content *(appeased)* or self-assured and pleased *(complacent)*.

Answer to Question 35:

ecologists, monogamous and biodiversity

This text is about plants and animals and their relationship, and *ecologists* study the interaction between organisms and their environment. There is nothing in the passage relating to codes and ciphers (what *cryptologists* study) or rocks and the composition of the earth (what *geologists* study).

The bees stay with a single flower, so the second blank needs to describe a relationship where you are with only one person – *monogamous*, not *polygamous* (a relationship between several people) or *hypergamous* (a relationship with someone of higher status or more wealth).

The passage claims that it is important for an ecosystem to have a larger number of species (in this case bee species), or *biodiversity*. Neither *anathemas* (despised or repugnant things) nor *surfeit* (an overabundance) make sense in this context.

Answer to Question 36:

an expedient, presumptively and implications

Expedient (suitable or advantageous) is the only valid choice for the first blank given that the method is also described as simple and useful. There is no reason to think that it is a bad idea *(imprudent)* or that it was unnecessary *(superfluous)*.

For the second blank the best choice is E – since the scientists are hopeful for the future of the enzyme it can hardly be *dubious* (unlikely) that it will be used to cure diseases. Since the scientists are "not yet sure" how exactly it will be used, *presumptively* (in all likelihood, presumably) is the best fit.

Curing diseases and reprogramming cells is a concrete, not an *abstract* use of the enzyme. The last blank has to be a word that is similar to possibilities or repercussions. *implications*.

Answer to Question 37:

physics, interference and observed

Gravity and surface tension refer to laws of *physics*, not *biology* or *geology*.

Being able to slide through a tiny hole or climb up the side of a glass implies that these laws are not in effect, or are not *interfering* with the movement of the superfluid.

And while *envisioned* could possibly work for the final blank, *observed* is much more appropriate, especially considering that scientists rarely make assumptions without experimenting and observing to check their validity.

Answer to Question 38:

an escalation, smaller-grained and an accelerated and expensive

That the erosion (wearing away of rocks and other deposits on the earth's surface) is substantial is clear from the phrase "large amounts of lost sediment." To *escalate* means to intensify or accelerate, and thus A is the correct answer.

D, E, and F could all be possibilities for Blank (ii), but the only option that would plausibly result in faster erosion is *smaller-grained*.

The final blank requires some inference. Given the information we have that beach nourishment causes fast erosion, *accelerated* and *never-ending* are appropriate descriptions of the cycle of erosion and replacement. *Ineffective* is possible, but not as good a fit as the other two options. We understand the process, so it is not *inexplicable*, and we are given no reason to believe it is *unhygienic*. It is safe to assume that having to replace the sand again and again is *expensive*, so G is the best choice.

Answer to Question 39:

immutable

Immutable means unchanging, and unchangeable. The size of an object is not changed and cannot be changed by distance from the viewer. Option A is the correct answer. Flexible is an antonym and suggests that the size of an object can and will change depending on the distance from the viewer. Stable suggests that object size is changeable, but remains temporary unchanged. Abiding suggests that the object remains unchanged because it adheres to a rule, rather than because it is of a constant size. Abiding, like stable includes the possibility of change in size. Uniform suggests that all objects are the same size.

Answer to Question 40:

interpretation

To interpret is to bring out the meaning of information or stimuli. Option B is the best choice for the blank. Insight is knowledge of the true nature of stimuli, usually through intuitive understanding, and does not apply. Translation changes information to fit new requirements. To elucidate is to explain something that is complicated. To adapt is to change for a new application. In this case, the sentence describes the process of receiving stimuli, then deriving or bringing out meaning by sorting through the available information.

Answer to Question 41:

ascertains

To ascertain is to find out definitely. If one assumes or theorizes, he or she guesses based on varying evidence. Since this passage refers to learning, ascertain is applicable making option C the best choice. To validate is to confirm what is already known. This passage describes the process of learning through repeated experiences, rather than validating prior knowledge. Disputes is an antonym for assumes and doesn't make sense in the sentence, because if one disputed which route was shorter, he or should would not like to adopt that route.

Answer to Question 42:

unheeded

To note information is to consciously acknowledge it is present. Information that is unheeded is noted, but not considered. Choice A is the best choice. Information that is rejected may not be noted. Considered is a synonym for "deserve focus" and does not fulfill the contrast suggested by the sentence. Abandoned suggests the information is considered, but later given up; this would suggest the information deserved and received focus, which again does not fit the contrast established in the sentence. Underestimated suggests the information is more important than the subject is aware of and doesn't make sense with the definition of signal detection.

Answer to Question 43:

appreciable

Appreciable stimuli are easily noticed. Negligible and imperceptible stimuli are not easily noticed. Pronounced and significant stimuli are substantially present, which means they may dominate an environment. The sentence does not indicate that the stimuli are strong and the examples indicate subtle stimuli making option E the best choice.

Answer to Question 44:

propel, constricts and depleted

To propel is to cause something to move forward. The contraction of the heart muscle moves blood forward and out of the muscle. To pitch is to throw, which does not apply to liquid moved through a closed system. Influence and project should be eliminated. Project is similar to pitch as it refers to throwing or casting something out. The sense of force and forward motion is not evident.

To constrict is to squeeze from all sides. To compress is to press together to create a solid mass. To cinch is to circle something with a tight grip. Constricts is the correct choice as it refers to the pressure exerted to send blood out of the heart.

Depleted means seriously decreased or exhausted. Blood depleted of oxygen must be enriched. Squandered means wasted. The oxygen in the blood is not wasted; rather it is consumed by the body systems. Augmented is an antonym, which means added to. As the blood travels the circulatory system different organs and systems use the oxygen. By the time the blood returns to the heart, the oxygen has been depleted making it the best choice.

Answer to Question 45:

procure and rudimentary

To annex is to attach, usually to something larger or more important. To procure is to obtain by some special means. To relinquish is to give up. Since the cells obtain nutrients, and release waste, the word procure is most accurate. If a cell were to annex nutrients, those nutrients would remain attached to the cell surface, rather than incorporated. Thus, procure is the most appropriate choice.

A rudimentary animal is simple with a very basic structure. Primitive suggests a lack of complete development, which does not apply since the sponge is completely developed; it is not a damaged or mutated creature. Vestigial, like primitive indicates the animal is left from another time. Vestigial, however, does not describe the complexity of the organism. A vestigial organism could be quite complex.

Answer to Question 46:

impairment and pervasive

Since diabetes leads to blindness, it is logical that it impairs vision. Impaired vision may result in diminished sight, but the words are not synonymous. Impaired means damaged, while diminished means only lessened or decreased. Stagnation is the slowing or stopping of an action, which does not apply.

Pervasive means widespread and has a negative connotation. Pervasive conditions are serious and difficult to control. So, pervasive is the correct answer. Circumscribed means controlled or contained. Capacious means roomy or capable of holding a great quantity and is not applicable.

Answer to Question 47:

cadre and secrete

A cadre is a group that works together on similar goals. The different glands in the endocrine system are a cadre as each gland releases a different hormone. A force is a group charged with a specific mission. It is clear that there are multiple "missions" of the endocrine system both inside and outside of the body. The crux is the pivotal point. The endocrine system is made up of glands; it is not a unique entity.

The reader will likely make a determination between disperse and secrete. To disperse is to scatter.

Since the hormones go directly into the blood stream, there is no scattering. The process of secretion is that of releasing a hormone into a system, in this case the circulatory system. Beget refers to giving birth or producing. Again, this sentence refers to the function of releasing the hormones, not creating or producing them.

Answer to Question 48:

osmose and deliquesce

The contrast for this word is between the action of the single-celled organisms that obtain nutrients directly, and the more complex organisms that have structures for obtaining and breaking down food sources. To osmose is acquire gradually and unconsciously, without effort. This concept directly contrasts the processes of multi-celled organisms. Thus, option A is the best choice for the blank.

Exude refers to output, not intake, and is not applicable. Cull is to select or choose. While the passage indicates that multi-cell organisms may select food sources, that point is not made about single-celled organisms. To extract nutrients multi-cell organisms dissolve or melt the food source. Deliquesce means to melt or dissolve. Flux is a general term for melting, but doesn't apply to liquefying elements. Coagulate is an antonym meaning to join elements of a liquid into a solid or semi-liquid.

Answer to Question 49:

heritable

Gene theory studies which traits are transmitted genetically. Since this passage mentions traits and genetics, one can assume Mendel studied traits that are transmitted to different generations. Bequeathed suggests a conscious action and selectivity, which is not accurate. Inbred does not apply as it refers to the process of breeding, not the resultant genetics. Maternal describes one line of genetic transfer. Acquired traits are those not heritable. Heritable is therefore the answer, as it refers to traits transmitted genetically.

Answer to Question 50:

extant

Extant cells are cells that already exist. The distinction between new cells deriving from extant cells and those cells simply appearing is the main point of this sentence. This sentence clearly makes the comparison. The required word must be a contrast to the idea of cells that "spontaneously appear." Inanimate cells are non-moving cells; it is not clear if these cells exist or spontaneously appear. Neither living, surviving, or mortal, describing the life-state of cells makes a specific contrast to "spontaneously appear."

Answer to Question 51:

foundation

Hooke's work was the basis for future theory, therefore, foundation is correct. Infrastructure is not accurate, as he did not build all the necessary components for future study. Hooke's theory was innovative in that it was new, but innovative does not include the notion that Hooke created a starting point for other scientists. Consequence suggests a cause and effect relationship. If one were to replace the blank with effect, the sentence would not make sense. Production refers to something that is created or produced. Hooke himself did not produce the cell theories that were to follow his discovery.

Answer to Question 52:

synergy

Synergy means cooperation or collaboration. The cells clearly do not simply co-exist. They work together for the functions to occur. There is nothing in the sentence to suggest agreement or communion. The cells could reasonably have conflicting functions necessary for processes to occur. Accord and intimacy also suggest relationships between the cells other than cooperation. Contention is an antonym and should be eliminated.

Answer to Question 53:

cooperatives

The important detail is that the individual cells in the group are specialized and that they work together. A cooperative is an organization of entities that works together for the benefit of all involved. An organism's functions would obviously benefit all of the component cells; thus, A is the answer. An aggregate is a collection of different units into a single body. This is not a completely inaccurate choice, but is not as precise as it does not indicate the cooperative nature of the body. A collective is similar to an aggregate, and, again, the concept of cooperation or benefiting the whole through group effort is not indicated. A division is a part of the whole. Unanimity refers to the state of being in agreement. Since the cooperative cells perform different functions, they are not in agreement.

Answer to Question 54:

orbits and analogous

The context of this sentence makes clear analogy. The behavior of electrons around the nucleus is a planetary model. That is, electrons orbit the nucleus as the planets orbit the sun in the solar system. To orbit is to revolve around another body in a specific path. To envelop is to cover completely. The electrons do not cover the nucleus. To converge is to move toward a single point. This passage describes the path of a rotation around a point, not a movement toward that point.

Since the comparison looks at similarities, the correct choice is analogous. Components which are analogous show likenesses or similarities. Components which are homologous are identical and are derived from shared sources. This term is generally applied to biological elements. Retrogression refers to a return to a prior development stage. There is no mention of evolution or development in this passage.

Answer to Question 55:

unalloyed and multifarious

An alloy is a metal created by combining two or more pure metallic elements. Elements, by definition, are pure. The metal is not alloyed, or combined with other metals or other elements. Elements are, therefore, unalloyed. Something that is adulterated is impure. As noted, an element is pure in that it is made of a single component and is not alloyed or combined with other components. Veritable is similar to literal and is used to indicate that something named is true, realistic, and not imaginary.

Multifarious describes something that occurs with great variety. A multifarious grouping of elements would include those with few, if any, common characteristics. In another context, a multifarious library might include books on tax law, religious tomes from different sources, and children's rhyming books about bears. Something that is homogenous is made up of many components that share some similarity. A homogenous library might contain mystery novels by different authors. Conglomerate describes a mass made of different, varied sources which remain whole, rather than blend together.

Answer to Question 56:

Inverse and familiar

Conforming can be eliminated from the choices, as it refers to actions that are similar and this passage describes actions that are dissimilar. The connection is an almost exact opposite; as one variable increases, the other decreases. Contradictory is similar in meaning, but not a direct opposite. The correct answer is inverse, meaning opposite.

Proverbial should be eliminated as the context does not apply. Mundane can mean dull, which is not supported with context. The word, obvious, after the blank indicates that the example is quite known or familiar. The correct response, therefore, is familiar.

Answer to Question 57:

conjunctly

This sentence is saying that even though we have two different types of law (criminal and civil) they both still maintain social order. Therefore, we can infer that they work as a team. "Perniciously" means "wickedly." There is no evidence given in this passage that civil and criminal law work "wickedly." The only implication is that they most likely work together. "Superciliously" means "condescendingly." Again, there is no implication that civil and criminal laws combine to function condescendingly. "Redundantly" means "superfluously." The sentence clearly describes the two as having separate purposes (with criminal laws having greater consequences), so they cannot be described as redundant. "Intractably" means "stubbornly." Again, there is no implication given that the two work "stubbornly" together. "Conjunctly" means "cooperatively." This makes sense. Since civil and criminal laws function in different ways, they would have to work conjunctly in order to maintain social order.

Answer to Question 58:

encumbrance and reticent

The passage is stating how the field of meteorology has been pulled, against its will, into the world of politics. This is described as being a burden on meteorologists. Note that the first blank is difficult to answer without reading the rest of the passage. Working in the context of political discourse is not inherently good or bad, so further reading is necessary to establish what answer to choose. After reading, however, it becomes clear that political discourse is undesirable for meteorologists. "Auspices" means backing, or support. Given what we learn about the relationship between political discourse and meteorology, this word doesn't fit. "Insight" means "intuition." Once again, this word does not describe how political discourse effects meteorology "Encumbrance" means "burden," or "hindrance." Given what we learn in the passage, political discourse would be a burden to the study of meteorology.

The second blank describes scientists being thrust into another world. Given the use of the word "thrust," we can infer they were forced to be there. Therefore, we want words that establish the personality of a person who does not want to be in a public situation. "Ostentatious" means "flashy." A person like this would want to be in public situations. "Conspiratorial" is a word that means of or relating to unsavory and secretive behavior. There's no evidence provided in the passage that suggest that meteorologists would want to partake in unsavory and secretive behavior. "Reticent" means "quiet," or "discreet." It makes sense that a quiet person would only enter a public forum when being "thrust" into it.

Answer to Question 59:

antagonistic and inscience

The passage is trying to establish the difficulties that arise in trying to promote new ideas in the world of academia. The first blank is talking about something happening to potential growth in the field of physics. Since this thing is happening "in spite of immense intellect," we can infer that it must be negative. "Correlated" means connected. This word doesn't describe growth being inhibited or promoted, so it doesn't work. "Supplanted" means replaced. This answer does not make sense in the context of the question. We are left with "Antagonistic," which means "opposed to," or "hostile." Having factors that are "opposed" to growth makes sense.

The second blank is the end of a list that states the obstacles a progressive person would face. We want a word that completes this list. "Eminence" means renown. This doesn't continue the tone of the list. "Acquiescence" means compliance. This is of course the opposite of what we want. "Inscience" means "ignorance." Ignorance would function like "entrenched logic" and "petty careerism" in inhibiting society from accepting new ideas.

Answer to Question 60:

enraptured, abstruse and charlatans

The passage states that Fiona is very interested in dreams and what they reveal about the dreamer. "Vindicated" means "justified." The passage doesn't state that Fiona in any way feels "justified" by her dreams. "Denounced" means "condemned." The passage doesn't talk of dreams condemning Fiona to anything, so this is wrong. "Enraptured" means "captivated." Given the amount of study Fiona has put into dreams, she can accurately be described as "captivated" by them.

For the second blank, the passage states that Fiona is convinced that dreams have logical impetuses, even if they aren't clear. "Debonair" means "charming." Having charming dreams would not prevent Fiona from understanding them. "Gentile" means "amiable." Having amiable dreams would not prevent Fiona from understanding them, either. "Abstruse" means "perplexing." This makes sense.

Fiona would have a hard time understanding perplexing dreams.

For the third blank, the passage does not seem confident that the experts are really experts. It even goes so far as to put "experts" in quotations to show Fiona's doubts. "Solemn" means "serious." If Fiona is referring to the experts ironically, she would not be calling them serious. "Guileless" means "honest." Again, if Fiona is referring to the experts in the field ironically then she would not be calling them honest. "Charlatans" means "fakes." If Fiona is referring to the experts in the field ironically then she clearly considers them fakes.

Answer to Question 61:

enigmatic, exorbitant and exhaustive

The paragraph says that it is difficult to locate the many organisms living in the ocean because of the space they have to live in. Our lack of experience with them gives the organisms a secretive quality. "Haughty" means "proud." Being rarely seen would not cause aquatic life to be "proud." "Vituperative" means "offensive." Again, being rarely seen would not make aquatic life offensive. "Enigmatic" means "mysterious." This accurately describes how aquatic life would appear to humans if we've rarely or never seen them before.

The second sentence stresses the sheer size of the ocean and describes how this size is perceived in terms of searching for marine life. It must be considered excessively large for that purpose. "Coquettish" means "demure." This personality trait does not explain how the size of the ocean would be perceived by those looking for life within it. "Ardent" means "zealous." Once again, this word does not describe how the ocean would be perceived by those trying to find life within it. We are left with "Exorbitant." This word means "excessive." This describes exactly how one would feel about the size of the ocean when searching it for life.

The last sentence stresses how understanding every aspect of marine life is necessary in order to attain a certain type of understanding about the ocean. This "certain type" of understanding must be complete understanding if it requires understanding everything, including microscopic organisms. "Diminutive" means "small." A small understanding would not require knowing how every microscopic organism functions within the ocean. "Reticent" means "shy." A "shy" understanding does not make sense. "Exhaustive" means "complete." This makes sense. A complete understanding of marine life would require knowing how everything, including microscopic organisms, function within the ocean.

Answer to Question 62:

vocations and exactitude

The first blank talks about how there are "things" that fall under the heading of biotechnology that one wouldn't expect. We want a word that describes what these "things" might be. By reading further into the passage we see various jobs listed – brewers of alcohol and agricultural developers. Therefore, we want a word that describes a job. "Verisimilitudes" means "truths." This does not describe a field of work and therefore is incorrect. "Denigrations" means "defamations." These are insults and not fields of work. "Vocations" means "life's work." This describes the jobs that unexpectedly fall into the category of "biotechnology."

The last sentence is comparing what you would expect to fall under the heading of "biotechnology" (medical procedures of a certain quality) with what you wouldn't expect ("rough-and-tumble" jobs). Therefore, we want a word that would contrast with the "rough-and-tumble" description given to the latter group of jobs. "Unsophistication" means "lack of refinement." This relates to "rough-and-tumble" and therefore is incorrect. "Fallacy" means "misconception." This word does not contrast the scientific procedures with the "rough-and-tumble" jobs. "Exactitude" means "precision." This word contrasts nicely with "rough-and-tumble."

Answer to Question 63:

inhospitable and foil

Desolate landscapes and *small populations* do not sound particularly promising, and the word missing in the first sentence must reflect that. *Germane* means *relevant*, which is not the best way to describe whether or not a location is suitable for business (in fact, *germane* more commonly refers to comments or topics). *Morbid*, on the other hand, is too extreme; it means *unwholesome* or *gruesome*. The correct answer is *inhospitable*, which simply means *unwelcoming* or *unfavorable*.

In order to fill in the second blank, you need to read the passage all the way through to the end. We are told that South Dakota has very low taxes; presumably, since the author sees fit to mention it, this is one reason why it is a good place to start a business. Places with high taxes, then, are probably not conducive to succeeding in business, and the missing word should reflect that. *Obviate* means to *anticipate and prevent*, but does not quite work in this sentence; it is generally used when the thing being prevented is unnecessary, impractical, harmful, etc. *Lampoon* is appropriately negative, but does not make very much sense in this context; it means *to ridicule* or *to satirize*. The correct answer is *foil*, which means *to impede* or *to prevent the success of*.

Answer to Question 64:

belligerent

This sentence is about the military successes of Ghengis Khan and the Mongols; the missing word could mean something like *aggressive*, but it could also just mean *effective*. The best way to solve it, then, is by process of elimination. *Rancorous* means *spiteful* or *maliciously resentful*; even for a description of a military leader, it is a rather strong word, and one that implies a moral judgment, so you should eliminate it. *Timorous (fearful or timid)* clearly will not work. *Disingenuous* means *insincere*; again, it suggests moral condemnation, but more importantly, there is nothing in this passage about Ghengis Khan's honesty or lack thereof - eliminate it. *Erratic* means *unpredictable* or *having no definite course*. It is probably not the best description of a successful leader, so you should check to see if the other remaining choice makes more sense. *Belligerent* means *warlike*, and is the correct answer.

Answer to Question 65:

impervious to and forestall

We know from the word *though* that the missing word in the first sentence must in some way contrast with the fact that women are unlikely to have X-linked disorders; check the answers and see if there is a word that makes sense, given this. *Inclined* to will not work, because there is no contradiction between the idea that women are *not inclined to genetic disorders* and the fact that they are not susceptible to X-linked conditions. *Intransigent* means *uncompromising* or *inflexible* and generally describes someone's attitude; it is hard to see what being *uncompromising towards* a disease means, or how it has anything to do with one's susceptibility - eliminate it. The correct answer is *impervious to (invulnerable or incapable of being injured)*.

To fill in the second blank, notice that we are told that women have a *normal gene* that produces *clotting factors*. Even if you don't know exactly what clotting factors are, you can almost certainly deduce that they make blood clot (and therefore prevent *life-threatening bleeds*). *Engender* is nearly the opposite of what we want; it means to *produce* or *cause*. To *mollify* means *to soften* or *to mitigate*; it is a better answer, since it means something like *to make less severe*, but it is more often used in the context of feelings rather than physical injuries. To *forestall* is the better option; it means *to prevent* or *to anticipate*.

Answer to Question 66:

partisan, soporific and eschew

To solve the first blank, you will need to use process of elimination to find the best answer. *Rancorous*, or *spiteful*, is a bit extreme; in the absence of further information, we should give even a politician the benefit of the doubt and assume he doesn't want to elicit actual hostility. *Indigenous* is not a very good choice either; it means *originating in a particular region*. Given the political context, *partisan (partial to a particular person or party)* makes the most sense.

We are then told that the candidate was probably *disappointed* by the speech's effect. If his goal was in fact to stir up partisan feelings, he would likely have been gratified by an *incendiary (tending to arouse or inflame)* effect - eliminate this choice. *Noxious* is probably too strong a word to be warranted in this context; it means *harmful* or *corrupting*. *Soporific*, which means *tending to cause sleep*, is the best answer.

In the final sentence, we are told that the candidate's speech was characterized by *reasoned argument*. To fill in the final blank, then, we need to find a word that will make the sentence read something *like the politician avoided inflammatory taglines in favor of reasoned arguments*. *Abhor (to loathe or to detest utterly)* is too strong a word, and does not really work with the sentence structure - one does not generally *abhor* something *in favor of* something else. *Preclude* is also not quite what we need; it means to *make impossible*. To *eschew*, however, means *to abstain* or *to avoid* and is the correct answer.

Answer to Question 67:

tractable, repudiate and abide by

You need to read at least the second sentence before attempting to fill in the first. We are told that we like to think of ourselves as firm in our beliefs, when in truth those beliefs are easily swayed. The first blank, therefore, must refer to this susceptibility to external suggestion. *Dogmatic* is nearly the opposite; it means *opinionated* or asserting *opinions in a doctrinaire manner*. *Fatuous (foolish)* is better, but is a bit too judgmental - eliminate it. You are left with *tractable*, which means *easily managed* or *yielding*. In order to fill in the last two blanks, you need to have some sense of what the sentence as a whole is saying; the gist seems to be that participants in the Asch study misjudged the length of a line *in the interests of conformity*. For the first blank, then, we need a word that means something like *ignore*.

Vituperate (vilify or berate) makes no sense in this context; there is no suggestion that the participants actively criticized their sensory perceptions. You have probably heard the phrase *garner evidence* before, but do not be led astray; *to garner* means *to gather*, which does not work here. *To repudiate*, on the other hand, works well; it means *to reject* or *to refuse to acknowledge*.

Finally, we need a word that means something like *agree with* to fill in the last blank. To *preclude* means *to make impossible*, while to *quibble with* means *to make trivial objections*; neither makes sense in this context. *Abide by (to act in accord with or to submit to)* is the correct answer.

Answer to Question 68:

ubiquitous

In this sentence we are looking for a word that will contradict the idea that radiation is *out of the ordinary* - perhaps *common* or something similar. *Ineffable (incapable of being expressed)* has to do with whether or not something can be described, which is not in question here - eliminate it. *Nebulous* means *hazy* or *indistinct*. It is not a very good choice, unless perhaps you imagine that it is hard to avoid indistinct things. In any case, it has nothing to do with being *out of the ordinary*, so you should be able to eliminate it. You can rule out *quiescent* for similar *reasons*; it might be hard to avoid something *dormant* simply because you don't know that it is there, but what would this mean in the context of radiation, and what does it have to do with being uncommon? If you can't answer these questions, you should eliminate the word. *Foolproof* means *never-failing* and is more commonly used to describe plans or ideas - eliminate it. The correct answer is *ubiquitous*, which means *present everywhere*.

Answer to Question 69:

indigenous and deleterious

As its name should tell you, an invasive species is an organism that is not native to a particular place but has moved in and is disrupting the local ecosystem. It is a threat to local plants and animals, so the first blank probably means something like native. Inveterate means firmly established by long continuance, but it more commonly refers to feelings, practices, or even diseases than it does to plants or animals. Pugnacious means quarrelsome or combative; there is nothing in the passage to suggest that native species are unusually aggressive, so you should eliminate it. This leaves you with indigenous, which means originating in and characteristic of a particular region and is the best answer.

To fill in the second blank, you simply need a general sense of the passage's point - that invasive species are harmful. Covert means concealed or secret. It is clear from the passage, however, that at least some invasive species have a very obvious effect on the environment (see, for example, the description of the emerald ash borer), so you should be able to eliminate this choice. Perfidious, on the other hand, is too strong a word; it means treacherous or disloyal and implies a malicious intent that insects presumably do not have. Deleterious, or injurious, is the best choice.

Answer to Question 70:

trenchant

We are told that the teacher was impressed by the student's comments, so presumably they were insightful. Urbane is probably an overstatement; it means reflecting elegance or sophistication. Pedantic, on the other hand, means ostentatious in one's learning, and has negative connotations - eliminate it. An equivocal, or deliberately ambiguous, answer would probably not impress the teacher, particularly because it implies an intent to deceive. Likewise, a *loquacious* observation is not particularly praiseworthy; it means *characterized by excessive* talk. The best answer is trenchant *(incisive or keen)*.

Answer to Question 71:

catalyst, heinous and opprobrium

The first sentence informs us that the death of Hu Yaobang caused the protests, so we are looking for a word that describes something that causes something else. An antidote (something that prevents or counteracts injurious or unwanted effects) causes improvement, but that clearly will not work in this sentence, which describes events culminating in a massacre. Imbroglio will also not work; it means a misunderstanding or an intricate and perplexing affair, and better describes the circumstances following Hu Yaobang's death than the death itself. The correct answer is catalyst, which means a thing that precipitates an event or change.

As for the final two blanks, you should be able to glean from the rest of the passage that the government responded to the protests in a particularly savage way that was probably not received well in other countries, so you should be looking for words in keeping with this. Redoubtable means formidable, and it often implies respect, which is clearly not appropriate here - eliminate it. Dubious means questionable and is also not a good choice; there is no question that the government's actions were unethical. You are left with heinous (hateful or totally reprehensible).

As for the last blank, encomium would certainly not be an appropriate response; it means a formal expression of high praise. Sanctimony is also a bad fit; it means pretended, affected, or hypocritical religious devotion, righteousness, etc. Opprobrium (reproach or censure) seems a quite likely reaction, however, and is the correct answer.

Answer to Question 72:

cumbersome, diaphanous and lithe

In the first sentence, we learn that female dancers' corsets, hoops, and high heels prevented them from taking center stage - probably because the costumes were simply too difficult to move in. Disheveled does not make very much sense; there is no indication that the dancers' costumes were routinely untidy or disordered, and even if they were, couldn't they simply fix them? Maladroit is not a good fit because it usually describes people or their actions, not clothing; it means inept or awkward. Cumbersome (burdensome or unwieldy) is the correct answer.

To fill in the last two blanks, think about the way this passage describes ballet dancers; they act the part of nymphs and spirits, they float effortlessly, and they are ethereal. Your answers need to mesh with these descriptions. Dulcet means soothing or melodious; it usually refers to sound, so it is probably not the best description of costumes. Meretricious (tawdry or based on pretense) is too negative a word. Diaphanous is the best answer; it means very sheer and light and fits in well with the passage's depiction of ballet dancers.

Brittle (easily damaged or destroyed) will not work well for the last blank; dancers' bodies may seem fragile, but the connotations of brittle are too negative for a passage that otherwise describes the dancers in flattering terms. Supine does not make sense; a dancer could hardly remain inactive or lying on her back. The best answer is lithe, which means supple or limber.

Answer to Question 73:

conspicuous

20 percent seems fairly significant, and the missing word probably reflects this. Temperate will not work; the amount of money in question does not suggest moderate or self-restrained behavior on the part of the teenagers. Nebulous means hazy or indistinct and does not make sense here, given that we are actually given an exact percentage. Ignominious (disgraceful or contemptible) is too strong a word - eliminate it. You may know that impecunious has something to do with money but do not be tricked into choosing it; it means having little or no money and does not make sense in this context. The correct answer is conspicuous (striking

or noticeable).

Answer to Question 74:

harbinger and corroboration

The statement that tornadoes are unpredictable is presented as counterevidence to an assertion made in the first sentence. This should clue you in to the kind of word you need for the first blank - specifically, a word implying that green skies predict tornadoes. Propagation means multiplication or dissemination and does not really make sense in this context - eliminate it. An incursion is an invasion or a harmful inroad, which still does not quite capture the notion that green skies precede tornadoes. The correct answer is harbinger (an omen).

As for the second blank, we are told that even radar is not an entirely reliable indicator of tornadoes, and that eyewitness accounts are also needed; the missing word must mean something like confirmation. Reciprocity means mutual exchange; it is somewhat awkward here, particularly given that we are not told that the eyewitness accounts require radar confirmation. Approbation means or commendation or official approval, and is again a bit out of place here; it implies an approving attitude rather than simple confirmation. The correct answer is corroboration, which means confirmation or authentication.

Answer to Question 75:

reprobate, tenuous and maligning

The first sentence describes Richard III, at least in Shakespeare, as murderous. Clearly we need a word that implies condemnation of some sort. Mendicant won't work; it simply means beggar, which a king is unlikely to be in any case. An iconoclast is a person who attacks traditional beliefs or institutions, and the passage gives us no reason to suspect Richard of subversive activities; regardless of whether or not he killed his nephews, he presumably did not attack the monarchy as an institution. Reprobate (a depraved or unprincipled person) is the correct answer.

Moving on to the next blank, we know from the use of however that the historians mentioned in the sentence must doubt Shakespeare's portrayal of Richard; they presumably believe that the evidence against him is weak. Whimsical means fanciful or given to fanciful notions; it is not normally used in the context of something as serious as evidence. Quotidian means ordinary or commonplace - something that would presumably have no effect on the veracity of the evidence. Tenuous means thin or unsubstantiated and is the best answer. F

Finally, in order to fill in the last blank, we need to find a word that deals with Shakespeare's handling of Richard's character. Renovating will obviously not work; someone who renovates a person's reputation would be restoring it to good condition. Commemorating also has connotations that are too positive for this context; to commemorate means to honor the memory of. Maligning (slandering or speaking ill of) is the correct answer.

Answer to Question 76:

restive

As you should be able to glean from the use of the word forced, the children are probably not happy to be inside; the correct answer needs to describe a plausible effect of keeping kids inside against their will for several days. Boorish means unmannered or crude. Unless the speaker in this sentence is particularly snobby, it does not make a lot of sense to describe children this way, given that no one expects them to be models of propriety - eliminate it. Phlegmatic (calm or not easily excited) is an even less apt description of the average child - particularly one who has been inside for a week. Gregarious means sociable. It is hard to see what connection this could have to staying inside; if anything, being cut off from other people for an extended period of time would seem likely to make one less sociable. Finally, feckless means ineffective or lazy. Again, it is a strange adjective to apply to children, who are not expected to be as productive as adults. Restive, on the other hand, fits well and is the correct answer; it means restless or stubborn.

Answer to Question 77:

mundane and tenacity

The use of the word even implies that the missing word goes one step beyond humble in describing these companies beginnings. Frugal is not entirely out of the realm of possibility - it means economical in use or expenditure - but ask yourself if it works in the context of the passage as a whole. The sentence has nothing to do with money, so frugal is probably not the best answer. Bogus, on the other hand, is unwarrantedly negative; we have no reason to think that these companies have origins that are counterfeit or not genuine. Mundane, however, works well with the second half of the sentence; it means banal or earthly, which a rice cooker surely is.

As for the second blank, we are looking for a quality - distinct from vision - that could help get a business off the ground. It is not inconceivable that presumption (bold or insolent behavior) could help a young business survive, but it is a somewhat negative that the sentence as a whole does not justify. You should eliminate sophistry for the same reasons; it means a tricky but generally fallacious method of reasoning. This leaves you with tenacity (perseverance), which is the correct answer.

Answer to Question 78:

contentious, brash and condone

You will definitely want to read the entire passage before attempting to tackle the first blank. The key information here is that some people believe that the language used in victimology risks blaming the victim. It would seem, then, that victimology sometimes deals with controversial or touchy subjects, and we need a word that reflects this. Salacious is not a good choice; although some people might take a salacious (lustful or obscene) interest in certain crimes, this passage does not deal with that. Propitious will not work either; it means favorable or auspicious. The best answer is contentious, which means characterized by argument or controversy.

Where the second blank is concerned, we are looking for a word describing behavior that might catch the attention of a criminal. Timorous seems unlikely. While it is not out of the question that a criminal might target someone, who seems fearful or timid, such is surely not the case in most crimes. Fulsome is too strong a word, even given the controversial nature of the term victim precipitation; it means offensive to good taste or sickening. The correct answer is brash, which means impertinent or, in this case, impetuous.

Finally, we need a word that means something like excuse for the final blank - excusing the crime is the natural consequence of blaming the victim. To provoke (to anger or to induce) might describe what, according to the theory of victim precipitation, the victim does, but it is not a good fit here - eliminate it. Rescind is too formal a word for this context; implicitly excusing the crime is not the same as officially invalidating or revoking it. You are left with condone, which means to disregard or to give tacit approval to.

Answer to Question 79:

renowned and poignant

If L'Orfeo is regarded as the first opera, it probably enjoys a fairly prestigious reputation. Incongruous (out of keeping or place or not harmonious in character) will not work, because one would expect the first opera to enjoy a *reputation. Unscathed (unharmed)* is not a good choice either, because it implies that L'Orfeo has escaped some threat to its reputation, which the sentence does not mention. *Renowned (celebrated or distinguished)* is the correct answer.

In order to fill in the second blank, you do not need to be familiar with the story of Orpheus. The brief description given to you should allow you to immediately eliminate *droll*; if a story involving a trip to the underworld were somehow *whimsically humorous*, the author would definitely make note of it. Given the respectful tone of the passage, you can also rule out *maudlin*, which means *foolishly sentimental*. The correct answer is *poignant*, which means *affecting* or *moving the emotions*.

Answer to Question 80:

phlegmatic, sluggard and abstain from

As this passage implies, the sloth has a reputation for being slow and lazy, and the first missing word will reflect that. Fulsome is too negative for the neutral and descriptive tone of the passage; it means offensive to good taste or sickening. Lugubrious means mournful or gloomy and has nothing to do with the subject of the passage. This leaves you with phlegmatic, which means not easily excited to action or display of emotion and is the correct answer.

Given this, the second blank must refer to a lazy or inactive person. Virago means an ill-tempered, scolding woman - eliminate it. Libertine is similarly irrelevant; it means a person who is morally or sexually unrestrained. Sluggard, however, fits perfectly; it refers to a person who is habitually inactive or lazy.

Finally, we know from the rest of the passage that sloths do not move frequently, so they must avoid physical activity. Inveigh against does not make sense; sloths do not protest strongly against physical activity, they simply refrain from it. There is also no indication that sloths go through an active period, so it cannot be that they wean themselves off (withdraw from) physical activity. The best answer is abstain from, which means to hold oneself back voluntarily.

Answer to Question 81:

pellucid and august

If the speaker was charmed by the Mediterranean, the missing word must be positive. For this reason, you can immediately rule out turbid (clouded because of stirred-up sediment). Quiescent means quiet or motionless. Although this is not a negative description, we are more likely to admire the stillness of a pond or lake than we are that of a sea or ocean. Pellucid is a better answer; it means translucent or limpid. The keys to filling in the second blank are the words grandeur, stately, and imposing. We need a word that conveys a similar sense of majesty. Irrevocable does not, and in any case it makes little sense to describe a relic as unable to be repealed or annulled. Portentous (ominous or momentous) is better, but often hints at an underlying threat or danger that does not make sense in this context. August (venerable or inspiring reverence) is the best answer.

Answer to Question 82:

confounded

As the second half of the sentence informs you, light has some unusual - and confusing - properties. The missing word could mean something as simple as *interested*, but it is possible that even these thinkers have found the nature of light perplexing, so we could also be looking for a word meaning *confused*. In either case, *placated* does not make sense, because even if scientists could be *appeased* by questions about light, why would they need to be appeased in the first place? *Fettered* is too strong a word; it means *confined* or *restrained*. *To implicate* means *to show to be involved in or to connect* or *relate to intimately* - eliminate it. Finally, *enervated* means *weakened* or *deprived of strength;* clearly scientists cannot have been too *weakened* by these questions, or they would never have made any progress. Eliminate it.
The best answer is *confounded (bewildered)*.

Answer to Question 83:

trifling, inadvertent and sagacious

The use of the word *seemingly* suggests that the details that *make all the difference* do not seem particularly important, so you should look for a word that means something like *insignificant*. It would no doubt be helpful to have an eye for *disparate* details - that is, details that appear *distinct* or *dissimilar* - in case they end up being related after all, but that is not what this sentence is about - eliminate it. *Spurious* means *not genuine, authentic,* or *true*. It does not make sense in this context, particularly given the later discussion of color; color can't be *inauthentic*. *Trifling* is the best answer; it means *trivial* or *insignificant*.

To fill in the second blank, we need a word that in some way contrasts with *powerful*, and that describes the effects of color on a person's mood. *Nugatory* means *of no real value*. It does somewhat contrast with *powerful*, but it also makes no sense in this sentence; if color can be an *effective tool* in marketing, clearly it does have value. *Salutary* is too specific; it means *healthful* or *wholesome*, and one can easily imagine a situation in which color could have a negative effect on one's mood. This leaves you with *inadvertent*, which works well with the notion that color could be written off as a *trifling detail*; it means *unintentional*.

Finally, the last blank requires a word that describes the kind of businessman who uses color effectively - *savvy* or something similar, perhaps. You may know that *impecunious* has something to do with money and be tempted to pick it for this reason - don't. It means *penniless,* which is more or less irrelevant to this sentence, unless the businessman is so poor that he can't afford a bucket of paint. *Officious (meddlesome or aggressive in offering one's services)* does not make sense either; the businessman in question is presumably looking out for himself rather than offering to help others. The correct answer is *sagacious (shrewd)*.

Answer to Question 84:

alacrity

In this question we are looking for a way of eating that might offend people with *impeccable manners*. *Efficacy* is probably not the correct answer. To begin with, it means *effectiveness,* which is not a word we usually associate with eating. It is also hard to imagine why anyone would object to *effective eating,* providing it was done politely - eliminate it. *Decorum* is the opposite of what we are looking for; it means *dignified propriety* and is precisely the sort of thing that would impress people who emphasize table manners. You can eliminate *adroitness* for the same reasons you eliminated *efficacy*; it means *skill* or *resourcefulness*. *Temperance* means *moderation* or *self-restraint* and would, again, probably go over well with the guests described in the sentence. This leaves you with *alacrity (briskness or readiness)*. Eating quickly could very well offend people who insist on proper table manners, so this is the best answer.

Answer to Question 85:

plethora

The fact that Petra was located on a trade route, as well as the fact that its architecture apparently utilizes at least two column styles, suggests that it was probably influenced by a variety of cultures. You can, therefore, immediately rule out *dearth,* which means *scarcity* or *lack*. *Imprecation* is irrelevant in this context; it means *a curse*. Eliminate it. Both *travesty (a debased likeness or imitation)* and *adulteration (debasement)* imply that the architecture of Petra is merely a corruption of other cultural styles. Given that the tone of this passage is in no way negative, you can eliminate both of these words. The correct answer is *plethora,* which means *abundance* or *excess*.

Answer to Question 86:

substantiate

It is important to note that this sentence is discussing the *hypothesized age* rather than simply *the age*. This means that the scientists already have a guess, and are merely trying to confirm it. It is for this reason that you can rule out *discern*, which means *to perceive* or *to recognize*. *To correlate* means *to bring into mutual* or *reciprocal relation*; it is hard to see what this could have to do with this sentence, particularly since there is no mention of anything the hypothesized age could be correlated with. Eliminate it. It is unlikely that the scientists would be trying *to gainsay* - or *dispute* or *contradict* - their own hypothesis, so you can eliminate this as well. To *palliate* means *to alleviate* or *to extenuate* and is clearly out of place in this context. The correct answer is *substantiate (to establish by proof or evidence)*.

Answer to Question 87:

ramifications and precipitate

The gist of the first sentence seems to be that studying viruses is important because its findings may affect other areas of medicine - the missing word probably means something like implications. Proscriptions is probably too specific; it means prohibitions, and while it is not inconceivable that a medical study might lead to some prohibitions or restrictions, this particular passage mentions nothing of the kind. You can eliminate exigencies (a state that demands prompt remedy or action or the need intrinsic to a situation) for the same reason. The best answer is ramifications (outgrowths or consequences).

The second half of the passage deals with the potentially harmful consequences of otherwise innocuous viruses, which, we are told, have been linked to certain forms of cancer. It would be unusual to use the word truncate in the context of a disease, but the context makes it a poor choice regardless; it means to shorten, which, when speaking of cancer, would be a good thing. To attenuate means to weaken or reduce in force - again, a desirable effect in the context of a disease. This leaves you with precipitate, which means to hasten the occurrence of.

Answer to Question 88:

abhorred, mandated and immaculate

As the first sentence of this passage implies, incest is taboo in many contemporary cultures, so you should look for a word that expresses strong censure or disapproval. Venial means not seriously wrong or excusable and is a near antonym. Ancillary will also not work; it means subordinate or auxiliary and would imply that society approved of, or at least tolerated, incest. The correct answer is abhorred (detested).

By contrast, the second blank requires a word that means something stronger than tolerated; if brother-sister marriages were actually used by the royal family for a specific purpose, they must have been approved of or even required. You can, therefore, rule out condoned (to overlook or to excuse). Rectified (remedied or righted) will not work in this sentence either, as it implies that brother-sister marriages were seen as a problem to be fixed. This leaves you with mandated, which means authorized or required.

To fill in the last blank, you will need to think about what the purpose of marrying within the royal family might have been. You can probably guess that the Egyptian royal family, like most royalty throughout history, wanted their line to remain untainted by *inferior* blood, so the missing word probably means something like *pure*. *Omnipotent* will not work because the missing word is modifying *bloodline* rather than *family*; the family almost certainly wished to remain *unlimited in power*, but it does not make much sense to refer to the bloodline in this way. *Empyreal* is also slightly off the mark; it means *pertaining to the sky* or *celestial*. As a matter of fact, the Egyptian royals were considered divine, but since this information is not provided in the passage itself, it is best to eliminate this answer. The correct answer is *immaculate*, or *free from spot* or *stain*.

Answer to Question 89:

superfluous and formidable

Even if you don't know what vestigial means, you should be able to figure out that the missing word must mean something like useless or unnecessary, because it is meant to contrast with the word valuable. Apocryphal means either false or of doubtful authorship or authenticity. It is mainly used to describe stories, and in any case, vestigial organs or behaviors aren't false - just unnecessary. Exiguous means scanty, meager, or small; given that there is no indication in the passage that vestigial organs or reflexes have dwindled or weakened in any way, it is probably not the best choice. The correct answer is superfluous (excessive or unnecessary).

To fill in the second blank, think about why appearing larger might help an animal faced with a predator - perhaps it makes the animal look more threatening. It is not clear why bristling fur would make an animal appear more obsequious (fawning or deferential), and even if it did, this would probably not help ward off a predator. Impassive is a slightly better choice - an animal that appears unmoved or calm in the face of a predator might make that predator think twice about its chances - but what does this have to do with looking larger? The best answer is formidable (causing fear or of discouraging strength or size).

Answer to Question 90:

reviled, lurid and obfuscate

We know from the word although that the first half of the first sentence is meant to contrast with the second half, so if The Picture of Dorian Gray is now an acclaimed work, it must have been ignored or even criticized at the time it was published. Vaunted, which means boasted of, is close to the opposite of what we are looking for, then. Expunged is better, but still not a good choice; it means erased or wiped out, which the novel clearly was not, given that it is still in existence today. The best answer is reviled, which means vilified or disparaged.

We don't have much to go on for the second blank, except that the novel was taken as an account of moral depravity; we can assume, at least, that the missing adjective is nothing complimentary. Histrionic, which means deliberately affected or overly dramatic, is somewhat plausible, but don't pick it until you've read through all the choices. Insipid is probably not correct; it means vapid or bland, which just doesn't seem a strong enough description for a supposedly immoral story. Lurid, on the other hand, ties in with the book's perceived immorality and is therefore the best choice; it means gruesome, shocking, or terrible in intensity.

The final blank clearly deals with the effect of social climate on the reception of a piece of art. Emblazon does not seem like a very good choice; it means to decorate with brilliant colors or to proclaim, whereas this passage is about the lack of recognition Dorian Gray received as a result of its social context. Atrophy (to affect with atrophy, which means degeneration, decline, or disuse) will not work either, unless you believe that social climate can affect the actual value (i.e. not the perceived value) of something. The correct answer is *obfuscate*, which means *to make obscure* or *unclear*.

Answer to Question 91:

lambent

Given that this sentence is discussing how brilliant the colors of a sunset appear, the missing adjective could very well mean something like vivid, bright, or simply beautiful. Fervid conveys the idea of intensity, but it is a better description of people or feelings than it is of colors; it means heated or vehement in spirit or burning. Plangent means having a loud deep sound or resonant and mournful. Even when it is used in the latter sense, it almost always refers to sounds - eliminate it. Do not be tricked into choosing crepuscular; it means of or pertaining to twilight, which is not the same as sunset. Winsome, again, is more usually associated with people than colors; it means winning or sweetly charming. The best answer is lambent (softly bright or glowing).

Answer to Question 92:

vociferous and unpalatable

For the first blank, we are looking for a word that, along with widespread, could describe objections - perhaps a word that conveys the intensity of the objections, like vehement or strenuous. Bombastic is probably not a good choice because of its negative connotations; we have no reason to believe that the author of this passage views the objections as high-flown or pretentious. Moribund (in a dying state or stagnant) contradicts the notion that the objections are significant enough that the governor incurred criticism for ignoring them. Vociferous (vocal or clamorous) is the best answer.

The second blank presumably requires a word like unpleasant - that is, a word that will explain the existence of widespread objections. Clearly the laws are not imminent (impending) because they are already in place. Execrable is simply too strong a word; it is difficult to imagine the governor defending his decision by acknowledging that the laws were utterly detestable. Unpalatable is a safer choice, because it simply means unpleasant or disagreeable.

Answer to Question 93:

forestall, onerous and wary

Most people would probably want something done about the *worst effects* of climate change - or any other problem, for that matter. To fill in the first blank, therefore, we need a word that means something like address or mitigate. Descry is not a good choice; it is not enough to discern or perceive the worst effects, and it is not clear how reducing emissions would accomplish this in any case. It is also hard to imagine how one could propitiate (appease or conciliate) climate change - generally speaking, only people are capable of being appeased. Forestall (prevent or anticipate) is the correct answer.

For the second blank, we need a word that explains why the companies mentioned in the passage feel they cannot comply with the law. Meretricious does not make sense; surely even a law that is tawdry or based on pretense can be followed, and in any case, there is nothing in the passage suggesting that the program is simply for show. Amorphous is slightly more plausible. It could very well be difficult to comply with a law that is unorganized or lacking definite shape. However, the final sentence should tell you that onerous (burdensome) is a better choice; concrete companies feel that cutting emissions is essentially impracticable.

The final blank requires a word that describes the relationship between concrete makers and the new law. There is no reason, based on this passage, to think that they are more cognizant (aware) of the law than any other company affected by it. Devoid simply does not make sense in this sentence; it means *not possessing*, and laws are not generally things that can be *possessed*. This leaves you with wary *(cautious towards or leery of)*, which is the correct answer.

Answer to Question 94:

beguiled

In this sentence, we are looking for a word describing an emotional state that something awe-inspiring might evoke. It is possible that something awe-inspiring could cause someone to be perturbed, but this would be slightly redundant coming after repulsed; the word sublime has basically positive connotations, so the missing word presumably describes an emotion that counterbalances the repulsion already mentioned. Eviscerated is even more unlikely; even if we take it metaphorically, a landscape that disembowels those who see it does not sound appealing in any way. To transcend means to rise above or go beyond or to surpass. It is quite likely that a sublime landscape might also appear transcendent, but given that this passage focuses more on the spectator's reactions to the landscape rather than the landscape itself, it is not a good fit here. Galvanized is also not a good choice; if the people in question were startled into sudden activity, we would almost certainly be told what it was they were suddenly inspired to do. The correct answer is beguiled, which means charmed or captivated.

Answer to Question 95:

dispassionate and jibe with

In the first sentence, we are looking for a word that describes observations in a way that contrasts with judgments based on unconscious beliefs and biases - that is, a word that means something like unbiased. Chary means cautious or wary and is often followed by of. It is not the best choice, but if you are unsure, set it aside and see if there is a more likely answer. Momentous (of great importance) won't work; if we truly believed our judgments were momentous, this in and of itself would be a self-serving bias. The best choice is dispassionate, which means impartial or calm.

As for the second blank, the fact that attractive people appear to be given preferential treatment suggests that we see physical appearance as an indication of overall intelligence and morality. The word we choose needs to reflect this. To ascribe to means to credit or attribute. It is a good description of our actions - we unconsciously ascribe a person's looks to his overall character - but it does not work in this particular sentence. Purport to is also slightly off the mark; it means to profess or to present the appearance of being, but it is generally followed by a verb rather than by a noun (something purports to do or be something). The correct answer is jibe with, which means to be in harmony with or to agree with.

Answer to Question 96:

nonplussed

If the *average person* only knows about three phases of matter, and the other phases of matter are *bizarre*, people would probably be *surprised* to learn about these other phases. *Contrite* doesn't make sense; why would someone be *remorseful* or *penitent* to learn about other phases of matter? *Saturnine* means *gloomy* or *taciturn*, which would surely be an extreme reaction to learning something new, even if it means your previous beliefs were mistaken. You can eliminate *dispirited (discouraged or dejected)* for the same reason. *Livid* would be even more of an overreaction; it means *enraged*. *Nonplussed (puzzled)* is the best answer.

Answer to Question 97:

moribund, torpid and foster

If virtually all efforts at community outreach had ceased, the group is probably not doing well - look for a word that reflects this. However badly the group is doing, however, it is not chimerical (unreal); it definitely exists if new members have joined it and are making plans to rehabilitate it. The group may be superannuated (antiquated or too old for use), but the fact that it is experiencing difficult times does not in and of itself imply that it is very old or obsolete. The best answer is moribund, which means in a dying state or stagnant.

To fill in the next blank, we need to look for a word that could conceivably describe the leadership of such a group - ineffective perhaps? Frowzy is probably not correct; it means slovenly or musty, which has no bearing on how well the group is functioning. Stringent is slightly more plausible, but would not necessarily cause problems for the group; strict or exacting leadership could be harmful if taken too far, but it could potentially accomplish a great deal as well. Torpid (inactive or slow) fits in well with moribund and is the correct answer.

Finally, the last sentence implies that the new recruits hope to stir up new interest in the group, so we need a word that means something like elicit or incite. To perpetrate means to commit or to execute and has generally negative connotations (as in, perpetrate a crime) - it is out of place here. Make sure that you do not mix up convoke and evoke; the former means to call together (as in, to convoke an assembly), while the latter means to elicit or draw forth. The best answer is foster (to promote the growth of or to encourage).

Answer to Question 98:

cursory, dynamic and harrowing

If van Gogh has a *highly distinctive style*, it probably does not require much time or effort to get a feel for it; the sentence is probably supposed to mean something like *even the idlest...* or *even the briefest...* so look for an adjective along those lines. *Perspicacious (having keen mental judgment or discerning)* will not work, given that it implies a good deal of knowledge. A *jaundiced* viewpoint would be unlikely to help you learn anything new; it is generally best to regard a work of art as objectively as possible, and *jaundiced* means *affected with prejudice. Cursory (hasty or superficial)* is the correct answer.

When working on the second blank, consider the phrases *bold brushstrokes* and *unusual emotional intensity*; whichever adjective we choose to modify colors needs to fit into the overall description of van Gogh's painting. Do not pick *incarnadine* simply because it looks like it may have something to do with colors; it can mean either *blood-red* or *flesh-colored*, so you should ask yourself if an artist is likely to paint only in shades of red. Unless neither of the other answers makes sense, this is probably not your best bet - eliminate it. *Funereal (mournful or dismal)* colors sound as if they might be muted; unless the *emotional intensity* of van Gogh's painting is of a consistently gloomy sort, this is probably not the best choice. The correct answer is *dynamic (characterized by force of personality, ambition, energy, new ideas, etc)*.

For the last blank, we need to find a word to describe a *struggle with mental illness*. If van Gogh's mental illness was only *affected (assumed artificially or feigned)*, the passage would certainly make note of it. *Iniquitous (wicked, sinful)* implies moral condemnation, which is surely unwarranted in the case of an illness. The correct answer is *harrowing*, which means *extremely distressing* or *grievous*.

Answer to Question 99:

precipitous

Even if you know nothing about the Himalayas, you are told that they have *jagged peaks*, which means that they will have steep or *sharp* drops as well. Do not be tricked into picking *nascent (beginning to exist or develop)* simply because you are told that the Himalayas are fairly young mountains; it does not make very much sense to describe *drops* this way. *Surreptitious* is too specific; although there may be *secret* or *stealthy drops*, it is unlikely that all of them will be hidden. *Overweening (conceited or exaggerated)* is generally used to describe a person or an attitude - not a physical object. *Notorious* is a somewhat plausible answer - very steep drops are likely to be *widely and unfavorably known* - but don't pick it until you have read all of the answers. *Precipitous (extremely or impassably steep)* is a better choice because it describes the drops themselves rather than an attitude towards them, and therefore better parallels *jagged peaks*.

Answer to Question 100:

tremulous, fulsome and confound

For the first blank, we are looking for a word to describe a kind of beauty that would suggest *extreme fragility*. Perhaps something like *delicate* or *wispy*. There is no reason that *inordinate (excessive)* beauty would necessarily imply fragility - eliminate it. *Mincing* is too negative a word for the neutral, even respectful, tone of this passage; it means *affectedly dainty* or *elegant. Tremulous*, which means *timid* or *quivering*, is the best answer.

As for the second blank, we know from the passage that some butterflies *advertise* their taste in *the hopes that a predator will not make the same mistake twice*. The butterflies must therefore be either poisonous or extremely bad-tasting. An *insidious* taste is not obvious enough to deter a predator; it means *stealthily treacherous* or *operating in an inconspicuous way but actually with grave effect*. And predators might actually seek out an elusive *(hard to express or define)* taste, provided it was a pleasant one. The correct answer is *fulsome (offensive or sickening)*.

Finally, we are told that some butterflies deal with predators by sporting *eye-shaped spots* on their wings; these spots probably either frighten or confuse predators. It is not clear how the spots could *placate (appease or conciliate)* a predator; it is not as if the butterflies are offering up their wings for consumption. Eliminate it. It is even less likely that the spots could *maim (mutilate or impair)* a predator. You are left with *confound*, which means to *perplex* and is the correct answer.

Answer to Question 101:

proscription and contentious

For the first blank, we obviously need a word that means something like *law* or *prohibition. Litigation (judicial proceeding in a court)* has to do with the law, but is not appropriate for this sentence; we need a word that means the ban itself, not what happens when a ban is broken. *Vituperation (violent denunciation)* expresses great depth of feeling but is not formal enough; it is easy to imagine someone denouncing something that is perfectly legal. The correct answer is *proscription (prohibition or the act of prohibiting).*

The key to filling in the second blank is the idea that different societies may define murder differently; as the second half of the passage informs us, someone who takes Buddhism seriously might regard even killing in self-defense as wrong. The definition of the crime, then, is *controversial* or *unclear*. It is going too far to say the definition is *fallacious (logically unsound or misleading)*; the basic idea behind outlawing murder is a good and sound one. Clearly, however, the definition is not *inclusive (comprehensive or including everything concerned)*, because some cultures could have a very restricted notion of what constitutes murder. *Contentious (characterized by argument)* is the correct answer.

Answer to Question 102:

filial, deference to and tenuous

To fill in the first blank, we need a word that describes the kind of obedience that *all parents expect*. You should be able to rule out *scrupulous* easily; not all parents expect *minutely careful* or *exact* obedience, and in any case, it makes no sense to speak of *degrees* of *exact* obedience. *Reciprocal (corresponding or given or felt by each toward the other, mutual)* makes even less sense, as it implies that all parents expect to obey their children, at least in some circumstances. The correct answer is *filial*, which simply means of, *pertaining to*, or *befitting a son or daughter.*

To fill in the second blank, think about what kind of parenting doesn't give children a *chance to exercise their own judgment* - presumably, one where the parents make all of the decisions. Clearly *intransigence towards (inflexibility towards)* will not work, because it implies that the children are doing whatever they want, regardless of their parents' orders. *Propensity for (natural tendency toward* is also a bad choice. To begin with, we do not normally speak of *absolute propensities* - it is somewhat like saying *absolute leanings*. In any case, the phrase *propensity for parental authority* is awkward and unclear; does it imply, for example, that the parents are naturally skilled at giving orders? If you cannot make sense of a sentence once you have tried out a word, that word is almost certainly incorrect. The best answer is *deference to (respectful submission or yielding to).*

Finally, we need a word to describe the *sense of self* possessed by children who grow up in authoritarian households. If they have low self-esteem and are not used to making decisions for themselves, it is a fair bet that they probably do not have a good grasp of who they are or what they want. *Mercurial (volatile or animated)* is not a completely implausible answer, given that it implies a somewhat unstable sense of self, but its connotations are too positive for this context; the author clearly disapproves of this parenting style and feels it has negative consequences. On the other hand, *dissolute (indifferent to moral restraints or licentious)* is too judgmental; the author obviously does not regard these children as in any way immoral. You are left with *tenuous (thin or weak)*, which is the correct answer.

Answer to Question 103:

apocryphal

As their name implies, *urban legends* are not the most reliable of stories, and in this sentence, we are looking for an adjective that reflects their *doubtful origins*. Many urban legends probably are *hyperbolic (exaggerated)*, but because this does not relate directly to their veracity (or lack thereof), you can eliminate it. The word *ephemeral* implies a kind of insubstantiality, but it means *short-lived*, which urban legends clearly are not. *Judicious* is nearly the opposite of what we are looking for; it means *discreet* or *sensible*. And while urban legends are sometimes *prurient (characterized by lascivious or lustful thoughts, desires, etc)*, this has nothing to do with their origins. The best answer is *apocryphal*, which means *false* or *of doubtful authorship or authenticity*.

Answer to Question 104:

disgruntlement, obtrusively and barrage

Most people don't like advertisements, and if they are seeing/hearing 3,000to 5,000 of them per day, they are probably fairly upset - the first missing word should reflect this. Although some commercials might be *edifying (instructive or beneficial)*, this passage clearly focuses on the downsides of advertising rather than the positives - eliminate *edification*. *Trepidation* is too strong a word; consumers are irritated by advertising, but they do not experience *tremulous fear* or *agitation*. The correct answer is *disgruntlement*, which means *discontent* or *sulky dissatisfaction*.

The second missing word probably also focuses on the frustration of consumers - *irritatingly*, perhaps. *Consummately* does not continue with this theme, and it would in any case be redundant coming directly after *effectively* (it means *completely* or *perfectly*). *Nefariously (wickedly* or *heinously)* is probably an overstatement; it is better to avoid such strongly condemnatory words unless you have a very compelling reason to believe the passage requires one. This leaves you with *obtrusively (obtrusive means meddlesome or blatant)*, which makes sense in the context of the passage without being repetitive.

Finally, we need to find a word to describe the kind of marketing we are exposed to - most likely one that once more draws attention to its prevalence or frequency. "Dearth" clearly will not work; it means *inadequate supply* or *lack*. *Parlance (a way of speaking or an idiom)* is not particularly relevant to this passage, which focuses on the quantity of ads we are exposed to, not on the kid of language they use. The correct answer is barrage, which means an *overwhelming quantity* or *explosion*, and therefore best conveys the notion that we are constantly subjected to ads of one kind or another.

Answer to Question 105:

gossamer

The sentence tells you that cirrus clouds are *wispy*, so the missing adjective probably has a similar or related meaning. *Halcyon* is not totally out of the question; it means *calm, tranquil,* or *carefree,* and can be used to describe weather. However, there may be a still better option, so don't pick it yet. *Sinuous* doesn't really work; something that *is wispy* could be *sinuous (curvy or winding)*, but they're not directly related, so in the absence of any other clues in the sentence, it's probably best to eliminate it. *Variegated* is also unlikely, particularly given that clouds generally appear white, and are therefore not *varied in appearance or color*. Lambent means *softly glowing*; again, it is possible that clouds might appear *lambent* - particularly during sunrise or sunset - but it isn't really a quality inherent to any particular type of cloud. The best answer is *gossamer*, which means *delicate, light,* or *gauzy*.

Answer to Question 106:

flippant and jocular

For this first blank, we need a word that can describe a sense of humor - preferably one that suggests an *inability to treat any subject seriously*. If anything, we would expect someone who is *erudite* to take things too seriously; it means *learned* or *scholarly*. Someone could have a *raucous (harsh or rowdy)* sense of humor, but *flippant (frivolously disrespectful or characterized by levity)* ties in more directly with the notion of taking things seriously (or not, as the case may be).

We most likely need another word meaning *joking* or *funny* for the second blank. Iconoclastic is probably too strong a term, even for someone who might be *frivolously disrespectful*; it means *attacking* or *ignoring cherished beliefs and long-held traditions*. *Equivocal (allowing the possibility of several different meanings, especially with intent to deceive)* is not a word usually used to describe jokes, because while jokes do often hinge on double meanings, they are not meant to be deceptive or tricky. The correct answer is *jocular*, which simply means *joking* or *facetious*.

Answer to Question 107:

expedient

If the traits in question help animals *survive long enough to mate*, they must be advantageous in some way - the missing word is most likely related to this. A trait that is merely *innocuous (harmless or inoffensive)* is unlikely to actually prove helpful - eliminate it. A *salient (prominent or conspicuous)* could prove good or bad, and therefore will not work in this context. *Titillating (exciting or arousing)* traits might attract potential mates, but the meaning is too specific for this passage, which seems to be discussing any and all traits that help an individual survive and reproduce. Don't pick *prolific (highly fruitful or highly productive)* simply because of the reference to mating; referring to a trait as *prolific* does not make very much sense. The best answer is expedient *(fit or suitable for some purpose or conducive to advantage or interest)*.

Answer to Question 108:

enigmatic, austere and fester

The key to filling in the first blank is to recognize that this passage is primarily about possible explanations for the Salem witch trials. Although the witch trials are somewhat *infamous (notorious or heinous)*, this does not have anything to do with what caused them - eliminate it. *Clandestine* is slightly off the mark; it means *executed with secrecy or deception, especially for purposes of subversion or deception*. Although the witch trials are mysterious, it is not as if anyone is concealing information about them, so you can eliminate this answer as well. The best answer is *enigmatic (perplexing or mysterious)*.

To fill in the second blank, we need a word to describe the *religious climate* at the time of the trials. You may very well know that the residents of Salem were members of the Puritan religion, which is notoriously strict, but even if you don't, you should be able to eliminate the wrong answers fairly easily. It is unlikely, for example, that *vitriolic (very caustic, scathing)* is the correct answer; it implies that the Puritans' religious beliefs were based on ill-will and malevolence, which is simply too extreme a statement to make about any religion. *Pristine*, on the other hand, has somewhat positive connotations and is therefore not suited to this context; it means *uncorrupted* or *unsullied*. The correct answer is *austere*, which means *strict, ascetic*, or *somber*.

Finally, the passage implies that the religious and socio-economic climate of Salem was conducive to *mass hysteria*; we are probably looking for a word that means something like *take root*, or *flourish*. *To convene* means *to cause to assemble*. It is generally used of people, and it implies a certain degree of formality which inappropriate in this context; it is not as if the *mass hysteria* was court-ordered. *To languish* means *to fade* or *to lose vigor* and is the opposite of what we are looking for. The correct answer is *fester (to rot or to rankle)*Answer to Question 1:

Answer to Question 109:

paradox and bombastic

This passage implies that Cyrano is of a somewhat contradictory nature; he *swaggers*, which suggests arrogance, but he is also *insecure*. Keep this in mind when filling in the first blank. An *archetype is an original model from which all things of the same kind are copied.* This passage does not discuss the effects of *Cyrano de Bergerac* on future literature, so you can eliminate this choice. *Cliche* is too negative a word for this passage, which is generally appreciative of the play; it means *a trite* or *hackneyed plot, character development, use of color, etc.* The correct answer is *paradox,* which means *any person, thing,* or *situation exhibiting an apparently contradictory nature.*

To fill in the second blank, we are looking for an adjective that can modify *words* and, probably, relate in some way to *swagger*. *Licentious means lewd or immoral* - something that this passage nowhere implies Cyrano to be. Eliminate it. *Iconoclastic (attacking or ignoring cherished beliefs and long-held traditions)* is slightly more plausible if you know anything about the play being discussed, but we still have no reason to believe, based on this passage that someone who is arrogant is also a revolutionary. This leaves you with *bombastic,* which means *high-flown* or *pompous,* and is often used to describe speech.

Answer to Question 110:

manifest, incumbent upon and abysmal

If people were surprised by this man's decision to teach, he must have had at least a passing interest in performing, so look for a word that reflects this. *Inordinate (not within proper or reasonable limits)* is too strong, given that it implies his interest was excessive and unhealthy. If his interest were merely *perfunctory,* however, it is unlikely anyone would be surprised; it means *hasty and superficial* or *indifferent. Manifest (evident or obvious)* is the correct answer.

Given that he decided to teach in spite of this, he must have felt it was important in some way - keep this in mind when filling in the second blank. *Inimical* to is certainly not the correct answer; he would surely no choose to do something that was *harmful* or *hostile* to him. On the other hand, he would have to have a fairly high opinion of himself to say that his decision was *munificent of (very generous of)* him. The correct answer is *incumbent upon (obligatory).*

As for the last blank, try to think of why he might feel obligated to teach - presumably because he feels that the *state of arts education in the public schools needs improving.* To say that arts education is *banal,* however, would be a bit harsh; the purpose of elementary and secondary arts programs isn't really innovation, so it would be unfair to criticize them as *hackneyed* or *trite. Odious* is also too strong a word, though for different reasons. It means *hateful* or *detestable,* which implies some degree of moral condemnation. The best answer is *abysmal,* which means *extremely bad* or *severe.*

Answer to Question 111:

indiscernible and brazen

Casual listeners are presumably not as attuned as researchers to the differences in question, so look for a word that means something like *unnoticeable. Pertinent* means *relevant,* which won't work in this context; the differences are presumably *relevant* to people other than *casual listeners* or the study would not have taken place. *Blatant (flagrant or conspicuous)* is the opposite of what we are looking for. The correct answer is *indiscernible (imperceptible).*

Where the second blank is concerned, we know from the word *condemn* that we are looking for a word with negative connotations that could describe a *romantically assertive* woman. *Garish* is not quite what we want; it means *crudely* or *tastelessly colorful, showy* or *excessively ornate,* and is not usually used to describe people.

Capricious, on the other hand, is not quite negative enough for this context; it means *erratic* or *flighty*, which are not strong enough criticisms to warrant *condemnation*. *Brazen (shameless or impudent)* is a better answer.

Answer to Question 112:

aegis

We are told that 3M is *diversified* and does business in a variety of different areas; clearly the sentence means to say that all of these branches fall under the control or *supervision* of 3M. *Vagaries* does not make sense; if all of its divisions were subject to its *unpredictable* or *erratic actions*, the business would probably not be successful. *Covenant* is more often used in a religious context; it means a *formal agreement*. An *opus* is a *composition* - either literary or musical - and is clearly irrelevant to this passage. *Tutelage*, on the other hand, implies that the different branches of 3M are more like apprentice companies; it means *instruction or guidance*. The best answer is *aegis (protection or support)*.

Answer to Question 113:

reaches, fathom and velocities and trajectories

The best answer for the first blank is *reaches*. *Reaches* suggests both the immensity and sense of the unknown that the rest of entry describes.

The best answer for the second blank is *fathom*. The rest of the entry is not concerned with measuring or explaining the universe, only imagining its immensity.

The best answer for the third blank is *velocities and trajectories*. This answer is the only one that refers to directional movement.

Answer to Question 114:

contend, coterie and cohesive style

The best answer for the first blank is *contend*. This answer best reflects that there is a debate among scholars.

The best answer for the second blank is *coterie*. A *coterie is a group of people*, whereas a *menagerie is a group of animals*; *gild* would be a possible answer, but gild here means to *coat in gold*.

The best answer for the third blank is *cohesive style*. The entry refers to a seamless collaboration between writers as a style, rather than a particular tone within the writing.

Answer to Question 115:

sequence, assistance and less coordination

The best answer for the first blank is *sequence*. The sentence indicates there are several gears to be shifted through, as in a *sequence*.

The best answer for the second blank is *assistance*. The entry must reflect the lack of action required from the driver.

The best answer for the third blank is *less coordination*. That a driver must shift a manual but do nothing in an automatic suggests less coordination is needed in an automatic.

Answer to Question 116:

lithe and associate

The best answer for the first blank is *lithe*.

The entry must be synonymous with the moves of a dancer, which are known to be *graceful*.

The best answer for the second blank is *associate*. The two things, *gazelles* and *dancers*, are being compared as similar to one another.

Answer to Question 117:

acumen and learned

The best answer to the first blank is *acumen*. This answer best refers to the education needed *to run a business*. The best answer to the second blank is *learned*. This also best relates back to the need for education in a particular area to run a business.

Answer to Question 118:

ore and composites

The best answer for the first blank is *ore*.

Unrefined and buried metals are best known as *ore*, whereas *magma* is *molten rock*.

The best answer for the second blank is *composites*. This entry indicates the combining of refined metals, whereas the others refer to the ore as it exists in the ground.

Answer to Question 119:

cognizant

The best answer is *cognizant*. The entry must refer to awareness, and no other choice fits.

Answer to Question 120:

precarious and origin

The best answer for the first blank is *precarious*. Although not a perfect answer, it best refers to the dangers of the long journey of a butterfly.

The best answer for the second blank is *origin*. The entry is concerned with location and travel distances.

Answer to Question 121:

localized

The best answer is *localized*. The subject is the location of the squirrels, rather than type, as the beginning of the sentence may suggest.

Answer to Question 122:

hurtle and extirpated

The best answer for the first blank is *hurtle*. The entry refers to fast, explosive movement, so this answer is better than *waft*.

The best answer for the second blank is *extirpated*. A meteor that is *extirpated* has completely disintegrated in the atmosphere, leaving nothing to fall to Earth.

Answer to Question 123:

rancor and moribund

The second sentence indicates that the reforms have been stalled *indefinitely*; in other words, they are *moribund*, the best choice for the second blank.

Given the *repressive* nature of the government and the status of the *reforms*, the best choice for the first blank is *rancor*, since it is more likely, in the context, that the people will resent the government than be loyal or disgusted.

Answer to Question 124:

cupidity and surfeit

The best choice for the first blank is *cupidity* since the sentence implies that the dictator had an excessive lust for material goods.

The clause following the dash indicates that the dictator had acquired an *overabundance*, or *surfeit* of material possessions.

Answer to Question 125:

probity

The best choice to fill in the blank is probity, since the passage indicates that the judge is upstanding and has considerable integrity.

Answer to Question 126:

assiduously

The best choice is assiduously. The sentence suggests that the group put consistent time and effort into the project - in other words, they worked assiduously.

Answer to Question 127:

effrontery

The passage suggests that the waiter was rude and presumptuous, so the best choice for the blank is effrontery.

Answer to Question 128:

loquacious

The best choice is loquacious. Although the seat mate being irascible or rapacious could explain why the writer was unable to read or sleep, the most logical choice in context is that he was very talkative, or loquacious.

Answer to Question 129:

espousing and grandiose

The best choice for the first blank is espousing. The second sentence points to an instance of a European ruler adopting, or espousing ties to ancient Rome.

The best choice for the second blank is grandiose, since it is the only choice that makes sense in context.

Answer to Question 130:

lucid

The passage indicates that Walt's presentation had the effect of making some previously unclear goals more accessible. Thus, the best choice is lucid; Walt's presentation was clear.

Chapter **7**

Introduction to Sentence Equivalence

Sentence Equivalence questions your ability to interpret and understand what you read, and also your ability to use vocabulary in context. Each Sentence Equivalence question will consist of a sentence with a single blank. You will be asked to choose the two words from among six that produce complete sentences with the most similar meanings.

The passages used for Sentence Equivalence questions will be drawn from a variety of topics, including the physical, biological and social sciences, the arts and the humanities, business and everyday life. As with other types of questions for the Verbal Reasoning component, you need not be an expert on the topics covered in Sentence Equivalence questions too. You will, however, need to read the passage carefully enough to understand what is being said, and be able to complete the sentence grammatically. All Sentence Equivalence questions will follow the same multiple-choice format. You will be given a sentence with a single blank, and will be given 6 options to fill in the blank. You will need to choose the TWO options that produce a grammatically correct sentence with the most similar meaning

What does a Sentence Equivalence question look like?

Sentence Equivalence questions will always be based off a single sentence. The sentence will have a single blank. You will be asked to read the sentence and get a feel for what two words from among six given will produce sentences with the most similar meaning. Below is an example of what a Sentence Equivalence question will look like on the GRE General Test:

Select the two answer choices that, when used to complete the sentence, fit the meaning of the sentence as a whole and produce completed sentences that are alike in meaning.

1. Under Stalin, the Soviet state showed many of the same BLANK tendencies of the Tsarist government it had replaced; dissent of any kind was stifled and political authority was centralized.

    [A] liberalizing

    [B] despotic

    [C] vicious

    [D] corrupt

    [E] oligarchic

    [F] autocratic

Answer Key

The answers to the above question are B. despotic and F. autocratic.

What skills do Sentence Equivalence questions test?

Like Text Completion questions, Sentence Equivalence questions test your ability to understand what you are reading and reason from incomplete information. However, Sentence Equivalence questions focus more on the meaning of a single sentence, so you'll need to be able to differentiate how different words complete the sentence. Some key skills that are tested include your ability to

- reason based on incomplete information

- understand the meaning of sentences

- understand high level vocabulary

- apply vocabulary in context

Key Facts about Sentence Equivalence questions

- Questions will be based off a single short sentence

- For each passage, you will need to fill in a single blank using the 6 options provided

- Passages will be on a variety of topics including the physical, biological and social sciences, the arts and the humanities, business and everyday life

- Questions will be answerable based on the information in the passage alone and your ability to apply vocabulary

- You will need to choose TWO options to fill in a single blank. Look for the two words that will produce two distinct, coherent, and grammatically correct sentences with similar meanings

Strategies for Sentence Equivalence Questions

Sentence Equivalence questions are the least time-intensive question type you will see on the Verbal Reasoning component. Time budgeting is important for every component of the test, however, assuming that you have managed your time well for other types of questions, you should have plenty to time to give the necessary attention to Sentence Equivalence questions. Like Text Completion questions, it is important that you read Sentence Equivalence questions with care. Do not skim Sentence Equivalence questions, since it is important that you understand exactly what the sentence means. Missing a key word in a Sentence Equivalence can spell disaster since the focus for these questions is very narrow. Given that each question is based on a single sentence, even a careful reading should not take very long. If you find yourself taking any more than a minute or so on a Sentence Equivalence, you should skip to another question and come back to it later if you have time.

As with the other types of questions on the Verbal Reasoning portion, do not let the subject matter of the passage throw you off - your ability to correctly answer these questions is independent of any expertise you may possess in the subject area of the passage. When answering Sentence Equivalence questions, you will need to be able to quickly assess the meaning of a sentence based on incomplete information, and have enough command of vocabulary to choose the words that will be the best fit to complete the sentence. You WILL NOT need to make any judgement about whether the passage is true or false.

The key skills for Sentence Equivalence questions are understanding the meaning of specific sentences and how individual words shape meaning. As you read the sentence, don't give the topic too much thought - focus on what the sentence means. Be sure to attend to important words that signal emphasis or qualification as these will help you decide which words will be the best fit for the blank. As with Text Completion, your vocabulary will play a role in your ability to do well on Sentence Equivalence questions. However, keep in mind that you will always be using words in context, so you won't necessarily need to know their exact meaning or dictionary definition. Also, remember that your task is to produce two sentences with the most similar meaning, not to find the two words with the most similar meaning.

- Read the passage carefully - do not skim

- Read the sentence carefully - do not skim

- Attend to key words that for sections of the passage that either closely match or negate the definition of one of the word options

- Apply vocabulary in context

What follows are some more specific strategies for answering Sentence Equivalence questions. In the next chapter, you'll have a chance to put your skills to the test through several practice questions and learn how to hone them in the answers and explanations that follow.

Review Vocabulary

Previous versions of the GRE featured sections that were specifically geared toward vocabulary. The GRE General Test no longer features these sections, but as has been noted previously, vocabulary is still very important. This is especially so for Text Completion and Sentence Equivalence questions, where you will need to have some idea of what some "big" words mean in order to fill in the appropriate blanks. Note that Sentence Equivalence questions focus on the meaning of the completed sentence more than on the meaning of any individual word, so you can often get away with having a ballpark understanding of what a word means. Nonetheless, anything that you can do to strengthen your vocabulary prior to the test will be helpful, since the test assumes a fairly high-level vocabulary. If you are not confident of your vocabulary, do what you can to improve it as preparation for the test (this will serve you well in graduate school as well). Again, there are many cases when you will not need to know a precise definition of a word, but you will need to have a general sense of what it means. There are several things you can do to improve your vocabulary for the test:

- Review lists of common "GRE words" such as the one included in this book

- Use a vocabulary builder

- Get a sense of key Greek or Latin root words and what they mean - many words in English are based on Greek or Latin words, and knowing the meaning of a few key Greek or Latin words can help you figure out the meanings of numerous English words

Read the Sentence Carefully

Before you try to fill in any blank, read the sentence carefully. Sentence Equivalence questions focus on the meaning of sentences, so you'll need to get a clear sense of what the sentence means without the blank filled in to get a clear sense of what words will effectively complete it.

Pay Special Attention to Significant Words

As with Text Completion questions, you should pay close attention to pivotal words in the sentence in Sentence Equivalence questions too. Key words can give tremendous insight into the meaning of the sentence and provide strong indicators of what word you will need to choose to complete the sentence correctly. Words like "although", "despite", "moreover" or "therefore" which either emphasize or qualify something that has been said are often especially significant, so look out for them and be sensitive to how they modify the meaning of the sentence.

Be Careful Not to Make Your Choice Solely on the Meaning of Words

It may sound counter-intuitive, but sometimes two words with very similar meanings will not necessarily produce sentences of similar meanings. When answering Sentence Completion questions, you might be tempted to simply select the two words from among the options that have the most similar meaning, and use them to answer the question. This is a bad strategy for two reasons. In the first place, sometimes there will be more than one pair of words that have similar meanings. Without focusing on the meaning of the sentence, you might choose the wrong pair, since you need to produce two grammatically correct, coherent sentences with similar meanings and not just find words that have similar meanings. The second reason is more counter-intuitive; however, sometimes the two words with the most similar meanings will not produce the two sentences with the most similar meanings. Keep this in mind and always focus on the meaning of the sentence, rather than on the meaning of the words you are choosing to complete it.

Try to fill in the blank with your own word before you look at the answer choices

As with Text Completion questions, you can try to think of words that will fill in the blank to complete the sentence and then compare them to the options given to see if you can find any similar words. Sometimes you'll be able to see words that obviously correspond to those you have already thought of to fill in the blanks; other times, you'll be able to eliminate words with opposite meanings. Either of these options will be helpful to you as you try to answer the question.

Always check your work

As with Text Completion questions, be sure that you always fill in the options that you choose to complete the sentence to make certain that your choices produce coherent, grammatically correct sentences with similar meanings. Remember that you need to satisfy all of these requirements in your answer.

Use Process of Elimination

Process of elimination is ALWAYS useful in answering any type of multiple-choice question, and Sentence Equivalence is no exception. Unless the answer is immediately obvious to you, you should always be looking to narrow your choices by getting rid of potential answers that don't fit, or don't make sense. When using process of elimination for Sentence Equivalence questions, always keep in mind what the goals of the question are. You need to find the two words that will produce two distinct sentences that are coherent, grammatically correct, and have similar meanings. If a word doesn't make sense in context, you can dismiss it. If a word doesn't fit grammatically into the sentence, you can dismiss it. Keep this in mind as you answer Sentence Equivalence questions, since it will help you eliminate inappropriate answer choices.

Chapter 8

Practice Questions for Sentence Equivalence

1.   Although the theory of the conservation of mass was not stated clearly until 1789, it had many
     _____ in the history of the physical sciences.

     A   originators

     B   derivatives

     C   forerunners

     D   antecedents

     E   imitators

     F   descendents

2.   Einstein's discovery of general relativity is a major turning point in the history of physics and _____
     a full century of further research.

     A   stimulated

     B   dampened

     C   abetted

     D   motivated

     E   debilitated

     F   vitalized

3.   Determinism, the notion that reality is independent of how we question or observe it, is the only
     conclusion that can be reasonably _____ from the classical form of Newtonian physics.

     A   imputed

     B   drawn

     C   ascertained

     D   calculated

     E   derived

     F   assumed

4. Chemical thermodynamics _____ measurements of thermodynamic properties and the application of mathematical methods to the study of chemistry.

   A entails

   B subsumes

   C constitutes

   D contains

   E involves

   F embodies

5. In accomplishing the seemingly impossible, the young woman was _____ by her desire to impress her parents.

   A inhibited

   B sedated

   C motivated

   D influenced

   E stymied

   F adjudicated

6. The sheer depth of space that must be traversed in order to locate even basic truths about the origins of our Universe has rendered _____ reasoning as one of the most effective way to shirk our empirical handicap.

   A inverse

   B deliberate

   C deductive

   D inferable

   E observable

   F obvious

7. The pervasive institutionalization of the notion that beauty must be suffered for has crippled the didactic efficacy of modern media and _____ the self-confidence of a whole generation of children.

    A   subverted

    B   undermined

    C   initiated

    D   rectified

    E   invigorated

    F   objectified

8. The differences in symptoms between the autism spectrum disorders and the anxiety conditions (such as obsessive-compulsive disorder) are often so _____ that a patient can go years without receiving a proper diagnosis.

    A   inconspicuous

    B   pervasive

    C   harmless

    D   debilitating

    E   subtle

    F   extravagant

9. He watched the peripheral artery bypass through the observation window and marveled at the doctor's _____, which justified the already-tremendous amounts of audaciousness necessary to perform such a procedure.

    A   aggression

    B   reticence

    C   proficiency

    D   contempt

    E   delusion

    F   expertise

10. I asked her to stop _____ me all the time about fixing the faucet in the spare room bathroom.

   [A] hounding

   [B] bearing

   [C] ferreting

   [D] badgering

   [E] weaseling

   [F] remonstrating

11. Gang related crime was _____ in that area; even the police were wary about entering after dark.

   [A] epidemic

   [B] endemic

   [C] curtailed

   [D] governable

   [E] exuberant

   [F] prevalent

12. The scent of freshly baked bread _____ into the room from the bakery below.

   [A] drifted

   [B] wafted

   [C] coasted

   [D] transmitted

   [E] poised

   [F] inured

13. The evening's _____ rays were enchanting to behold as they lit the horizon with their amazing display of colour.

   A   twilight

   B   diurnal

   C   crepuscular

   D   noontide

   E   enlightened

   F   modicum

14. It is quite remarkable to see a book in such _____ condition; I've never seen a 17th-century first edition of that high standard before.

   A   sanitary

   B   untarnished

   C   purified

   D   pristine

   E   immaculate

   F   adulterated

15. In all respects, the designs were unpopular with the masses, they were both _____ and unpractical.

   A   sophisticated

   B   ill-bred

   C   clumsy

   D   gauche

   E   butterfingered

   F   couth

16.   In spite of his apparent knowledge of historical figures, Henry was a/an _____ when it came to well-known French Impressionists.

   A   dilettante

   B   unskilled

   C   amateur

   D   dabbling

   E   connoisseur

   F   proficient

17.   You could see why Annette was his muse; she had a healthy complexion and a/an _____ mane of golden tresses that cascaded down her back.

   A   barren

   B   profuse

   C   elaborate

   D   plenteous

   E   pretentious

   F   luxuriant

18.   Rows of breathtakingly beautiful and _____ marble columns stretched the length of the basilica, watching over the 15th-century church's exceptional mosaic floor.

   A   clement

   B   ornate

   C   embroidered

   D   baroque

   E   dowdy

   F   garish

19.   Despite its _____ dimensions, the office space was still undersized for our needs.

       A   capacious

       B   abundance

       C   expansive

       D   brimming

       E   minute

       F   discrepant

20.   The marketing team _____ a new campaign to boost sales.

       A   connived

       B   contrived

       C   devised

       D   schemed

       E   blueprints

       F   casted

21.   It is known that many firms engage in misleading and often _____ accounting practices to inflate their short-term profits.

       A   counterfeit

       B   infamous

       C   fraudulent

       D   villainess

       E   dubious

       F   slanderous

22. Due to recession, companies have learnt to be _____ with their marketing budgets and not spend outlandishly.

    A gluttonous

    B frugal

    C altruistic

    D lavish

    E parsimonious

    F miserly

23. Archaeologists have found evidence that _____ tribes made baskets for collecting and storing food.

    A old-fashioned

    B primitive

    C obsolete

    D trampled

    E antiquated

    F archaic

24. There was great public outrage when the _____ publication appeared in the media talking about the existence of child slavery in first world countries.

    A quarrelsome

    B controversial

    C metaphysical

    D doubtful

    E polemic

    F cantankerous

25. Socialists often decry the _____ excesses of most capitalist societies.

   A materialistic

   B nonconforming

   C indolent

   D capitalism

   E victorian

   F bourgeois

26. Brazil and Argentina discussed the importance of gathering genetic information from the _____ tribes that live in the Amazonas region.

   A homegrown

   B inherited

   C alien

   D indigenous

   E aboriginal

   F inbred

27. The economic _____ between first world countries and third world countries have increased since the 1950s.

   A disparities

   B burrow

   C disagreeable

   D hole

   E animosity

   F discrepancies

28. After such a lengthy illness, her complexion was still _____; she obviously needed a few more days of repose.

   A hearty

   B salubrious

   C bilious

   D albino

   E vigorous

   F sallow

29. The effects of urban gentrification is an ongoing tale of winners and losers; some residents benefit from the _____ of business investment and improved school quality that come with the improvements in neighborhoods, but other residents are displaced as rents increase and property taxes rise.

   A profusion

   B abridgement

   C ardor

   D parapet

   E accretion

   F culmination

30. The Internet provides a window into cultures that may be unfamiliar from the ones in which we live; a quick Internet search can provide _____ into how people from other cultures live, how they interact with one another, and what is important to them.

   A perspicacity

   B erudition

   C sagacity

   D sapience

   E apotheosis

   F proclivity

31. Technology has led to many changes in the time spent on household responsibilities; with the adoption of appliances such as microwaves, washing machines, and vacuum cleaners into the home, the time spent on household tasks have _____ tremendously compared to the substantial time spent on household duties a century ago.

    A   bated

    B   minified

    C   masticated

    D   attenuated

    E   impinged

    F   augmented

32. The human body's immune system is a powerful biological process that is responsible for fighting off thousands of harmful organisms; when the immune system is working properly, the body is protected from dangerous bacteria, but when it is impaired the body is vulnerable to a _____ of dangerous, disease-carrying microbes.

    A   plethora

    B   surfeit

    C   legion

    D   consanguinity

    E   peculation

    F   extolment

33. A microscope contains one or more lenses that magnify the image of the organism placed on its focal plane; depending on the power of the lens, the microscope can allow people to _____ view the cells of organisms with little to no effort.

    A   mendaciously

    B   salubriously

    C   adventitiously

    D   fastidiously

    E   punctiliously

    F   exiguously

34. To make identifying one animal from another more _____, scientists from different societies have devised various classification systems, but now some scientists are advocating the creation of a single, universal animal classification system for all cultures across the globe to adopt.

   A   tamable

   B   vociferous

   C   resplendent

   D   quiescent

   E   glib

   F   tractable

35. Though both protons and neutrons are housed in the nucleus of an atom, the protons but not the neutrons define the electric charge of the nucleus; neutrons contribute to the mass of the nucleus, but they have no electric charge to _____ to the nucleus.

   A   extenuate

   B   impart

   C   bestow

   D   remit

   E   bequeath

   F   ossify

36. The nucleus is the most _____ part of an atom; a nucleus's significance lies in that the majority of the atom's mass is located in the nucleus, and, in living organisms, the nucleus is the site where DNA lives and begins to be interpreted by the cell.

   A   effulgent

   B   substantive

   C   epochal

   D   indispensable

   E   recondite

   F   evidentiary

37. Metabolism is a word that is often _____ with weight loss, but metabolism is associated with many more processes than regulating a person's ability to convert fat to energy; it can refer to all of the chemical reactions that occur inside the cells of living organisms.

   A affiliated

   B colligated

   C caviled

   D distended

   E ensconced

   F abrogated

38. The exact timing of hurricane season depends on the part of the world under _____, but meteorologists have determined that on average the month of May is the most active month for hurricane activity worldwide while the month of September usually has the least hurricane activity.

   A cogitation

   B consideration

   C circumlocution

   D introspection

   E expatiation

   F rumination

39. Though a significant number of countries are governed as democracies, the government structures that exist around the world are far from _____; along with democracies, an assortment of ruling systems including theocracies, technocracies, constitutional monarchies, absolute monarchies, and dictatorships are in use today.

   A bilious

   B lachrymose

   C homogenous

   D undifferentiated

   E discrete

   F disjointed

40. European imperialism redrew the borders of many African nations from the ones that existed before the colonizers arrived; many groups that were _____ before the Europeans' arrival found themselves, as a result of conquest, part of new nations that contained historically unacquainted ethnic groups by the time European rule ended.

   A   sequestered

   B   parochial

   C   insular

   D   sectarian

   E   illiberal

   F   catholic

41. America's founding fathers used compromise to _____ disagreements that arose when assaying the emerging government; for example, the founders determined the best solution would be to create a two-house legislative body in order to suppress conflicts that arose between two factions over how citizens would be represented in the national government.

   A   quell

   B   castigate

   C   emulate

   D   exacerbate

   E   obviate

   F   precipitate

42. The social stigma associated with a conviction for a serious crime can present nearly _____ obstacles for someone attempting to re-enter society and contribute to the citizenry after completing a period of incarceration; a criminal record can prevent a person from finding employment or even voting in certain jurisdictions.

   A culpable

   B dogmatic

   C intransigent

   D emollient

   E recalcitrant

   F florid

43. The components that make up a culture vary depending on the group in question; shared language, experiences, history, food, and language are some of the delineating elements distinguishing one culture from another, but a powerful, albeit intangible, aspect of what defines a culture is an _____ bond members feel for one another.

   A irascible

   B execrable

   C inextirpable

   D illustrious

   E opprobrious

   F indelible

44. Media are some of the most effective tools cultural influencers can use to spread their messages to the widest possible audience; some use media to influence others in _____ ways, forwarding fashion and hairstyle trends for example, while others employ media to incite dissension and societal upheaval.

    A innocuous

    B aberrant

    C injurious

    D banal

    E equivocal

    F exorbitant

45. Extensive liberal arts study was once considered an integral component of a quality education, but as societies have become more technologically, dedicating years to studies in classic literature or philosophy are more often perceived as _____ endeavors that should be set aside for training in more practical study in the sciences or in medicine.

    A erudite

    B lofty

    C asinine

    D obtuse

    E chary

    F fetid

46. After the fall of the Iron Curtain, multinational corporations acquired companies in countries that had been part of the Soviet Bloc and _____ problems at every level of their new possessions.

    A encountered

    B took on

    C happened upon

    D affronted

    E emulated

    F studied

47. Although it might not seem apparent to the _____ observer, a watch has more mass when it is wound up than when it is not because when its spring is put into tension, that is, when it is wound up, it experiences an increase in the potential energy it bears and thus it increases in mass.

   A casual

   B concerned

   C curious

   D dispassionate

   E heedless

   F interested

48. Belief in evolution is based on evidence, otherwise it would be _____.

   A inconceivable

   B implausible

   C questionable

   D incontestable

   E probable

   F cogitable

49. Males and females can have different management styles, leading sometimes to misunderstandings and when the misunderstandings are not resolved, they can result in decreases in a company's _____.

   A creativity

   B edge

   C effectiveness

   D productivity

   E potency

   F adaptability

50. Affirmative action programs aimed at increasing the number of women and minorities in upper management can sometimes lead to the white males in the company feeling _____.

   A boorish

   B apprehensive

   C unassertive

   D unfazed

   E uneasy

   F worrisome

51. More so than other types of cells, animal cells are fragile and remain _____ to changes in their immediate environment.

   A receptive

   B sensible

   C sensitive

   D sensual

   E sensorial

   F subject

52. When a company's name becomes synonymous with the product it sells, the company loses its distinctive _____ and other companies can sell similar products as if they were selling the same product as the original company.

   A ability

   B advantage

   C dominance

   D edge

   E stranglehold

   F superiority

53.   When workers are invited to use their own individual ingenuity and imagination to solve problems
      confronting the company, they get a chance to believe that they are _____ to the company and
      the company is frequently able to become stronger.

      A   fundamental

      B   indispensable

      C   integral

      D   intrinsic

      E   significant

      F   vital

54.   Bruegel's paintings are _____ for their vivid colors and realistic representations of peasant
      scenes such as vomiting and brawling at inns.

      A   eye-catching

      B   famous

      C   glaring

      D   notable

      E   remarkable

      F   tawdry

55.   Except for the _____ example of "The Necklace," Maupassant's short stories are not known for
      surprise endings, most of his work emphasizes characterization and the exploration of sexuality.

      A   famous

      B   great

      C   ignominious

      D   infamous

      E   notorious

      F   preeminent

56. The music of the ballet and its composer were _____ in the government-run media and the composer was forced to repudiate his work or risk losing his livelihood.

   A aspersed

   B degraded

   C disgraced

   D exculpated

   E repudiated

   F traduced

57. In response to negative attention in the press following a public performance of his opera, Shostakovich subtitled his next work "An artistic response to just criticism," although many _____ listeners heard sarcasm coming through the seemingly happy moments of the music.

   A discriminative

   B intensive

   C intelligent

   D perceptive

   E sharp-witted

   F veteran

58. Totalitarian governments usually feel threatened by any individual voice that becomes _____ they do what they can to silence such potential problems.

   A eminent

   B noteworthy

   C recognizable

   D salient

   E significant

   F visible

59.   Ann Rand wrote that copyrights and patents are a way of _____ a most basic property right, the
       right to profit from the product of one's own mind.

       [A]   effectuating

       [B]   legislating

       [C]   observing

       [D]   promulgating

       [E]   protecting

       [F]   validating

60.   In his "Letter from Birmingham Jail," Martin Luther King catalogued the multitude of abuses
       experienced by African Americans living in the 1960's in the United States and _____ a course
       for change.

       [A]   calculated

       [B]   drafted

       [C]   framed

       [D]   organized

       [E]   prepared

       [F]   schemed

61.   Martin Luther King's justly famous "Letter from Birmingham Jail," was written in response to a/
       an _____ statement by "Eight Alabama Clergymen" that had been published in newspapers
       throughout the United States.

       [A]   disreputable

       [B]   famous

       [C]   oppugnant

       [D]   opprobrious

       [E]   shoddy

       [F]   vicious

62. Study after study has _____ that when women and men have similar levels of education and similar jobs and work histories, that men earn more than women and that even when they are children, women tend to see themselves earning less money than men when they become adults.

A manifested

B projected

C publicized

D revealed

E uncloaked

F unveiled

63. When Joseph Stalin attended the premier of Shostakovich's opera "The Nose," he left early, apparently offended by the _____ plot and shocked by the progressive music of the score.

A ebullient

B gamey

C impish

D phlegmatic

E puckish

F ribald

64. When the Japanese attacked Pearl Harbor on 7 December 1941, their ultimate aim was not to totally defeat the United States, but to win a war of attrition so they could eventually have _____ over the peoples and products of the Eastern Pacific Rim, an outcome the United States would never have accepted.

A ascendance

B clout

C hegemony

D privileges

E management

F reign

65. As Franz Liszt said, the _____ influence on the musicians of the late 19th century that is, the musicians of the Romantic Period, was the work and towering legacy of Ludwig van Beethoven, the late classical composer who died in 1827.

     A ancillary

     B distinguished

     C notable

     D preponderant

     E sovereign

     F auxiliary

66. At the beginning of the twentieth century, it appeared that Russia was going to become the center of the musical and literary world, but instability in the country and the 1917 October Revolution put an end to any _____. Russia might have enjoyed.

     A clout

     B importance

     C place

     D privilege

     E superintendence

     F sway

67. Charles Dickens is known for the clearly defined characters he creates, his vivid descriptions of settings, and for his efforts to use his work to raise public consciousness about the _____ practices of privileged groups in British society of his time.

     A beneficial

     B benignant

     C co-optive

     D deceptive

     E deleterious

     F exploitive

68.   In 2010, an electrician who had worked for Pablo Picasso revealed that he had in his possession a/an
_____ of Picasso's work spanning the entire creative career of the artist.

   A   argosy

   B   collection

   C   cornucopia

   D   repository

   E   stockpile

   F   wellspring

69.   The Trinidadian author, V. S. Naipaul, won the Nobel Prize for literature in 2001, but is widely
_____ by Caribbeanists for his allegedly negative portrayals and views of the Caribbean and its
people.

   A   chided

   B   excoriated

   C   exculpated

   D   sanctioned

   E   libeled

   F   slandered

70.   After World War Two, many were _____ by the contrast between the unprecedented
technological progress of the preceding years and the inability of human societies to get along with
each other.

   A   addled

   B   agitated

   C   cozened

   D   deluded

   E   graveled

   F   stunned

71.   Karl Popper's most important contribution is his statement that if a hypothesis is to have scientific
      _____ it must be testable, that is, there must be a way that can potentially show that the theory is
      wrong.

      A   condition

      B   capacity

      C   position

      D   rank

      E   standing

      F   status

72.   Rather than putting so much _____ in definitions, Karl Popper wrote that it would be better to
      carefully phrase one's sentences so that the various meanings of the words used would not matter and
      people would argue less about words.

      A   credit

      B   dubiety

      C   force

      D   hope

      E   progeny

      F   stock

73.   Because the military, economic and social life of any society is _____ by that of other countries,
      few things take place in any nation that are not related to events in bordering countries.

      A   accommodated

      B   conditioned

      C   habituated

      D   inured

      E   primed

      F   recast

74. Although in the past biologists kept the subfields of biology separate, in recent years the emphasis has been on the study of the biological phenomena that living things have in common, a search for _____, characteristic of twentieth-century scientific inquiry.

   A   universals

   B   specifics

   C   details

   D   circumscription

   E   generality

   F   precision

75. There is a/an _____ similarity between a 1929 picture of frightened citizens crowding the streets around the New York Stock exchange on the first day of the October Stock Market crash that ushered in the Great Depression and pictures taken seventy-two years later of New Yorkers looking up at the World Trade Center towers on September 11, 2001.

   A   eerie

   B   curious

   C   interesting

   D   striking

   E   surprising

   F   uncanny

76. The facts that all living cells come from pre-existing living cells and all living cells use the same _____ to transmit DNA from one generation to another, pose problems for those who seek to determine the origin of the first living cell.

   A   determinant

   B   impetus

   C   ingredient

   D   means

   E   mechanism

   F   median

77. Although the human body has been studied intensively for centuries, it should not be thought that there is nothing more to learn; scientists will be making _____ discoveries about the body for as long as there are scientists.

     A   germinal

     B   innovative

     C   ingenious

     D   novel

     E   original

     F   primal

78. Two developments that greatly aided advancement in biology in the 17th century were the growth of scientific societies and the further development of the microscope; one aided individual discovery and the other aided _____ among professionals of what had been discovered.

     A   dispersal

     B   dissipation

     C   collection

     D   concentration

     E   dissemination

     F   propagation

79. Although spontaneous generation was debunked in 1688, belief in it persisted for two more centuries until the 1870's, when Louis Pasteur definitively _____ that it could not occur.

     A   adduced

     B   disconfirmed

     C   divulged

     D   evinced

     E   publicized

     F   substantiated

80. Mendel's study of heredity and his imaginative deductions based on the work were completed in the 1860's, but his discoveries did not become widely known until after 1900, largely because an influential botanist of the 1860's failed to see the _____ of Mendel's work and did not lend Mendel his support.

   A preeminence

   B prominence

   C renown

   D significance

   E substantiveness

   F worth

81. _____ dreams of wealth will do you little good as an entrepreneur; research suggests that those with a concrete business plan are twice as likely to succeed as those without.

   A Nebulous

   B Sagacious

   C Craven

   D Cogent

   E Dubious

   F Fervid

82. Edgar Allan Poe's _____ tales of crumbling mansions and dying women are perennial favorites among those with a taste for horror and mystery.

   A whimsical

   B morbid

   C saturnine

   D sublime

   E droll

   F esoteric

83. Ernest Shackleton became famous for his _____ efforts to ensure the survival of his team during the Endurance Expedition; after months of coping with the harsh Antarctic conditions, Shackleton made an 800-mile open-boat voyage in the hopes of seeing his companions rescued.

   A   erudite

   B   dogged

   C   phlegmatic

   D   desultory

   E   preternatural

   F   indefatigable

84. In the musical Camelot, Mordred exposes Lancelot and Guinevere's _____ love affair in his efforts to overthrow King Arthur, Guinevere's husband.

   A   inchoate

   B   noisome

   C   clandestine

   D   discrete

   E   illicit

   F   gauche

85. For scientists concerned about climate change, the recent prevalence of "extreme weather" - hurricanes, droughts, and the like - is an alarming _____ of things to come.

   A   portent

   B   vagary

   C   harbinger

   D   antithesis

   E   enigma

   F   imbroglio

86. Living in groups of up to eighty individuals and engaging in behaviors such as mutual grooming, the chimpanzee is one of nature's most _____ animals.

   A indigenous

   B ascetic

   C peripatetic

   D redoubtable

   E gregarious

   F extroverted

87. When asked where he had been, the suspect _____ spinning an elaborate story but failing to provide any evidence of his whereabouts.

   A fawned

   B equivocated

   C quaffed

   D prevaricated

   E transgressed

   F palpitated

88. Although one-third of the world's population is thought to be infected with tuberculosis, the disease may remain _____ for several years; in many cases, it never becomes active at all.

   A restive

   B inimical

   C latent

   D fulsome

   E quiescent

   F discreet

89. In nineteenth-century Europe, female behavior was subject to the most stringent of social rules; women who _____ convention and had children out of wedlock were often treated as outcasts.

   A wafted

   B extolled

   C flouted

   D spurned

   E disinterred

   F condoned

90. Although Galileo maintained that his theory of heliocentrism was compatible with Christian belief, Church leaders did not agree, and ultimately brought him before the Inquisition where he was forced to _____ his beliefs.

   A repudiate

   B beatify

   C preclude

   D foment

   E accrue

   F abjure

91. Although many people assume that research and development tax credits are only available to large companies with money to invest in on-site laboratories and the like, the truth is that even small businesses can be eligible for tax benefits, provided that their work is innovative and their management _____.

   A shrewd

   B supine

   C adroit

   D dogmatic

   E ineluctable

   F meretricious

92. The mother _____ her child for stealing money from his sister's piggy bank.

  A   placated

  B   castigated

  C   flustered

  D   vilified

  E   upbraided

  F   descried

93. As its name suggests, the "corpse flower" emits a strong and _____ odor that is highly unpleasant to humans.

  A   pusillanimous

  B   effete

  C   fetid

  D   hirsute

  E   noisome

  F   florid

94. Joan of Arc, a peasant girl with no military training and with only her religious convictions to guide her, showed great _____ in asking the Dauphin to entrust her with the French army.

  A   temperance

  B   temerity

  C   mettle

  D   recreancy

  E   paean

  F   fecklessness

95.   The relatively _____ weather of northern Europe is in large part due to the Gulf Stream, a warm ocean current originating in the waters off of Florida.

    A   provident

    B   torpid

    C   aseptic

    D   benign

    E   inveterate

    F   propitious

96.   The rich and, to some people, strident sound of bagpipes is a far cry from the more _____ tones of so many other instruments.

    A   mellifluous

    B   dulcet

    C   lithe

    D   obstreperous

    E   abstruse

    F   stentorian

97.   The fearsome crashing of thunder, which makes so many children _____ and seek their parents, has a surprisingly simple explanation; each bolt of lightning heats the surrounding air, causing it to expand so rapidly that it breaks the sound barrier.

    A   clinch

    B   quail

    C   demur

    D   rebuff

    E   cower

    F   simper

98. Thomas Hobbes, who famously remarked that life in a "state of nature" is "nasty, brutish and short," believed that the _____ of society are all that prevent humanity from succumbing to its basest urges.

  [A] cabals

  [B] idylls

  [C] proscriptions

  [D] vacillations

  [E] prohibitions

  [F] derelictions

99. Although it seems unlikely that the average person's tastes are as discriminating as those of a _____ it is nevertheless true that 90 percent of restaurants fail within one year of opening.

  [A] tyro

  [B] wag

  [C] virago

  [D] libertine

  [E] connoisseur

  [F] epicure

100. The audience was unimpressed with the lecture; despite the speaker's dazzling rhetoric and considerable charisma, it was clear that his claims were _____.

  [A] fervid

  [B] specious

  [C] picaresque

  [D] fallacious

  [E] officious

  [F] feckless

101. To those unfamiliar with Middle Eastern dance, the countless sequins and tassels worn by belly dancers may seem excessive or even _____ however, by accentuating the dancer's movements; such embellishments serve a practical purpose.

    [A] tawdry

    [B] piquant

    [C] voluble

    [D] raffish

    [E] aberrant

    [F] diaphanous

102. Animals that deal with the seasonal shortage of food by hibernating typically _____ themselves beforehand in order to store up enough energy for the winter months.

    [A] incense

    [B] preen

    [C] glut

    [D] recast

    [E] enervate

    [F] gorge

103. Efforts to address the so-called "glass ceiling" have met with only _____ success; although women are twice as likely as men to startup businesses, only 3 percent of these female-owned businesses generate revenue of over $1 million.

    [A] middling

    [B] halcyon

    [C] equivocal

    [D] ecumenical

    [E] sophomoric

    [F] garrulous

104. The teacher was of a _____ disposition, and frequently lashed out at her students over perceived insults.

  A stygian

  B fatuous

  C turbid

  D irascible

  E splenetic

  F recondite

105. Research suggests that those with a _____ for math may have inherited their skills from their parents; a 2009 study revealed that the development of the part of the brain used in calculations is overwhelmingly governed by genetics.

  A mendacity

  B aptitude

  C recidivism

  D eloquence

  E dereliction

  F propensity

106. As anthropologists know, certain practices and beliefs unite the _____ cultures of the world; every known civilization, for example, has practiced some form of religion.

  A inimitable

  B profligate

  C disparate

  D palatial

  E myriad

  F prolix

107. The unique and sometimes visionary premises of independent films are proof of what writers and directors can achieve when not _____ by concerns of money and popularity.

   A   fettered

   B   emaciated

   C   obviated

   D   macerated

   E   satiated

   F   constrained

108. Although the Chinese economy has been growing rapidly for three decades, there is some concern that this expansion will slow as more and more people obtain college degrees; those with a university education will no doubt be _____ to accept the low-paying factory jobs that have contributed to China's success.

   A   crass

   B   nonplused

   C   disinclined

   D   loath

   E   urbane

   F   frantic

109. In order to get the most out of your batteries, keep them at room temperature; cold, for example _____ the chemical reaction that generates power, so the battery must work harder to produce the same amount of power.

   A   retards

   B   vituperates

   C   bedizens

   D   impedes

   E   ameliorates

   F   piques

110. Even during his lifetime, Caligula had a reputation for moral _____; one account had him ordering his guards to throw a group of innocent spectators into the Colosseum's arena to be devoured by wild animals.

    A desuetude

    B finesse

    C probity

    D degeneracy

    E insularity

    F turpitude

111. His _____ disposition was infectious; it was impossible to talk to him and remain unmoved by his enthusiasm.

    A ineffable

    B ebullient

    C blithe

    D lachrymose

    E verdant

    F edacious

112. Terms used in everyday language are not necessarily the most scientifically _____ as the case of the organism known as "seaweed" illustrates; contrary to what its name suggests, seaweed is actually a member of the kingdom Protista.

    A admonitory

    B insouciant

    C felicitous

    D sententious

    E expedient

    F quixotic

113. Given the events that preceded the couple's separation, it is hardly surprising that the divorce proceedings were marked by ill-will and _____.

A   vituperation

B   indolence

C   obloquy

D   vacillation

E   doggerel

F   abeyance

114. Because they can go for several years without erupting, it can be difficult to determine which volcanoes are extinct and which are merely dormant - a _____ state of affairs.

A   disconcerting

B   extenuating

C   trenchant

D   ominous

E   inimitable

F   luculent

115. Given that they account for roughly half of America's GDP, it would be a mistake to _____ the importance of small businesses.

A   broach

B   denigrate

C   glean

D   sanction

E   lionize

F   disparage

116. Faberge eggs are known for the incredibly _____ designs; the first one ever made opened to reveal a gold yolk, which itself concealed a gold hen and a miniature diamond replica of the Russian Imperial Crown.

    A sumptuous

    B ubiquitous

    C ostentatious

    D incipient

    E prudish

    F lugubrious

117. The movement of gas molecules is rather _____; particles move quickly and more or less randomly.

    A belligerent

    B turgid

    C volatile

    D irrevocable

    E frenetic

    F malleable

118. The world's oceans are home to many bizarre and fascinating creatures, but few are more _____ than the octopus, which has three hearts, no bones, and an intelligence level that far exceeds that of other invertebrates.

    A prosaic

    B extant

    C inscrutable

    D enigmatic

    E nascent

    F incredulous

119. The "Trail of Tears" owes its _____ name to the thousands of Cherokees who suffered and often died during their forced relocation westward.

      A   petrous

      B   imperious

      C   pugnacious

      D   evocative

      E   doleful

      F   salubrious

120. It is clear that Mozart, who wrote his first opera at the age of eleven, displayed _____ musical abilities from his earliest years.

      A   prodigious

      B   grandiloquent

      C   preternatural

      D   epicurean

      E   refractory

      F   brazen

Explanatory Answers

Answer to Question 1:

forerunners and antecedents

The blank needs to be filled by a word that refers to things that came before 1789; derivatives, descendents, and imitators can therefore be ruled out from the start. Originators could be used in the sentence, but is not equivalent to any of the other options, leaving antecedents and forerunners.

Answer to Question 2:

stimulated and motivated

The negative dampened and debilitated do not belong in the sentence. Abetted fits well in the sentence, but emphasizes the notion that Einstein's work helped the work that followed, which may be true, but such a meaning is not equivalent to the meaning of any of the other options. Vitalize is what can happen to something already in existence. Since work based on Einstein's discovery did not exist until after the he had made the discovery, the discovery did not vitalize the work that came after it, instead the discovery stimulated or motivated the work that followed.

Answer to Question 3:

drawn and derived

In the sentence, drawn and derived refer to a conclusion based on Newton's physics. The other options refer to actions and/or thought processes, none of which are equivalent to each other or to drawn or derived.

Answer to Question 4:

entails and involves

In the sentence, entails and involves indicate that when one does chemical thermodynamics, one also does "measurements of thermodynamic properties and . . ." Subsumes means "take the place of," constitutes means "is the same as," embodies means represents, and contains would indicate that chemical thermodynamics is some sort of container for "measurements. . ."

Answer to Question 5:

motivated and influenced

Motivated and influenced convey that the "young woman" was inspired by "her desire to impress her parents." Inhibited, sedated, and stymied suggest different levels of negative influence and do not fit well in the sentence. Adjudicated, has no other similar word among the options.

Answer to Question 6:

deductive and inferable

This passage is saying that humans do not possess the capabilities, scientifically, to explicitly see the scientific truths that we want to see. Therefore, we must rely on something to overcome our "empirical handicap." "Inverse" means to render in the opposite direction. This would not help us understand faraway truths because it would just make them equally distant in another capacity. "Deliberate" means slow and careful. This looks like a good answer at a glance but just because you work slowly at something you lack the scientific capability to do doesn't mean you'll ever get there. You're still terminally unequipped. "Observable" means capable of being seen. This misses the entire point the sentence is going for: these things can't be seen. You can't use "Observable" evidence to study something that is implied to be unobservable. "Obvious" means easy to ascertain. This answer is also wrong because the entire point of the sentence is that these Universal truths are not easy to ascertain. This leaves "Deductive" and "Inferable." Both of these words mean capable of being apprehended through inference. This is exactly what would be needed to overcome lack of direct observation: the ability to work backwards and reason the existence of a concept. Therefore, c and d are correct.

Answer to Question 7:

subverted and undermined

This sentence is saying that modern superficial standards have damaged the media, and done something to children. If it damaged all of modern media then it can be safely assumed that it damaged children, too. "Initiated" means began. If superficiality-initiated confidence then it would be helping children, so that answer must be wrong. "Rectified" means fixed. Again, since superficiality is described as doing damage then this answer cannot be correct. "Invigorated" means strengthened. Again, this sentiment is the opposite of what the sentence wants to convey. To invigorate confidence would be a good thing, "Objectified" means portrayed, often with negative connotations. But it is beauty that is being objectified, not the self-confidence of children. The self-confidence of children is collateral damage. Therefore, "Subverted" and "Undermined" are the correct answers. They both mean damaged or weakened. The modern superficiality is damaging the self-confidence of young children. This makes perfect sense. So, a and b are correct.

Answer to Question 8:

inconspicuous and subtle

This sentence is saying that very different conditions can be misdiagnosed because there is "something" about the differences in their symptoms that cause them to be confused. This "something" must be a vagueness that renders them easily confused. "Pervasiveness" means prevalence. The amount of the symptoms wouldn't hinder a doctor's ability to differentiate between them. "Harmless" means non-threatening. The harmlessness of the differences wouldn't affect a doctor's ability to differentiate between symptoms, either. "Debilitating" means incapacitating. If the differences were debilitating it would actually make proper diagnosis easier because they would have such different effects on a patient. "Extravagant" means excessive. Again, excessive differences would make proper diagnosis easier. We want differences that are hard to notice. That leaves us with "Inconspicuous" and "Subtle." These both mean difficult to locate. Differences in symptoms that follow these two descriptions would, in fact, be difficult to spot and would lead to misdiagnosis. a and e are correct.

Answer to Question 9:

proficiency and expertise

"Aggression" means violence or hostility. This doesn't work in the sentence because violence is not a characteristic a doctor must possess to perform a difficult surgery. "Reticence" means reserve or quietness. This answer also does not complete the sentiment of the sentence because it's already been established that the doctor is audacious. "Reticence" would contradict the word audacious. "Contempt" means disdain or scorn. There is no reason to believe that disdain or scorn would aid a doctor in completing a complicated surgical procedure. "Delusion" is misunderstanding. Again, misunderstanding the topic at hand would not help a doctor perform a surgery – it would hinder him or her. This leaves "Proficiency" and "Expertise." Both of these words mean aptitude or skill. A doctor would certainly need to compliment his or her daring with an equal amount of ability. Therefore, choices c and f are correct.

Answer to Question 10:

hounding and badgering

If we read the sentence, we get the sensation that the person is annoyed by being asked repeatedly to fix a problem. The words hounding, and badgering are the best options because both of these words mean to annoy or irritate repeatedly. The other word choices bearing, ferreting and weaseling have nothing to do with reminding a person to constantly do something. They are words that mean to move or in a certain way (bearing), to look for something persistently (ferreting), and to cheat somebody (weaseling). Remonstrating means to protest or object strongly to something and would not complete the sentence properly.

Answer to Question 11:

endemic and prevalent

In the above sentence, we are led to believe that there is a lot of crime in the area and even the police are hesitant to go in after nightfall. The two words that would best complete the sentence would be endemic and prevalent. Epidemic refers to the wide spread of virus, curtailed means something has been lessened, governable would mean that the problem was controllable and exuberant means exciting, lively or happy - all of which would not complete the above sentence in a logical manner.

Answer to Question 12:

drifted and wafted

The correct word option is one that means to come through. The correct word choices are drifted and wafted. The words coasted, transmitted, poised and inured make no sense when completing the above sentence. Coasted means to sail or slide by, transmitted means to emit a signal or information, poised means to be calm or balanced, and inured means to become an advantage or to make someone become accustomed to something disagreeable such as children to sex and violence.

Answer to Question 13:

twilight and crepuscular

The keyword in the sentence above is evening. We are looking for words that refer to the evening, words such as twilight and crepuscular. Diurnal refers to the day time, noontide refers to 12 o'clock noon, enlightened means to become aware of and modicum is a tiny portion or a limited quantity.

Answer to Question 14:

pristine and immaculate

In the above sentence, the words remarkable, condition and high standard all lead us to believe that the missing word describes how well the book has been preserved. Sanitary is used to describe how clean something is e.g. a hospital, untarnished is mainly used for metals or for describing a person's reputation, purified refers to something that has been through a purifying process and adulterated means something that has been manipulated or tampered with. The only two-word choices left are pristine and immaculate. These two-word choices refer to the excellent condition of a book that generally would not be, because of its age.

Answer to Question 15:

clumsy and gauche

Clumsy and gauche are the only two-word options possible because they are the only options that complete the sentence logically Clumsy and gauche in this sentence both mean crude or badly done. Sophisticated would not make any sense in the sentence since the designs were unpopular and unpractical. The word choice ill-bred refers to a person who is impolite while butterfingered is used to describe a person who is extremely clumsy and drops things. Lastly, couth is used to describe something or someone extremely sophisticated.

Answer to Question 16:

dilettante and amateur

The key phrase in the sentence is in spite of. This phrase leads us to believe that there is a contrast in ideas and the missing word most likely means lack of knowledge or not being profuse in a subject. The word choices that would best fit this idea would be dilettante and amateur. The word unskilled refers to a person's skill and has nothing to do with knowledge, dabbling is the action of taking a superficial interest in something; connoisseur and proficient both mean being an expert or extremely knowledgeable on the topic.

Answer to Question 17:

profuse and plenteous

The word choices that don't make sense in the sentence are barren, elaborate, pretentious and luxuriant. Barren means not being able to bear fruit, arid and dry, elaborate is usually not used to describe a person's hair unless we're describing their hairstyle, pretentious describes someone who makes claims of undeserved self-importance and, luxuriant is generally used with vegetation (or material riches) and means profuse or very fertile. It is generally not used with hair unless we're referring to hair growth. Therefore, the word options, profuse which means abundant and plenteous which means generous are the correct answers.

Answer to Question 18:

ornate and baroque

Ornate and baroque are the best words to describe the marble columns. The rest of the words do not complete the sentence in a meaningful way. Clement is used to refer to mild weather, embroidered is something that has been sewn with a picture or design, dowdy means dull or boring and from the context of the sentence the columns are not dull or boring. Garish means loud and flashy which is also unlikely in a beautiful and elegantly designed 15th-century church.

Answer to Question 19:

capacious and expansive

Here, in the above sentence, the keywords are despite and undersized, and because despite is used when there is a contrast in ideas, we are looking for a word that would mean the opposite of undersized, a word that means spacious. Capacious and expansive would therefore be the most logical word choices. Abundance means a large quantity but cannot be used here because we must say 'abundance of' something, brimming is normally used when something exceeds its capacity as in a liquid; minute refers to something very small and the word discrepant means disagreeing and would not logically make sense in the sentence.

Answer to Question 20:

contrived and devised

In the above, the marketing team has done something to improve sales. We are looking for a word that means planned or came up with; therefore, the best word options to complete the sentence logically would be contrived and devised. The word connived also means to come up with, however it has a negative connotation as does the word schemed; as a consequence, neither word would complete the sentence in a meaningful way. Blueprints are plans or designs drawn up by architects and casted means to throw or to make an impression of.

Answer to Question 21:

fraudulent and dubious

Here, the main idea is that something is being done by firms, something to inflate their profits and something that is misleading or dishonest. The best options to replace the missing word would be fraudulent and dubious. Counterfeit means an imitation. In this sentence, it cannot be used because you cannot make a counterfeit accounting practice, although you can make counterfeit documents or money. Infamous means to be notorious and is generally used to describe people, villainess is a quality used to describe a person who acts like a villain or that is evil and, slanderous means to tell lies about a person to discredit him.

Answer to Question 22:

frugal and parsimonious

The keyword in the sentence is "recession". Companies are now doing something with their marketing budgets that they probably didn't use to do before the recession when markets were buoyant. We are looking for a word that means "to be careful with money". The most logical answers to complete the sentence would be frugal and parsimonious which both mean to be cautious with money. Miserly has a negative connotation and refers to being cheap or mean with money. Gluttonous means to be voracious, altruistic means to be generous and to give to good causes and lavish would mean to be extremely generous, all of which a company would not be inclined to do during times of financial difficulty.

Answer to Question 23:

primitive and archaic

While most of the word options mean, to some extent, something that is outdated or old, not all of them can be used in the above sentence. Old-fashioned and antiquated are used to describe something that is out of date, not fashionable or something that is not really used anymore. Obsolete is used for something that is no longer used or is useful. Trampled makes no sense because it means to walk over forcibly. The two options left are primitive and archaic, both refer to something ancient that is generally no longer in existence.

Answer to Question 24:

controversial and polemic

The key phrase here is child slavery; and a publication (book or news article) about such a topic that might cause some controversy. Hence the correct missing word options are controversial and polemic. Quarrelsome means to cause a fight and while the topic is controversial; it is unlikely to cause fights. Metaphysical is a term meaning without physical presence and does not complete the sentence logically. Cantankerous is used to describe a person who is grumpy or bad humored.

Answer to Question 25:

materialistic and bourgeois

The best word choices to complete the sentence are materialistic and bourgeois. The two words socialists and capitalist are keywords because they help determine the missing word. Socialists disapprove of capitalists; they would not like excessive spending on material things. Socialists also disapprove of the rich or wealthy middle-class, i.e. the bourgeois. Knowing this allows us to choose materialistic and bourgeois as the correct word options. Nonconforming, indolent, Victorian and capitalism would not make any sense in the above sentence. Nonconforming has nothing to do with excesses, indolent means lazy, Victorian is an adjective that refers to Victorian England and capitalism is an ideology and not used as a word to describe excesses.

Answer to Question 26:

indigenous and aboriginal

The word missing from the above sentence is a synonym of the word native - as in native tribes. Indigenous and aboriginal are both words used to designate native peoples of a land. Homegrown is not possible because you cannot grow a tribe, nor is it likely you can inherit a tribe. It also would not make sense to gather genetic data from an alien tribe. The word inbred is not possible because it means the interbreeding or exchange of ideas within a culture or people.

Answer to Question 27:

disparities and discrepancies

The word options disparities and discrepancies are the best options to complete the sentence since the words refer to the economic difference between first and third world countries. While the word hole and burrow are synonyms for gap, they are not used in an economic sense. Animosity means hateful or spiteful while disagreeable means something that is not agreeable. Neither option would make sense when used in the above sentence.

Answer to Question 28:

bilious and sallow

The word options hearty, salubrious and vigorous are all synonyms of the word healthy, and if a person is ill, his/her complexion is not going to be healthy. Albino is a type of genetic condition and does not make sense in the sentence. The two possible answers would be bilious and sallow. Both words are adjectives used to describe a person who is not looking very healthy or well.

Answer to Question 29:

profusion and accretion

This question stem sets up a contrast; some residents are displaced while others enjoy the new additions to the community. The missing answer will support the idea of addition or growth in the community. Choice (B)-abridgement (meaning to shorten or condense) is the opposite of growth. Choice(C)-ardor (meaning great emotion or passion), Choice (D)-parapet (meaning fortification consisting of a low wall and, Choice(F)-culmination (meaning conclusion) are all off-topic for this sentence. The correct answers are Choice(A) profusion – meaning extreme abundance and Choice (E)-accretion (meaning a gradual increase in size, as through growth or external addition

Answer to Question 30:

perspicacity and sagacity

The Internet is providing a window or a look into other cultures; the missing word will provide a similar meaning to "a look" or "insight". Choice(B)-erudition and Choice(D)-sapience both mean intelligence which is the incorrect idea for this sentence. Choice (E)-apotheosis (meaning the epitome of perfection or the elevation to the status of a deity) and Choice (F)-proclivity (meaning tendency or inclination) are off-topic for the question stem. The correct answer choices are Choice (A)-perspicacity (meaning insight or understanding) and Choice (C)-sagacity (meaning insight and wisdom).

Answer to Question 31:

bated and minified

The sentence presents a change over time; Previously, household tasks took up substantial time, but the appliances have changed that tremendously Therefore, the correct answer will support the idea of the tasks being reduced. Choice(E)-impinged (meaning to infringe upon or advance beyond the normal limit) and Choice(F)-augmented (meaning making something greater in number or strength) are the opposite meanings needed for the missing word. Choice(C)-masticated (meaning to bite or grind with the teeth) and Choice(D)-attenuated (meaning reduced in strength) both mean reduced but with the wrong connotation to suit the question stem. The correct answers are Choice(A)-bated (meaning diminished) and Choice (B)-minified (meaning lessened).

Answer to Question 32:

plethora and legion

The question stem indicates that there are thousands of harmful organisms in the body. Without the immune system, these numerous organisms could attack the body. The correct answer will correspond with the idea of "numerous" or "thousands". Choice (B)-surfeit (meaning the state of being more than full), Choice (D)-consanguinity (meaning a close relation or connection, particularly a blood relationship), Choice (F)-extolment (meaning an expression of approval and commendation), and Choice (E)-peculation (meaning a fraudulent appropriation of funds entrusted in your care but owned by someone else) are all off-topic for this question stem. The correct answers are Choice (A)-plethora and Choice (C)-legion both of which mean a large number.

Answer to Question 33:

fastidiously and punctiliously

The microscope allows people to see something as small as an organism's cell easily; therefore, we can deduce the correct answer will support the idea of seeing better or more clearly. None of the incorrect answers fit into the scope of the sentence; Choice(A)-mendaciously (meaning in an untruthful manner), Choice (B)-salubriously (meaning healthy to the mind or body), Choice (C)-adventitiously (meaning associated by chance and not integral) do not correspond with "in detail". Choice (F)-exiguously (meaning deficient in amount or quality or extent) also does not make sense in the sentence. The correct answers are Choice(D)-fastidiously and (E)punctiliously, which both mean painstakingly and carefully.

Answer to Question 34:

tamable and tractable

The message of the sentence is that scientists created a naming system to make identifying one animal for another more of something. Naming systems help to define and categorize things, so we can deduce these systems likely make identifying animals easier or more manageable. The missing word likely have a similar connotation to "simpler" or "manageable". Choice (B)-vociferous (meaning conspicuously and offensively loud), Choice (C)-resplendent (meaning having great beauty), Choice(D)-quiescent (meaning being quiet and still), and Choice(E)-glib (meaning slick or insincere speech) are all off-topic for this question stem. The correct answers are Choice (A)-tamable (meaning controllable) and Choice (F)-tractable (meaning easily managed).

Answer to Question 35:

impart and bestow

The question stem describes what the neutrons contribute to the nucleus; the neutrons contribute to the mass of the nucleus but do not contribute to the electric charge of the nucleus. The correct answer will align with the idea of contributing or transferring from one to another. Choice (A) extenuate (meaning to lessen the importance) and Choice (F) ossify (meaning to become hard and bony) are incorrect because they do not refer in any way to contributing. Choice (D) remit (meaning to give money) and Choice (E) bequeath (meaning to give possessions in the case of death) both mean to contribute in some way, but they are incorrect because they carry the wrong connotation for the sentence. The correct answers are (B) impart – meaning to transmit or pass on and (C) bestow – meaning to give or transfer an honor.

Answer to Question 36:

substantive and indispensable

The question stem describes the nucleus as providing major functions for the atom. The missing word will reflect this – that the nucleus is a significant part of an atom. Choice(A)-effulgent (meaning brilliant or radiating) and Choice(E)recondite (meaning confined to and understandable by only an enlightened inner circle) do not fit the scope of the sentence. Choice (C)-epochal (meaning so significant that it brings about a new era), and Choice (F)-evidentiary (meaning important based on evidence) all refer to some aspect of the word "significant", but the connotation of each word is not fitting for the question stem. The correct answers are (B)substantive – meaning important or essential and (D)indispensable– meaning necessary or vital.

Answer to Question 37:

affiliated and colligated

For this question, the missing word is defined in the sentence: metabolism is associated with more processes than just converting fat to energy. The correct answer will have a similar meaning to "associated". None of the incorrect answers support the idea of "associated"; Choice (C)-caviled (meaning to quibble or make unnecessary objections), Choice (D)-distended (meaning to swell, to inflate, to bloat), Choice (E)-ensconced (meaning to fix or settle firmly), and Choice (F)-abrogated (meaning to formally abolish) all do not fit within the scope of the sentence. The correct answers are Choice (A)-affiliated (meaning to associate) and Choice (B)-colligated (meaning to make a logical connection).

Answer to Question 38:

consideration and expatiation

The key idea in this sentence "have determined"; by this we know meteorologists have studied or examined hurricane activity in order to draw conclusions about its timing. The missing word will correspond with the idea of an examination or the undertaking of a study. Choice (A)-cogitation (meaning deep thought), Choice (D)-introspection (meaning contemplation), and Choice(F)-rumination (also meaning contemplation) do relate to examining, but the connotation is not proper for this sentence. These three words refer to examining for the purpose of understanding and not examining for the purpose of analyzing. Choice (C)-circumlocution (meaning a lengthy, round-about expression) is off-topic for this sentence. The correct answers are Choice (B)-consideration (meaning the process of weighing carefully) and Choice (E)-expatiation (meaning a discussion that enlarges a topic).

Answer to Question 39:

homogenous and undifferentiated

The message of the sentence is that there are many different types of governments in place around the world; in other words, the governments throughout the world are far from "the same". The correct answer will mean "the same". Choice(A)-bilious (meaning irritable or ill-tempered) and Choice(B)-lachrymose (meaning sorrowful) are incorrect as they do fit the scope of the sentence. Choice(E)-discrete (meaning separate) and Choice(F)-disjointed (meaning unconnected) have similar meanings, but they do not mean "the same". The correct answers are Choice(C)-homogenous (meaning of the same nature) and Choice-(D)undifferentiated (meaning the same kind or lacking diversity).

Answer to Question 40:

sequestered and insular

Imperialism resulted in ethnic groups that were once unacquainted with each other now living in the same nation. The correct answer will reflect the first part of the story – that these nations were not in close contact. Choice(B)-parochial (meaning narrow-minded and restricted to new ideas) and Choice(E)-illiberal (meaning close-minded and intolerant) both mean restricted, but they are incorrect because they refer to the restriction of opinions rather than of any physical space. Choice (C)-sectarian (meaning a subgroup of a larger group) and Choice(F)-catholic (meaning including a wide variety of things or all-embracing) are the opposite of the idea or groups not in close contact. The correct answers are Choice(A)-sequestered (meaning secluded from others) and Choice(C)-insular (meaning isolated).

Answer to Question 41:

quell and obviate

The founding fathers are attempting find solutions to disagreements, or in other words, suppressing or eliminating conflict. The correct answer will have a similar meaning to "suppressing" or "eliminating". Choice (D)-exacerbate (meaning to increase bitterness or violence), and Choice (F)-precipitate (meaning to hasten or bring about) are incorrect; they are both the opposite of the needed meaning. Choice(B)-castigate (meaning to criticize harshly) and Choice (C)-emulate (meaning to strive to equal or excel) do not fit the scope of the sentence. The correct answers are Choice(A)-quell (meaning to stamp out) and Choice (E)-obviate (meaning to do away with).

Answer to Question 42:

intransigent and recalcitrant

In this sentence, having a criminal record prevents someone from taking part in basic social functions. The correct answers will support the idea of a criminal record as a significant obstacle. None of the incorrect answers all do not support the idea of a criminal record as a hard-to-get-around obstacle. : Choice(A)-culpable (meaning deserving blame or censure), Choice(B)-dogmatic (meaning pertaining to a code of beliefs), Choice(D)-emollient (meaning softening to the skin), Choice (F)-florid (meaning flush with a rosy color) The correct answers are Choice(C)-intransigent (meaning entrenched) and Choice(E)-recalcitrant (meaning stubbornly resistant).

Answer to Question 43:

inextirpable and indelible

The sentence lists many components of culture but highlights that a powerful component is a type of bond members feel. A bond is a connection that fastens things together, so the correct answer will support the idea of a strong or powerful tie. None of the incorrect answers support this idea: Choice(A)-irascible (meaning grouchy or cranky), Choice(B)-execrable (meaning abominable and utterly despicable), Choice (D)illustrious-(meaning famous or prominent), and Choice(E)-opprobrious (meaning offensive and disgraceful). The correct answers are Choice(C)-inextirpable (meaning indestructible or unable to erase) and Choice(F)-indelible (meaning permanent and lasting).

Answer to Question 44:

innocuous and aberrant

The message of the sentence is that the media can be used in multiple ways; some people use media in one way while others use media in another way. One way is disruptive to society, but the other way - the contrast to disruptive - is exemplified by fashion and hairstyle trends. Choice (C)-injurious (meaning to cause harm) is incorrect; this word provides a similar idea to disruptive or destructive, and we need a word that means the opposite. Choice(E)-equivocal (meaning doubtful or uncertain) is incorrect as the sentence describes very certain ways the media influences others. Choice(B)-aberrant (meaning deviating from the normal) and Choice(E)-exorbitant (meaning exceeding or outside of customary limits) do not fit the scope of the sentence; using media to forward fashion trends is actually quite normal. The correct answers are (A)innocuous – meaning harmless and (B) banal – meaning commonplace, ordinary, or usual. These two words do not have exactly the same meaning, but both of them fit into the sentence in a way that makes sense overall.

Answer to Question 45:

erudite and lofty

The liberal arts education is now seen as an area of study not practical for today's society. The correct answer must evoke the opposite of "practical" and "down-to-earth". Choice (C)-asinine (meaning lacking intelligence or foolish) and Choice (D)-obtuse (meaning not quick or alert in perception, feeling, or intellect) both relate to learning, but both are incorrect because neither provides a contrast with "practical". Choice(F)-fetid (meaning foul-smelling, putrid, stinking) is not relevant to this question stem. Choice(E)-chary (meaning cautiously or suspiciously reluctant to do something) does not fit in this sentence; no indication is given that anyone dedicating years of study to liberal arts should be cautious or suspicious). The correct answers are (A)erudite – meaning scholarly and (B) lofty – meaning high-minded both provide a direct contrast with the idea of a practical, down-to-earth education.

Answer to Question 46:

encountered and happened upon

Affronted, emulated, and *studied,* would indicate that the corporations took various specific actions in response to the problems. *Took on* would suggest the likely scenario that the corporations learned about the problems and took steps to solve them. The correct options, *encountered* and *happened upon,* have no similar words among the options and indicate only that the corporations came into contact with problems, not that they did anything in response to these problems.

Answer to Question 47:

casual and dispassionate

The pairs *casual/dispassionate* and *curious/interested* fit in the sentence, but the correct options agree with the context of the sentence because the fact that a watch increases in mass when wound would not be necessarily surprising to someone who was thinking (i.e. *curious* and *interested*) about the issue. *Heedless* is similar in meaning to *casual* and *dispassionate* but has a negative sense not entailed in the correct options. Similarly, *concerned* is similar to *curious* and *interested.*

Answer to Question 48:

inconceivable and implausible

Inconceivable and *implausible* indicate that the concept or idea at issue would not be possible. All *inconceivable* and implausible ideas are also questionable, but since not all questionable ideas are not *inconceivable* and *implausible*, *questionable* cannot be a correct choice *Cogitable* would mean that evolution could be imaginable, and *incontestable* and *probable* are positive terms where the sentence requires negative words such as *inconceivable* and *implausible*. Also, none of the incorrect options mean the same as any of the other options.

Answer to Question 49:

effectiveness and productivity

While all the options fit will in the blank, only *effectiveness* and *productivity* refer in the sentence to the same *concept* and so all other options are incorrect.

Answer to Question 50:

apprehensive and uneasy

Boorish, unassertive, and *worrisome* can be ruled out because they have to do with different ways of *interacting* with others. *Unfazed* would mean that the *white males* in question are not bothered by company policy, a meaning at odds with the sense of the sentence. The remaining options, *apprehensive* and *uneasy*, are similar in meaning and fit well in the sentence.

Answer to Question 51:

sensible and sensitive

Sensitive and *sensible* imply only that the cells easily detect changes in their environment. The other terms suggest varying types of reaction to changes in the environment.

Answer to Question 52:

advantage and edge

Ability can be rejected because the sense of the sentence conveys the idea that *ability* is not what the company risks losing. Dominance, *stranglehold,* and *superiority* would suggest that being distinctive *necessarily* leads to controlling the market, when in fact distinctiveness merely provides a competitive *edge* or *advantage*.

Answer to Question 53:

indispensable and vital

The difference between the correct options and the other choices is that the wrong choices suggest that while the employee may be important to the company, if the company had hired someone else, that person would be just as important. Using your own creativity is contributing something that only you can provide, making you feel *vital* and *indispensable*.

Answer to Question 54:

notable and remarkable

The *sentence* presents Bruegel's work in a positive light and thus *glaring* and *tawdry* do not fit in the sentence. *Eye-catching* has no synonym. *Famous* could be used as a synonym for either *remarkable* or *notable*, but *remarkable* and *notable* do not necessarily include the notion of fame, indicating only that vivid colors and realistic representations are an important dimension of the artist's work, whether he be *famous* or not.

Answer to Question 55:

infamous and notorious

Notorious, infamous, and *ignominious* could be used as synonyms, but *ignominious* suggests insignificance, unlike the first two terms which suggest a degree of fame. *Famous* could be used because something infamous is also famous, but infamous and notorious entail a touch of negativity not present in the more neutral famous. *Great* and *preeminent* could also be used as synonyms, but they contradict the sense of the sentence.

Answer to Question 56:

aspersed and traduced

Exculpated must be rejected because it is a positive term where all the others are negative. *Disgraced, degraded,* and *repudiated* imply different meaning and none carry the notion, as do traduced and *aspersed,* that untrue things where said about the individual and music.

Answer to Question 57:

discriminative and perceptive

All the terms would fit in the sentence and be true. The correct options fit best in the sentence because they center in on the specific trait needed to discern the sarcasm, while the other terms are more general.

Answer to Question 58:

eminent and salient

Salient and *eminent* refer to a particular status gained by the *individual voice,* the other terms, except for *visible,* suggest that the *voice* is worth listening to, but do not necessarily imply that anyone actually is listening. *Visible* suggests, similar to the correct options, that people can hear the *voice* but does not imply that anyone is listening.

Answer to Question 59:

effectuating and observing

The *options* relate closely to each other, but only the correct options convey the idea of putting into practice the basic property right. The other options refer to things that can be done *about* the right.

Answer to Question 60:

drafted and framed

The correct options refer to charting a course. *Organized* and *prepared* suggest a degree of control over the coming *course* of action not supported by the rest of the sentence. *Calculated* and *schemed* also do not fit the sense of the sentence.

Answer to Question 61:

oppugnant and opprobrious

The correct options mean offensive. *Disreputable* and *famous* agree with the sense of the sentence, but *famous* conveys that there may have been something positive about the letter, while *disreputable* is a negative term. *Shoddy* and *vicious* have no synonyms among the options.

Answer to Question 62:

manifested and revealed

Projected and *publicized* would suggest that the information obtained became widely available and well known. *Uncloaked* and *unveiled* suggest that the information had been concealed. The correct options, agreeing with the sense of the sentence, indicate only that the information was discovered.

Answer to Question 63:

gamey and ribald

Puckish, impish, and *ebullient* suggest that the plot was lively, but a lively plot would seem unlikely to offend *anyone*. *Phlegmatic* has no synonyms among the options, leaving *ribald* and *gamey* which suggest that the play had some potentially obscene content which would seem likely to offend.

Answer to Question 64:

ascendance and hegemony

The incorrect options refer to specific types/levels of control not necessarily entailed in the generalized terms *ascendance* and *hegemony*. *Clout* refers to the influence over people, but is not usually used in reference to influence over products. *Privileges* is vague compared to the correct options, and *management* and *reign* refer to more specific types of influence than *ascendance* and *heemony*.

Answer to Question 65:

preponderant and sovereign

The correct options convey that Beethoven exerted an overwhelming influence on his successors. *Distinguished* and notable do not agree with towering, and *ancillary* and *auxiliary* suggest a weaker degree of influence than conveyed by the rest of the sentence.

Answer to Question 66:

superintendence and sway

The correct options convey the notion of a controlling or leading influence. *Clout, privilege, importance,* and *place* can be used interchangeably in the sentence, as they suggest a degree of influence, but do not indicate a controlling or leading influence.

Answer to Question 67:

co-optive and exploitive

Exploitive and *co-optive* convey the idea of the oppression of the weak by the strong and so fit better than the other words. *Deceptive* and *deleterious* have no synonyms among the options. The synonyms *benignant* and *beneficial* do not agree with the sense of the sentence.

Answer to Question 68:

argosy and cornucopia

Argosy and *cornucopia* suggest a treasure trove of objects, while the other terms are more neutral. *Wellspring, while* more positive than the other wrong choices, would incorrectly suggest that the group of Picasso's work was replenishable.

Answer to Question 69:

chided and excoriated

The near synonyms *exculpated* and *sanctioned* are positive terms that do not agree with the sentence. The correct options agree with the objective tone of the sentence and thus fit better than *libeled* and *slandered*.

Answer to Question 70:

addled and graveled

The correct options refer to being confused by something. *Deluded* and *cozened* refer to being misled by something, a meaning not in accord with the rest of the sentence. *Agitated* and *stunned* refer to emotional states not necessarily in agreement with each other.

Answer to Question 71:

standing and status

The correct options convey that the hypothesis will be useful to science if it is testable. *Position* and *rank* refer to places *on* a continuum rather than the on-or-off sense of *status* and *standing*. *Capacity* and *condition* have no synonyms among the options.

Answer to Question 72:

credit and stock

Credit and *stock* convey the idea of faith or trust. *Force* is close to *stock* but *credit* is closer. *Dubiety* and *progeny* have no synonyms among the options.

Answer to Question 73:

conditioned and primed

The correct *options* convey the notion that events in one country are influenced by those in another. The synonyms *habituated* and *inured* do not agree with the sense of the sentence and *recast* and *accommodated* have no synonyms among the options.

Answer to Question 74:

universals and generality

The *phrase* that *living things have in common* requires the options *universals* and *generality*. The synonyms *specifics* and *details* do not go well with *have in common* nor do *circumscription* and *precision*.

Answer to Question 75:

eerie and uncanny

Eerie and *uncanny* agree with the overall tone of the sentence and especially the word *frightened*. *Interesting* and *striking* on the one hand, and *curious* and *surprising*, on the other, suggest a more neutral emotional response not in keeping with the sentence.

Answer to Question 76:

means and mechanism

The *correct* options are the only synonyms in the list. Do not be misled by median vs. medium.

Answer to Question 77:

novel and original

While *innovative* and *ingenious* fit fairly well in the sentence, *novel* and *original* fit better because the *emphasis* of the sentence is on new discoveries, not on whether the discoveries are *innovative* or *ingenious*. *Germinal* and *primal* have to do with the beginnings of things, and do not fit well in the sentence.

Answer to Question 78:

dissemination and propagation

Dissemination and *propagation* refer to a purposeful spreading of ideas, while *dispersal* and *dissipation* refer to *random* scattering. *Collection* and *concentration* do not work as synonyms in the sentence.

Answer to Question 79:

evinced and substantiated

The *correct* options indicate that Pasteur showed that spontaneous generation could not occur. *Divulged* and *publicized* don't fit well with *definitively*, and *adduced* and *disconfirmed* have no synonyms in the options.

Answer to Question 80:

significance and worth

Preeminence, prominence, and *renown* refer to the visibility of something and *substantiveness* refers to the reality of something. Since the sentence indicates that in the 1860's, Mendel's work was important, but not famous, that is, not preeminent, prominent or renowned; the correct options are the best choices.

Answer to Question 81:

Nebulous and Dubious

It is clear from the sentence structure that the missing word is meant to contrast with the second half of the sentence; we are told that *concrete business plans* lead to success, and we are looking for something that will *do you little good*. If you know the meanings of the answer choice, you should be able to eliminate a few of them relying solely on common sense. *Sagacious* means *wise*, and surely wise dreams stand a good chance of becoming a reality. *Cogent* means *convincing* and is usually used to describe arguments. Your best clue, however, is the use of the word *concrete* - whatever answers we pick must mean something like hazy or indistinct. *Craven* means *cowardly*, and *fervid* means *ardent* or *intense* - *eliminate* them. This leaves you with *nebulous* and *dubious*, which mean *indistinct* and *questionable*, respectively.

Answer to Question 82:

morbid and saturnine

This sentence focuses on the kind of writing Poe is known for; *horror, mystery,* and *crumbling mansions* are all fairly dark words, so the description probably means something like *frightening* or *grim*. Even if you are unsure of their exact meanings, you might now that *whimsical* and *droll* have positive connotations, and can therefore eliminate them. *Esoteric* describes something that appeals to a very narrow range of people - not something that is a *perennial favorite* - so you can eliminate it. *Sublime* means *elevated* or *lofty*, and while it is not inconceivable that an author's work might be described as *sublime, ask* yourself if the word really has anything to do with the rest of the sentence - it doesn't. The correct answers are *morbid* and *saturnine*, which mean *gruesome* and *gloomy*.

Answer to Question 83:

dogged and indefatigable

The gist of this sentence seems to be that Shackleton overcame many obstacles in order to keep his team safe, so the answer probably has to do with perseverance. *Desultory* means *inconsistent* - almost the opposite of what we need. *Phlegmatic* means *apathetic* or *sluggish* - another quality that would do a person little good in an emergency. *Erudite* and *preternatural* mean *learned* and *extraordinary* or *unnatural*. Neither of these has very much to do with the rest of the sentence, but if you are tempted to answer *preternatural*, check to see if there is another word with a similar meaning (there isn't). You are left with *dogged* and *indefatigable*, which mean *persistent* or *tenacious* and untiring.

Answer to Question 84:

clandestine and illicit

If you don't know the story of King Arthur, you should at least be able to gather from the sentence that Lancelot and Guinevere's relationship is adulterous and that it must have been a secret at one point if Mordred is able to *expose* it. Look at the answer choices and see if there is a word that might make sense in the context of the sentence. *Noisome* means *offensive* or *noxious* and usually describes a smell; there is no evidence *suggesting* that the writer of the sentence has such a strongly negative opinion on the subject, but even if you were tempted to pick this as your answer, the fact that there are no near-synonyms for it among the other answers should dissuade you. Do not confuse *discrete* with *discreet* - *discrete* means *discontinuous* or *distinct* and doesn't make sense in this context. *Inchoate* means *rudimentary* and, again, does not have much to do with the rest of the sentence. *Gauche* means something like *tactless*; this should strike you as an understatement in the context of the sentence, but if it doesn't, you will probably realize that the other remaining answers - *illicit* and *clandestine* - have much more similar meanings and are a better fit.

Answer to Question 85:

portent and harbinger

If scientists *concerned about climate change* find extreme weather *alarming*, they probably see it as an early effect of climate change, so the missing word must mean something like *preview* or *sign*. If the current bad weather were the *antithesis* of what is to come, there would be little reason for alarm, because *antithesis* means the *direct opposite*. *Vagary* means *an unpredictable event* or *action*. It is often pluralized, but if you don't know this, use common sense; scientists think the current weather is part of a predictable process. *Enigma* and *imbroglio* mean a *puzzle* and a *misunderstanding* or *confusing situation*, neither of which is relevant in this context. This leaves you with *portent* and *harbinger*, which both mean *omen*.

Answer to Question 86:

gregarious and extroverted

Notice that the sentence is discussing the social behaviors of chimpanzees; you have probably seen *indigenous* used to describe animals, but it means *native to a particular region* and has nothing to do with the rest of the sentence. The sentence tells us that chimpanzees live in large groups and interact with each other, so the answer probably has something to do with how sociable they are. *Ascetic*, which means *austere*, clearly does not work. *Peripatetic* means *wandering* or *itinerant*; the sentence says nothing about the movements of chimpanzees, so you can eliminate it. *Redoubtable* means *formidable* or *fearsome* and, again, does not have much to do with the sentence as a whole. *Gregarious* and *extroverted*, however, both mean something like *sociable*, and are therefore the correct answers.

Answer to Question 87:

equivocated and prevaricated

The sentence gives us reason to believe that the suspect is not being truthful; he *spins* a story but does not back it up with evidence. The missing word probably has to do with dishonesty. Although you might associate *suspects* with transgressing, do not be taken in; this particular sentence has nothing to do with the suspect breaking a law. You might also think a suspect would *fawn* - that is, act in a servile manner - towards his interrogators, but the sentence is not about this, and you can eliminate it. *To palpitate* means to *flutter* or *beat rapidly* and often describes a heartbeat. *To quaff* means to *drink deeply*. This leaves you with *equivocated* and *prevaricated*, which have very similar meanings; both have to do with speaking ambiguously or hedging in order to hide the truth.

Answer to Question 88:

latent and quiescent

If the disease may never become *active*, the missing word must mean something like *inactive*. Do not be fooled into thinking *restive* means *at rest*; its real meaning is *restless*, and is nearly the opposite of what you want. *Inimical* means *harmful*, which diseases certainly are, but it doesn't describe a disease that is currently inactive. *Fulsome* means *offensive* or *disgusting* - eliminate it. *Discreet* means *prudent* and is used to describe people or their actions and behavior. This leaves you with *latent* and *quiescent* - the former means *present but not visible* and the *latter* means *quiet* or *inactive*.

Answer to Question 89:

flouted and spurned

If women who had children out of wedlock were treated as outcasts, their actions were most likely seen as a violation of conventional social standards, so the missing word should mean something like *ignored* or *broke with*. *To condone* means *to pardon* or *approve* - nearly the opposite of what we want. *To extol* can be eliminated for similar reasons; it means *to praise*. *Wafted* and *Disinterred* have little to do with the sentence; the *former* means *to carry lightly* or *to float*, and the *latter* means to *exhume* or *unearth*. *Flouted* and *spurned* are the correct choices; both have to do with ignoring or rejecting something.

Answer to Question 90:

repudiate and abjure

You have probably already heard of Galileo's appearance before the Inquisition, but if you haven't, this sentence informs you that he got into trouble with the Church for claiming that the sun was the center of the solar system. Clearly the *Church leaders* mentioned in the sentence did not approve of his *beliefs*. This should help you to rule out beatify; the Church would hardly have *officially blessed* Galileo's ideas. *Foment* means *to foster* or *to stir up*, and because the Church was interested in squashing Galileo's beliefs, not encouraging them, you can eliminate this. *Preclude* means *to prevent*, and *accrue* means *to accumulate* - eliminate them. The correct answers are *repudiate* and *abjure*, which mean *to renounce* or *to reject*.

Answer to Question 91:

shrewd and adroit

The sentence suggests that while small businesses can get tax breaks, it may require a bit more effort, because they lack the resources available to larger companies. Their *management* probably needs to be skillful and determined, and we want a word that reflects this. *Meretricious* definitely does not work; it means *showy* or *based on pretense*, and we need a word that describes genuinely skillful management. *Dogmatic* means *stubborn* or *dictatorial*, and implies an arbitrary adherence to a set of rules (*dogma*); it has a negative connotation, and we are looking for a positive word. *Supine* and *ineluctable* simply are not relevant to the sentence; the former means *lying on one's back* and the latter means *certain* or *inescapable*. *Shrewd* (*astute*) and *adroit* (*skillful*) are the best answers.

Answer to Question 92:

castigated and upbraided

Most mothers would be upset to learn that their child has been stealing, so the correct answer likely reflects displeasure - *scolded*, perhaps, or something similar to it. *To placate* means *to pacify* or *appease*; a son caught stealing might try to placate his mother, but the mother probably has little interest in calming her son down. You may confuse *descry* with *decry*, but the former actually means *to discern* or *see*, which has nothing to do with the rest of the sentence - eliminate it. The son might be *flustered* (*upset* or *confused*) by his mother's criticism, but her primary goal is probably not to upset him but rather to teach him a lesson, so you can eliminate this answer. *To vilify* means *to disparage* or *to speak ill of*; it is a strong word, and it is hard to imagine a mother doing this to her son, no matter how upset she is. This leaves you with *castigated* and *upbraided*, which both mean *scolded* or *reprimanded*.

Answer to Question 93:

fetid and noisome

As the sentence itself states, a plant named after a corpse probably has a fairly bad odor. You might be tempted to pick *florid* simply because it looks as if it has something to do with flowers (which it does - think *floral*), but it means *ruddy* or *ornate*, neither of which works particularly well as a description of an odor. *Effete* and *pusillanimous* both have negative connotations, but neither fits into this sentence; the former means *worn out* or *degenerate*, and the latter means *cowardly*. *Hirsute* means *hairy* and is similarly out of place in this context. You are left with *fetid* and *noisome*, which are both commonly used to refer to offensive odors.

Answer to Question 94:

temerity and mettle

For most peasants, the thought of saying anything at all to the Dauphin was probably somewhat daunting, so Joan of Arc must have had great self-confidence and/or courage to make such an enormous demand. *Temperance* means *self-restraint* and *recreancy* means *cowardice*. Neither of these would have gotten her very far, so you can eliminate them. *Fecklessness* means *ineffectiveness* or *laziness* and can be eliminated for similar reasons. *Paean* is wholly unrelated to the sentence; it refers to a song of joy or praise. The correct answers are *temerity* and *mettle*; the former means *boldness* (with a hint of recklessness or audacity) and the latter means *courage*.

Answer to Question 95:

benign and propitious

If you are unfamiliar with the Gulf Stream, use common sense; a warm current probably moderates what would otherwise be a cold climate (it is *northern* Europe, after all). Given this, you should be able to eliminate most of the answer choices. *Provident* means *having foresight* - not a quality we generally associate with weather of any kind. *Aseptic* is similarly out of place in this context; it means *sterile* or *free from germs*. It makes little sense as a description of weather - eliminate it. *Inveterate* means *firmly established by long continuance* and is more commonly used to describe feelings or beliefs. *Torpid* means *sluggish* and has negative connotations; it is not inconceivable that someone might describe weather this way - say, during a hot and humid summer - but before you pick it, check to make sure there are no better answers. *Benign* and *propitious*, which mean *pleasant* and *favorable,* are more in line with the probable meaning of the sentence, and are therefore the best answers.

Answer to Question 96:

mellifluous and dulcet

This sentence establishes a contrast between the *strident* sound of bagpipes and the sound of other instruments, so the missing word probably means *gentle* or *smooth. Stentorian* is commonly used to describe sounds, but it means *loud* or *resounding,* so you can eliminate it. *Lithe* means *supple* or *limber* and more commonly refers to bodies or other physical objects. *Obstreperous* means *unruly* or *boisterous* - almost the opposite of what we are looking for. *Abstruse* means *hard to understand* or *esoteric,* and makes no sense in this context; the author nowhere mentions whether certain instruments are more intellectually challenging than others. The correct answers are *mellifluous* and *dulcet,* which mean *sweetly flowing* and *melodious.*

Answer to Question 97:

quail and cower

As we all know, and as the sentence tells us, many children are afraid of thunder, so we are looking for a verb that expresses that fear. *To rebuff* generally requires an object, and in any case has little to do with this sentence; it means *to reject* or *snub.* You can eliminate *clinch,* which means *to settle something decisively,* for similar reasons; it is generally used when a question or issue has been resolved, which is not the case in this sentence. *To demur* means *to take exception* or *to object,* and again, does not make sense in this context. Only by a great stretch of the imagination are the children *objecting* to anything here, so you should eliminate this answer. *To simper* means *to smile in a silly way* or *to smirk;* it has a negative connotation that the context here does not warrant. Moreover, people who are frightened usually do not smile in any manner at all. You are left with *quail (to lose heart or courage)* and *cower (to recoil or flinch).*

Answer to Question 98:

proscriptions and prohibitions

In this question, we are looking for something that could *prevent* people from following their natural instincts - laws or rules, perhaps. *Idyll* can refer either to a kind of pastoral poem or to a pleasant event or episode, neither of which seems likely to dissuade people from anything. A *cabal* is a group of conspirators. It has a fairly specific meaning, and does not fit into this sentence; how often do you hear about the *cabals* of society? The phrase itself makes little sense, given that cabals are secretive rather than sanctioned by society. Eliminate this answer. A society prone to *vacillations (states of indecision or fluctuations)* would almost certainly be unable to exercise the kind of control Hobbes seems to have in mind, so you can eliminate this answer as well. *Dereliction* is wrong for similar reasons; it means *neglect (as in dereliction of duty)* and again, could hardly act as a deterrent. The correct answers are *proscriptions* and *prohibitions,* which both refer to a formal ban on something.

Answer to Question 99:

connoisseur and epicure

The missing word in this sentence refers to someone with *discriminating* tastes - particularly with regards to food. A *tyro* is a novice - not someone we would expect to have very developed tastes. Eliminate it. *Wag* and *virago* do not relate to the rest of the sentence; the former means *a person given to droll humor* and *the latter is a loud* and *overbearing woman.* Neither of these has anything to do with food or taste, so they are most likely not the correct answers. A *libertine* - or *dissolute man* - might enjoy food, but would probably not be particularly discriminating. This leaves you with *connoisseur* and *epicure;* the former is a *discerning judge* of the arts or food, and the latter is a *person with refined tastes, especially in food or wine.*

Answer to Question 100:

specious and fallacious

The speaker spoke well and was charming, but the audience was still dissatisfied; perhaps his claims were simply false. *Fervid* claims are characterized by intense feeling or passion; this is no way incompatible with *dazzling rhetoric and considerable charisma,* and there is no reason to believe the audience would find it off-putting. Eliminate this choice. *Picaresque* simply does not make sense in this context; it describes a specific kind of episodic narrative, often featuring a roguish hero. *Officious* means *aggressive in offering one's services* and is out of place in this sentence; *claims* are generally not officious, because they are simply statements, not offers of help. *Feckless* means *ineffective* or *lazy* - not the best choice anyway, given that it more usually describes a person, but the fact that there are no near-synonyms among the other answer choices should lead you to eliminate it. You are left with *specious* and *fallacious,* which mean, respectively, *apparently good but lacking real merit* and *logically unsound.*

Answer to Question 101:

tawdry and raffish

The word *even* should tell you that we are looking for a word that goes beyond *excessive,* and the *countless sequins* and *tassels* sound a bit flashy; we want an adjective that captures these qualities. Do not be tricked into choosing *diaphanous;* while it is often used in reference to clothing or fabric, it means *sheer* or *gauzy* - not something we would associate with heavy ornamentation. *Piquant* means *pleasantly biting* or *interesting* and does not convey any sense of excess - eliminate it. *Aberrant (departing from the norm)* does not work particularly well either; although dance costumes may differ from everyday clothing, they are hardly unheard of. *Voluble* means *talkative* and is not a word used to describe clothing. *Tawdry* and *raffish* are the correct answers; they mean *gaudy* and *flashy* or *vulgar,* respectively.

Answer to Question 102:

glut and gorge

This sentence implies that animals that hibernate do so in order to avoid having to look for food in the winter; they have to get energy from somewhere, though, so they probably eat more than usual before hibernating, and the word we choose should reflect this. *To incense* means *to anger;* using it reflexively does not make very much sense, and in any case, it would not help an animal store up energy. *To preen* means *to dress oneself smartly* or *to trim* or *dress fur* or *feathers,* and again, does not really work; if anything, preening would seem to require energy. You might think that *enervate* has something to do with gathering energy, but it actually means *to deprive of force or weaken* - eliminate it. *To recast* means *to remodel* or *to refashion;* it does not make very much sense in this sentence, unless you take it extremely figuratively and imagine the animal restructuring itself into a creature with a lower metabolism. *Glut* and *gorge* are much better choices, because both mean something like *to feed* or *fill to excess.*

Answer to Question 103:

middling and equivocal

The explanation following the semi-colon, as well as the word *only,* should tell you that the efforts have been at best partially successful. *Halcyon* means *calm* or *peaceful* and therefore is irrelevant to this sentence. *Garrulous* means excessively *talkative* and again, does not make sense here. *Ecumenical* refers to something that pertains to the entire Christian religion; it would be strange if these efforts were successful only in Christian circles. Eliminate it. *Sophomoric* means *immature,* which is more commonly used to describe people or actions than facts (i.e. the results of the *efforts* here mentioned). You are left with middling (*mediocre* or *average*) and equivocal (*questionable* or *dubious*).

Answer to Question 104:

irascible and splenetic

Someone who lashes out probably has a quick temper, so we are looking for a word that means *easily angered*. You might associate the word *recondite* with teaching or academics (it means *esoteric* or *dealing with very profound or difficult subject matter*) but it does not make sense here, where the teacher's profession is essentially unrelated to the topic of the sentence, which is her personality. *Fatuous* has an appropriately negative connotation - it means *foolish* - but there is nothing in the sentence that suggests that the teacher is dim-witted. *Stygian* means *gloomy* or *hellish*, and *turbid* means *clouded* or *confused*. They do not work particularly well as descriptions of people, so you should eliminate them. The correct answers are *irascible* and *splenetic*, which both describe someone who is easily provoked.

Answer to Question 105:

aptitude and propensity

It is clear from the context that we are looking for a word that means something like *skills*; a word implying innate aptitude would be even better, given that the ability in question is inherited. Do not be led astray by eloquence; it does indeed imply skill, but it means *the art of using language with fluency and aptness* and does not pertain to math. *Mendacity* has a negative connotation and does not work with the rest of the sentence anyway (it means *the quality of being untruthful*). You can eliminate *recidivism* for similar reasons; it means *repeated relapse* and is often used in the context of criminal activity. *Dereliction* means *neglect* and can also be ruled out. This leaves you with *aptitude* and *propensity*, both of which describe a natural skill in or inclination towards something.

Answer to Question 106:

disparate and myriad

This sentence focuses on the similarities between different cultures, but implies that there are many differences (only *certain* beliefs are shared). For this reason, you might guess (correctly) that the missing word means something like *different* or *varied*. If this does not occur to you while reading the sentence, though, don't worry; you should be able to rule out the incorrect choices based on how well they work in the sentence. *Inimitable* means *matchless* or *incapable of being copied*, which does not make very much sense in this context; surely no culture is perfect, and in any case, the sentence refers to all cultures regardless of whether or not the author deems them *matchless*. *Profligate* makes even less sense; it means *immoral* or *extravagant*. Again, there is no reason to believe that the author is speaking of only one kind of culture, so you can eliminate this choice as well. Palatial (*resembling a palace*) and *prolix* (wordy or *lengthy*) do not describe any form of culture particularly well. You are left with disparate and myriad, which work well in the sentence; the former means *dissimilar* or *distinct*, and the latter means *many* or *of a great number*.

Answer to Question 107:

fettered and constrained

The implication here is that writers and directors cannot exercise their creativity when they are forced to think about how well their movies will be received; the missing word must mean something like *burdened* or *inhibited*. *Obviated* makes no sense in this context; it means *to anticipate* and *prevent* and is generally used in the context of an event or set of circumstances. *Emaciated* means *very thin* or *wasted*. It has a negative connotation, but is probably not the best choice, unless you imagine the writers and directors being preyed upon by their concerns. In any case, it has no near synonym among the other answers, so you should be able to eliminate it. *To macerate* has a very specific meaning that clearly does apply to this sentence; it means *to soften* or *separate by steeping in a liquid*. *To satiate* means *to satisfy fully* or *in excess* and once again does not work in this sentence, which implies that the writers and directors are not satisfied. The correct answers are *fettered* and *constrained*, which both mean *restrained*.

Answer to Question 108:

disinclined and loath

For the most part, people attend universities so that they can find better jobs - usually jobs that don't require manual labor. Therefore, the missing word must mean something like *unwilling*. *Urbane* means *sophisticated* and obviously has nothing to do with factory jobs, so you can eliminate it. The only reason people might be *frantic* to accept low-paying jobs is a shortage of jobs generally, which is not the issue in question here. *Crass* and *nonplused* do not make much sense either; the former means *without refinement* or *obtuse*, and the latter means *at a loss* or *puzzled*. The best answers are *loath* (*averse* or *unwilling*) and *disinclined* (*lacking desire* or *unwilling*).

Answer to Question 109:

retards and impedes

This question requires a bit of logical thinking; if the battery is working harder but not producing more power, the cold must somehow inhibit its ability to work. *To ameliorate* clearly will not work; it means *to make better* and is the opposite of what we are looking for here. *To bedizen* (*to dress* or *adorn in a showy way*) simply makes no sense. *To vituperate* and *to pique* are also out of place; the former means *to berate* and the latter means *to excite* or *to wound* (*someone's feelings*). They are more commonly used in the context of social interactions, and do not work well in describing the speed of a chemical reaction. You are left with *retard* and *impede*, which both mean *to slow* or *to hinder*.

Answer to Question 110:

degeneracy and turpitude

Clearly, a mass murderer is not exactly a moral person. The answer probably reflects Caligula's lack of morals. *Desuetude* refers to a state of disuse; it is not the best description of someone's character. *Finesse* (*subtle skill*) and *probity* (*uprightness*) will certainly not work in this sentence. If anything, Caligula's actions reveal a complete lack of uprightness. Nor are they subtle enough to justify the use of *finesse*; a person with finesse might bend moral rules, but not so obviously ignore them. It is difficult to see what *insularity* (*pertaining to islands* or *isolated*) could have to do with the rest of the sentence; there is, for example, no indication that Caligula is following some narrow-minded moral code of his own. The best answers are *degeneracy* and *turpitude*, which mean *a state of deterioration* or *degradation* (*particularly in terms of morality*) and *depravity*, respectively.

Answer to Question 111:

ebullient and blithe

The correct answers must have something to do with *enthusiasm* and/or the ability to lift other people's spirits - *cheerful* or *optimistic*, perhaps. *Lachrymose* means *tearful* or *tending to cause tears* - the opposite of what we are looking for. *Verdant* has generally positive connotations, but it means *fresh and green* or *inexperienced* and is not the best fit in this sentence. *Edacious* means *consuming* or *voracious* and does not make sense in this context either. *Ineffable* (*incapable of being expressed*) does not work well, only because the speaker is able to describe this person's disposition (*enthusiastic*). This leaves you with *ebullient* (*overflowing with fervor or enthusiasm*) and *blithe (joyous or carefree).*

Answer to Question 112:

felicitous and expedient

This sentence deals with the scientific inaccuracy of a word, so the answer most likely means something like *accurate*. *Insouciant* means *carefree* and does not really make sense in this context - indeed, the sentence implies that scientific language is exceedingly careful. *Sententious* means *given to moralizing* or *given to pithy sayings* - neither of which are usually associated with science. *Quixotic* means *romantic* or *impulsive (think Don Quixote)* and once again doesn't work in the context of scientific language. *Admonitory* means *cautionary*; it is not out of the question that scientists might admonish us about certain issues, but this is hardly the point of scientific language, and you should eliminate it. You are left with *felicitous* and *expedient*, which mean, respectively, *well-suited* or *apt* and *fit for a particular purpose.*

Answer to Question 113:

vituperation and obloquy

The answer will complement *ill-will*, so we should look for a word with a fairly negative meaning that makes sense in the context of a divorce. *Doggerel*, a kind of lowbrow poetry, will certainly not work, given that it has no bearing on the subject of the sentence. *Indolence (idleness)* does not seem particularly likely either; it is difficult to be lazy while actively angry at someone. *Abeyance* is a temporary state of inactivity or a deferral and is similarly unsuitable in this context. *Vacillation* - or a *state of indecision* - does not fit in with ill-will either, as it would seem to imply some second thoughts or misgivings about the proceedings. This leaves you with *vituperation* and *obloquy*, which both refer to abusive and condemnatory language.

Answer to Question 114:

disconcerting and ominous

Not knowing whether a volcano is active sounds potentially dangerous and therefore worrisome, and the missing word presumably reflects this. *Inimitable* means *matchless* and has generally positive connotations - clearly not what we are looking for here. *To extenuate* means *to serve to make something seem less serious* (as in an *extenuating factor* in a court case); it does not make sense in this sentence because there is no mention of anything that requires excusing. *Trenchant* and *luculent* are also bad choices; the former means *incisive* or *effective* and the latter means *clear* or *con6vincing*. *Disconcerting* (*disturbing*) and *ominous* (*threatening* or *foreboding*) are the correct answers.

Answer to Question 115:

denigrate and disparage

Half of America's GDP is clearly a significant amount, so the answer probably means something like *overlook* or *discount*. *Lionize* is the near-opposite of what we are looking for; it means *to treat as a celebrity*. *Glean* does not make sense either; it means *to learn* or *to discover*, and if small businesses truly are important, surely we should want people to learn about it. *Broach* (*to mention for the first time*) will not work; it is usually followed by *the subject* or *the issue*, and in any case, the author of this sentence presumably wants this topic to be brought up and discussed. *To sanction* means *to authorize* or *to ratify* - a far cry from *discounting*. The best answers are denigrate (*to treat something as lacking in value*) and disparage (*to speak slightingly of something*).

Answer to Question 116:

sumptuous and ostentatious

As you can no doubt see from the description, Faberge eggs are highly ornamented and perhaps even a bit over-the-top; the correct answers will reflect this. *Ubiquitous* (*present everywhere*) definitely does not work; Faberge eggs are meant to stand out and be unique, and it is not as if we see replicas of them wherever we go. *Lugubrious*, which means *excessively sorrowful* or *melancholy*, is simply not warranted; the author never indicates that the eggs' patterns are sorrowful in any way. Someone or something that is *prudish* is *excessively proper* or *modest*, which clearly is not the case of expensive luxuries like these eggs. *Incipient* means *beginning to exist*. The phrase *incredibly incipient* designs is awkward and confusing; does it imply that the designs are in some way unfinished? If you have to struggle to make a word work in the sentence, it is almost certainly not the correct answer - eliminate *incipient*. This leaves you with *sumptuous* and *ostentatious*, which mean *entailing great expense* or *lavish* and *intended to attract notice* or *impress*, respectively.

Answer to Question 117:

volatile and frenetic

We are looking for a word that describes quick and random movement. *Turgid* makes little sense; it means *swollen* or *overblown*. It is not a particularly apt word for describing movement, and even if it were, *swollen* movement does not sound as if it would be fast. *Belligerent* does not work either; unless the author is speaking metaphorically, gas molecules - or molecules of any kind - cannot be *warlike* or *aggressively hostile*. *Irrevocable* means *unalterable* and malleable means *adaptable* - eliminate them. Clearly the particles' movements are not unalterable if they are constantly changing, and nowhere does the author imply that their movements can be influenced by humans. The correct answers are *volatile* (*unstable* or *fluctuating*) and *frenetic* (*frenzied, here used somewhat figuratively*).

Answer to Question 118:

inscrutable and enigmatic

As the list of traits should make clear, we are looking for a word that goes beyond *bizarre and fascinating*. Given this, *prosaic* - or *commonplace* - is out of the question. You might be *incredulous* (*skeptical* or *disinclined to believe*) while reading about the octopus, but it is not a good description of the octopus itself - eliminate it. *Extant* means *in existence* and does not work well in this sentence; it is in any case difficult to be *more* in existence than something else, and this alone should dissuade you from picking this as your answer. You can also reject *nascent* (*beginning to exist*); nowhere does the sentence say that the octopus is a brand-new species. The best answers are *inscrutable* (*not easily understood*) and *enigmatic* (*mysterious*).

Answer to Question 119:

evocative and doleful

The missing word here describes the name *The Trail of Tears*, rather than the event itself, so while the answer could be something like *sad*, it could also mean something like *descriptive*. *Petrous (stony)* will not work regardless. *Imperious* and *pugnacious* do not make sense either; the former means *overbearing*, and the latter means *quarrelsome*. It is generally best to avoid loaded or judgmental terms unless the issue in question is a clear-cut case of right and wrong; in this sentence, it is inaccurate and even insensitive to characterize the name as *overbearing*. *Salubrious (promoting health)* is also out of the question; it is hard to imagine what this would mean when describing a name or a word. This leaves you with *evocative*, meaning *suggestive* (*tending to evoke*), and *doleful*, meaning *sorrowful*.

Answer to Question 120:

prodigious and preternatural

As this sentence makes clear, Mozart was extremely - and anomalously - skilled; the missing word should reflect that. You might think *grandiloquent* may perhaps sound promising, but it actually means *lofty* or *pretentious*. *Pretentious* is not a word usually used to describe a skill - you simply have the skill or you don't. In any case, its negative connotations are not justified by the sentence. *Brazen* is also a negative word; it means *shameless* or *impudent*. Again, while you might display your skills in a brazen manner, it does not make sense to describe the skills themselves *as brazen*. *Refractory* (*stubborn* or *disobedient*) simply does not make sense; how can an ability be *stubborn*? *Epicurean* means *fond of* or *adapted* to luxury and generally refers to tastes rather than skills. The best answers are *prodigious* (*extraordinary* or *wonderful*) and *preternatural* (*exceptional with a hint of uncanny*).

This page is intentionally left blank

Chapter **9**

Practice Test 1

Y ou are about to begin a Practice Test. The Test has two sections. The time allotted for each section is marked at the beginning of the section. Work on one section at a time. Use a timer to keep track of the time limits for every section.

Try to take the Practice Test under real test conditions. Find a quiet place to work, and set aside enough time to complete the test without being disturbed.

At the end of the test, check your answers by referring to the Answers Key and Explanatory Answers. Pay particular attention to the questions that were answered incorrectly.

Section 1

Time: 30 minutes

20 Questions

Select one entry for the blank. Fill the blank in the way that best completes the text.

1.   After taking Prof. Wilson's class, Alex found that he had _____ chemistry - he loved the topic and quickly grasped even advanced concepts.

| an aversion to |
| an affinity for |
| an adherence to |
| a censure for |
| a forum for |

For Questions 2 to 4, select the <u>two</u> answer choices that, when used to complete the sentence, fit the meaning of the sentence as a whole <u>and</u> produce completed sentences that are alike in meaning.

2. Many organisms have symbiotic relationships with one another, but the particular nature of the long-term relationship varies depending on the organisms; in some cases, one or both of the members are harmed by the relationship while in other instances the relationship is _____ to both parties.

    A propitious

    B pusillanimous

    C fulsome

    D maudlin

    E tenuous

    F opportune

3. The wide array of diversity among the human species is observable through examining internal and external traits; externally, human diversity can be seen through the vast differences in hair color, height, eye color, and body structure present, but diversity also presents itself in less _____ ways such as blood type and disease susceptibility.

    A macroscopic

    B ocular

    C purblind

    D telescopic

    E risible

    F viscid

4.   The poetry of Robert Frost and the music of Mozart are similar in that beneath an apparently _____ surface there is a world of meaning that to some may seem inaccessible.

   A   idiosyncratic

   B   prosaic

   C   recherche

   D   unrefined

   E   unremarkable

   F   transcendent

Question 5 is based on the following passage.

It is a fact of <u>the current state of cosmology</u> that the greatest set of evidence for dark matter comes from this galactic gravitational data. Scientists have even made galactic curves describing the rotational properties of stars versus the distance from the galactic center. When the gravitational data is plotted it can be shown that only a small portion of the observed speeds are explicable by classical computations. In other words, there is <u>a scarcity of visible mass in the observed galaxies</u> to attribute the sum total of gravitational effects to visibly observable stars planets and galaxies. Thus, the simplest way to explain this galactic mystery of insufficient mass is to <u>hypothesize a non-detectable type of mass</u> known as dark matter which can be the cause for the gravitational effects.

Select only one answer choice.

5.   In the paragraph given, the three underlined portions play which of the following roles?

   Ⓐ   theorem and axioms

   Ⓑ   cause and effect

   Ⓒ   point and counterpoint

   Ⓓ   problem and solution

   Ⓔ   procedural order of events

Question 6 is based on the following passage.

Many experts are very concerned about the bee decline, known as Colony Collapse Disorder, or CCD. The notable scientist Albert Einstein once said, "If the bee disappears from the surface of the earth, man would have no more than four years to live. No more bees, no more pollination... no more men!" When he said this over fifty years ago, many people quickly dismissed it. However, it is now generally accepted that, without the bees, mankind would have a difficult time living. Many experts today agree with Einstein's prediction, or believe that mankind would not be able to survive. With most people scared of bees, or unable to see their true value, it is becoming important to spread the word before it is too late.

Select only one answer choice.

6. The author of this passage uses a quote from Albert Einstein for which of the following purposes?

   Ⓐ To show that scientists have known about the importance of bees for more than fifty years

   Ⓑ To demonstrate that, just because Einstein was highly regarded in math and physics, he was not considered an expert in biology

   Ⓒ To show that experts eventually came to agree with Einstein

   Ⓓ To use an outside authority to lend support to his position

   Ⓔ To demonstrate Einstein's ability to make accurate predictions outside of his area of expertise

For Questions 7 and 8, for each blank, select one entry from the corresponding column of choices. Fill all blanks in the way that best completes the text.

7. Rather than create energy, electrical power plants convert other forms of energy into electricity for transmission and use in homes, business, and industry. For example, fuel (i) _____ from petroleum is burned and the heat from that chemical reaction is converted via generators into electricity. Energy (ii) _____, but is never really "used up." Certain sources of energy, like coal, oil, and natural gas, may become scarce, but energy is present in many different forms, and using all of the potential energy on the planet is an impossibility.

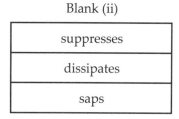

Blank (i)	Blank (ii)
cleaved	suppresses
derived	dissipates
aggregated	saps

8.   The following paper studies the intonation of native and non-native Russian speakers when reciting Blok's poem Neznakomka. After analyzing the intonation of "standard" Russian poetry (i) _____, it examines how non-native speakers consciously and sub-consciously (ii) _____ the intonation of native speakers when reading poetry. The resulting data shows that the use of rising intonation is closely mirrored among participants with a range of familiarity with Russian poetry. The author looks at cultural and societal conditions to (iii) _____ how this poetic intonation is learned.

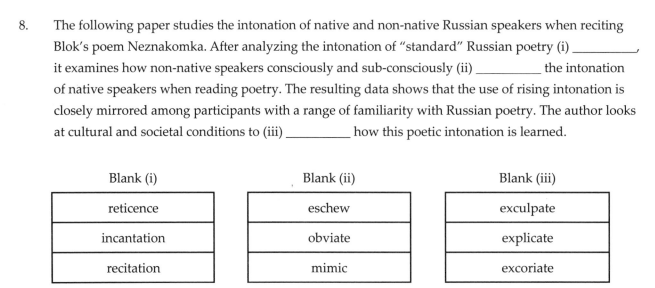

Blank (i)	Blank (ii)	Blank (iii)
reticence	eschew	exculpate
incantation	obviate	explicate
recitation	mimic	excoriate

Question 9 is based on the following passage.

A variant of the observer's <u>paradox</u> is named for the Hawthorne Works, a factory built by Western Electric, where efficiency engineers in the 1920s and 1930s were trying to determine if improved working conditions such as better lighting improved the performance of production workers. The engineers noted that when they provided better working conditions in the production line, efficiency increased. But when the engineers returned the production line to its original conditions and observed the workers, their efficiency increased again. The engineers determined that it was merely the observation of the factory workers, not the changes in the conditions in production line that increased the measured efficiency.

Select only one answer choice.

9.   In the context of this passage, which of the following is the best definition of paradox?

Ⓐ   an instance of a paradoxical phenomenon or reaction

Ⓑ   an opinion that conflicts with common belief

Ⓒ   a statement or proposition that seems self-contradictory or absurd but in reality expresses a possible truth

Ⓓ   any person, thing, or situation exhibiting an apparently contradictory nature

Ⓔ   a self-contradictory and false proposition

For each blank, select one entry from the corresponding column of choices. Fill all blanks in the way that best completes the text.

10. When the waters (i) _____, they were able to assess the devastation caused by the flooding. The town had been completely (ii) _____ - no building had escaped extensive and costly damage.

Blank (i)
diverged
abated
coalesced

Blank (ii)
expunged
decimated
assimilated

Questions 11 to 13 are based on the following passage.

Because the gravitational field created by the Moon weakens with distance from the moon, it exerts a slightly harder tidal force on the side of the Earth facing the Moon than on the opposite side. The Moon thus tends to <u>stretch</u> the Earth slightly along the line connecting the two bodies. The solid Earth deforms a bit, but ocean water, being fluid, is free to move much more in response to the tidal force, particularly horizontally. As the Earth rotates, the magnitude and direction of the tidal force at any particular point on the Earth's surface change constantly; although the ocean never reaches equilibrium - there is never time for the fluid to <u>catch up</u> to the state it would eventually reach if the tidal force were constant - the changing tidal force nonetheless causes rhythmic changes in sea surface height.

11. Select the sentence that explains why the force of the moon's gravitational pull on the Earth is different from its force on the ocean.

For Questions 12 and 13, select only one answer choice.

12. In the context of this passage, the two underlined words play which of the following roles?

Ⓐ They provide ideas that are tangential to the main idea of the passage.

Ⓑ They contribute to the progression of ideas in the passage.

Ⓒ They provide clarity and unity for the ideas expressed in the passage.

Ⓓ They help the layman to more clearly understand the effects of the moon's gravitational pull on the Earth and the oceans.

Ⓔ They provide a balanced perspective on the topic.

13.   For which of the following commercial enterprises would the information in the passage be more useful?

Ⓐ A meteorologist predicting the weather

Ⓑ A fishing fleet launching its boats

Ⓒ A scientist compiling research

Ⓓ A high school student presenting a project

Ⓔ An oil company building a drilling platform

Select one entry for the blank. Fill the blank in the way that best completes the text.

14.   The press secretary's _____ answers to probing questions about policy satisfied the journalists without actually revealing any new information.

abject
interminable
candid
adroit
diligent

For each blank, select one entry from the corresponding column of choices. Fill all blanks in the way that best completes the text.

15.   Bixby loved to (i) _____ his own virtue for supporting numerous charities, but many who knew him as the most ruthless businessman in the community believed he was merely attempting to conceal his (ii) _____.

Blank (i)
disseminate
extol
foment

Blank (ii)
avarice
magnanimity
penury

Select the two answer choices that, when used to complete the sentence, fit the meaning of the sentence as a whole and produce completed sentences that are alike in meaning.

16.   Reducing the nation's dependence on fossil fuels is an important _____ in the platforms of the major political parties.

   A   plank

   B   detriment

   C   component

   D   goal

   E   deterrent

   F   theme

Questions 17 and 18 are based on the following passage.

Vitz makes the case that selfism is simply bad science and a warped philosophy. The little clinical evidence that does exist is mostly based on empirical observations and doesn't stand the test of solid scientific problem solving. He exposes flaws in each step of the process, from stating the problem, forming and testing the hypothesis, to testing the conclusion. He also identifies several philosophical contradictions and, in some cases, actual misrepresentations. The spread of this bad science and faulty philosophy is believed by the author to have contributed to the destruction of families. Additionally, the entire recovery group mentality convinces the person with "low self-esteem" that their ills are due to trauma inflicted on them in the past. Recovery group therapy strokes the patient with self-pity thereby convincing the clients that they are victims. Once labeled, the "victim" now assumes the attitude of victimhood.

Select only one answer choice.

17.   If clinical means applying objective or standardized methods to the description, evaluation, and modification of human behavior, which of the following definitions most clearly explains the use of the word "empirical" in this passage?

   Ⓐ   pragmatic

   Ⓑ   relating to medical quackery

   Ⓒ   provable or verifiable by experience or experiment.

   Ⓓ   depending upon experience or observation alone

   Ⓔ   theoretical

Consider each of the three choices separately and select all that apply.

18.   Identify the idea in the passage that lacks any support.

     [A]   The spread of this faulty science has destroyed families.

     [B]   Evidence to support the science was gathered in a subjective manner.

     [C]   Self-pity leads to an attitude of victimhood.

Questions 19 and 20 are based on the following passage.

Though all cotton has a large carbon footprint for its cultivation and production, organic cotton is considered a more sustainable choice for fabric, as it is completely free of destructive toxic pesticides and chemical fertilizers. Many designers have begun experimenting with bamboo fibre, which absorbs greenhouse gases during its life cycle and grows quickly and plentifully without pesticides. Even with this, bamboo fabric can cause environmental harm in production due to the chemicals used to create a soft viscose from hard bamboo. Some believe hemp is one of the best choices for eco fabrics due to its ease of growth, though it remains illegal to grow in some countries. These facts make recycled, reclaimed, surplus, and vintage fabric arguably the most sustainable choice, as the raw material requires no agriculture and no manufacturing to produce.

For Questions 19 and 20, select only one answer choice.

19.   In the context of this passage, what is the best definition for the word "vintage"?

     (A) old-fashioned; dated

     (B) representative of the best and most typical

     (C) of lasting interest and importance; venerable; classic

     (D) a time of origin

     (E) a group of people or objects of the same period

20. How do the facts in this passage provide support for the position stated in the last sentence?

Ⓐ The facts list all of the other choices available, leaving only those listed in the last sentence as suitable alternatives.

Ⓑ The facts effectively recognize both points of view regarding each choice, preventing the reader from making objections to the statements.

Ⓒ The facts are based on scientific research, and, as such, provide proven support for the author's position.

Ⓓ The author uses the rhetorical technique of part-to-whole to show how all of the facts are related, establishing a solid base for his position.

Ⓔ The author uses emotionally- charged words like destructive and harm to sway the reader to his point of view.

Section 2

Time: 30 minutes

20 Questions

Question 1 is based on the following passage.

In society you will not find health, but in nature. Unless our feet at least stood in the midst of nature, all our faces would be pale and livid. Society is always diseased, and the best is the most so. There is no scent in it so wholesome as that of the pines, nor any fragrance so penetrating and restorative as the life–everlasting in high pastures. I would keep some book of natural history always by me as a sort of elixir, the reading of which should restore the tone of the system.

Select only one answer choice.

1. Which of the following, if true, would most effectively strengthen the author's argument?

    (A) Full immersion in a natural surrounding is essential for avoiding ill health.

    (B) Nature has restorative qualities that far surpass any medical treatment.

    (C) Reading about nature is an inadequate form of restoring health to the mind and body.

    (D) Every person reacts to nature in a similar way, and its benefits affect everyone in the same way regardless of personal perspective.

    (E) Thriving cities are healthier than other cities, yet their inhabitants still require the benefits that nature can provide.

Questions 2 and 3 are based on the following passage.

The idea behind the concept of cream skimming in business is that the "cream" - high value or low-cost customers, who are more profitable to serve - would be captured by some suppliers (typically by charging less than the previous higher prices, but still making a profit), leaving the more expensive or harder to service customers without the desired product or service at all or "dumping" them on some default provider, who is left with fewer of the higher value customers who, in some cases, would have provided extra revenue to subsidize or reduce the cost to service the higher-cost customers, and the loss of the higher value customers might actually require the default provider to have to raise prices to cover the lost revenue, thus making things worse.

Select only one answer choice.

2.   Consider the information in the passage and select the scenario that would be considered cream skimming.

      Ⓐ Colleges refusing to accept high-school students with low GPA's.

      Ⓑ A retail outlet conducting a private sale

      Ⓒ Health insurance companies rejecting applications from people with pre-existing conditions

      Ⓓ A company's decision to hire the handicapped

      Ⓔ A school district's freezing wages for its highest-paid employees.

Consider each of the three choices separately and select all that apply.

3.   Some states use school vouchers which allow parents to select the school they want to attend. How might this be considered cream skimming?

      Ⓐ Parents can choose to send their children to schools where all of the students are high performing.

      Ⓑ Lower performing schools are left with underachieving or learning-disabled students who may need more expensive services, putting a strain on their budgets.

      Ⓒ Removing high-achieving students from a school will reduce its success in athletic competition.

For Questions 4 and 5, for each blank, select one entry from the corresponding column of choices. Fill all blanks in the way that best completes the text.

4.   At the opera, I was surrounded by people who would not be considered members of an (i) _____ group, but they enjoyed the performance more than the sequin-clad women who came to participate in the high-society ritual. In the cheap seats there was enthusiastic applause and a lack of (ii) _____ movement compared with the fidgeting evident in the orchestra seats below. Surely this is indicative of the (iii) _____ masses' interest in listening to the opera rather than participating in a social ritual that has little to do with the music itself.

Blank (i)	Blank (ii)	Blank (iii)
elite	overwrought	turgid
opulent	tacit	impecunious
verdant	restive	torpid

5.   The first order of business in any mediation is to (i) _____ tensions between conflicting parties by projecting an aura of calm impartiality and demonstrating (ii) _____ interest in the claims of both sides without becoming overwhelmed by the dispute.

Blank (i)
mollify
diffuse
deprecate

Blank (ii)
ostensible
categorical
specious

Questions 6 to 9 are based on the following passage.

An alternative to extinction is that Neanderthals were absorbed into the Cro-Magnon population by interbreeding. This would be counter to strict versions of the Recent African Origin, since it would imply that at least part of the genome of Europeans would descend from Neanderthals, who left Africa at least 350,000 years ago.

Genetic studies indicate some form of hybridization between archaic humans and modern humans had taken place after modern humans emerged from Africa. An estimated 1 to 4 percent of the DNA in Europeans and Asians (i.e. French, Chinese and Papua probands) is non-modern, and shared with ancient Neanderthal DNA rather than with sub-Saharan Africans (i.e. Yoruba and San probands).
No evidence supporting this has been found in mitochondrial DNA analyses of modern Europeans, suggesting at least that no direct maternal line originating with Neanderthals has survived into modern times.

Jordan, in his work Neanderthal, points out that without some interbreeding, certain features on some "modern" skulls of Eastern European Cro-Magnon heritage are hard to explain. In another study, researchers have recently found in Pestera Muierilor, Romania, remains of European humans from 30 thousand years ago who possessed mostly diagnostic "modern" anatomical features, but also had distinct Neanderthal features not present in ancestral modern humans in Africa, including a large bulge at the back of the skull, a more prominent projection around the elbow joint, and a narrow socket at the shoulder joint. Analysis of one skeleton's shoulder showed these humans, like Neanderthal, did not have the full capability for throwing spears.

An analysis of a first draft of the Neanderthal genome by Richard E. Green et al. from Max Planck Institute for Evolutionary Anthropology in Leipzig, Germany released in May 2010 indicates interbreeding may have occurred. "Those of us who live outside Africa carry a little Neanderthal DNA in us," said Paabo, who led the study. "The proportion of Neanderthal-inherited genetic material is about 1 to 4 percent. It is a small but very real proportion of ancestry in non-Africans today," says Dr. David Reich of Harvard Medical School in Boston, who worked on the study. This research compared the genome of the Neanderthals to five modern humans from China, France, sub-Saharan Africa, and Papua New Guinea. The finding is that about 1 to 4 percent of the genes of the non-Africans came from Neanderthals, compared to the baseline defined by the two Africans. This indicates a gene flow from Neanderthals to modern humans, i.e., interbreeding between the two populations. Since the three non-African genomes show a similar proportion of Neanderthal sequences, the interbreeding must have occurred early in the migration of modern humans out of Africa, perhaps in the Middle East. No evidence for gene flow in the direction from modern humans to Neanderthals was found. The latter result would not be unexpected if contact occurred between a small colonizing population of modern humans and a much larger resident population of Neanderthals. A very limited amount of interbreeding could explain the findings, if it occurred early enough in the colonization process.

6. Select the sentence that supports a possible argument that the physical characteristics of Neanderthals made it unlikely that they were hunters.

Consider each of the three choices separately and select all that apply.

7. The author of the passage provides the information about the DNA results primarily in order to accomplish which of the following?

   A   Proving that no direct maternal link to Neanderthals exists today

   B   Supplying an alternative theory to extinction as the cause of the disappearance of the Neanderthals

   C   Providing an example of a research model

For Questions 8 and 9, select only one answer choice.

8. Consider the structure of the entire passage and decide which of the following is a major weakness in paragraph 3.

   Ⓐ The information is inconsistent with the information in the remainder of the passage.

   Ⓑ It is irrelevant to the purpose of the passage.

   Ⓒ The ideas in it are inadequately developed.

   Ⓓ It interrupts the progression of ideas.

   Ⓔ It fails to provide any clarification of the topic.

9. Based on the information in the passage, which of the following in addition to DNA provides proof of Neanderthal influence on modern European populations?

    Ⓐ The discovery of Neanderthal DNA in Asian populations

    Ⓑ The rise of Cro-Magnon populations

    Ⓒ Physical remains found in Romania

    Ⓓ The lack of gene flow from modern humans in the direction of Neanderthal populations

    Ⓔ The diet of Middle Eastern populations

For Questions 10 to 13, select the two answer choices that, when used to complete the sentence, fit the meaning of the sentence as a whole and produce completed sentences that are alike in meaning.

10. In many ancient cultures, comets were infamous _____ of doom.

    Ⓐ foreseers

    Ⓑ oracles

    Ⓒ improvidences

    Ⓓ harbingers

    Ⓔ omens

    Ⓕ outriders

11. Rembrandt was extremely _____; his paintings are so lifelike that many say they feel that the people in his portraits are watching them.

    Ⓐ dexterous

    Ⓑ conventional

    Ⓒ adroit

    Ⓓ ineffectual

    Ⓔ feckless

    Ⓕ beneficial

12. Each atom's position in a molecule is _____ by the nature of the chemical bonds attaching it to other atoms in the molecule.

    A governed

    B conjectured

    C negotiated

    D prefigured

    E influenced

    F determined

13. _____ the laws governing a given system is facilitated by considering the energy and entropy of the system.

    A Assimilating

    B Articulating

    C Describing

    D Comprehending

    E Uncovering

    F Understanding

Select one entry for the blank. Fill the blank in the way that best completes the text.

14. I found the novel's hero _____ - he seemed like a dull mixture of literary cliches, almost totally devoid of life and originality.

desultory
recondite
insipid
variegated
venal

For each blank, select one entry from the corresponding column of choices. Fill all blanks in the way that best completes the text.

15.   David loved to (i) _____ his knowledge of mathematics, even going so far as to offer tutoring to other students. Despite this, his grasp of the field was actually quite (ii) _____ and he was often unable to recall important rules or solve difficult problems.

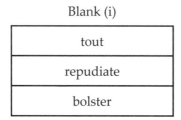

Blank (i)	Blank (ii)
tout	brazen
repudiate	tenuous
bolster	didactic

For Questions 16 and 17, select one entry for the blank. Fill the blank in the way that best completes the text.

16.   The atmosphere at the party was _____; everyone was sociable and in good spirits.

dour
convivial
frenetic
quotidian
placid

17.   The works of many modern composers can be very difficult for the untrained listener to appreciate or enjoy; they are more concerned with _____ music theory than with beauty or accessibility.

plausible
esoteric
versatile
tractable
disconcerting

Questions 18 to 20 are based on the following passage.

Edward III (1312–1377) was king of England from 1327 until his death, and is noted for his military success. Restoring royal authority after the disastrous reign of his father, Edward II, Edward III went on to transform the Kingdom of England into one of the most formidable military powers in Europe. His reign saw vital developments in legislation and government - in particular the evolution of the English parliament - as well as the ravages of the Black Death. Edward was crowned at the age of fourteen, following the deposition of his father. When he was only seventeen years old, he led a coup against his regent, Roger Mortimer, and began his personal reign. After a successful campaign in Scotland in 1333, he declared himself rightful heir to the French throne in 1337, starting what would become known as the Hundred Years' War.

For Questions 18 to 20, select only one answer choice.

18.   In the context of this passage, which of the following best describes the function of Roger Mortimer

     (A)   He served as the guardian of Edward III.

     (B)   He was the leader of the parliament.

     (C)   He was responsible for deposing Edward II.

     (D)   He ruled the country.

     (E)   He wrote important pieces of legislation.

19.   Based on the information in the passage, which of the following is likely a characteristic of the reign of Edward II?

     (A)   Lack of effective leadership

     (B)   Repression of the citizenry

     (C)   Failure to expand the British Empire

     (D)   Failure to prevent the Black Plague

     (E)   Living in debauchery

20.   Considering that the Hundred Years War was being waged during the last forty years of Edward III's life and reign, which of the following might be an accurate statement?

    Ⓐ   The number and scope of King Edward's military successes may have reduced or weakened his troops sufficiently to prevent a quick closure to the war with France.

    Ⓑ   The French military had sufficient numbers of troops and weapons to hold off the English for a protracted amount of time.

    Ⓒ   Because wartime is generally a time of prosperity, Edward deliberately prolonged the war in order to fill the coffers of the royal treasury

    Ⓓ   Rebels from Scotland provided the French with secret information to aid their cause.

    Ⓔ   His father, Edward II, was so hated by the French that they were determined to prevent his son's victory.

Answer Key

Section 1

1. an affinity for

2. A. propitious
   F. opportune

3. A. macroscopic
   B. ocular

4. B. prosaic
   E. unremarkable

5. B. cause and effect
   D. To use an outside authority to lend support to his position

6. (i) derived
   (ii) dissipates

7. (i) recitation
   (ii) mimic
   (iii) explicate

8. D. any person, thing, or situation exhibiting an apparently contradictory nature

9. (i) abated
   (ii) decimated

10. The solid Earth deforms a bit, but ocean water, being fluid, is free to move much more in response to the tidal force, particularly horizontally.

11. D. They help the layman to more clearly understand the effects of the moon's gravitational pull on the Earth and the oceans.

12. B. A fishing fleet launching its boats

13. adroit

14. (i) extol
    (ii) avarice

15. A. plank
    C. component

16. C. provable or verifiable by experience or experiment

17. B. Evidence to support the science was gathered in a subjective manner

18. C. Self-pity leads to an attitude of victimhood

19. A. old-fashioned; dated

20. B. The facts effectively recognize both points of view regarding each choice, preventing the reader from making objections to the statements.

Section 2

1.   B. Nature has restorative qualities that far surpass any medical treatment.

2.   C. Health insurance companies rejecting applications from people with pre-existing conditions

3.   B. Lower performing schools are left with underachieving or learning-disabled students who may need more expensive services, putting a strain on their budgets.

4.   (i) elite
     (ii) restive
     (iii) impecunious

5.   (i) mollify
     (ii) categorical

6.   Analysis of one skeleton's shoulder showed these humans, like Neanderthal, did not have the full capability for throwing spears.

7.   B. Supplying an alternative theory to extinction as the cause of the disappearance of the Neanderthals

8.   C. The ideas in it are inadequately developed.

9.   C. Physical remains found in Romania

10. D. harbingers
     E. omens

11. A. dexterous
     C. adroit

12. A. governed
     F. determined

13. D. Comprehending
     F. Understanding

14. insipid

15. (i) tout
     (ii) tenuous

16. convivial

17. esoteric

18. D. He ruled the country.

19. A. Lack of effective leadership

20. A. The number and scope of King Edward's military successes may have reduced or weakened his troops sufficiently to prevent a quick closure to the war with France.

Explanatory Answers

Section 1

Answer to Question 1:

The best choice is "affinity" since the second clause indicates that Alex both liked chemistry, and had a natural aptitude for it.

Topic: Everyday Topics

Answer to Question 2:

The question stem sets up a pair of opposites. Some organisms are harmed by the relationship while others are the opposite of harmed. The correct answer will have a similar meaning to helpful or beneficial. Choice(B)-pusillanimous (meaning lacking in courage) and Choice (E)-tenuous (meaning very thin or lacking substance) are off-topic for the sentence. Choice(C)-fulsome (meaning excessively ingratiating) and Choice (D)-maudlin (meaning tearfully sentimental) have somewhat similar meanings but are not relevant to the question stem. The correct answers are (A)propitious – meaning presenting favorable circumstances and Choice(F)-opportune (meaning suitable or advantageous for a particular purpose).

Topic: Everyday Topics

Answer to Question 3:

Human diversity reveals itself in different ways. Some aspects of human diversity can be seen on the outside, but humans can also be in diverse in ways than visible ones. Therefore, we can deduce that the correct answer will create the phrase "less visible" in the question stem. Choice (C)-purblind (meaning having greatly reduced vision) and Choice (D)-telescopic (meaning visible with a telescope) both relate to vision but have the improper connotations for the sentence: both have to do with the act of seeing something rather than observing. Choice(E)-risible (meaning arousing or provoking laughter) and Choice (F)- viscid (meaning having the sticky properties of an adhesive) are off-topic for this sentence. The correct answers are (A) macroscopic – meaning visible to the naked eye and (B) ocular – meaning visible.

Topic: Biological Science

Answer to Question 4:

The correct options refer to the unimposing surface of the poetry and music of the individuals refers to and agrees with the contrast implied in the sentence between what appears on the surface and what is present beneath the surface. Recherche and transcendent do not contrast surface and the underlying reality and so do not agree with the sense of the sentence. Unrefined could be seen as similar to the correct options, but the correct options do not imply a lack of refinement. Idiosyncratic has no synonyms among the options.

Topic: Arts and Humanities

Answer to Question 5:

As a result of the current state of cosmology and the scarcity of visible mass in the observed galaxies, scientists have resorted to creating a hypothesis about a non-detectable type of mass. In other words, the cause of classical computation's failure to explain all of the data is caused by the current state of cosmology and further complicated by the scarcity of visible mass. The effect is the creation of a hypothesis to explain the gravitational effects.

The best choice is B. Because there is no argument, there is no point and counterpoint. There is a problem with explaining the gravitational effects, but a hypothesis is not a solution. A procedural order of events would most likely be used when explaining how to do something. A theorem is a mathematical statement whose truth can be proved on the basis of a given set of axioms or assumptions.

Topic: Physical Science

Answer to Question 6:

Although lacking strong conviction, this brief passage is persuasive in nature. In the last sentence, the author tells the reader that it is important to spread the word before it is too late. Because Albert Einstein is universally recognized as a great scientist, "dropping" his name into the piece is an effective strategy for adding weight to the author's claim that the collapse of bee colonies is a legitimate concern. The reader is likely to think," Well, if Einstein says so, it must be true." D is the best choice. The author doesn't need to use the Einstein quote to show that knowledge of the bees' importance is more than fifty years old, nor does proving that Einstein is not an expert in biology add anything to his position. While it is appropriate to show that the experts eventually agreed with Einstein, that is not the original purpose for including his words. In this context, there is no need to demonstrate Einstein's predictive abilities. The best choice is D.

Topic: Biological Science

Answer to Question 7:

Derived is correct because it refers to any fuel product derived from petroleum including gasoline, fuel oil, etc. Fuel is not aggregated or combined into a collection. Something is cleaved when it is cut from a whole making it an incorrect choice.

To dissipate is to spread out and gradually become less and less concentrated, until it seems not to exist. To suppress is to prevent energy from being expressed. That which saps energy gradually diminishes the supply. The key to this question is the idea that energy is never really "used up." Therefore, it continues to exist, it is only widely dissipated.

Topic: Physical Science

Answer to Question 8:

The text is about people reading poetry aloud, or reciting. Incantation has a similar meaning, but is used almost exclusively for reading or chanting spells and magical words. If we keep reading past the second blank, we discover that the data shows that all the participants "mirror" each other. Therefore, we need a word that means that all the speakers use the same intonation. Mimic, or copy, is the only word that conveys this meaning. Looking at the last three choices, exculpate (to clear from blame), explicate (to explain in detail), and excoriate (to criticize), it is clear that the only logical choice is explicate.

Topic: Arts and Humanities

Answer to Question 9:

The correct answer is D. The example of the factory workers does not include an opinion, a statement, or a proposition; therefore, neither B, C, nor E can be correct. In the case of this passage, there was no paradoxical phenomenon or reaction; there was a paradoxical outcome. A is not the best choice. Because the situation of the factory workers exhibited contradictions in the results of improvements made and removed, D is the best choice of answer.

Topic: Social Science

Answer to Question 10:

When the waters abated, they were able to assess the devastation caused by the flooding. The town had been completely decimated - no building had escaped extensive and costly damage. Flood damage can only be fully gauged after the flood has receded, so the best choice for blank one is "abated". The second sentence indicates that the town had suffered severe damage during the flooding - in other words, it was "decimated".

Topic: Everyday Topics

Answer to Question 11:

The correct answer is "The solid Earth deforms a bit, but ocean water, being fluid, is free to move much more in response to the tidal force, particularly horizontally. "Because the earth is solid and, therefore, more rigid, it has less flexibility in its reaction to the moon's gravitational pull. The fluid water is able to react with more flexibility to the moon's gravitational pull.

Topic: Physical Science

Answer to Question 12:

The best choice is D. The author of the passage has used terms that help the average reader of the text to understand what happens as the moon exerts its gravitational pull on the Earth. In the case of the phrase, "catch up", the author is actually explaining the idea of equilibrium. A is incorrect for two reasons: the words do not express ideas and they are not tangential to the meaning of the passage. The progression of ideas in the passage is logical and is not aided by the use of these two words, eliminating B. They may provide clarity, but they do not unify the ideas in the passage; that function would be served by transitions. C is not the best choice. Balance occurs when more than one idea is presented in an equal manner. The passage has only one idea, so a balanced perspective is not one of the author's goals. E is not the correct choice.

Topic: Physical Science

Answer to Question 13:

Neither a meteorologist, a scientist, nor a student would be likely engaging in a commercial enterprise. Choices A, C, and D can be eliminated. An oil company is a commercial enterprise, but the construction of a drilling platform takes a considerable amount of time to complete, so the cycle of tides would have no effect on the prolonged construction. E is not the best answer. A fishing fleet relies on daily reports of high and low tides to time the launching of its boats. That timing is affected by the position of the earth relative to the moon. B is the best answer.

Topic: Physical Science

Answer to Question 14:

The press secretary's adroit answers to probing questions about policy satisfied the journalists without actually revealing any new information

The sentence suggests that the press secretary managed to satisfy questions about the policy without actually giving away any secrets. In other words, he answered the questions skillfully or "adroitly".

Topic: Everyday Topics

Answer to Question 15:

Bixby loved to extol his own virtue for supporting numerous charities, but many who knew him as the most ruthless businessman in the community believed he was merely attempting to conceal his avarice.

The sentence suggests a contrast between the way people perceive Bixby, and the way he wants people to perceive him. The only choice that makes sense for the first blank is "extol". The second clause tells us that Bixby is a ruthless businessman, and that he is thought to have a quality that contrasts with the virtue that he tries to project, so the best choice for blank two is "avarice", which is usually regarded as a vice rather than a virtue.

Topic: Everyday Topics

Answer to Question 16:

A plank in a campaign is a position that a political party takes on an issue. The plank becomes part of the campaign and is thus a component of the platform. Theme fits the sentence well, but as used in the sentence, plank and component refer to something integral to the platform, not something that could be incidental. The negative detriment and deterrent fit poorly in the sentence because a positive or neutral term is plainly needed. Goal cannot be right because a goal is something one is trying to achieve. The goal of a campaign is to win the election. A component or plank of a platform cannot be its goal.

Topic: Social Science

Answer to Question 17:

The passage states that the clinical evidence that exists is based largely on empirical observation, so the reader might be led to select D as the correct answer. However, the author goes on to criticize the steps taken to arrive at the empirical data and should lead the reader to the conclusion that experiments were performed. The correct answer is C. The author reveals that he examined each step of the process and proceeded to list the elements of the experiment conducted concerning selfism. C is the only choice that has the word experiment in the definition. Pragmatic means practical and does not suit the context of this passage, so A is incorrect. Quackery is akin to charlatanism or fakery. He was using legitimate techniques, so B does not apply. These techniques also eliminate D as a correct choice. He was not being merely theoretical, either. E is not the correct choice.

Topic: Arts and Humanities

Answer to Question 18:

Evidence in this brief passage is scanty for any of the ideas presented, however, there is some development of the ideas expressed in choices B and C. Choice A, according to the passage, is simply the author's opinion, and nothing else in the passage supports it.

Topic: Arts and Humanities

Answer to Question 19:

The best choice is A. Vintage fabric is basically fabric that was designed and manufactured in an earlier time. It may be representative of the best, choice B, only if it represented, for example, the most successful creations of a renowned designer. In that case, it may also be of lasting importance or classic, as in choice C. Choice D generally refers to a product that is distinguished from others like it by the year or era in which it was produced. This would apply to fabric if a specific era were identified such as the late 1960's and early 1970's – 70's vintage tie-dye. They are wines of last season's vintage would be an example of choice E.

Topic: Everyday Topics

Answer to Question 20:

The best answer is B. When attempting to persuade an audience, it is important to recognize the opposition's point of view. The reader is less likely to be formulating objections instead of paying attention to the author's argument. There likely is scientific evidence to support the harmful results of using cotton and bamboo to make fabric, but it is not the technique that strengthens the author's position. There are emotionally-charged words in the passage, but the author is not using that appeal to sell his position. The argument is logically laid out.

Topic: Everyday Topics

Section 2

Answer to Question 1:

The correct answer is (B).

(B) is the correct answer. The author states that people would not be healthy "unless [their] feet at least stood in the midst of nature" and goes on to say that "society is always diseased". By avoiding any mention of the possibility of relying on doctors and medicine to enjoy good health without the aid of nature, the author rests his argument on the power of nature alone, as choice (B) states.

(A) is incorrect in identifying 'full immersion' as the required dose for curing ill health through exposure to nature; by explaining the benefits of simply reading about nature, the author demonstrates how even a small, indirect dose of nature is beneficial.

(C) is also incorrect, as the author feels that reading about nature is indeed adequate, saying that doing so "should restore the tone of the system".

Choice (D) incorrectly states that everyone reacts to nature similarly, which refutes the author's claim that "to the sick, indeed, nature is sick, but to the well, a fountain of health". In this way, the author differentiates between the ways that people can view nature depending on what they expect to see.

In making the claim that "society is always diseased, and the best is the most so", the author says that the best societies have the most disease, thus refuting choice (E) which says that better cities have less disease.

Topic: Arts and Humanities

Answer to Question 2:

The best choice is C. Insurance companies reject applicants with pre-existing conditions because the cost-to-benefit ratio is too small or, sometimes, nonexistent. They must use the premiums from healthy subscribers to cover their claims, thus reducing the level of profit to the company. Colleges do accept the best students from the pool of applicants. They do want the "cream of the crop". However, it does not benefit them financially to do so, since the cost of educating each student is the same. Even though a retail store may conduct a private sale, they are still reducing the prices on their goods, obtaining no financial benefit. A company's decision to hire the handicapped may have long-term benefits, but, initially, may cost the company money in training and physical accommodations. A school district's decision to freeze wages at the highest levels may simply be a cost-saving measure. If those employees leave to seek work elsewhere, the district may benefit from being able to higher lower-cost applicants, but that is not guaranteed.

Topic: Business

Answer to Question 3:

Choices A and C might happen. Choice A fails to show how this is cream skimming. Choice C is not necessarily true. That school may still have great athletes. The best choice is B. It provides a reason why this school is affected by cream skimming.

Topic: Business

Answer to Question 4:

In order to fill in the first blank, you need to read the rest of the passage to discover that the author is talking about sitting in "the cheap seats" compared with the "high-society" members sitting in expensive orchestra seats. Thus the first blank must be about a group that is not part of the wealthy class. An elite group is high class or selective, and therefore A works best in this context. Opulent (luxurious, plentiful) is similar in meaning, but elite captures all the important facets of not just wealth but exclusion. The second blank is a comparison between fidgeting and a lack of some kind of movement. Restive movement (impatient or nervous) is very similar to fidgeting and therefore makes the contrast parallel. The final blank is asking for a description of the group the author is sitting with. Before they were described as not the elite or high-society. Impecunious means poor and therefore is the correct answer.

Topic: Arts and Humanities

Answer to Question 5:

Blank (i): Correct Answer A

Candidates must refrain from jumping to option B, thinking diffuse (or scattered) means defuse, or mollify. Mollify (A), to soften or mitigate, makes sense in the context of the sentence and is the correct answer. Option C must be eliminated because to deprecate, or earnestly express disapproval of the tensions between the two parties would clearly not help in any mediation.

Blank (ii): Correct Answer E

Expressing ostensible or a mere outward show of appearance would likely seem false and do little to promote the mediation process, hence D can be eliminated. Categorical (E) or absolute interest would demonstrate sincerity and promote mediation or a structured process to achieve agreement, making E the correct answer. Specious (F) interest, on the other hand, would be misleading or duplicitous, so this option must be eliminated.

Topic: Business

Answer to Question 6:

Analysis of one skeleton's shoulder showed these humans, like Neanderthal, did not have the full capability for throwing spears.

Although Neanderthals could have used other means to hunt, their anatomy disallowing for the ability to throw a spear could be used to support an argument that they did not hunt.

Topic: Biological Science

Answer to Question 7:

The correct choice is B. The passage does state the information in choice A, but it is not the primary focus of the passage. The author also reveals how the research was done to show that populations outside of Africa carry some Neanderthal DNA, but the purpose is to support the first sentence of the passage, an alternative to the extinction theory, thus eliminating C and supporting B as the answer.

Topic: Biological Science

Answer to Question 8:

The correct answer is C. The information in this brief paragraph does relate to the purpose of the passage stated in the first sentence of the passage, eliminating A as the correct choice. It is also relevant to the purpose of the passage, so B is not the correct choice. It does not interrupt the progression of ideas because it follows another paragraph about genetic information, so D is not the correct choice. Although the information is brief, it does help to clarify the author's premise, eliminating E as the correct choice. If one compares the depth of the information to that of paragraph 5, it comes up short, making C the correct choice.

Topic: Biological Science

Answer to Question 9:

The presence of Neanderthal DNA in Asian populations is not support for its existence in European populations, even though they likely resulted from the same migration out of Africa, so A is not the correct choice. The existence of Cro-Magnon humans is not, in itself, support for the idea, eliminating B as the correct choice. The lack of gene flow from modern to Neanderthal populations is simply another outcome of the research; D is not the best choice. The diet of Middle Eastern populations is largely a result of the food available in that region and does not provide support for the idea. E is incorrect. The passage provides examples from discovery of remains in Romania that supports the idea of Neanderthal influence on modern populations, making C the correct choice.

Topic: Biological Science

Answer to Question 10:

Answers: D and E. The only possible answers are harbingers and omens. Improvidence means to not foresee future events whereas foreseers and oracles are people that tell the future. The word outrider is used to describe a mounted attendant or person who clears the way for vehicle. Harbingers and omens are warnings or indicators of future events.

Topic: Everyday Topics

Answer to Question 11:

Answers: A and C. In the sentence, it is mentioned that Rembrandt's paintings seem to be alive, an effect that only a very talented or skillful artist could achieve. Adroit and dexterous both mean very skillful. Conventional means traditional and beneficial would not complete the sentence properly because we don't know if his paintings benefited anybody. Feckless is not a good word option because we don't know if Rembrandt was irresponsible or not from the sentence and ineffectual means to not produce the proper effect which would not make sense in the above sentence.

Topic: Arts and Humanities

Answer to Question 12:

Governed and determined have the sense of dictate, and both terms indicate a stronger affect that influenced. The other choices have no synonyms among the options and thus cannot be correct.

Topic: Physical Science

Answer to Question 13:

In the sentence, comprehending and understanding refer to knowledge of the "laws governing a given . . ." Uncovering would refer to finding out what the laws are, articulating would refer to identifying the laws, describing would refer to explaining them, and assimilating would refer to making the laws a part of oneself. None of the incorrect choices thus have any synonyms among the options.

Topic: Social Science

Answer to Question 14:

I found the novel's hero insipid - he seemed like a dull mixture of literary cliches, almost totally devoid of life and originality.

The best choice is "insipid" since it is synonymous with many of the other words used to describe the hero.

Topic: Everyday Topics

Answer to Question 15:

David loved to tout his knowledge of mathematics, even going so far as to offer tutoring to other students. Despite this, his grasp of the field was actually quite tenuous and he was often unable to recall important rules or solve difficult problems.

The first sentence suggests that David liked to boast about his knowledge of mathematics, so the best choice for the blank is "tout". The second sentence suggests that David's pretensions to knowledge lack substance, and that his grasp of the field isn't as strong as he claims, so the best choice for the second blank is "tenuous".

Topic: Arts and Humanities

Answer to Question 16:

The atmosphere at the party was convivial; everyone was sociable and in good spirits.

The best choice is "convivial", since that is the word that best fits the description of the atmosphere as sociable and cheerful.

Topic: Everyday Topics

Answer to Question 17:

The works of many modern composers can be very difficult for the untrained listener to appreciate or enjoy; they are more concerned with esoteric music theory than with beauty or accessibility.

The passage is about the difficulty of the average untrained listener being able to understand the work of modern composers. The implication is that works by modern composers require an understanding of aspects of music theory that very few people have. Therefore, the best choice for the blank is "esoteric".

Topic: Arts and Humanities

Answer to Question 18:

The correct answer is D. The passage reveals that Edward III was crowned at the age of fourteen but did not begin his personal reign until he reached the age of seventeen. Someone would have ruled the country in those three years, and it could not have been Edward II as he had been deposed. The passage also reveals that Edward III led a coup against Roger Mortimer. The purpose of a coup is to remove the head of state. Edward III would not have been legally eligible to reign the country until he reached the age of majority.

Topic: Social Science

Answer to Question 19:

The passage reveals that the reign of Edward II was disastrous. The reader must determine from the information provided the reasons for this disaster. Edward II may have repressed the citizens, failed to expand the British Empire, and/or lived a life of debauchery, but there is insufficient evidence to come to those conclusions. According to the third sentence, the Black Plague occurred during the reign of Edward III, so there is no cause to attribute the ravages of that disease to Edward II. Although it is a fairly general statement, A is the best answer. Because Edward III is credited with restoring royal authority, the reader can assume that Edward II did not have sufficient authority to rule effectively, a result of poor leadership.

Topic: Social Science

Answer to Question 20:

The correct answer is A. Since all of the choices are suppositions, the reader should look for the most logical based on the information given in this short passage. The writer reveals that Edward III was noted for his military success. Even successful campaigns generate a loss of troops and weapons. It may be that he entered into a conflict with France before his military had sufficiently recovered from other campaigns. There is no evidence in the passage to support the other choices.

Topic: Social Science

This page is intentionally left blank

Chapter **10**

Practice Test 2

Y ou are about to begin a Practice Test. The Test has two sections. The time allotted for each section is marked at the beginning of the section. Work on one section at a time. Use a timer to keep track of the time limits for every section.

Try to take the Practice Test under real test conditions. Find a quiet place to work, and set aside enough time to complete the test without being disturbed.

At the end of the test, check your answers by referring to the Answers Key and Explanatory Answers. Pay particular attention to the questions that were answered incorrectly.

Section 1

Time: 30 minutes

20 Questions

Questions 1 to 4 are based on the following passage.

Cognitive psychology is one of the more recent additions to psychological research, having only developed as a separate area within the discipline since the late 1950s and early 1960s following the "cognitive revolution" initiated by Noam Chomsky's 1959 critique of behaviorism and empiricism more generally. The origins of cognitive thinking such as computational theory of mind can be traced back as early as Descartes in the 17th century, and proceeding up to Alan Turing in the 1940s and '50s. The cognitive approach was brought to prominence by Donald Broadbent's book *Perception and Communication* in 1958. Since that time, the dominant paradigm in the area has been the information processing model of cognition that Broadbent put forward. This is a way of thinking and reasoning about mental processes, envisioning them as software running on the computer that is the brain. Theories refer to forms of input, representation, computation or processing, and outputs. Applied to language as the primary mental knowledge representation system, cognitive psychology has exploited tree and network mental models. Its singular contribution to AI and psychology in general is the notion of a semantic network. One of the first cognitive psychologists, George Miller is well-known for dedicating his career to the development of WordNet, a semantic network for the English language. Development began in 1985 and is now the foundation for many machine ontologies. This way of conceiving mental processes has pervaded psychology more generally over the past few decades, and it is not uncommon to find cognitive theories within social psychology, personality psychology, abnormal psychology, and developmental psychology. In fact, the neo-Piagetian theories of cognitive development have fully integrated the developmental conception of changes in thought with age with cognitive models of information processing. The application of cognitive theories to comparative psychology has driven many recent studies in animal cognition. However, cognitive psychology dealing with the intervening constructs of the mental presentations is not able to specify: "What are the non-material counterparts of material objects?" For example, "What is the counterpart of a chair in mental processes, and how do the non-material processes evolve in the mind that has no space?" Further, what are the very specific qualities of the mental causalities, in particular, when the causalities are processes? The plain statement about information processing awakes some questions. What information is dealt with, its contents, and form? Are there transformations? What is the nature of process causalities? How do subjective states of a person transmute into shared states, and the other way around? Finally, yet importantly, how is it that we who works with cognitive research are able to conceptualize the mental counter concepts to construct theories that have real importance in real everyday life? Consequently, there is a lack of specific process concepts that lead to new developments, and create grand theories about the mind and its abysses.

The information processing approach to cognitive functioning is currently being questioned by new approaches in psychology, such as dynamical systems, and the embodiment perspective.
Because of the use of computational metaphors and terminology, cognitive psychology was able to benefit greatly from the flourishing of research in artificial intelligence and other related areas in the 1960s and 1970s. In fact, it developed as one of the significant aspects of the inter-disciplinary subject of cognitive science, which attempts to integrate a range of approaches in research on the mind and mental processes.

1.   Select the sentence that presents an analogy for the information processing model of cognition mentioned in the underlined portion of the passage.

Consider each of the three choices separately and select all that apply.

2.   Which of the following is true about the emergence of cognitive theory in psychology?

   A   Its emergence occurred as a reaction to criticism about behaviorism

   B   It emerged as a result of the development of Artificial Intelligence

   C   It emerged as the need grew for a semantic network for the English language

For Questions 3 and 4, select only one answer choice

3.   What function is served by the series of questions at the end of the second paragraph of the passage?

   (A)   To encourage the reader to conduct more research

   (B)   To illuminate the shortcomings in cognitive theory

   (C)   To demonstrate the theory's usefulness in Artificial Intelligence

   (D)   To validate research concerning animal cognition

   (E)   To serve as rhetorical questions

4. Considering the evolution of cognitive psychology, select from the following statements the one that is most likely accurate.

    Ⓐ Because of the breadth of knowledge available to scientists today, there is likely to be little change in behavior theory.

    Ⓑ Because the scope of cognitive theory is too narrow, it will always be used in conjunction with other theories of behavior.

    Ⓒ Because its roots go back to the 17th century, cognitive theory will always be perceived as outdated.

    Ⓓ Because cognitive psychology has such close ties to technology, it is likely to change or be replaced by more appropriate theories of behavior as technology advances.

    Ⓔ Because the nature of psychology is cyclical, older theories will come back into fashion, and cognitive theory will go out of fashion.

For Questions 5 and 6, select the two answer choices that, when used to complete the sentence, fit the meaning of the sentence as a whole and produce completed sentences that are alike in meaning.

5. The electoral candidates were not allowed to _____ contributions for their political campaigns.

    A   hawk

    B   scope

    C   seek

    D   solicit

    E   sequester

    F   drum

6.   Due to stricter security measures, all factory workers are required to sign an agreement stating that they will _____ safety guidelines.

   A   concede

   B   abide

   C   dissolve

   D   evanesce

   E   repudiate

   F   acquiesce

Question 7 is based on the following passage.

   A good logo works in the simplest form. It is a memorable representation of your brand and inspires confidence in your customers. It should be fresh and original -- without visual cliches or amateur effects. A logo is well-designed when it looks as good on a business card as it does on a web page or a billboard. To be functional, a good logo must reduce well to simple black & white or grayscale for use on faxes or in newspaper ads. The best logos are elegantly simple.

Select only one answer choice.

7.   After reading this passage, decide which of the following is the best advice for people who are creating a logo for their business.

   (A)   In order to get the viewer's attention, use eye-catching colors in the design.

   (B)   Because it is a visual representation of your company, invest in a professionally designed logo.

   (C)   To inform the viewer, list all of your products and/or services on your logo.

   (D)   To inspire confidence in your clients, list endorsements and/or awards on your logo.

   (E)   To demonstrate that your company works in partnership with its clients, include an image of a handshake in the logo.

Select one entry for the blank. Fill the blank in the way that best completes the text.

8.   Subconsciously, humans tend to fear the worst, often in defiance of solid facts and empirical evidence
        to the contrary. Without realizing it, we all tend to give more credence to the negative than the positive,
        and we tend to hear and believe _____ predictions, no matter how outlandish, over predictions that
        tomorrow is going to be pretty much like today.

labyrinthine
abstruse
fustian
grandiloquent
pernicious

**For each blank, select one entry from the corresponding column of choices. Fill all blanks in the way that
best completes the text.**

9.   The (i) _____ of Good King Gustav may indeed have been (ii) _____ by the notoriety of his
        brother, Bad King George, whose reign was characterized by lavish parties for the aristocracy and (iii)
        _____ taxes on the poor. Over time these onerous taxes caused widespread poverty and starvation,
        and were subsequently rescinded by King Gustav when he reassumed the throne.

Blank (i)	Blank (ii)	Blank (iii)
beneficence	obfuscated	exorbitant
reticence	apotheosized	inchoate
insouciance	bolstered	antediluvian

Questions 10 and 11 are based on the following passage.

   An antioxidant is a molecule capable of inhibiting the oxidation of other molecules. Oxidation is a
chemical reaction that transfers electrons from a substance to an oxidizing agent. Oxidation reactions can
produce free radicals. In turn, these radicals can start chain reactions. When the chain reaction occurs in a cell,
it can cause damage or death. When the chain reaction occurs in a purified monomer, it produces a polymer
resin, such as a plastic, a synthetic fiber, or an oil paint film. Antioxidants terminate these chain reactions by
removing free radical intermediates, and inhibit other oxidation reactions. They do this by being oxidized
themselves, so antioxidants are often reducing agents such as thiols, ascorbic acid or polyphenols.

Select only one answer choice.

10. In the context of this passage, which is the best definition of the word, "reducing"?

     (A) to correct (as a fracture or a herniated mass) by bringing displaced or broken parts back into their normal positions

     (B) to become diminished or lessened

     (C) to be turned into or made to equal something

     (D) to change (an element or ion) from a higher to a lower oxidation state

     (E) to lower in degree, intensity, etc.

Consider each of the three choices separately and select all that apply.

11. According to the passage, which of the following is true about free radicals?

     [A] Understanding the action of free radicals on a purified monomer has enabled scientists to help in the design of numerous products that enhance the lifestyle of humans.

     [B] Understanding the action of free radicals on cells can lead scientists to create products that will inhibit aging and prolong life.

     [C] Understanding the action of free radicals on cells has led scientists to conclude that the production of free radicals should be avoided.

Questions 12 to 14 are based on the following passage.

The little boxfish is quite a speedy fellow, jetting through water at speeds of six body lengths per second. This isn't just a feat of strength though; the fish's cube-like shape is an important contributor to its aerodynamic qualities. Engineers who tested its abilities were stunned to find a boxfish replica able to slip through air far more efficiently than the most compact cars around. This, they concluded, was due to the fish's bony outer skin, which provided maximum strength while maintaining minimum weight. Tiny vortexes form in the water around the fish providing stability and outstanding maneuverability.

12. Select the sentence that contradicts the generally accepted idea that parabolic curves allow for more efficient flow of air over and under surfaces in motion.

Questions 13 and 14, select only one answer choice.

13.   Understanding that the boxfish's structure provides maximum strength while maintaining minimum weight one should be able to observe the practical use of this principal in which of the following projects?

   Ⓐ Building a log cabin

   Ⓑ Erecting a skyscraper

   Ⓒ Laying railroad tracks

   Ⓓ Designing a bridge

   Ⓔ Flying a kite

14.   The author's word choices in the first sentence of the passage are intended to have what effect?

   Ⓐ To prepare the reader for the technical information to follow

   Ⓑ To set a light-hearted tone for the remainder of the passage

   Ⓒ To set a formal tone for the remainder of the passage

   Ⓓ To create a question in the mind of the reader

   Ⓔ To enable the reader to call to mind similar scenarios

For each blank, select one entry from the corresponding column of choices. Fill all blanks in the way that best completes the text.

15.   Although Tom tried to (i) _____ .Mary by taking her out to her favorite restaurant, she remained (ii) _____ in her anger.

Blank (i)	Blank (ii)
peruse	obsolete
placate	mollified
obviate	obdurate

For Questions 16 and 17, select the two answer choices that, when used to complete the sentence, fit the meaning of the sentence as a whole and produce completed sentences that are alike in meaning.

16.   Belief in evolution is based on evidence, otherwise it would be _____.

     A inconceivable

     B implausible

     C questionable

     D incontestable

     E probable

     F cogitable

17.   At first the new employee approached his job with vigor, but his enthusiasm soon _____ and now he risks losing his position.

     A alleviated

     B vanished

     C burgeoned

     D dwindled

     E waned

     F elongated

For Questions 18 to 20, select one entry for the blank. Fill the blank in the way that best completes the text.

18.   Susie showed the classic symptoms of seasonal depression. In the spring and summer, she always had a smile on her face and loved to spend time with her friends, but in the winter months she became _____ and withdrawn.

jubilant
fulminating
forlorn
morbid
rueful

19. Many consider the reign of Louis the XIV to be the _____ of absolutism in France. During his long rule, power was centralized under his direct authority to an unprecedented degree.

substantiation
vindication
nadir
apogee
prototype

For each blank, select one entry from the corresponding column of choices. Fill all blanks in the way that best completes the text.

20. Few who are not already versed in Russian history realize that the (i) _____ for the revolution in 1917 was not systematic action by the Bolsheviks, but rather a series of (ii) _____ strikes and protests that eventually forced the abdication of the Tsar. Only after months of rule by a provisional coalition did the Bolsheviks decisively seize power.

Blank (i)	Blank (ii)
hierarchy	inscrutable
impetus	orchestrated
paradigm	disparate

Section 2

Time: 30 minutes

20 Questions

Select the two answer choices that, when used to complete the sentence, fit the meaning of the sentence as a whole and produce completed sentences that are alike in meaning.

1. The statue of the town's founder sits in a stone _____ overlooking the town square, which makes it look enthroned.

    A estuary

    B crypt

    C burrow

    D cloister

    E alcove

    F recess

2. Her music _____ everyone in the room with a sense of peace and tranquility.

    A affusion

    B doused

    C cleansed

    D imbued

    E inoculated

    F infused

For Questions 3 and 4, for each blank, select one entry from the corresponding column of choices. Fill all blanks in the way that best completes the text.

3.   (i) _____ in his field·and hailed as the Father of modern psychology, Dr. Sigmund Freud was not without his fair share of (ii) _____ including an addiction to cocaine and a/an (iii) _____ affair with his wife's sister that spanned decades.

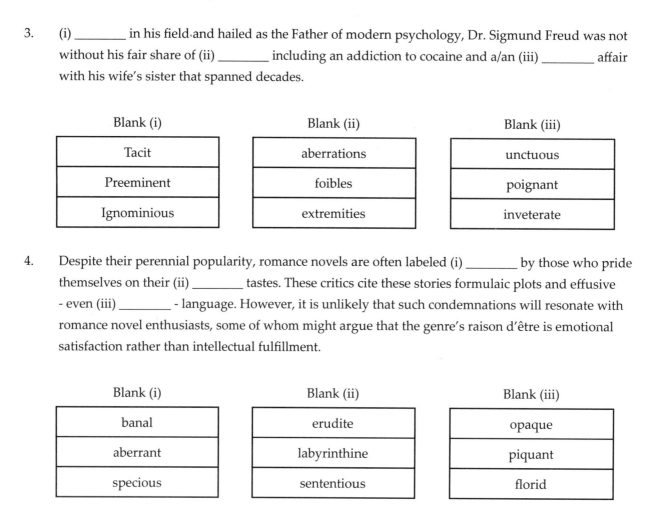

Blank (i)	Blank (ii)	Blank (iii)
Tacit	aberrations	unctuous
Preeminent	foibles	poignant
Ignominious	extremities	inveterate

4.   Despite their perennial popularity, romance novels are often labeled (i) _____ by those who pride themselves on their (ii) _____ tastes. These critics cite these stories formulaic plots and effusive - even (iii) _____ - language. However, it is unlikely that such condemnations will resonate with romance novel enthusiasts, some of whom might argue that the genre's raison d'être is emotional satisfaction rather than intellectual fulfillment.

Blank (i)	Blank (ii)	Blank (iii)
banal	erudite	opaque
aberrant	labyrinthine	piquant
specious	sententious	florid

Question 5 is based on the following passage.

A value chain is a chain of activities for a firm operating in a specific industry. Products pass through all activities of the chain in order, and at each activity the product gains some value. The chain of activities gives the products more added value than the sum of the independent activities' value. It is important not to mix the concept of the value chain with the costs occurring throughout the activities. A diamond cutter, as a profession, can be used to illustrate the difference of cost and the value chain. The cutting activity may have a low cost, but the activity adds much of the value to the end product, since a rough diamond is significantly less valuable than a cut diamond.

Select only one answer choice.

5.   Based on the underlined portion of the text, which of the following statements is accurate?

      (A) The value of an item is in direct proportion to the cost of the activities completed to produce it.

      (B) Not all of the activities in a value chain add the same amount of value to the finished product.

      (C) The first step in a chain of activities adds the most value to the finished product.

      (D) Only low-cost activities add high value to the item being created.

      (E) Although the retailer who sells the manufacturer's finished product may determine the price of the item, he does not contribute to the value of the item

Questions 6 to 8 are based on the following passage.

Wetter climates brought upon by ice ages starting 2 million years ago greatly increased excavation of the Grand Canyon, which was nearly as deep as it is now by 1.2 million years ago. Volcanic activity deposited lava over the area 1.8 million to 500,000 years ago. At least 13 lava dams blocked the Colorado River, forming lakes that were up to 2,000 feet (610 m) deep. The end of the last ice age and subsequent human activity has greatly reduced the ability of the Colorado River to excavate the canyon. Dams in particular have upset patterns of sediment transport and deposition. Controlled floods from Glen Canyon Dam upstream have been conducted to see if they have a restorative effect. Earthquakes and mass wasting erosive events still affect the region.

For Questions 6 to 8, select only one answer choice.

6.   The primary purpose of this passage is to

      (A) Provide a timeline of events that shaped the Grand Canyon

      (B) Reveal when the last ice age ended

      (C) Show the scope of the Grand Canyon

      (D) How wetter climates are preferable to dry ones

      (E) Tell the reader that deep lakes once existed in the area

7.   The author includes information about manmade dams primarily to

Ⓐ Show how human intervention has affected the Grand Canyon

Ⓑ Demonstrate how engineers can control natural forces

Ⓒ Demonstrate the progress of human achievement

Ⓓ Show how water is supplied to towns in the area

Ⓔ Compare them to lava dams

8.   A person most likely to find this information helpful would be

Ⓐ Someone writing a doctoral thesis

Ⓑ A park ranger preparing a presentation for a group of students

Ⓒ A family planning a vacation

Ⓓ The native people living on the floor of the Grand Canyon

Ⓔ Engineers planning to build a new dam

Select the two answer choices that, when used to complete the sentence, fit the meaning of the sentence as a whole and produce completed sentences that are alike in meaning.

9.   Although the company grew from $16+ billion in revenue in 1990 to $126+ billion in 2005, recent managerial decisions have _____ affected its finances and its long-term stability is threatened.

Ⓐ ultimately

Ⓑ negatively

Ⓒ positively

Ⓓ significantly

Ⓔ adversely

Ⓕ especially

Question 10 is based on the following passage.

Psychodynamics is another type of covariation information that is important in the effort of understanding the causes of social behavior. Distinctiveness refers to how unique the psychodynamics is to the particular situation. There is a low distinctiveness if an individual behaves similarly in all situations, and there exists a high distinctiveness when the person only shows the behavior in particular situations. If the distinctiveness is high, one will attribute this behavior more to the context instead of personal characteristics.

Select only one answer choice.

10.   Based on the information in this passage, select the situation below that portrays high distinctiveness.

   Ⓐ   A generally garrulous woman speaks to everyone she meets at the supermarket.

   Ⓑ   A generally laconic man avoids greeting everyone he meets at church.

   Ⓒ   A generally lugubrious best man smiles at everyone in the receiving line at a wedding.

   Ⓓ   A generally confident detective provides unequivocal answers while testifying in a criminal case.

   Ⓔ   A generally enigmatic undercover agent provides polysemous responses while under interrogation.

Question 11 is based on the following passage.

Local grocery stores in North town, Maine, report a significant increase in the sales of freezer bags during the months of September and October each year.
Select only one answer choice.

11.   All of the following could account for the increased sales EXCEPT

   Ⓐ   The stores take inventory at the end of August and again at the end of October, so they acquire precise numbers relating to the sales of freezer bags during the intervening months.

   Ⓑ   The manufacturers of the freezer bags offer deep discounts to grocery retailers during those months, and the stores pass on the savings to their customers.

   Ⓒ   The stores offer a wide variety of bulk fruits and vegetables at considerable savings over smaller quantities of those same fruits and vegetables.

   Ⓓ   A large number of North town residents have large vegetable gardens which they harvest throughout the month of September.

   Ⓔ   North town is home to many hunters, most of whom participate in the annual moose hunt, which occurs for one week in September and an additional week in October.

For Questions 12 and 13, for each blank, select one entry from the corresponding column of choices. Fill all blanks in the way that best completes the text.

12.   In recent times, the practice of filibustering, by which one party can effectively block the passage of any legislation that does not have overwhelming support in the senate, has come under scrutiny. Many critics have pointed out that the practice of the filibuster is merely (i) _____. Nonetheless, it is an important check that keeps a simple majority from (ii) _____ its agenda on a sizable minority.

Blank (i)
obstructionist
antiquated
spiteful

Blank (ii)
recalibrating
positing
foisting

13.   Millions of visitors travel every year to see the (i) _____ natural beauty of Yellowstone National Park in Wyoming. However, this peaceful landscape belies the (ii) _____ nature of our world's geology. 640, 000 years ago, Yellowstone was the scene of a (iii) _____ volcanic eruption and the geysers that draw tourists are themselves the result of continued volcanism

Blank (i)
grandiose
lackadaisical
idyllic

Blank (ii)
tangential
mercurial
rudimentary

Blank (iii)
surreptitious
cataclysmic
quotidian

Questions 14 and 15 are based on the following passage.

Artists like Bill Haley and the Comets adapted the work of the Black artists to come up with their own sound. The music's solid rhythm and heavy back beat inspired new forms of dancing. Soon there were stars - Chuck Berry, Jerry Lee Lewis, Little Richard, and Carl Perkins. Due to the prejudices of the times, Disc Jockey Alan Freed coined the name "rock and roll," ironically using a term that was slang for sex in the Black community at that time. Its initial appeal was to middle class white teenagers who soon came to feel it was their own. In this era, so called 'race music' was largely censured by America's white establishment as being too rebellious, sexual and anti-social to be acceptable.

Consider each of the three choices separately and select all that apply.

14.   What can the reader infer about the culture of the period discussed in this passage?

   [A]   Considerable levels of discrimination prevailed.

   [B]   Numerous genres of music were evolving.

   [C]   Middle class white teenagers defied their parents.

Select only one answer choice.

15.   Which of the following is a structural weakness of this passage?

   Ⓐ   There is too little evidence to support the claim.

   Ⓑ   The use of indefinite pronouns without sufficient references leads to some confusion while
         reading the passage.

   Ⓒ   The comparative nature of the passage is not evident.

   Ⓓ   Too little information is provided about the people identified in the passage.

   Ⓔ   The tone of the piece is not consistent from beginning to end.

Select the <u>two</u> answer choices that, when used to complete the sentence, fit the meaning of the sentence as a whole <u>and</u> produce completed sentences that are alike in meaning.

16.   The company and the industry analysts who have studied it, _____ its success to skillful
         management, honest dealings, and involvement in the local community.

   [A]   delegate

   [B]   credit

   [C]   limit

   [D]   ascribe

   [E]   portray

   [F]   aspire

Questions 17 and 18 are based on the following passage.

The CSI effect is any of several ways in which the exaggerated portrayal of forensic science on crime shows such as *CSI: Crime Scene Investigation* influences its public perception. The term most often refers to the belief that jurors have come to demand more forensic evidence in criminal trials, thereby raising the standard of proof for prosecutors. Although this belief is widely held among American legal professionals, several studies have shown that crime shows are unlikely to cause such an effect. There are several other manifestations of the CSI effect. Greater public awareness of forensic science has increased the demand for forensic evidence in police investigations, which in turn has significantly increased workloads for crime laboratories.

For Questions 17 and 18, select only one answer choice.

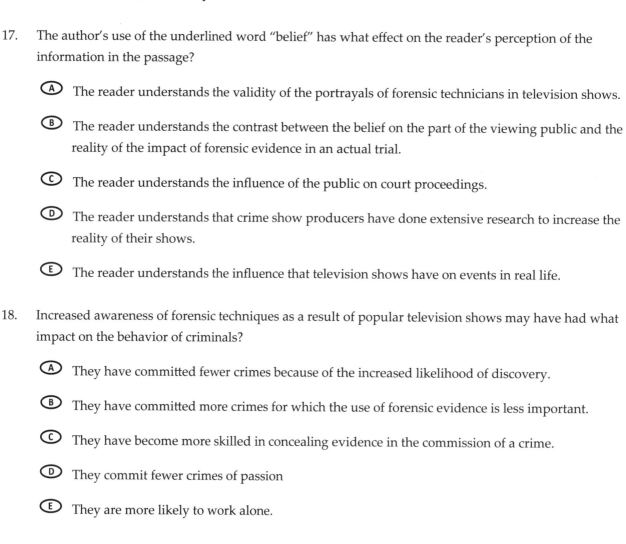

17.   The author's use of the underlined word "belief" has what effect on the reader's perception of the information in the passage?

    Ⓐ   The reader understands the validity of the portrayals of forensic technicians in television shows.

    Ⓑ   The reader understands the contrast between the belief on the part of the viewing public and the reality of the impact of forensic evidence in an actual trial.

    Ⓒ   The reader understands the influence of the public on court proceedings.

    Ⓓ   The reader understands that crime show producers have done extensive research to increase the reality of their shows.

    Ⓔ   The reader understands the influence that television shows have on events in real life.

18.   Increased awareness of forensic techniques as a result of popular television shows may have had what impact on the behavior of criminals?

    Ⓐ   They have committed fewer crimes because of the increased likelihood of discovery.

    Ⓑ   They have committed more crimes for which the use of forensic evidence is less important.

    Ⓒ   They have become more skilled in concealing evidence in the commission of a crime.

    Ⓓ   They commit fewer crimes of passion

    Ⓔ   They are more likely to work alone.

For Questions 19 and 20, for each blank, select one entry from the corresponding column of choices. Fill all blanks in the way that best completes the text.

19.   The novels of Thomas Hardy often (i) _____ the ambitions of the increasingly mobile working classes with the realities of Victorian society. Both The Mayor of Casterbridge and Jude the Obscure are (ii) _____ of this theme, showing the tragic consequences of working-class men (iii) _____ their traditional role through ambition.

Blank (i)	Blank (ii)	Blank (iii)
supersede	paradigmatic	obviating
juxtapose	redolent	subverting
conflate	derivative	comprising

20.   Ron's (i) _____ remarks about the economy were (ii) _____ to productive discussion. Although he showed no understanding of the subject, his attitude was smug and overbearing.

Blank (i)	Blank (ii)
erudite	conducive
jubilant	inimical
fatuous	incongruous

Answer Key

Section 1

1. Since an analogy is a comparison between like feature of two things, the comparison between the brain and a computer is appropriate and provides another way for the reader to view the information processing model of cognition.

2. A. Its emergence occurred as a reaction to criticism about behaviorism

3. B. To illuminate the shortcomings in cognitive theory

4. D. Because cognitive psychology has such close ties to technology, it is likely to change or be replaced by more appropriate theories of behavior as technology advances.

5. C. seek
    D. solicit

6. B. abide
    F. acquiesce

7. B. Because it is a visual representation of your company, invest in a professionally designed logo.

8. labyrinthine

9. (i) beneficence
    (ii) bolstered
    (iii) exorbitant

10. D. to change (an element or ion) from a higher to a lower oxidation state

11. A. Understanding the action of free radicals on a purified monomer has enabled scientists to help in the design of numerous products that enhance the lifestyle of humans

    B. Understanding the action of free radicals on cells can lead scientists to create products that will inhibit aging and prolong life

12. Engineers who tested its abilities were stunned to find a boxfish replica able to slip through air far more efficiently than the most compact cars around.

13. E. Flying a kite

14. B. To set a light-hearted tone for the remainder of the passage

15. (i) placate
    (ii) obdurate

16. A. inconceivable
    B. implausible

17. D. dwindled
    E. waned

18. forlorn

19. apogee

20. (i) impetus
    (ii) disparate

Section 2

1. E. alcove
    F. recess

2. D. imbued
    F. infused

3. (i) Preeminent
    (ii) aberrations
    (iii) inveterate

4. (i) banal
    (ii) erudite
    (iii) florid

5. E. Although the retailer who sells the manufacturer's finished product may determine the price of the item, he does not contribute to the value of the item.

6. A. Provide a timeline of events that shaped the Grand Canyon

7. A. Show how human intervention has affected the Grand Canyon

8. B. A park ranger preparing a presentation for a group of students

9. B. negatively
    E. adversely

10. C. A generally lugubrious best man smiles at everyone in the receiving line at a wedding.

11. A. The stores take inventory at the end of August and again at the end of October, so they acquire precise numbers relating to the sales of freezer bags during the intervening months.

12. (i) obstructionist
    (ii) foisting

13. (i) idyllic
    (ii) mercurial
    (iii) cataclysmic

14. A. Considerable levels of discrimination prevailed.

15. C. Middle class white teenagers defied their parents.

16. B. The use of indefinite pronouns without sufficient references leads to some confusion while reading the passage.

17. B. credit
    D. ascribe

18. B. The reader understands the contrast between the belief on the part of the viewing public and the reality of the impact of forensic evidence in an actual trial.

    C. They have become more skilled in concealing evidence in the commission of a crime.

19. (i) juxtapose
    (ii) paradigmatic
    (iii) subverting

20. (i) fatuous
    (ii) inimical

Explanatory Answers

Section 1

Answer to Question 1:

This is a way of thinking and reasoning about mental processes, envisioning them as software running on the computer that is the brain.

Topic: Social Science

Answer to Question 2:

The correct choice is A. The first paragraph of the passage clearly mentions Noam Chomsky's critique of behaviorism. Cognitive theory has practical applications for Artificial Intelligence, but neither is the result of the other. George Miller has applied cognitive theory to the creation of a semantic network, but the development of cognitive theory did not rely on it.

Topic: Social Science

Answer to Question 3:

The correct answer is B. The sentence prior to the list of questions informs the reader that cognitive theories are unable to specify certain ideas. That is a shortcoming for those who want a clearer understanding of the science. There is no call on the part of the author to researchers, so A is not correct. The article reveals how cognitive theory relates to Artificial Intelligence, but these questions do not support that relationship, eliminating C as an appropriate choice. D should be the easiest choice to eliminate as the questions are not specific enough to enable the reader to reach this conclusion. These are not rhetorical questions; they are questions that need answering to support the validity of cognitive psychology. E is not the correct answer.

Topic: Social Science

Answer to Question 4:

The correct answer is D. Cognitive behavior theory has already merged into cognitive science. Because of its influence in Artificial Intelligence, which, itself, is still changing and expanding, it is likely that cognitive behavior theory will have to keep pace. A is not correct because human knowledge is always expanding and all disciplines adapt to that expansion. There is no evidence that the scope of this branch of psychology is too narrow, so B cannot be the correct choice. C simply refers to the history of theories associated with cognitive psychology. The information in E may be correct, but there is no evidence in the passage to support it.

Topic: Social Science

Answer to Question 5:

C and D. We are looking for words that would pair up with the keyword *contributions*, and in this instance, we can seek or solicit a contribution. The other words would not complete the sentence because sequester means to isolate or seclude, hawk means to sell, and scope refers to the aim or purpose of something. The word drum would be correct if it were used with the preposition up as in "drum up" which would then mean "to come up with".

Topic: Business

Answer to Question 6:

B and F. The correct answers are B and F because in the sentence the workers are asked to sign a document agreeing to something. In this case, it would be to follow safety guidelines. The other word options would not complete the sentence logically. The word concede means to give into or admit to as in to concede victory, dissolve means to cause to disappear, evanesce means to dissipate like vapor and repudiate means to refuse or reject something.

Topic: Business

Answer to Question 7:

It might be a good idea to use eye-catching colors in your design, but some colors wash out completely in a black-and-white reproduction, making A less than the best advice. Choices C and D will likely make the logo too busy and detract from the visual message, so they are inappropriate choices. The advice in choice E includes incorporating a visual cliché in the logo. The handshake has been overused and makes the business too similar to other enterprises. The best advice is to have the logo created by professionals who have experience in this area. A professional created logo should be worth the expense making option B the best choice.

Topic: Business

Answer to Question 8:

If we give preference to the negative and improbable as the passage makes clear, it stands to reason that we would undoubtedly tend to believe the worst predictions, realistic or not. Labyrinthine (A), meaning twisted and complicated does not fit in the context of the sentence and must be eliminated. Similarly, abstruse (B), meaning recondite or difficult to understand, does not relate and must be eliminated. C, fustian, means bombastic, and like options A and B is irrelevant to the passage, as is grandiloquent (D), meaning the tendency to use elevated embellished language. Pernicious (E), however meaning causing insidious harm, effectively describes the kind of predictions those with a predilection for bad news would believe and is the correct answer to this question..

Topic: Arts and Humanities

Answer to Question 9:

Blank (i): Monikers used in the sentence focus on the juxtaposition of good and bad, suggesting that the modifier needed will have to do with the goodness of Good King Gustav. Beneficence (A), meaning goodness, is a fit, while reticence (B), meaning reluctance or quality of being reserved, and insouciance (C), meaning cheerfulness, have nothing to do with goodness, and must be eliminated. A is the correct answer.

Blank (ii): The sentence focuses on a cause-effect relationship, and it can be inferred that George's "badness" has increased and/or supported the perception of Gustav's "goodness." Hence, we can say that the beneficence of Good King Gustav has been supported, not obfuscated (D), or made unclear, by the notorious behavior of his brother. Option D can be eliminated. Apotheosized (E) is not a fit for blank (ii) as beneficence, the subject of this sentence, cannot be glorified or praised. Bolstered (F), however, means supported, lifted, or strengthened and makes sense in the context of the sentence, making F the correct answer.

Blank (iii): If the taxes on the poor were onerous, we can safely infer they were exorbitant (G) or exaggerated/ high. Such taxes would not be described as inchoate (H), meaning neophyte or incipient as this makes little sense in the context of the sentence. Similarly, antediluvian (I), meaning ancient/antiquated does not fit in the context of the sentence as antediluvian does not speak to the onerous nature of the taxes. G is the correct answer.

Topic: Social Science

Answer to Question 10:

The correct answer is D. This definition mentions oxidation specifically. The purpose of an antioxidant is to lower the oxidation state. Choice A is a medical definition having to do with setting a broken bone. B is related to losing weight. An example for choice C might be the following statement: We were all reduced to tears by the scene in the movie. Choice E refers to reducing one's speed on the highway.

Topic: Physical Science

Answer to Question 11:

The correct choices are A and B. In the case of choice A, the author lists products that result from this reaction; they include products like plastic and paint film that do, indeed, make positive contributions to our lifestyle. In the case of choice B, the reaction can lead to damage and death. Learning how to prevent damage to or death of cells can inhibit the aging process. C is incorrect because of the benefits explained in the action of free radicals on a purified monomer.

Topic: Physical Science

Answer to Question 12:

This sentence explicitly states that the boxfish, despite its lack of curved surfaces, is able to slip through air for more efficiently than most compact cars, the majority of which have curved shapes.

Topic: Biological Science

Answer to Question 13:

In the construction of a log cabin, great weight is concentrated in the outside structure, making it dissimilar to the boxfish. The exterior structure of modern skyscrapers might seem visually similar to the structure of a boxfish, but the concrete reinforced beams carry great weight as does the center structure of the building. Railroad tracks do not have a visible three-dimensional structure. The structure of a bridge is dense and heavy. A well-designed kite has a lightweight, rigid framework and is affected by air currents in much the same way as the fish is affected by water currents. The best choice is E.

Topic: Biological Science

Answer to Question 14:

The word "fellow" is informal and has a positive connotation. The author's description of this "fellow" "jetting" about is light-hearted in nature. The reader should not expect to be weighed down with detailed facts about the boxfish. There is no demand by the author to create a question about the material to follow, nor does the author suggest that the reader think about previous experiences or similar situations. The most appropriate choice is B.

Topic: Biological Science

Answer to Question 15:

The clue to blank one is in the second clause - Mary is angry. The first clause suggests that Tom is trying to calm, or "placate" Mary's anger. However, the "although" at the beginning of the first clause suggests that Tom hasn't been successful - Mary is still unmoved in her anger, so the best choice for the second blank is "obdurate".

Topic: Everyday Topics

Answer to Question 16:

In conceivable and implausible indicate that the concept or idea at issue would not be possible. All inconceivable and implausible ideas are also questionable, but since not all questionable ideas are not inconceivable and implausible, questionable cannot be a correct choice. Cogitable would mean that evolution could be imaginable, and incontestable and probable are positive terms where the sentence requires negative words such as inconceivable and implausible. Also, none of the incorrect options mean the same as any of the other options.

Topic: Biological Science

Answer to Question 17:

Wane and dwindle refer to something decreasing, not necessarily that the thing has disappeared, ruling out vanished as a possible answer. Alleviate can be used for wane, but it usually refers to the lessening of negatives such as symptoms of diseases. Burgeon and elongate refer to an increase in size, but burgeon means to get bigger, while elongate indicates a length increase. Further, since the sentence requires a word in the blank relating to something getting smaller, neither burgeoned nor elongated can be used.

Topic: Business

Answer to Question 18:

The best choice is "forlorn", since there is no reason to suppose that Susie's depression leads to morbidity.

Topic: Social Sciences – Psychology

Answer to Question 19:

The only two choices that make sense in context are "prototype" and "apogee". "Prototype" would suggest that Louis was a completely new kind of ruler, which seems implausible. "Apogee" is the best choice because it suggests that Louis' reign was the height of French absolutism.

Topic: Arts and Humanities

Answer to Question 20:

The best choice for the first blank is clearly "impetus", since the passage is concerned with explaining how the Russian Revolution began and developed. The fact that the revolution was not started by "systematic action by the Bolsheviks" and that there were "months of rule by a provisional coalition" suggest that the strikes and protests were only loosely related, so the best choice for the second blank is "disparate".

Topic: Arts and Humanities

Section 2

Answer to Question 1:

1. E and F. The best options to complete the missing word are alcove and recess; both words refer to an indentation or an opening. The other word choices would not complete the sentence in a logical manner because estuary refers to the mouth of a river, a crypt is a type of tomb, burrow is a hole in the ground and cloister generally refers to a type of room in a monastery or rectory

Topic: Everyday Topics

Answer to Question 2:

D and F. The word choices infusion, doused, cleansed and inoculated do not complete the sentence logically because affusion is the act of pouring water on as in a baptismal, doused means to throw liquid on, cleansed means to get rid of impurities and inoculated is a synonym for the word vaccinated. The only word choices left to complete the missing word are imbued and infused which both mean to permeate or inspire.

Topic: Everyday Topics

Answer to Question 3:

Blank (i): Tacit (A), meaning silently understood, does not describe a person so renowned as to be called the father of modern psychology and can be eliminated. Preeminent (B), however, means foremost, and effectively describes the father of modern psychology. Ignominious (C), meaning contemptible or discreditable possibly describes the "real Freud," but blank (i) clearly describes the other Freud, the preeminent one hailed as the father of psychology. Option B is the correct answer.

Blank (ii): Freud's problems are critical to selecting the right answer here. They are more than mere foibles (E), or harmless eccentricities. They are not extremities (F) as this word, when applied to humans refers to the parts of our bodies at the extreme ends of our limbs…fingers and toes. Cocaine and a protracted affair with one's sister-in-law are notorious deviations from the norm or aberrations, making option D, the correct answer to this question.

Blank (iii): Readers can ascertain from the passage that Freud's affair with his sister-in-law was long-lasting and must consequently look for the answer that conveys a sense of duration. Unctuous (G) means groveling or sycophantic and must be eliminated. Poignant (H), meaning keenly distressing, must also be eliminated. The passage does not support this option. Inveterate (I), however, means long-lasting and makes sense within the context of the sentence. Option I is the correct answer.

Topic: Arts and Humanities

Answer to Question 4:

You will probably need to read the entire passage before attempting to tackle the first sentence. We are told that critics of romance novels dislike their "formulaic plots" and "effusive language." These should strike you as rather learned objections, and the critics making them probably consider their tastes fairly highbrow. "Labyrinthine" means "complicated" or "tortuous" and does not work well in the context of describing someone's preferences - eliminate it. You might consider these critics somewhat "sententious" ("self-righteous" or "given to pithy sayings"), but it is unlikely that they would "pride" themselves on this. The best answer for the second blank is "erudite," or "scholarly." With this filled in, you should be able to fill in the first blank as well by asking yourself what kind of criticism someone with "erudite" tastes might make. "Aberrant" seems too extreme, and in any case, something that is "perennially popular" is hardly "deviating from the norm." "Specious" is a common enough criticism, but it does not really work in this context; it means "apparently good but lacking in real merit," and it is doubtful whether these critics would even characterize romance novels as "apparently good." "Banal," however, works perfectly; it means "trite" or "commonplace." Finally, to fill in the last blank we need to find a word similar to "effusive" but stronger. Effusive language is probably not "opaque" ("difficult to understand" or "obscure"), so you can eliminate this choice. "Piquant" has a rather positive connotation; it means "interestingly provocative or lively" and does not convey the sense of excess we need here. "Florid," which means "flowery" or "excessively ornate," is the correct answer.

Topic: Arts and Humanities

Answer to Question 5:

The correct choice is E. Although a retailer sets the price for an item he sells, he has performed no action on the item that would alter its value. It has come from the manufacturer in its finished form. A is incorrect because some of the activities may add more value than others. B is not correct because all of the activities may add the same amount of value, depending on the product being created. C may be true in some cases but not true in others. In the case of the diamond cutter, a low-cost activity adds great value to the product, but a high-cost activity may also add high value to the item, ruling out D as the best answer.

Topic: Business

Answer to Question 6:

A is the best answer. The author mentions the deep lakes and the last ice age, but they are merely facts that add information to the overall purpose of the passage; B and D can be eliminated. The author does not reveal the scope of the entire canyon; C is incorrect. The passage does not compare wet and dry climates, so D can be eliminated.

Topic: Physical Science

Answer to Question 7:

The correct answer is A. Humans have made the decisions to build dams along the mighty rivers in America. The author reveals the effect that dams have had on the formation of the canyon. B and C are too broad in nature. There is no mention of the dams' supplying water to towns. The purpose of the piece is not to compare and contrast, eliminating E as the correct answer.

Topic: Physical Science

Answer to Question 8:

This information is too general to be of much help in someone writing a doctoral thesis, so A is not the correct answer. A family planning a vacation would be more interested in activities around the Grand Canyon than in this brief history of its formation, eliminating C as the best choice. The native people living there consider the floor of the canyon their ancestral home and more likely to be interested in the myths and legends of the site than in its geographical history. Engineers must focus on the features that exist in the present rather than historical information; E is not the correct choice. From this list of possibilities, B is the best choice. Teachers will expect their students to learn something about the Grand Canyon, but would not want the students to be overloaded with facts. This amount of information might be sufficient and have some relevance as the students are actually viewing the canyon, making B the best answer.

Topic: Physical Science

Answer to Question 9:

Positively can be ruled out because of its non-negative meaning. Ultimately would make the sentence vague. The other options fit well, but since negatively and adversely agree in meaning and specifically indicate that the decisions have been bad for the company, they are better than significantly and especially. Especially, further, indicates that the decisions affected not just finances, but that the finances were harder hit than other parts, while significantly provides no indication if the decisions affected other aspects of company operations.

Topic: Business

Answer to Question 10:

To qualify as highly distinctive behavior, the individual should act in a manner contrary to his or her normal actions. A garrulous woman is one who talks a lot and would be expected to behave in that manner everywhere she goes, eliminating A as the correct choice. A laconic man is generally silent and remains so at church, so B is also incorrect. A confident detective providing unequivocal responses is no surprise, nor is an undercover agent giving responses that have more than one meaning. Neither D nor E is correct. C is the best choice. A lugubrious – or mournful – best man would be out of character if he smiles. His behavior is dependent upon the context, in this case, the happy occasion of his friend's wedding.

Topic: Social Science

Answer to Question 11:

The correct answer is A. This choice, in essence repeats the prompt. It provides no reason for the increase in sales; it reveals how the stores arrive at their numbers. Answer choice B provides a good reason for increased sales, lower prices. If this is an annual event, shoppers are likely to anticipate it and buy enough freezer bags to last them several months or until the next sale. Answer choice C also suggests a reason for the bump in sales. Shoppers may take advantage of the bulk prices and freeze quantities of lower priced fruits and vegetables for future use. In addition, customers who have large gardens will need to preserve their harvests and may choose freezing as the best option. Answer choice D is, therefore, incorrect. Answer choice E presents another reasonable scenario that explains the increase in sales of freezer bags. Hunters who bag a moose will need to freeze most of the meat.

Topic: Business

Answer to Question 12:

The best answer for the first blank is "obstructionist", since it relates back to the idea in the first sentence that the filibuster is a tool for blocking, or obstructing legislation. The word "nonetheless" at the start of the final sentence signals the introduction of an opposing point of view. "Foisting" fits the context best, given its negative connotation - the suggestion is that the filibuster has good consequences that weren't noted in the first two sentences.

Topic: Social Science - Political Science

Answer to Question 13:

The best choice for the first blank is "idyllic"; although "grandiose" might seem like an appropriate choice, it connotes excess as well as grandeur, and that does not fit well with the description of the landscape as "peaceful" in the next sentence. The "however" that begins the next sentence indicates a qualification of the original description. Neither "tangential" nor rudimentary make sense in context, so "mercurial" is the best word for the second blank. Similarly, "cataclysmic" is the only word that makes sense in context for the third blank.

Topic: Physical Science – Geology

Answer to Question 14:

There is sufficient evidence in the passage to support choice A, especially in the use of the phrases "prejudices of the times" and "race music". Since the only genre discussed in the passage is rock and roll, it would be incorrect to select B as the answer. The last sentence reveals that the white establishment censured this music, while the white teens adopted it as their own, defying the beliefs of their elders. C would also be a correct choice.

Topic: Arts and Humanities

Answer to Question 15:

A well-structured paragraph has easily identifiable parts and all of the points are clear to the reader. In this case, the writer has used indefinite pronouns without clear antecedents, or references, causing some confusion in the mind of the reader. "Its initial appeal" leaves the reader wondering what it is. A second "it" in the same sentence adds to the ambiguity. There is no claim being made on the part of the author; the piece is not comparative in nature anyway; and no tone exists because the piece is simply expository. Choices A, C, and E can be eliminated as choices. It is true that the author does not provide information about the people named in the piece, but it does not matter in this context. The correct answer is B.

Topic: Arts and Humanities

Answer to Question 16:

Credit and ascribe convey that the company and the analysts believe that the company's management, honesty, and community involvement are responsible for its success. None of the other options agree with each other or fit well in the sentence.

Topic: Business

Answer to Question 17:

The correct answer is B. Belief is not proof. It is believed that the shows have had an impact on juries and prosecutors, but there is no proof of that.

Topic: Everyday Topics

Answer to Question 18:

The correct answer is C. The passage reveals the increased use of forensic evidence to investigate crime and the impact that it has had on the prosecutors who try the cases in court. Because of the increased likelihood of being caught, criminals will have to be more careful about leaving forensic evidence at a crime scene. There is no evidence that fewer crimes are being committed, eliminating A as the correct choice. Choice B is not logical; forensic evidence is probably a factor in the investigation of all crimes. Crimes of passion happen in the heat of the moment, without any thought to the consequences, so knowledge of forensic techniques would not prevent them. D is incorrect. It may be that criminals will be more likely to work alone to reduce the risk of forensic evidence being left at a crime scene, but the sole perpetrator would still need to use more skill to avoid leaving such evidence. E is not the best choice.

Topic: Everyday Topics

Answer to Question 19:

The best choice for the first blank is "juxtapose", since the sentence indicates that Hardy's novels evaluate the consequences of combining two disparate threads in Victorian life. The best choice for the second blank is "paradigmatic" since the passage indicates that the two works mentioned are especially good examples of the theme under discussion. The best choice for the third blank is "subverting", since the passage indicates that Hardy's heroes incur tragic consequences by trying to break free of or overthrow their traditional roles.

Topic: Arts and Humanities – Literature

Answer to Question 20:

To make any decision about filling in the blanks, it is necessary to read the second sentence, which indicates that Ron had nothing to offer the discussion. Realizing this, the best choice for the first blank is "fatuous" since this fits with the description of Ron as both smug and ignorant. "Incongruous" might work for the second blank, but the better choice is "inimical", which suggests, in keeping with the second sentence, that Ron's comments are the opposite of productive.

Topic: Everyday Topics

Chapter 11

Practice Test 3

Y ou are about to begin a Practice Test. The Test has two sections. The time allotted for each section is marked at the beginning of the section. Work on one section at a time. Use a timer to keep track of the time limits for every section.

Try to take the Practice Test under real test conditions. Find a quiet place to work, and set aside enough time to complete the test without being disturbed.

At the end of the test, check your answers by referring to the Answers Key and Explanatory Answers. Pay particular attention to the questions that were answered incorrectly.

Section 1

Time: 30 minutes

20 Questions

Question 1 is based on the following passage.

'Yes, it is marvelous and more than marvelous this triumph of the sciences that my modest rent-charge stimulates you annually to record; nor do I wonder less at what my lecturers have said of humane letters and the fine arts, of the history of all times and of my time, of Erasmus whom I remember, and that age of the Renaissance (as you call it) in which (so you say) I lived. But there is one matter, one science (for such we accounted it) of which they seem to have said little or nothing; and it happens to be a matter, a science, in which I used to take some interest and which I endeavored to teach. You have not, I hope, forgotten that I was not only an English judge, but, what is more, a reader in English law.'

Select only one answer choice.

1.   The two underlined portions play which of the following roles?

    Ⓐ They extend the meaning of the ideas that precede them.

    Ⓑ They reveal skepticism about the validity of remarks made by the person that the speaker is addressing.

    Ⓒ They provide a contrast in point of view to the third parenthetical phrase.

    Ⓓ They reveal the speaker's disagreement with the characteristics of the Renaissance.

    Ⓔ They provide a transition from the ideas in the first half of the passage to those in the second half.

For Questions 2 and 3, select the two answer choices that, when used to complete the sentence, fit the meaning of the sentence as a whole and produce completed sentences that are alike in meaning.

2.   That strange _____ was built using a very simple but innovative architectural design method.

   A   disassemble

   B   chassis

   C   dwelling

   D   groundwork

   E   edifice

   F   habitant

3.   Whether to go to Cancun or to Rio was a _____ for Helen since she had never been abroad before.

   A   vacillation

   B   plight

   C   impasse

   D   quandary

   E   certitude

   F   conundrum

Question 4 is based on the following passage.

Last winter, Mogul Mountain Ski Resort reduced the price of its lift tickets by thirty percent. Despite the price cut, Mogul Mountain's ticket sales were twenty percent less than the previous three years.

Select only one answer choice.

4.   Which of the following best explains the discrepancy?

     Ⓐ   A nearby ski resort slashed lift ticket prices by forty percent.

     Ⓑ   Mogul Mountain hosted Olympic downhill trials during the traditional public-school winter break.

     Ⓒ   One of the mountain's snow making machines was broken for a month.

     Ⓓ   The mountain invested in new skis and boots for its rental shop.

     Ⓔ   The prices of meals at the base lodge increased by twenty percent.

Question 5 is based on the following passage.

Bacterial and viral infections are caused by two different types of microorganisms. The bacteria are very small unicell organisms that can be found everywhere around us: in the air, in the food that we eat, in the soil, and millions of them are on the surface of our skin and in our bodies. The bacteria are so small that a single glass of drinking water contains millions of them. Most bacteria are harmless and are kept in control by our immune system. Some of them are even useful and help us absorb vitamins and aid digestion as well. The pathogenic bacteria are the "bad bacteria" as they are the ones causing infections that kill millions of people every year. Bacterial infections that can damage our health considerably are cholera, tuberculosis, bubonic plague and anthrax.

Consider each of the three choices separately and select all that apply.

5.   Based on the information in this passage, what might logically be the topic of the subsequent paragraph?

     ☐ A   How viruses interact with humans

     ☐ B   How the use of antibacterial cleansers affect human interaction with bacteria

     ☐ C   How bacterial infections are treated

Question 6 is based on the following passage.

Once an all human endeavor based mainly upon changes in barometric pressure, current weather conditions, and sky condition, forecast models are now used to determine future conditions. Human input is still required to pick the best possible forecast model to base the forecast upon, which involves pattern recognition skills, teleconnections, knowledge of model performance, and knowledge of model biases. The chaotic nature of the atmosphere, the massive computational power required to solve the equations that describe the atmosphere, error involved in measuring the initial conditions, and an incomplete understanding of atmospheric processes mean that forecasts become less accurate as the difference in current time and the time for which the forecast is being made (the range of the forecast) increases. The use of ensembles and model consensus help narrow the error and pick the most likely outcome.

Consider each of the three choices separately and select all that apply.

6.   According to the passage, which of the following is true about the use of technology to predict the weather?

    A   The use of technology has not replaced the human factor in weather forecasting.

    B   Increased understanding of atmospheric processes would enable long range forecasts to become more accurate.

    C   The introduction of more sophisticated technology has made weather forecasting virtually error free.

For each blank, select one entry from the corresponding column of choices. Fill all blanks in the way that best completes the text.

7.   The Canadian rock band Rush has long been (i) _____ for the way in which they move (ii) _____ between time signatures within a song. On the performers level this is a (n) (iii) _____ and on the presentation level it is quite impressive when this can be pulled off while still maintaining an audiences' interest. This smooth transitioning through time-signatures is amongst the reasons that Rush has become reveled in the rock world.

Blank (i)	Blank (ii)	Blank (iii)
reviewed	suddenly	complex feat
lauded	awkwardly	rote process
criticized	seamlessly	uninteresting activity

Select one entry for the blank. Fill the blank in the way that best completes the text.

8.   In the early 20th century various composers took it upon themselves to break the mold of the Romantic
      era of symphonic music which was characterized by simple lyricism and influenced by the classical
      adherence to gentle tonality. These composers were criticized for placing the _____ task
      upon their audiences of tolerating the dissonant cacophony created in their compositions.

diffident
innocuous
contumacious
onerous
extemporaneous

**For each blank, select one entry from the corresponding column of choices. Fill all blanks in the way that
best completes the text.**

9.   The story of Kaspar Hauser has captured the popular imagination for generations. After his mysterious
      appearance on the streets of Nuremberg in 1828, some speculated that he was the legitimate heir to
      the House of Baden who had been robbed of his inheritance as part of a (i) _____ plot. Although
      popular media has continued to lend credence to the theory that Hauser was the (ii) _____ of the
      House of Baden, professional historians have tended to (iii) _____ this claim.

Blank (i)	Blank (ii)	Blank (iii)
utilitarian	scion	debunk
beneficent	predecessor	corroborate
nefarious	prelate	repudiate

Questions 10 to 12 are based on the following passage.

The American Civil War was followed by a boom in railroad construction. 56,000 miles (90,000 km) of
new track were laid across the country between 1866 and 1873. Much of the craze in railroad investment was
driven by government land grants and subsidies to the railroads. At that time, the railroad industry was the
nation's largest employer outside of agriculture, and it involved large amounts of money and risk. A large
infusion of cash from speculators caused abnormal growth in the industry as well as overbuilding of docks,
factories and ancillary facilities. At the same time, too much capital was involved in projects offering no
immediate or early returns.

For Questions 10 to 12, select only one answer choice.

10.   According to the information in this passage, which of the following might be a correct assumption on the part of the reader?

   Ⓐ   The expansion of the railroad made it easier to move goods and people to heretofore inaccessible places.

   Ⓑ   The speculative nature of the railroad expansion led to a financial crisis.

   Ⓒ   Because financial institutions relied on the expanded railroads to transport gold and currency, train robberies increased.

   Ⓓ   The expansion of the railroad provided many jobs for slaves that had been freed as a result of the Civil War.

   Ⓔ   The expansion of the railroad coincided with other advances in the technology of the era.

11.   Which of the following statements is the least likely explanation for the railroad boom's occurring closely after the end of the Civil War?

   Ⓐ   Displaced southern plantation owners were eager to move their families and household possessions to the northern states.

   Ⓑ   The labor needed to build the railroad would have been in short supply during the Civil War because virtually all able-bodied men were called to fight.

   Ⓒ   Citizens of the America were hopeful about the future of the country since the reunification of the North and the South and expressed that optimism in expanding the railroad, among other endeavors.

   Ⓓ   Factories that had been producing items for the war effort were available to make the products necessary for building railroads.

   Ⓔ   Because many businesses had suffered during the war, their owners were looking for a means to recover financially and saw the railroads as an opportunity to do so.

12.   The author's tone is best described as

   Ⓐ   sarcastic

   Ⓑ   realistic

   Ⓒ   factual

   Ⓓ   cautionary

   Ⓔ   skeptical

For each blank, select one entry from the corresponding column of choices. Fill all blanks in the way that best completes the text.

13. Scientists have long sought a single theory to explain all physical (i) _____. One such theory is string theory, which would, if true, (ii) _____ quantum mechanics and general relativity. However, despite its promise as complete "theory of everything", string theory has been criticized by detractors for failing to provide (iii) _____ support for its claims.

Blank (i)	Blank (ii)	Blank (iii)
phenomena	interpolate	vitriolic
matter	reconcile	coherent
fecundity	reify	empirical

Select the two answer choices that, when used to complete the sentence, fit the meaning of the sentence as a whole and produce completed sentences that are alike in meaning.

14. Although an organization may have a formal leadership structure, there can frequently be an informal leadership structure in operation that influences the organization in _____ ways.

   A   categorical

   B   complex

   C   deep

   D   orphic

   E   profound

   F   uncanny

Questions 15 to 17 are based on the following passage.

Author George Leonard discusses in his book Mastery how homeostasis affects our behavior and who we are. He states that homeostasis will prevent our body from making drastic changes and maintain stability in our lives even if it is detrimental to us. Examples include when an obese person starts exercising, homeostasis in the body resists the activity to maintain stability. Another example Leonard uses is an unstable family where the father has been a raging alcoholic and suddenly stops and the son starts up a drug habit to maintain stability in the family. Homeostasis is the main factor that stops people changing their habits because our bodies view change as dangerous unless it is very slow. Leonard discusses this dilemma as the media today only encourages fast change and quick results.

15. Select the sentence that best states the reason for the frequency with which people with drug and alcohol addictions return to rehabilitation facilities for further treatment.

For Questions 16 and 17, select only one answer choice.

16. What purpose is served in this passage by the author's including the example of the unstable family in the fourth sentence?

Ⓐ To introduce emotional homeostasis in addition to physical homeostasis

Ⓑ To show how homeostasis is maintained in a dysfunctional family

Ⓒ To show how the media today influence family dynamics

Ⓓ To argue that sons are more likely than daughters to replace a father's negative behavior with negative behavior of their own

Ⓔ To demonstrate the family dynamic that has resulted from today's fast-paced lifestyle

17. Which of the following, if true, undermines the premise of the passage?

Ⓐ Parents have cochlear implants provided for their deaf child.

Ⓑ Dieters who lose ten pounds generally reward themselves with food.

Ⓒ Families eat dinner at the same time every day.

Ⓓ Children of alcoholics marry alcoholics.

Ⓔ Twelve-step programs are successful.

Select the two answer choices that, when used to complete the sentence, fit the meaning of the sentence as a whole and produce completed sentences that are alike in meaning.

18.   Bach's "Brandenburg Concertos" brought the concerto groso form to a new height, yet there is no evidence that they were ever performed in his lifetime, or that the nobleman to whom he sent them ever _____ the receipt of the now world-famous compositions.

       A   acknowledged

       B   conceded

       C   disputed

       D   recognized

       E   revealed

       F   unveiled

For Questions 19 and 20, for each blank, select one entry from the corresponding column of choices. Fill all blanks in the way that best completes the text.

19.   The first world was has been overshadowed in the popular imagination by World War II, but its length, violence, and the widespread changes it brought shocked people who lived through it. A war that everyone thought would be over within months turned into a (i) _____ stalemate of four long years; the (ii) _____ waste of life in the trenches was unprecedented in its bloodiness; and the war led directly to the (iii) _____ of four great empires.

Blank (i)	Blank (ii)	Blank (iii)
recalcitrant	querulous	accretion
protracted	anachronistic	demise
divergent	wanton	disparity

20.   After several (i) _____ abuses came to light, the military promised to (ii) _____ the use of torture in its detainment facilities.

Blank (i)	Blank (ii)
absurd	propagate
fatuous	gainsay
egregious	abjure

Section 2

Time: 30 minutes

20 Questions

Questions 1 to 6 are based on the following passage.

Britannica Online defines art as "the use of skill and imagination in the creation of aesthetic objects, environments, or experiences that can be shared with others." By this definition of the word, artistic works have existed for almost as long as humankind: from early pre-historic art to contemporary art; however, some theories restrict the concept to modern Western societies. Adorno said in 1970, "It is now taken for granted that nothing which concerns art can be taken for granted any more: neither art itself, nor art in relationship to the whole, nor even the right of art to exist." The first and broadest sense of art is the one that has remained closest to the older Latin meaning, which roughly translates to "skill" or "craft." A few examples where this meaning proves very broad include *artifact, artificial, artifice, medical arts, and military arts*. However, there are many other colloquial uses of the word, all with some relation to its etymology.

The second and more recent sense of the word art is as an abbreviation for *creative art* or *fine art*. Fine art means that a skill is being used to express the artist's creativity, or to engage the audience's aesthetic sensibilities, or to draw the audience towards consideration of the finer things. Often, if the skill is being used in a common or practical way, people will consider it a craft instead of art. Likewise, if the skill is being used in a commercial or industrial way, it will be considered commercial art instead of fine art. On the other hand, crafts and design are sometimes considered applied art. Some art followers have argued that the difference between fine art and applied art has more to do with value judgments made about the art than any clear definitional difference. However, even fine art often has goals beyond pure creativity and self-expression. The purpose of works of art may be to communicate ideas, such as in politically, spiritually, or philosophically motivated art; to create a sense of beauty; to explore the nature of perception; for pleasure; or to generate strong emotions. The purpose may also be seemingly nonexistent.

Art can describe several things: a study of creative skill, a process of using the creative skill, a product of the creative skill, or the audience's experience with the creative skill. The creative arts (*art as discipline*) are a collection of disciplines (*arts*) that produce artworks (art as objects) that are compelled by a personal drive (*art as activity*) and echo or reflect a message, mood, or symbolism for the viewer to interpret (art as experience). Artworks can be defined by purposeful, creative interpretations of limitless concepts or ideas in order to communicate something to another person. Artworks can be explicitly made for this purpose or interpreted on the basis of images or objects. Art is something that stimulates an individual's thoughts, emotions, beliefs, or ideas through the senses. It is also an expression of an idea and it can take many different forms and serve many different purposes. Although the application of scientific knowledge to derive a new scientific theory involves skill and results in the "creation" of something new, this represents science only and is not categorized as art.

1.   Select the sentence that best supports the definition of art as being all-inclusive.

For Questions 2 and 3, consider each of the three choices separately and select all that apply.

2.   The Britannica definition implies which of the following about art?

       A   Until it is shared with others, an aesthetically created object cannot be considered as art.

       B   The application of skill without imagination is not art.

       C   Imagination, alone, is not sufficient to create art.

3.   The structure of this passage serves which of the following purposes?

       A   To persuade the reader to employ his or her aesthetic sensibilities to the viewing of art

       B   To expand upon the Britannica Online definition of art

       C   To convince the reader that scientific applications are not considered art

For Questions 4 to 6, select only one answer choice.

4.   Considering the information in the second paragraph of the passage that distinguishes art from craft, which of the following would be considered a craft functioning as art?

       Ⓐ   A handmade wooden frame for a picture

       Ⓑ   A knit afghan draped over the back of a sofa

       Ⓒ   A quilted wall hanging

       Ⓓ   A macrame plant holder

       Ⓔ   A punched-tin lampshade

5.   The author of the passage proposes that the purpose of works of art may be to communicate ideas, such as in politically, spiritually, or philosophically motivated art. Which of the following would be an example of art as communication of ideas?

       Ⓐ   a portrait of the artist's mother

       Ⓑ   a rural landscape

       Ⓒ   a still life of fruit

       Ⓓ   a propaganda poster

       Ⓔ   a cubist rendering of a self portrait

6.   In the final paragraph of the passage, the author is primarily concerned with

   Ⓐ Creating a more inclusive definition of art that reflects a more contemporary point of view

   Ⓑ Persuading the reader to participate in art

   Ⓒ Putting the definition of art into layman's terms

   Ⓓ Distinguishing between art and science

   Ⓔ Countering claims made by earlier critics of art

Question 7 is based on the following passage.

Having a pet may help people achieve health goals, such as lowered blood pressure, or mental goals, such as decreased stress. There is evidence that having a pet can help a person lead a longer, healthier life. In a study of 92 people hospitalized for coronary ailments, within a year, 11 of the 29 without pets had died, compared to only 3 of the 52 who had pets. Pet ownership has been shown to significantly reduce triglycerides and thus heart disease risk in the elderly. A recent study concluded that owning a pet can reduce the risk of a heart attack by 2% and that pets are better than medication in reducing blood pressure. Owning a pet can also prolong survival of a heart attack.

Select only one answer choice.

7.   Based on the information in the passage, which of the following is a weakness in the author's position?

   Ⓐ The author fails to identify the type of pet required to obtain these therapeutic results.

   Ⓑ The author fails to identify other conditions in addition to coronary disease that might be ameliorated by pet ownership.

   Ⓒ The author ignores the dilemma of people who cannot have pets due to allergies or living conditions.

   Ⓓ The author fails to identify alternative means to achieve and sustain good health for people with heart disease.

   Ⓔ The author fails to discuss how pet ownership can lead to better mental health.

For Questions 8 to 10, for each blank, select one entry from the corresponding column of choices. Fill all blanks in the way that best completes the text.

8.   In telecommunication systems, broadcast signals can be (i) _____ allowing someone to broadcast over someone else's network. For example, if station A were (ii) _____ a signal to people tuned into their station it would be possible for station B to have their own signal be distributed over station A's network. This signal intrusion is accomplished when station B sends a stronger signal to station A's transponder.

Blank (i)
interjected
interpolated
appropriated

Blank (ii)
transcribing
simulcasting
circulating

9.   The relaxing of policies concerning lending practices has created problems for some small business owners. Small business owners often turn to larger companies and banks to receive loans to help them manage the expenses of their business. Unfortunately, nowadays, there is little regulation concerning (i) _____ which has put many small business owners in a position where they are (ii) _____ into so much debt that their ability to gain a profit is (iii) _____ by the mounting interest on their loans.

Blank (i)
profiteering
usury
piracy

Blank (ii)
bilked
slighted
coerced

Blank (iii)
obscured
abrogated
hampered

10.   Van Gogh was a man of many contradictions. Although he was prone to periods of (i) _____, much of his art is marked by (ii) _____ use of color.

Blank (i)
temerity
depression
indolence

Blank (ii)
an exuberant
a capricious
a mundane

Question 11 is based on the following passage.

Wear and tear is a form of depreciation which is assumed to occur even when an item is used competently and with care and proper maintenance. For example, repeated impacts may cause stress to a hammer's head. In the normal use of a hammer for its designed task, this stress is impossible to prevent, and any attempt to eliminate it would make the hammer useless. At the same time, it is expected that the normal use of a hammer will not break it beyond repair until it has gone through a certain amount of use.

Select only one answer choice.

11.   If the condition stated in the underlined portion of the text is not met, which of the following is likely to be impacted?

   Ⓐ   The salesperson's commission

   Ⓑ   The replacement warranty

   Ⓒ   The product placement in the showroom

   Ⓓ   The retailer's markup

   Ⓔ   The wholesaler's markup

For Questions 12 and 13, select the two answer choices that, when used to complete the sentence, fit the meaning of the sentence as a whole and produce completed sentences that are alike in meaning.

12.   He had to tread lightly in crafting his own breakfast cereal mascot; the _____ lawyers from other companies knew the importance of brutally snuffing out even the most minor of competitors through the court system.

   Ⓐ   bellicose

   Ⓑ   compromising

   Ⓒ   international

   Ⓓ   careful

   Ⓔ   pugnacious

   Ⓕ   quixotic

13.   One effect of public education is to eliminate the idiosyncrasies that make each person a one of a kind, so that what was once a unique snowflake gets _____ into a drop of water little different from all the other drops of water in the world.

[A]   commuted

[B]   deformed

[C]   disfigured

[D]   exchanged

[E]   reduced

[F]   rendered

For Questions 14 to 16, for each blank, select one entry from the corresponding column of choices. Fill all blanks in the way that best completes the text.

14.   Reading Heidegger for the first time can be difficult even for someone well-versed in philosophy: his writing can be highly (i) _____, thanks to his use of obscure terminology and his frequent invention of new words. Nonetheless, once the reader learns to cope with this (ii) _____ difficulty, Heidegger's work becomes as accessible as that of any philosopher.

Blank (i)	Blank (ii)
histrionic	impenetrable
lucid	topical
opaque	arbitrary

15.   The challenger uttered (i) _____ about his opponent during the campaign, often completely misrepresenting the (ii) _____ voting record in an attempt to gain political advantage through character assassination.

Blank (i)	Blank (ii)
palavers	incumbent's
panegyrics	neophyte's
calumnies	senator's

16. Archaeological evidence suggests that our human ancestors were hunter-gatherers prior to the rise of agriculture. Hunter-gatherer societies were often highly mobile, or even (i) _____, dues to the variable availability of food to support (ii) _____ or hunting.

Blank (i)
desultory
nomadic
meticulous

Blank (ii)
dissembling
foraging
proselytizing

Questions 17 and 18 are based on the following passage.

Roy Baumeister, a social and personality psychologist, argues that blaming the victim is problematic from an explanatory point of view and perhaps it is not necessarily fallacious. He argues that showing the victim's responsibility can be insightful contrary to typical explanations of violence and cruelty, which incorporate the trope of the innocent victim. According to Baumeister, in the classic telling of "the myth of pure evil," the innocent, well-meaning victims are going about their business when they are suddenly assaulted by wicked, malicious evildoers. In actuality, the situation is more complicated and it is mostly - though not always - the case that the victim has done something to provoke the ire of the "evildoer", although the subsequent actions may outweigh the scale of the "victim's" initial offense.

For Questions 17 and 18, select only one answer choice.

17. In this context, what is the best definition of the underlined word, "trope"?

     (A) the principle of organization according to which matter moves to form an object during the various stages of its existence

     (B) a word or expression used in a figurative sense

     (C) a phrase, sentence, or verse formerly interpolated in a liturgical text to amplify or embellish

     (D) a company of actors or other performers

     (E) an assemblage of persons or things

18. According to the author, which of the following is generally true about the perpetrator –and –victim relationship?

Ⓐ The victim is always physically inferior and, therefore, dominated by the perpetrator.

Ⓑ Their roles are always equal in the conflict

Ⓒ Each satisfies an emotional need in the other

Ⓓ Although their roles may be unequal, both are partners in the conflict.

Ⓔ It is mythic in scope and outcome

For Questions 19 and 20, select the two answer choices that, when used to complete the sentence, fit the meaning of the sentence as a whole and produce completed sentences that are alike in meaning.

19. Sometimes when we see an overweight person, we think that they cannot control their diet and that if they exercised more they would be healthy, but the problem may be that they have physical _____ such as a failing lymph system.

Ⓐ barriers

Ⓑ challenges

Ⓒ dilemmas

Ⓓ issues

Ⓔ obstacles

Ⓕ quandaries

20. More so than other types of cells, animal cells are fragile and remain _____ to changes in their immediate environment.

Ⓐ receptive

Ⓑ sensible

Ⓒ sensitive

Ⓓ sensual

Ⓔ sensorial

Ⓕ subject

Answer Key

Section 1

1. B. They reveal skepticism about the validity of remarks made by the person that the speaker is addressing.

2. C. dwelling
    E. edifice

3. D. quandary
    F. conundrum

4. B. Mogul Mountain hosted Olympic downhill trials during the traditional public-school winter break.

5. A. How viruses interact with humans

6. A. The use of technology has not replaced the human factor in weather forecasting.

    B. Increased understanding of atmospheric processes would enable long range forecasts to become more accurate.

7. (i) lauded
    (ii) seamlessly
    (iii) complex feat

8. D. onerous

9. (i) nefarious
    (ii) scion
    (iii) repudiate

10. B. The speculative nature of the railroad expansion led to a financial crisis.

11. A. Displaced southern plantation owners were eager to move their families and household possessions to the northern states.

12. D. cautionary

13. (i) phenomena
    (ii) reconcile
    (iii) empirical

14. C. deep
    E. profound

15. He states that homeostasis will prevent our body from making drastic changes and maintain stability in our lives even if it is detrimental to us.

16. A. To introduce emotional homeostasis in addition to physical homeostasis

17. E. Twelve-step programs are successful.

18. A. acknowledged
    D. recognized

19. (i) protracted
    (ii) wanton
    (iii) demise

20. (i) egregious
     (ii) abjure

Section 2

1.   Some art followers have argued that the difference between fine art and applied art has more to do with value judgments made about the art than any clear definitional difference.

2.   A. Until it is shared with others, an aesthetically created object cannot be considered as art.

     B. The application of skill without imagination is not art.

     C. Imagination, alone, is not sufficient to create art.

3.   B. To expand upon the Britannica Online definition of art

4.   C. A quilted wall hanging

5.   D. a propaganda poster

6.   A. Creating a more inclusive definition of art that reflects a more contemporary point of view

7.   E. The author fails to discuss how pet ownership can lead to better mental health.

8.   (i) appropriated
     (ii) circulating

9.   (i) usury
     (ii) coerced
     (iii) hampered

10. (i) depression
     (ii) an exuberant

11. B. The replacement warranty

12. A. bellicose
     E. pugnacious

13. A. commuted
     F. rendered

14. (i) opaque
     (ii) topical

15. (i) calumnies
     (ii) incumbent's

16. (i) nomadic
     (ii) foraging

17. B. a word or expression used in a figurative sense

18. D. Although their roles may be unequal, both are partners in the conflict.

19. B. challenges
     D. issues

20. B. sensible
     C. sensitive

Explanatory Answers

Section 1

Answer to Question 1:

Quite often, parenthetical phrases extend the meaning of the words preceding them. That is not the case in this passage. The speaker uses them to comment on what the "you" in this passage has said at some previous time. Those comments reveal some skepticism on the part of the speaker. He is not sure he agrees with what "you" have said or believe. These parenthetical phrases affect the tone of this passage. The correct choice is B.

Topic: Social Science

Answer to Question 2:

Answers: C and E. The key phrase is architectural design. It alludes to the idea that the missing word must be some type of building; for this reason, dwelling and edifice are the correct answers. Chassis usually refers to the outside or framework of a vehicle. Habitant refers to the person who lives in an environment or habitat, a resident and is not logical here. Groundwork is the basic preparation for something and disassemble means to take apart both of which do not make sense in the sentence.

Topic: Everyday Topics

Answer to Question 3:

Answers: D and F. In the sentence, Helen has been given a choice. She must choose between two places that she has never been to before. It is likely that this choice is causing her difficulties. Consequently, the correct word options are quandary and conundrum because both words refer to having to make a difficult or confusing choice. The options vacillation, plight, impasse and certitude would not complete the sentence in a logical way. Vacillation means the inability to take a stand on an important issue, plight refers to a hardship, Helen wasn't at an impasse because an impasse is a deadlock or position where there is no escape. Last of all, certitude refers to a feeling of being certain and doesn't complete the sentence logically.

Topic: Everyday Topics

Answer to Question 4:

The correct answer is B. The traditional school winter break is likely to be a busy time for any ski resort. Parents and children can take advantage of the break to enjoy a family ski vacation. If Mogul Mountain hosted an Olympic trial, one or more of its downhill runs along with the ski lifts would not be available for the public to use. Athletes and coaches would likely be housed in any hotels for the time period, making them also unavailable to the public. Limiting public access to the mountain during this vacation week would have a serious effect on lift ticket sales. Answer A is incorrect, because the reader doesn't know the original prices of tickets at Mogul Mountain or the nearby resort. Mogul Mountain's reduced ticket prices may still be lower than those at the other resort. The other resort may not have the same or as many amenities as Mogul Mountain, so lower ticket prices there may have no effect on Mogul's attendance, anyway. Answer choice C is incorrect, because there may have been enough snow to make the snow making machine redundant. New equipment in the rental shop should make skiing at Mogul Mountain more attractive rather than have a negative effect on ticket sales, so answer choice D is incorrect. Whether or not increased meal prices in the base lodge would have an effect on lift ticket sales depends on the original prices and how many skiers typically buy meals there. Answer choice E is incorrect.

Topic: Business

Answer to Question 5:

The first sentence of the paragraph introduces the topic of both bacterial and viral infections. This passage deals only with bacteria and human interaction. It is realistic to expect that the focus of the next paragraph would be the virus and human interaction. Because the author had introduced the topic of viral infections, the next paragraph should deal with viruses in the same manner by explaining what kind of organism it is, where it can be found, etc., until he lists what viruses can do to damage one's health. In other words, what the writer must do in this case is to provide a similar treatment of the other topic introduced at the beginning of this passage. A is the best choice.

Topic: Biological Science

Answer to Question 6:

Choice C can be eliminated based on the last sentence of the passage. The likelihood of error has been narrowed but not eliminated. Both A and B are correct. Humans are still needed to interpret the data, making A the correct choice. The passage states that incomplete understanding of atmospheric processes affects the ability to generate long range forecasts, supporting choice B.

Topic: Physical Science

Answer to Question 7:

The key to answering this question is to address blank ii by noting that in the last sentence we find 'smooth transitioning' which indicates the proper selection of seamlessly because the concepts are related. Suddenly and awkwardly would go against the underlying notion here. For blank i we can also find in the last sentence the band is stated as being 'reveled' which relates to being celebrated or 'lauded' making this the best selection. Reviewed would be general and carries neither a positive nor negative connotation, in this problem we are led to believe that Rush is positively reviewed, whereas 'criticized' is closer to a negative review. 'Complex feat' works best for blank iii because it is hinted that moving through time-signatures is not a simple thing to do, 'rote process' opposes the idea of a 'complex feat' and 'uninteresting activity' goes against the underlying sensibility that moving through time-signatures is 'quite impressive'.

Topic: Arts and Humanities

Answer to Question 8:

What we are looking for here is a word that aligns with the notion that audiences were displeased by their music and found it burdensome to tolerate this music; the term 'onerous' best serves this purpose as it means something which is a burden to bear. 'Diffident' is not a good term as it would imply that the audience lacked confidence in listening to the music, the degree of the audience's confidence is not expressed in this passage. 'Innocuous' is a poor fit because it is presented in the passage that the music was offensive to the audience, and 'innocuous' means to be inoffensive, so this is opposite of what we are going for. 'Contumacious', having to do with a stubborn rejection, is not a good match, although the audience may have felt rebellious about tolerating this music, it is not indicated that the issue was their stubborn rejection of it. 'Extemporaneous' indicates that the audience was not prepared for the task, which may be true, but the idea of doing something extemporaneously has more of a pro-active connotation whereas the audience concerns were more of a reactive nature.

Topic: Arts and Humanities

Answer to Question 9:

The best choice for the first blank is "nefarious" since the other options can be ruled out. In the next sentence, the "although" indicates that the first clause will be qualified by the second clause. Since we have already learned that the popular belief is that Hauser was the successor to the House of Baden, "scion" is clearly the best choice for the first blank, while the qualifying "although" lets us see that historians hold a contrary view, so we are left to choose between "debunk" or "repudiate". "Debunking" connotes that the claim has been conclusively disproven, an interpretation not supported by the passage. Therefore, "repudiate" is the best solution.

Topic: Arts and Humanities – History

Answer to Question 10:

The author of this passage uses several words and phrases to highlight the risky nature of this rapid expansion of the railroad: craze, risk, speculators, abnormal, no immediate or early returns. These should lead the reader to conclude that all of this risk may have led to a financial crisis, or answer B. There is no evidence in the passage to support the other conclusions.

Topic: Business

Answer to Question 11:

The question asks the reader to make a best guess based on the information in the passage. The war certainly had an impact on the ability to pursue normal commercial activities. It is true that virtually every able-bodied man in the country participated in the fighting and would have been unavailable for other pursuits, so B is a likely conclusion. The Civil War was demoralizing for the citizens of America, and they likely would have embraced an opportunity to engage in a rebuilding effort, making C another acceptable choice. During war time, it is typical for factories to shift their efforts to support the war and to cease production of peacetime goods; D is a likely conclusion. The author mentions investment in railroads in the passage, and business owners might, indeed, have been looking for what appeared to be a sure way to recoup wartime losses, so E is also an appropriate conclusion. A is the only conclusion that is doubtful.

Topic: Business

Answer to Question 12:

Since tone describes the author's attitude toward his subject, the reader should be able to deduce that the writer is presenting this information as a warning against jumping on the band wagon and incurring too much risk. He is being cautionary, so the correct answer is D. It is tempting for individuals to invest in the latest technology. However, when the returns are not immediate or early, one's money can be tied up for a long period of time. Regardless of the historical era in which the technology is created, the investor should be skeptical about the reality of the return. Although the author wants the reader to view these opportunities with skepticism, that is not his tone in this piece, eliminating E as the correct choice. Although the writer is presenting facts, he is using them to achieve a larger purpose. C is not correct. The choice of words would be different if the author were being sarcastic.

Topic: Business

Answer to Question 13:

"Phenomena" is the best choice for the first blank, since the physical world contains more than just matter. The first sentence explains string theory's ambition to provide a unified theory of physics; from this, the word that best fits the context of the second sentence is "reconcile". Since we have already learned that one of string theory's key claims is theoretical unity or coherence, the word that best fits the last sentence is "empirical".

Topic: Physical Science – Physics

Answer to Question 14:

The correct options indicate that the informal leadership structure has a fundamental and all-pervading influence on the organization. The other options indicate an influence that is less pervasive. Uncanny and orphic are similar in meaning, but orphic implies something almost magical, while uncanny has no such sense.

Topic: Business

Answer to Question 15:

The word in this sentence that makes it the best choice is "detrimental". Drug and alcohol addictions are detrimental. Even so, addicts find it difficult to stop those behaviors because doing so upsets a balance to which the body has become accustomed. The next-to-last sentence in the passage may seem like an appropriate choice, but it fails to identify detrimental behaviors.

Topic: Biological Science

Answer to Question 16:

The correct answer is A. Just as a dieter's body reacts negatively to a reduced intake of food, so does a dysfunctional family react to a drastic change. In this case, the emotional balance of the family is upset. Because the author is listing examples of instability as a result of change, B is not the best choice. The author does mention the influence of the media on people's expectations of change but does not relate it specifically to family dynamics, eliminating C as the correct choice. The passage is not persuasive in nature, so there is no argument. He simply uses the son's using drugs as an example; that is not always the case. D is incorrect. The passage is not about fast-paced lifestyles, making E an incorrect choice.

Topic: Biological Science

Answer to Question 17:

The best answer is E. Cochlear implants enable many deaf children to hear. In this way, the hearing parents do not have to change their means of communication; it remains stable. Dieters reward their successes with food. Because they have denied themselves food for the sake of the diet, their use of it as a reward creates a temporary sense of balance. Families who have established daily routines feel comfortable; the unpredictable is upsetting. Children of alcoholics marry alcoholics because that is the behavior that they understand and are comfortable with. The success of twelve-step programs for any number of addictions demonstrates that, with help, people can change their behavior even when it threatens both their physical and their psychological homeostasis.

Topic: Biological Science

Answer to Question 18:

The synonyms revealed and unveiled are synonyms, but suggest that there was something covered up. Conceded also implies some negative sense, but like disputed, has no synonym among the options. The neutral acknowledged and recognized indicate, agreeing with the sense of the sentence, that the receipt of the concertos was not necessarily concealed; it was just ignored.

Topic: Arts and Humanities

Answer to Question 19:

The best choice for the first blank is "protracted" since the phrase indicates that the war surprised people by going on for a long time. The best choice for the second blank is "wanton", since neither of the other two choices makes sense, and "wanton" serves to indicate the brutality of trench warfare. The best choice for the last blank is "demise"; here, either a cursory knowledge of history, or the recognition that neither of the other options make sense indicate that "demise" is the best choice.

Topic: Arts and Humanities – History

Answer to Question 20:

The best choice for the first blank is "egregious". The passage suggests that some unusually bad "abuses" happened in the detainment facility, and "egregious" conveys that. The best choice for the second blank is "abjure", since it makes sense in context that the military would likely say that it was going to give up, or "abjure" the abuses.

Topic: Everyday Topics

Section 2

Answer to Question 1:

This sentence follows what some suggest are the differences between art, craft, and applied art. The sentence suggests that those differences are based on value judgments, which are inherently subjective. The first sentence of the second paragraph equates creative art and fine art, saying that the term art applies to both.

Topic: Arts and Humanities

Answer to Question 2:

All three are correct. Though some might argue that art exists for art's sake, this definition requires that the art be shared with others to be considered art. Choice B could apply to simply copying what someone else has done; it requires skill but no imagination. One may have a great imagination, but the inability to translate that imagination into an object, environment, or experience prevents the creation of art.

Topic: Arts and Humanities

Answer to Question 3:

The correct choice is B. The Britannica Online definition appears at the beginning of the passage and concisely defines art. The writer then endeavors to clarify and provide examples of what has been considered art throughout time, including changes in interpretation of the definition. Art is intended to engage the viewer's aesthetic sensibilities. Art should do the work, not the viewer, eliminating A as a correct choice. The passage is not persuasive in nature. It is expository, so C is not correct.

Topic: Arts and Humanities

Answer to Question 4:

The correct answer is C. A quilted wall hanging is the only object from the list of choices that is not being used in a practical way. The other four objects in the list, though handmade, are serving a functional rather than artistic purpose.

Topic: Arts and Humanities

Answer to Question 5:

The passage states that the purpose of works of art may be to communicate ideas, such as in politically …

motivated art. The only item in the list that communicates an idea is a propaganda poster, most of which are created for political reasons with the intention of causing the viewer to take some action. A portrait may be done for pleasure or to express beauty. A rural landscape or still life of fruit may also be expressions of beauty or an experiment in perspective. An artist may complete a cubist self-portrait as an experiment. The correct answer is D.

Topic: Arts and Humanities

Answer to Question 6:

The correct answer is A. The author of the passage uses transition words like "second" to let the reader know that a progression of ideas is in progress. It is appropriate for the reader to assume that the last paragraph is also the last in a series of definitions. This definition also expands on the Britannica Online definition in the first paragraph of the passage. The passage is not persuasive in nature, eliminating both B and E as correct choices. C is not the best choice because the passage is relatively free of technical language, eliminating the need to simplify the terminology to make it more understandable. The statement about science is simply an addition to the end of the last paragraph and does distinguish between art and science, but that is not the primary purpose of the paragraph.

Topic: Arts and Humanities

Answer to Question 7:

The best answer is E. The topic sentence claims that pet ownership can help one achieve both physical and mental health goals. The remainder of the passage focuses solely on health goals.

Topic: Everyday Topics

Answer to Question 8:

In this passage we are talking about a broadcast being taken over; once we have that in mind we can begin figuring out our missing terms. In blank i we are looking for the term that best describes a situation where someone takes over someone else's signal. In this case that term is 'appropriated', which means to take over something for one's own usage. 'Interjected' refers to abruptly speaking, especially when interrupting someone else. In the passage it is not indicated that anyone is interrupting someone else by speaking suddenly. Further 'interjection' is more appropriate to the context of a discussion. 'Interpolated' has to do with inserting additional material into already present material, especially as concerns text, such as interpolating pictures into a text. In the passage it is not a matter of adding a signal to the other signal, but rather replacing one signal with another. For blank ii we want a term that is closest to the broadcasting or transmitting of the signal. 'Circulating' as in distributing something from one person to the next within a network fits best here since it addresses the idea of a signal being distributed or broadcasted. 'Transcribing' has to do with writing something down which is not at issue here. 'Simulcasting' is tempting since it refers to the idea of broadcasting a signal through different mediums at the same time. If it was specified that the station was transmitting the same signal through different mediums then simulcasting would fit well, however, this is not suggested in the passage.

Topic: Physical Science

Answer to Question 9:

The main message of this passage is that larger businesses and banks give loans that are needed by smaller businesses to simply stay in business but charge interest rates that are so high that the small businesses remain in debt. Blank (i) requires a specific word that refers to the practice of lending and charging very high interest rates, this is the meaning of the term 'usury'. Though the banks and larger business are likely participating in 'profiteering' this isn't the specific practice being discussed here. 'Piracy' is not a good fit because it refers to an outright stealing of other people's property. In blank (ii) 'coerced' is the best fit. The idea that the small business owners were 'coerced' into debt relates to the notion that they were forced to take on the debt in order to avoid losing their business. 'Bilked' would imply that the small business owners were cheated into the debt. However, this is not supported by the passage as there is no mention of the banks and large businesses deceiving the small business owners, presumably the small business owners are aware of the interest rate. 'Slighted' has to do with being insulted by not being given one's due respect. It does not make much sense to consider that the small business owners were insulted which led to their debt. Blank (iii) requires a word which will indicate that the small business owners' ability to profit is being hindered by the large sums of interest they owe. 'Hampered' is a good word for this purpose because it means to hinder or impede the progress of something. 'Abrogated' has to do with repealing something and in this case would suggest that the mounting interest on loans is doing away with the gain in profit. One must currently possess something to have it repealed. It is not presented that the small business owners are currently able to gain profit therefore that ability cannot be 'abrogated'. The ability to gain a profit being 'obscured' by the interest rates would imply that the interest rates are making it difficult to understand the ability to gain a profit, which does not make sense in the context of this passage.

Topic: Business

Answer to Question 10:

Right away, phrase "was a man of many contradictions" suggests that we may see opposing aspects of Van Gogh's personality. An additional clue is provided by the second sentence beginning with "although" - we can immediately infer from this structure that the second clause will present information that mitigates what we have learned from the first clause. The only two words from the choices given that make sense in context are "depression" and "exuberant".

Topic: Arts and Humanities - Art History

Answer to Question 11:

The correct answer is B. Should the item break or fail before it has gone through a certain amount of normal use, it has not lived up to its expectations. A warranty will cover unexpected failure of an item, generally within a specified period of time. The salesperson earns his commission at the time of sale, and it is not affected by the failure of the item. Product placement is determined by the popularity of an item. The retailer's and wholesaler's markups are determined by the cost of the item to them and are not affected by failure of the item.

Topic: Business

Answer to Question 12:

This sentence describes a man who is careful as he treads around lawyers because they will quickly sue for any indiscretion. Therefore, we can characterize these lawyers as looking for a fight. "Compromising" means negotiating or conceding. Lawyers who succeed in eliminating the competition cannot be described as "Compromising." "International" means hailing for another country. The lawyers may very well be international but that doesn't explain why they would be so eager to sue somebody. "Careful" means alert and watchful. Again, these lawyers may very well be careful but that doesn't explain the swift cruelty with which they act. "Quixotic" means impractical. These lawyers are obviously described as very competent so "Quixotic" makes no sense in this context. We are left with "Bellicose" and "Pugnacious." These two words both mean belligerent and aggressive. Those are the exact characteristics that lawyers would have if they pride themselves on brutally eliminating the competition. a and e are correct.

Topic: business

Answer to Question 13:

The correct options refer only to change in a neutral manner. Reduced fits the sense of the sentence, but has no synonyms among the options. Deformed and disfigured are negative terms out of keeping with the rest of the sentence and exchanged implies back and forth inter-change not in keeping with the sense of the sentence.

Topic: Arts and Humanities

Answer to Question 14:

The first blank is best filled by "opaque", since the sentence is discussing Heidegger's lack of clarity. The "nonetheless" in the second sentence signals a change of tone; we are given to understand that, although Heidegger may be difficult to understand at first, he can become clear with deeper study - thus "topical" is the best choice to complete this sentence.

Topic: Arts and Humanities

Answer to Question 15:

The best choice for the first blank is "calumnies" since the sentence suggests that the challenger used denigrating and misleading rhetoric about his opponent; since nothing in the sentence tells us what office the candidates are running for, "incumbent" is the best choice for the second blank.

Topic: Everyday Topics

Answer to Question 16:

The best answer for the first blank is "nomadic", since the sentence indicates that hunter-gatherers were, at least "highly mobile", and possibly even nomads. The only plausible choice for the second blank is "foraging".

Topic: Social Science

Answer to Question 17:

The most effective strategy for selecting the meaning of an unknown word is to replace it in the sentence with the suggested definition and then decide which is the best fit. In this passage, the author is using the phrase, innocent victim, in a faintly ironic sense, as his claim is that the victim is not entirely innocent. He is using the phrase "innocent victim" as a figure of speech. The definition that best fits in this case is B. The definition in D is actually for the word, troupe, and the definition in E is for the word, troop. A is a scientific definition as in the word heliotrope which describes any species of plant whose blossoms turn toward the sun. Choice C is the simplest to eliminate because of its very specific meaning in the context of religion.

Topic: Social Science

Answer to Question 18:

The correct answer is D because, in the words of the author, it is contrary to popular opinion, which is the basis of his reasoning. There is no evidence to support the idea that the victim is physically inferior to the perpetrator, nor that each satisfies an emotional need in the other, eliminating A and C. The author reveals that the action of the "evil doer" may outweigh those of the victim, negating the idea expressed in choice B that they are equal. The author uses the word myth in this context to diminish the idea of the perpetrator's acting out of an evil impulse, so E is incorrect.

Topic: Social Science

Answer to Question 19:

The synonyms obstacle and barrier imply something concrete to be overcome. The synonyms dilemma and quandary imply there is something to be figured out. The correct options are more general than the other two sets of synonyms and do not imply any particular type of problem and thus agree better with the sentence than the other options.